DISCIPLINED
ENTREPRENEURSHIP

DISCIPLINED ENTREPRENEURSHIP

24 STEPS TO A SUCCESSFUL STARTUP

BILL AULET

Ethernet Inventors Professor
of the Practice of Entrepreneurship
MIT Sloan School of Management

EXPANDED & UPDATED

WILEY

Published by John Wiley & Sons, Inc., Hoboken, New Jersey.
Published simultaneously in Canada.

For general information on our other products and services or for technical support, please contact our Customer Care Department within the United States at (800) 762-2974, outside the United States at (317) 572-3993 or fax (317) 572-4002.

Wiley also publishes its books in a variety of electronic formats. Some content that appears in print may not be available in electronic formats. For more information about Wiley products, visit our web site at www.wiley.com.

Library of Congress Cataloging-in-Publication Data

Names: Aulet, Bill, 1958- author.
Title: Disciplined entrepreneurship : 24 steps to a successful startup /
   Bill Aulet.
Description: Expanded and updated. | Hoboken, New Jersey : Wiley, [2024] |
   Includes index.
Identifiers: LCCN 2023048232 (print) | LCCN 2023048233 (ebook) | ISBN
   9781394222513 (cloth) | ISBN 9781394222537 (adobe pdf) | ISBN
   9781394222520 (epub)
Subjects: LCSH: New business enterprises—Management. | Entrepreneurship.
Classification: LCC HD62.5 .A935 2024 (print) | LCC HD62.5 (ebook) | DDC
   658.1/1—dc23/eng/20240108
LC record available at https://lccn.loc.gov/2023048232
LC ebook record available at https://lccn.loc.gov/2023048233

Cover Design and Illustration: Marius Ursache
Author Photo: Courtesy of the Author

SKY10085723_092324

To Lisa, my wife of over four decades. How she puts up with me, I have no idea, but I got so lucky and am eternally grateful.

To my deceased parents, Becky and Herb Aulet, who gave me everything.

And to my sons and their significant others, Kenny and Liz, Tommy and Zach, Kyle, and Chris and Sophia.

And to granddaughters, Caroline and Avery, the best gifts Happah could ever have hoped for.

Family is the foundation for everything else. And I hit the jackpot!

CONTENTS

PREFACE

OVER 15 YEARS AGO, when I was asked to lead a core entrepreneurship course at MIT, I looked for a book that taught the basics of entrepreneurship that I had learned the hard way in over two decades as an entrepreneur in startups as well as a large organization. I was confident that there was a book out there that was rigorous, actionable, and accessible.

Turned out I was wrong. There was no such book.

Many of the books I came back to were excellent and had great material I had found helpful along my journey to entrepreneurship enlightenment, including Geoffrey Moore's *Crossing the Chasm*, W. Chan Kim and Renée Mauborgne's *Blue Ocean Strategy*, Stefan Thomke's *Experimentation Works: The Surprising Power of Business Experiments*, Brian Halligan and Dharmesh Shah's *Inbound Marketing*, Steve Blank's *Four Steps to the Epiphany*, Eric Ries's *Lean Startup*, Ash Maurya's *Running Lean*, Marc Randolph's *That Will Never Work*, and Alex Osterwalder and Yves Pigneur's *Business Model Generation*. More recently, the books have gotten more comprehensive, like *Zero to IPO* by Frederic Kerrest and *See, Solve, Scale* by Danny Warshay. These are all great books that truly advance the field of entrepreneurship, and I will reference many of them in this book. I believe that each book, along with other material I've collected over the years (like the concepts of Design Thinking, Jobs To Be Done, Simon Sinek's talks, and lessons from IBM as well as Procter & Gamble, to name but a few more), provide valuable insights that are applicable at the right time and context of the product conception, development, and launch. But what I needed was a one-stop concise guide summarizing key principles but also, equally importantly, directions about when and how to use them.

Since what I wanted wasn't out there, I did what so many instructors do—I started to construct a reader for the course. *Disciplined Entrepreneurship* is a direct descendant of that reader. It comes not only from my decades of experience as an entrepreneur but also from my experience teaching entrepreneurship at MIT, as well as from workshops I have taught around the world. Just as I teach in this book, I iterated and refined this approach with thousands of great entrepreneurs.

This book does not provide an algorithm that guarantees you success, because that is not possible. Every situation is different and, when successful, the outcome is something that never previously existed. Everyone's path is also unique. As such, as much as we might wish, there is not a singular surefire path to success.

As such, this book is designed as a rigorous but accessible guide for first-time and repeat entrepreneurs. It provides a prescriptive framework and integrated toolbox of tools, which will achieve this goal of creating an economically sustainable organization. This process can be used for "for profit," not-for-profits, and in fact almost any organization to increase their impact using the rules of a free market. It is an efficient and effective way to bring new products to market.

The 24-step process as presented is sequential in that you know what you should be doing next, but it is definitely not linear because there will be constant iterating on the work you've done in previous steps. Insights gained in early steps give you critical knowledge for later steps. That being said, entrepreneurship is about speed, and you should err on the side of action; make a decision, keep moving, and go back and refine your answers later—but keep moving.

While there are other elements to consider, from culture and team to sales, financing, and leadership, the foundation of a successful innovative new venture is the product (which could be a replicable service) that is created and delivered to a customer who enthusiastically accepts and pays for it, and so that is the focus of this book.

To be clear, this is not the only path to success, and there are many successful entrepreneurs who have not read this book. But when you analyze their success, you will see the same principles described herein.

Some people tell me that entrepreneurship should not be disciplined, but chaotic and unpredictable—and it is. But it is just in such situations where a framework to attack the problem in a systematic manner will be most valuable. This is exactly the book I wish I had 30 years ago when I fully committed to be an entrepreneur.

Special Note on this Expanded and Enhanced 10th-Anniversary Edition

Why a new version and what is different?

Well, looking back now, I am blown away by the success of this book.

When it was released, I joked that I hoped it was successful enough to get me on my favorite TV show at the time, *The Colbert Report*. Well, that never happened, but in every other way, it far exceeded my expectations of what impact it would have.

It has been translated into over two dozen languages, over 300,000 copies have been sold, it has been the basis for five online courses that have been taken by hundreds of thousands more on every continent and in most nations in the world, and is used in hundreds (probably thousands) of institutions today to teach entrepreneurship. Every week I have multiple interactions from people telling me how *Disciplined Entrepreneurship* really helped them. I will never forget the e-mail I got from someone I had never met from Zimbabwe who said simply, "Thank you. For the first time in my life I see a path to economic freedom."

How is this possible with a book where I tried to create the fewest new concepts I could? At the book's core were ideas and concepts that others had come up with that I had tested, determined that they worked, and summarized in an accessible way.[1] My goal was not grandiose but rather simple: making entrepreneurship success accessible to all. Turns out there was a big demand for this.

I somewhat half truthfully say that if I had known this was going to happen, I could never have written it. I would have agonized about it much more before releasing it to the publisher. As the book was adopted by so many people, I began to see the imperfections and areas to improve it. Five years ago, I made an attempt to fill in the gaps and add what new things I had learned by writing an entirely new book, *Disciplined Entrepreneurship Workbook*, meant to complement the original book. Still, I knew that the original needed to be redone. So much was learned and had changed since it was released, but I also knew now it was a daunting task. I needed a push.

First, I had a new colleague full of energy who joined me over three years ago in teaching the foundational course at MIT, Paul Cheek. He is not just a tremendous instructor, but he extended the material and showed how it could be even more impactful by creating a follow-on course. He kept pushing me to update the book. But that was not enough.

Secondly, it has been said there has never been a better invention to get things done than a deadline. Paul combined with a wonderful prodding publisher on the other side knew this. They got me to agree to set the tenth anniversary as a deadline to get this update of the original (or "OG" as my Wiley publisher Shannon Vargo calls it). This new edition is designed to cover the material in the OG but even more concisely. In addition, it integrates key parts of the *Disciplined Entrepreneurship Workbook* into a single book. Updated examples were in order as well. There were also new materials to be covered, especially with the rapid advances in go-to-market strategies and technologies. Generative AI, for example, has been a game changer. Finally, there is a treasure trove of additional materials that are now available online, fully coordinated with the book for those entrepreneurs or entrepreneurship educators who want more.

An important design point for this book was that it fit very well with Paul's book being released at the same time, *Disciplined Entrepreneurship Startup Tactics: 15 Tactics to Turn Your Business Plan into a Business* (Link to Disciplined Entrepreneurship Tactics website: startuptactics.net). As I mentioned about Paul earlier, he has been running a well-received follow-on course to the material in this book. The two books complement each other like peanut butter and jelly. Similar to how I tested the original *Disciplined Entrepreneurship* manuscript with hundreds of students before publishing, the pairing of these two books has also been tested with our students and the results have been fantastic. To say I am excited about these books coming out together is an understatement.

---

[1] Reminds me of the story about the great rock and roll musician George Thorogood. When asked why he didn't write more of his own songs, he said, "Because Chuck Berry already wrote all the good songs." I can relate.

So, when I started and was asked to make my reader into a book, I honestly thought, does the world really need another entrepreneurship book? My initial answer was, probably not, but what the heck. You miss 100% of the shots you don't take. Today, I am in a totally different mindset. I know the corpus of books and materials out in the world for entrepreneurs and I am very confident that this book and Paul's book will be very meaningful contributions. I hope you agree after reading the book, and if you do, please share with others because there is no doubt that with the many seemingly intractable problems we face as humans, we need more high-quality and better-connected entrepreneurs. They are the ones who historically have been at the center of solving the world's greatest challenges—and they will be so in the future. Go forth and contribute to the solution. Read on.

Note on examples in this book: Many of the examples in this book come from student work done in the courses I teach at MIT and elsewhere. I have altered some of them to better illustrate best practices and pitfalls for various steps but kept the essence of the situation. The projects described by the examples might not have turned into full-fledged companies, depending on the decisions the student teams make after completing their coursework, but their examples are valuable in an educational context nonetheless.

INTRODUCTION

News Flash: Entrepreneurship Can Be Taught!

WE KNOW IT IS IN THERE, BUT WE JUST CAN'T SEEM TO FIND THAT ENTREPRENEURSHIP GENE

Entrepreneurship is nurture, not nature. Everyone can be an entrepreneur and it can be taught.

THE FIRST QUESTION I ask when I begin a new course or workshop is, "Do you think entrepreneurship can be taught?" Invariably a silence comes over the group. They wiggle uncomfortably in their seats. Some amiably agree, telling me that is why they came to class in the first place. After a polite back and forth, someone will invariably say what is on the mind of many in the room: "No, either you are an entrepreneur or you are not." That person, once empowered, begins to passionately argue the case.

I have to say that I tend to like this person, in large part because that person would have been me in the not too distant past. But now I know that entrepreneurship can be taught. I experience it every day in the courses I teach at the Massachusetts Institute of Technology (MIT) and around the world.

When we look at Jeff Bezos, Steve Jobs, Bill Gates, Oprah Winfrey, Elon Musk, Richard Branson, Jack Ma, Mark Zuckerberg, Tope Awotona, Sara Blakely, and all the other highly visible entrepreneurs, they seem to be different from us. They seem extraordinary. But each of their successes is a result of great products (or replicable services) that made them successful, not the result of some special gene.

To be a successful entrepreneur, you must have great and innovative products. All of the other factors that influence success are nothing without a product that creates value for a customer for which someone will pay the company or organization. And the process of making a great product that people will pay for can be taught. *Disciplined Entrepreneurship* will teach you how to systematically improve your odds of achieving this goal.

In this book I present a disciplined step-by-step approach to creating a new venture. This framework is useful both in a classroom setting and for those who want to create a new company that serves a new market outside the classroom. Before we begin, though, we must tackle several common myths about the entrepreneur that often hamper those wishing to start new companies or teach students how to do so.

Ten Common Myths About Entrepreneurship That Must Go

There are many misconceptions about what entrepreneurship is and what makes for a successful entrepreneur that could well be extrapolated from movies like *Steve Jobs* and *The Social Network*. These myths are not just untrue but they are detrimental mental models to creating successful entrepreneurs.

1. **Entrepreneurship is about mercurial individuals.** While the entrepreneur as a lone, often disagreeable hero is a common narrative, a close reading of the research tells a different story. Teams start companies. Importantly, a bigger team actually adds to the odds of success. *More founders = better odds of success.*[1] **The truth is that entrepreneurship is a team sport,** and that gets truer every day as the world gets more complex.

---

[1] Roberts, Edward B., *Entrepreneurs in High Technology: Lessons from MIT and Beyond*, Oxford University Press, New York, 1991, p. 258.

Despite what you see in the movies, research shows that entrepreneurship is not an individual sport but rather a team sport where collaboration is crucial to success.

2. **Entrepreneurs succeed because they have special charisma.** You may have heard about Steve Jobs's "reality distortion zone" and entrepreneurs being able to sell "ice to Eskimos." This implies that it takes great charisma to be successful; but the opposite is more likely true. While charisma may be effective for a short period, it is difficult to sustain and, in the end, will be counterproductive. Great entrepreneurs produce real value for their customers. The truth is that entrepreneurs need to sell real value. They need to delight their customers because the best salesperson you can ever have is not someone you can hire, but instead it is your own customers. Research shows that more important than being charismatic, entrepreneurs need to be effective long-term communicators, recruiters, and salespeople not just with customers but with all of their stakeholders. **Authenticity is much more important than charisma.**

3. **Entrepreneurs are born, not made.** As the cartoon at the beginning of this chapter suggests, an entrepreneurship gene has and will not be found. Some believe that personality traits like being flamboyant or risk-taking are correlated with successful entrepreneurship, but that line of thinking is misguided. Instead, there are real skills that can be taught, which increase the odds of success. They are not genetically gifted to a few lucky souls. MIT professor Ed Roberts's research shows that the more times people start companies, the more likely they are to be successful. As you will see in this book, being successful in entrepreneurship is not a matter of gut feeling or instincts, but rather a systematic process that can be taught. **Entrepreneurship is nurture, not nature.**

4. **Entrepreneurs are successful because they are smarter than the rest of us.** Again, watching movies and reading books, you might think this because, as they say, "History is written by the victors." I can tell you firsthand that it is not true; entrepreneurs are not smarter than "the rest of us." When you see successful entrepreneurs, they are successful because they get obsessed (not passionate but obsessed) with solving a problem and learning everything they need to know to solve that problem better than anyone else. This might appear like intelligence (and there must be some level of intelligence) but it is much, much more about **focus on becoming an expert in one area** than general intelligence.

5. **You have to love risk to be an entrepreneur.** This myth frames the issue incorrectly and must be addressed. Entrepreneurs don't like risk in areas they can't control. They understand that risk, like temporary failure or adversity, is part of the process of becoming great. There is no place in the world where there is no risk, and that is becoming increasingly truer every day. **What entrepreneurs learn is how to take intelligent informed risk.** This is where they have some agency and some advantage where the risk-reward ratio indicated it is rational to pursue the opportunity.

6. **Entrepreneurs are lucky.** I will not deny there are some entrepreneurs who just get lucky, but most engineer their luck. In his book *Outliers*, Malcolm Gladwell describes how very successful people identify a new opportunity in the future and then work hard to get their "ten thousand hours"[2] of preparation in by the time the opportunity becomes real. **By working smart and hard, entrepreneurs make their own luck; they don't depend on random events happening.**

---

[2] "Ten thousand hours" is a seemingly arbitrary number. Rather than focus on the specific number, I suggest you focus on the fact that they spent a lot of time and effort preparing before the day they saw the window of opportunity opening up, and hence they were well prepared beyond others.

While good entrepreneurs might appear to be lucky, that luck is often by design. They see a future opportunity and they work diligently to be prepared to take advantage of it when it happens.

7. **Entrepreneurs are successful because they came up with a novel idea.** As I have written about elsewhere,[3] the original idea is the single most overrated thing in entrepreneurship. As my colleague at MIT Professor Bengt Holmstrom, Nobel Laureate, says with regard to first-mover advantage, "There are three letters missing: D-I-S"—meaning it is often actually a disadvantage. The person with the original idea most often loses to others in the end. Another former colleague, Professor Matt Marx, now chair and faculty director of entrepreneurship at Cornell University, showed in his research that successful companies start with an idea and then focus on a customer and do a process called "switchbacks"[4] until they figure out what works. Netflix co-founder Marc Randolph describes in his brilliant book *That Will Never Work* how every original idea is flawed and it is only through iteration that it becomes viable. **An idea is necessary to catalyze a team into action, but much more important is executing effectively on a viable idea that will evolve over time.** This is all much easier and more likely to happen with a disciplined process and a strong team.

---

[3] "The Most Overrated Thing in Entrepreneurship" by Bill Aulet, https://www.d-eship.com/articles/the-most-overrated-thing-in-entrepreneurship/

[4] Switchbacks are the very pronounced or sharp turns a road makes when it goes up a particularly steep hill to make the ascent more manageable—a good analogy.

While necessary to get started, the idea (or technology) is ultimately the least important factor in determining success.

8. **You need to be young to be a successful entrepreneur.** Going back to point number one, entrepreneurship is a team sport where having multiple perspectives is critical. It is not a bad idea to have young people on your team, but the research shows that working with young people does not equal success. Another one of my colleagues here at MIT, Professor Pierre Azoulay, showed in his research that the average age at founding for the 1,000 fastest-growing new ventures was 45. While we do not want to discount the contribution of young members on a team, his research suggests that the idea of the young, tech-savvy entrepreneur is a myth, and that successful entrepreneurship is more likely to come with age and experience.

9. **Entrepreneurs succeed at a rate of less than 10%.** I often ask groups what they believe the success rates of startups is. Success would be defined as being in business five years after founding. The responses are consistently in the range of 1–5% and the high might be 10%. It is perceived as a long shot. I am not sure where these perceptions come from but I can tell you that students who come out of our programs at MIT have a five-year survival rate of almost 70%.[5] Is this the right metric for success? I have qualms about that for sure, because many of the people who did not succeed according to this metric still go on to be some of our most successful entrepreneurs, so it can be misleading. Still, the point is that **if you know what you are doing, entrepreneurship is not as risky as is generally perceived.** In fact, it is a way to control your destiny.

---

[5] "10 Years of delta v: An Impact Study," https://entrepreneurship.mit.edu/delta-v-10-year-study/

10. **Entrepreneurs are undisciplined.** In fact, it is quite the opposite. Entrepreneurs must have extraordinary discipline to be successful. This was one of the most fundamental insights that led to the name of this book. The first decade of my business career (the 1980s), I worked at IBM, a company known at the time for extreme discipline in all aspects. I looked down on the entrepreneurs of my time like Gates, Jobs, and Mitch Kapor as being undisciplined. Then I started my own company and I realized they had a more important discipline than I had. My discipline had to do with dressing, meeting etiquette, calendar integrity, and other such things. What I quickly realized was that those things did not matter unless they led to getting profitable customers who paid me. Why? Because if I did not get profitable customers who paid me and told other customers how great our products were, we did not make payroll, whereas I never worried a day while I was at IBM about making payroll. This urgency created a focus that gave my startup an unrelenting personal discipline that was at a level far beyond what I had at IBM. **Entrepreneurs have to have the spirit of a pirate to be different but they also have to have the discipline of a Navy SEAL to execute successfully**.

SUCCESSFUL ENTREPRENEURSHIP

SPIRIT
OF A PIRATE

SKILLS
OF A NAVY SEAL

Successful entrepreneurship is a balance of thinking differently, combined with strong self-discipline regarding executing once you have determined the direction.

Five Useful Mental Models About Entrepreneurship

On the flip side of the myths that are detrimental to us in trying to understand entrepreneurship, there are five lenses in which it is helpful to view entrepreneurship.

1. **Entrepreneurship is a craft, not a science or art.** The end product of successful entrepreneurship is always unique and new. As such, there cannot and will never be an algorithm to make someone a successful entrepreneur. On the other hand, it is not some mystical process like art. Entrepreneurship is in the middle as a craft. It is like pottery where everyone can do it and create unique results but there are also first principles that can be taught to increase the quality of your results. To become better at a craft requires understanding both the first principles (i.e., the theory) and even more so, how to apply them (i.e., the practice). This can only be properly taught in an apprenticeship model. This is to say that you cannot truly learn entrepreneurship just by reading this book or watching videos; you also have to apply it

The sciences are well-defined and deterministic; art is the opposite. Entrepreneurship is a craft that sits between these two ends of the spectrum.

multiple times (i.e., "get your reps in") looping back and forth between theory and practice with some mentoring to become an expert.[6]

2. **Entrepreneurship is a mindset, a skill set, and a way of operating.** Entrepreneurs have to be not just willing but should also take joy in being different and significantly improving the status quo. Entrepreneurs start with a "hacking" mindset that there is a better way to do things than what we are doing today and it will be really fun and rewarding to find a better way and implement it. They must understand that it will not be easy and there will be a lot of adversity along the way, but they love going on that roller coaster journey and are willing to pay that price. They have to "love the game," as my colleague Nagarjuna Venna describes it. Once you have that spirit and understanding, the rest of it—entrepreneurship skills and way of operating—can be taught. It requires the four Hs, as we talk about at MIT: the heart (spirit/mindset), the head (knowledge/theory), the hands (practice/capability), and the home (community-based way of operating to be able to utilize resources beyond your control).[7] While it all starts with a mindset (heart), it must be complemented with the other three Hs as well.

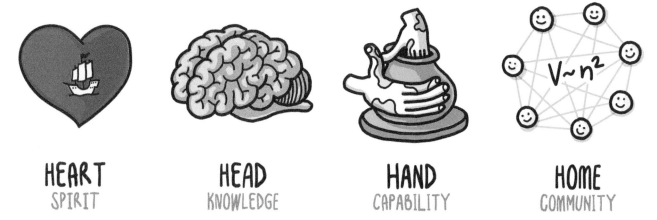

HEART
SPIRIT

HEAD
KNOWLEDGE

HAND
CAPABILITY

HOME
COMMUNITY

The four Hs summarize four key pillars to becoming a successful entrepreneur—and it all starts with the Heart.

---

[6] For a full article on this topic, see https://www.d-eship.com/articles/entrepreneurship-is-a-craft-and-heres-why-thats-important/
[7] Harvard Business School Professor Howard Stevenson with great insight defined entrepreneurship as the pursuit of opportunity beyond resources controlled.

3. **Everyone is capable of entrepreneurship.** I often have people tell me they are not entrepreneurs, to which I reply "not true!" We are all born entrepreneurs and it is the system that stifles it in us. Since the beginning of time, people have been making things, trading things, and providing services to survive. It is a Darwinian characteristic for humans. It is only since the industrial revolution that we altered our educational and societal systems to focus on managing large organizations. Entrepreneurship by necessity has famously flourished and proliferated in places like Israel, South Africa, Vietnam, and China, and I assure you that even the most reluctant person you know would become entrepreneurial quickly when given a choice between death and hustling to survive.[8]

4. **Entrepreneurship is more than startups.** We must expand our view of entrepreneurs beyond simply people who create startups backed by venture capital. Entrepreneurs are needed and certainly can exist inside already established organizations. They can be in nonprofits, academia, government, and faith-based organizations. They should be ubiquitous in our society. Entrepreneurs are efficient, effective, and creative problem solvers who thrive in times of change. They don't fear change but rather see it as an opportunity. With change coming at us at an increasingly rapid pace, it is essential that all of us have an entrepreneurial mode in all facets of our lives, not just in startups.

5. **Sustained and successful entrepreneurship as we will talk about in this book is an ethical activity.** While entrepreneurship, as we will be teaching in this book, utilizes one of the most powerful forces the world has ever seen, capitalism, it is not simply about profiteering. To be a sustained success, entrepreneurs have to have a "raison d'être" (French for "reason for existence"). We will be talking more about this in depth in Step 0 but now it is important to know that this raison d'être needs to be more than simply making money. No new venture, initiative, or product has a journey that always goes well. It will have down times when it makes more sense economically to jump to Goldman Sachs or some other more lucrative job. If the only thing holding your team to your effort is money, they will leave at exactly the point when you probably need them the most to avoid a downward death spiral. There must be some great mission tying the organization together and keeping the team together through the inevitable ups and downs. That is the raison d'être that is a higher cause than profiteering.

In summary, have confidence going forward in this book, knowing that if you have the mindset, you can be taught how to be a successful entrepreneur.

---

[8] For more on this topic, see https://www.d-eship.com/articles/featured/all-people-are-born-entrepreneurs-then-society-takes-this-away/

Definition of Entrepreneurship

The first rule you are taught in engineering is before trying to solve a problem, define your terms. Let's start with the most basic: What is entrepreneurship in the most succinct definition possible? An economist (which I am not, but I work with lots of them) would define entrepreneurship along the lines of the following:

> An entrepreneur creates a new economically sustainable organization where there was none before. She does this by creating value for someone. That is a necessary but not sufficient condition. The second criterion is that the entrepreneur should extract value (i.e., some payment or "rent") for the value that she produces. The third criterion is that the rent extracted exceed the costs of running the business on an ongoing basis while also paying off any debts or other obligations from those providing the initial resources to create the new organization. That is a definition in the simplest terms.
>
> The person or organization may or may not be the one realizing the value created by the company, such as Google, which creates value for you, the end user, doing the internet searches, but they extract their rent from advertisers to make the organization economically sustainable. The person who pays the rent is called the economic buyer and in fact there could be multiple economic buyers. The money they provide must exceed the costs of continuing to run the business and also be sufficient to pay off those who funded the development of the organization. Again, this is an exercise not in simply creating value but also extracting sufficient value so as to be at a minimum self-sufficient. This definition also applies to doctors, dentists, lawyers, IT service companies, grocery stores, nail salons, restaurants, consultants, nonprofits, and academic institutions (foundations and donors can be economic buyers too but they need to be convinced the entrepreneur is providing real value).

This describes entrepreneurs in general and at the most basic level. Let us now advance to the next level to talk about two fundamentally different types of entrepreneurs.

Distinguishing Two Distinct Types of Entrepreneurship

Entrepreneurship is about creating a new business where one did not exist before. That definition seemed clear until my colleagues Professors Fiona Murray and Scott Stern and I spent a good deal of time talking to various organizations about how to promote entrepreneurship in different regions of the world. We found that when we said "entrepreneurship" to people, it could mean at least two extremely different things—a discrepancy that had important ramifications, because each type of entrepreneurship has dramatically different objectives and needs.[9]

Small and Medium Enterprise (SME) Entrepreneurship

The first type of entrepreneurship is small and medium enterprise (SME) entrepreneurship. This is the type of business that is likely started by one person to serve a local market and it grows to be a small or medium-size business that serves this local market. It is most often closely held, likely a family business, and control is important. The business "rewards" for these founders are primarily in the form of personal independence and cash flow from the business.

These businesses generally do not need to raise as much money, and when money is injected into these businesses, the resultant increase in revenue and jobs created is relatively rapid. These entrepreneurs and enterprises can be geographically dispersed and the jobs they create are for the most part "non-tradable" jobs in that they cannot be outsourced to someplace else to reduce costs. Frequently these businesses are service businesses or retailers of other companies' products. The key distinguishing factor is their focus on local markets.

Innovation-Driven Enterprise (IDE) Entrepreneurship

Innovation-driven enterprise (IDE) entrepreneurship is the riskier and more ambitious of the two. These entrepreneurs arc aspiring to serve markets that go well beyond the local market. They are looking to sell their offering at a global or at least at a regional level.

These entrepreneurs are more often teams, and they are building their business off some technology, process, business model, or other innovation that will give them significant competitive advantage, as compared to existing companies. They are interested in creating impact more than they are interested in control, and they often have to sell equity in their company to support their ambitious growth plans.

While they are often slower to start, they tend to have more impressive exponential growth when they do get customer traction. Growth is what they seek, at the risk of losing control of their company and having multiple owners. While SME companies tend to grow up and stay relatively small (but not always), IDE companies are more interested in "going big or going home." To achieve their ambitions, they have to become big and fast-growing to serve global markets.

---

[9] Aulet, Bill, and Fiona Murray, "A Tale of Two Entrepreneurs: Understanding Differences in the Types of Entrepreneurship in the Economy," May 2, 2013, Kauffman Foundation research paper, https://www.kauffman.org/entrepreneurship/reports/a-tale-of-two-entrepreneurs-understanding-differences-in-the-types-of-entrepreneurship-in-the-economy/

IDE entrepreneurship creates companies that have "tradable" jobs, which means they could and may well be moved geographically out of a region when it makes the overall business more competitive. It is also generally the case that any injection of investment or money requires a much longer time to show results in terms of incremental new revenues or jobs.

In the short run the SME model will be more responsive, but with patience, the IDE ventures have the capacity to produce profound results, as we have seen with companies like Apple, Google, Hewlett-Packard, and other publicly traded companies.

Our Focus Is Innovation-Driven Enterprise   A healthy economy consists of both types of entrepreneur-ship and both have their strengths and weaknesses. Neither is better than the other. But they are substantively different enough that they require different mindsets and different sets of skills to be successful. Therefore, in this book, rather than teach "entrepreneurship," I will teach IDE entrepre-neurship, because it is what I know best, having co-founded and/or run three companies (Cambridge Decision Dynamics, SensAble Technologies, and Viisage) based on innovation.

What Is Innovation?   Innovation has become an increasingly clichéd term, but it has a simple definition, which I have adapted from Ed Roberts:[10]

$$\text{Innovation} = \text{Invention} * \text{Commercialization}$$

I modify Roberts's definition, which involved addition, because innovation is not a sum of invention and commercialization, but a product. If there is commercialization but no invention (invention = 0), or invention but no commercialization (commercialization = 0), then there is no innovation.

The invention (an idea, a technology, or some sort of intellectual property) is important, but the entrepreneur does not need to create the invention. In fact, the inventions that lead to innovation-driven companies often come from elsewhere. Such was the case with Steve Jobs, who identified others' inventions (the computer mouse created by Xerox PARC is the most famous example) and commercialized them effectively through Apple. Likewise, Google has made most of its money through AdWords, the text-based, keyword-driven advertisements on their search results pages. A different company, Overture, had invented such advertisements, but Google was successful through its commercialization of Overture's invention.

---

[10] Roberts, Edward B., "Managing Invention and Innovation," *Research-Technology Management*, January-February 2007, p. 35. Roberts's original definition is "Innovation = Invention + Exploitation." I have changed the word "exploitation" to the simpler word "commercialization."

These examples show that the capability to commercialize an invention is necessary for real innovation. An entrepreneur, then, serves primarily as the commercialization agent.

I very consciously do not use the word "technology-driven" entrepreneurship because innovation is not limited to technology. Innovation can come in many varieties, including technology, process, business model, positioning, and more.

Some of the most exciting innovations of our time are at their core business model innovations, such as Airbnb, Uber, Google, iTunes, Salesforce.com, Netflix, and Zipcar, among others. They are enabled by technology, yes. Zipcar would find it difficult to maintain its large network of cars without keyless-entry technology for its members. But at its core, Zipcar's innovation is treating a rental car as a substitute for owning a car, rather than as temporary transportation for car owners and business travelers visiting far-flung areas. Zipcar doesn't have to understand the intricacies of its technology to be successful, but it has to understand what it means for its customers to "collaboratively consume."

As technology becomes more and more commoditized, you will see more non-technology centric innovations that leverage technology. Innovations in other areas including (but not limited to) business model (i.e., how you extract rent) or go-to-market (GTM; i.e., how you create and fulfill demand for your product) are already becoming more important in many cases, and that trend will continue.

SME Entrepreneurship	IDE Entrepreneurship
Initially focus on addressing local markets only.	Focus on global/regional markets. The company is based on some sort of innovation (tech, business process, model) where they can go global or across regions.
"Non-tradable jobs"—jobs that must be performed locally (e.g., restaurants, dry cleaners, and service industry.).	"Tradable jobs"—jobs that do not have to be performed locally.
Most often family businesses. People who start them seek to maintain control, even at the expense of high growth. Likely an individual-driven founder group.	More diverse ownership base as the focus of founders is on high growth and creating company market value. More team-oriented group of founders.

SME Entrepreneurship	**IDE Entrepreneurship**
The company grows at a linear rate. When you put money into the company, the system (revenue, cash flow, jobs, etc.) will respond quickly in a positive manner.	The company starts by losing money, but will have exponential growth. Requires investment. When you put money into the company, the revenue/cash flow/jobs numbers do not respond quickly.

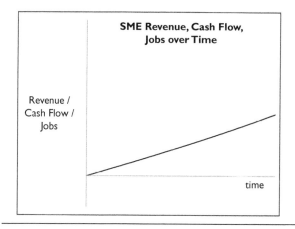

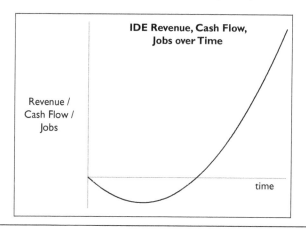

Source: Aulet, Bill, and Fiona Murray, "A Tale of Two Entrepreneurs: Understanding Differences in the Types of Entrepreneurship in the Economy," May 2, 2013, Kauffman Foundation research paper, https://www.kauffman.org/entrepreneurship/reports/a-tale-of-two-entrepreneurs-understanding-differences-in-the-types-of-entrepreneurship-in-the-economy/

ADDITIONAL RESOURCES

There are additional resources for this step at www.d-eship.com/intro. These materials include:

- Case Study: What Explains MIT's Success in Entrepreneurship?
- Article from USASBE 2018 Annals of Entrepreneurship Education and Pedagogy: *What I've Learned About Teaching Entrepreneurship* by Bill Aulet.

Additional resources will be added as new and updated examples and information become available.

Moving from Introduction to Action and the 24 Steps

In this introduction I have spent time carefully defining the key areas of focus for this book (i.e., entrepreneurship, innovation) and cleared up some misperceptions. I have described the context and the frameworks that have been successful to make more successful entrepreneurs. You should have a sense of what is coming. Now it is time to get to work on the specific steps of how to build your innovation-driven venture.

SIX THEMES OF THE 24 STEPS

THE 24 STEPS ARE discrete, actionable tasks but they can be grouped into six themes. Ideally, the steps should be done in numerical order but this is not always how it works in the real world. If you happen to get to later steps before the earlier ones, don't freak out but be cautious. Make sure you go back with urgency and complete the previous steps so you have a strong foundation for your business.

Each step builds off the ones before it, so they should be seen as cumulative and sequential. That being said, they are *not linear,* where you complete a step and never return to it. You continually go back and update earlier steps as you get more information later in your journey.

With the above understanding, these themes present a proven general outline of how to create a sustainable innovation-based business.

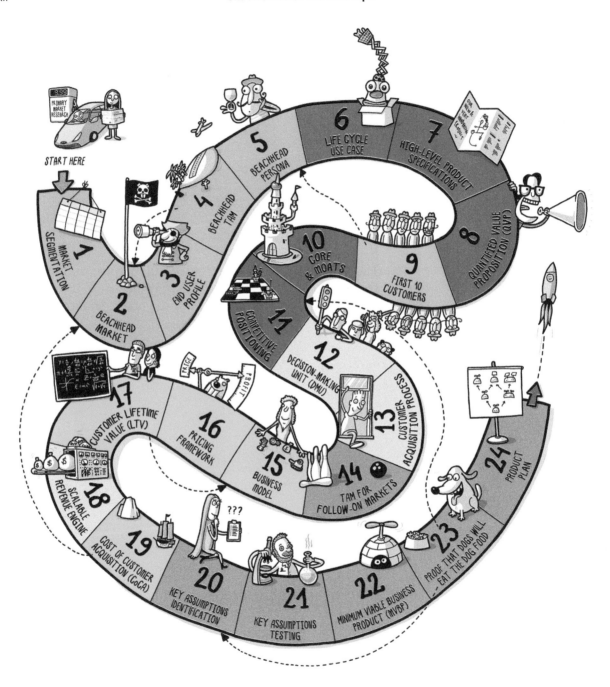

WHO IS YOUR CUSTOMER?

1. Market Segmentation
2. Beachhead Market
3. End-User Profile
4. Beachhead Market TAM
5. Beachhead Market Persona
9. First 10 Customers

WHAT CAN YOU DO FOR YOUR CUSTOMER?

6. Full life cycle use case
7. High-level product specifications
8. Quantified value proposition
10. Core & moats
11. Chart your competitive position

HOW DOES YOUR CUSTOMER ACQUIRE YOUR PRODUCT?

12. Decision-making unit (DMU)
13. Customer acquisition process
18. Scalable revenue engine

HOW DO YOU MAKE MONEY OFF YOUR PRODUCT?

15. Business model
16. Pricing framework
17. Customer lifetime value (LTV)
19. Cost of customer acquisition (CoCA)

HOW DO YOU DESIGN AND BUILD YOUR PRODUCT?

15. Key assumptions identification
16. Key assumptions testing
17. Minimum viable business product (MVBP)
19. Proof that dogs will eat the dog food

HOW DO YOU SCALE YOUR BUSINESS?

14. TAM size for follow-on markets
24. Product plan

Who Is Your Customer?	What Can You Do for Your Customer?	How Does Your Customer Acquire Your Product?	How Do You Make Money off Your Product?	How Do You Design and Build Your Product?	How Do You Scale Your Business?
Step 1. Market Segmentation	6. Full Life Cycle Use Case	12. Determine the Customer's Decision-Making Unit (DMU)	15. Design a Business Model	20. Identify Key Assumptions	14. Calculate the Total Addressable Market Size for Follow-on Markets
2. Select a Beachhead Market	7. High-Level Product Specification	13. Map the Process to Acquire a Paying Customer	16. Set Your Pricing Framework	21. Test Key Assumptions	24. Develop a Product Plan
3. Build an End User Profile	8. Quantify the Value Proposition	18. Design a Scalable Revenue Engine	17. Calculate the Lifetime Value (LTV) of an Acquired Customer	22. Define the Minimum Viable Business Product (MVBP)	
4. Calculate the Total Addressable Market Size (TAM) for the Beachhead Market	10. Define Your Core		19. Calculate the Cost of Customer Acquisition (CoCA)	23. Show That "The Dogs Will Eat the Dog Food"	
5. Profile the Persona for the Beachhead Market	11. Chart Your Competitive Position				
9. Identify Your Next 10 Customers					

1. Market Segmentation
   a. **What?**

   Brainstorm and identify how your idea/technology can serve a variety of potential end users. Primary market research (PMR) is then used to fill out a matrix.

   b. **Why?**

   It is crucial to start the process with the customer and work everything back from there.

2. Select a Beachhead Market
   a. **What?**

      Select one market segment from Step 1 where you feel you have the highest odds of success while also giving you legitimacy and strategic assets to grow further.
   b. **Why?**

      As a startup you have limited resources and focus is essential.
3. Build an End User Profile
   a. **What?**

      Use PMR techniques to build out a robust demographic and psychographic description of your end user.
   b. **Why?**

      There are three reasons: (1) to keep the focus on the end user, (2) to deepen your understanding of the primary customer, and (3) to calculate the TAM in the next step.
4. Calculate the Total Addressable Market (TAM) Size for the Beachhead Market
   a. **What?**

      Estimate the revenue per year you will get in your Beachhead Market if you achieve 100% market share.
   b. **Why?**

      To make sure your Beachhead Market is not too big or too small.
5. Profile the Persona for the Beachhead Market
   a. **What?**

      Identify one actual real end user in your Beachhead Market who best represents your End User Profile.
   b. **Why?**

      Creates great focus in your organization and serves as a touchstone for all decisions going forward.
6. Full Life Cycle Use Case
   a. **What?**

      Describe the full longitudinal experience of the persona and what opportunity there is for improvement.

　　b. **Why?**

　　This will provide invaluable information for future steps to create specificity with regard to solutions, value, and accessing the customer.

7. High-Level Product Specification

　　a. **What?**

　　Create a visual description of the product as well as making a simple draft brochure, landing page, or digital representation of the proposed product.

　　b. **Why?**

　　You need to make sure your team and the customer all have a common agreement on what the product is.

8. Quantify the Value Proposition

　　a. **What?**

　　Summarize in as concrete a way as possible the value your product will create for the target customer.

　　b. **Why?**

　　Customers buy based on value; it needs to be clear that you can show it.

9. Identify Your Next 10 Customers

　　a. **What?**

　　Create a list of the next 10 customers after the Persona who closely fit the end user profile.

　　b. **Why?**

　　Validates the Persona and all the assumptions you have made so far.

10. Define Your Core

　　a. **What?**

　　Determine the single thing that you will do better than anyone else that will be very difficult for others to copy.

　　b. **Why?**

　　Having a clear definition of your Core will allow you to focus your limited resources to build and reinforce it.

11. <u>Chart Your Competitive Position</u>
    a. **What?**

    Represent visually your position relative to the other alternatives in the Persona's top two priorities.

    b. **Why?**

    Customers don't care about your "core" but they do care about benefits relating to their priorities.

12. <u>Determine the Customer's Decision-Making Unit (DMU)</u>
    a. **What?**

    Determine all the people who are involved in making the decision to acquire your product—including influencers.

    b. **Why?**

    This starts the process to determine the Cost of Customer Acquisition (CoCA).

13. <u>Map the Process to Acquire a Paying Customer</u>
    a. **What?**

    Detail how the DMU decides to buy your product. Particular focus will be made to identify Windows of Opportunity and Triggers (Step 13A) where they are most open to acquiring.

    b. **Why?**

    This will be critical input to determine the length of the sales cycle and identify critical bottlenecks in the process.

14. <u>Calculate the Total Addressable Market Size for Follow-on Markets</u>
    a. **What?**

    Calculate the annual revenues from the top follow-on markets after you are successful in your Beachhead Market.

    b. **Why?**

    It shows the potential that can come from winning your beachhead and motivates you to do so quickly and effectively.

15. <u>Design a Business Model</u>
    a. **What?**

    Review the different types of way to get paid for your product and choose the best one aligned with all key stakeholders' interests.

b. **Why?**

Wise selection of a value extraction Business Model can dramatically reduce CoCA, increase Lifetime Value (LTV) of an Acquired Customer, and provide you with competitive advantage.

16. Set Your Pricing Framework

a. **What?**

Determine a framework to test pricing for your new product and decide on what the initial price will be.

b. **Why?**

Small changes in pricing can have a huge impact on your profitability.

17. Calculate the Lifetime Value (LTV) of an Acquired Customer

a. **What?**

Estimate the Net Present Value (NPV) of the total profits you will get from a new customer over the time period they will be your customer.

b. **Why?**

To complete the unit economics, you now need to estimate and understand the drivers of the LTV and it should get to at least 3X the CoCA.

18. Design a Scalable Revenue Engine

a. **What?**

Visually map the short-, medium-, and long-term way you will create and fulfill demand for your product.

b. **Why?**

This will be critical input to calculating the CoCA over time.

19. Calculate the Cost of Customer Acquisition (CoCA)

a. **What?**

Estimate the total marketing and sales expense in a given period to get new customers and divide this by the number of new customers.

b. **Why?**

The unit economics are a simple but effective proxy for how sustainable and attractive your business will be as it scales.

20. <u>Identify Key Assumptions</u>
    a. **What?**

    Identify key assumptions to be tested before you begin to make heavy investments in product development.

    b. **Why?**

    It will be faster and much less costly now to test the assumptions and allow you to preserve valuable resources and adjust as needed.

21. <u>Test Key Assumptions</u>
    a. **What?**

    Test, through a series of small and inexpensive experiments, each of the individual assumptions you have identified in Step 20.

    b. **Why?**

    This scientific approach will allow you to understand which assumptions are valid and which ones are not, then adjust when the cost of doing so is much lower and it can be done much faster.

22. <u>Define the Minimum Viable Business Product (MVBP)</u>
    a. **What?**

    Define that the minimal product you can use to start the iterative customer feedback loop—where the customer gets value from the product and pays for it.

    b. **Why?**

    You must reduce the variables in the equation to get the customer feedback loop started with the highest possibility of success with simultaneously the most efficient use of your scarce resources.

23. <u>Show That "The Dogs Will Eat the Dog Food"</u>
    a. **What?**

    Offer your MVBP to your target customer and obtain quantitative metrics regarding the adoption rate of the product, the value the target customer is getting from the product, and proof that someone is paying for the product.

    b. **Why?**

    Numbers don't lie. Show concrete evidence and don't rely simply on anecdotal evidence.

24. <u>Develop a Product Plan</u>

    a. **What?**

    Develop a longer-term plan to add functionality so you can address additional markets over time.

    b. **Why?**

    It is important to think ahead and have a plan so your team is ready to keep moving forward after the MVBP.

Note: **Primary Market Research (PMR; see Step 1A)** *is the fuel that will drive this whole process. The process only works if you get quality input from a quality PMR process. Garbage in, garbage out. Quality PMR fuel into the process, gold out.*

TRACKING YOUR PROGRESS: THE DISCIPLINED ENTREPRENEURSHIP (DE) CANVAS

WHILE THE 24 STEP diagram from the previous pages is a great single image to summarize the process, my colleagues at MIT and I have learned it is also extremely helpful to have a one-page summary or canvas to track your progress. This is how the DE Canvas came about.

Originally, we used the Business Model Canvas by Alex Osterwalder and then the Lean Model Canvas by Ash Maurya. While we found initial enthusiasm and use for them, we also found the limitations in these for what we wanted to do. Neither embedded explicitly the important sequential logic and depth that we desired and so we built our own customized canvas around the 24 Steps. The DE Canvas extends beyond the 24 Steps to make sure the entrepreneur considers other important factors to make a successful and scalable new venture. It should be noted as well that in addition to vetting startups and startup ideas, the DE Canvas has been used extensively in existing organizations as well to improve their profitability and growth.

What Is the DE Canvas, and Why Is It Important?

The DE Canvas is a one-page overview of the Disciplined Entrepreneurship approach to entrepreneurship. It includes all of the 24 Steps but also two other critical areas: (1) the elements you start your business with, and (2) the overall financials of your new venture. There are 10 boxes in the canvas (a nice visual symmetry) with a sequential order. That does not necessarily mean they must be done in that order, but it does convey the cumulative nature of the steps.

The early steps form the foundation for the later steps. This is similar to the 24 Steps. For example, it is ineffective, inefficient, and unsustainable to develop a Quantified Value Proposition in Box #3 (Value Creation) if you don't know who your customer is, which is Box #2 (Initial Market). Similarly, if you do not know who your customer is, it would be unproductive to proceed to thinking about competitive positioning, how to generate revenue from the product, and how to build out your organization. While building a new venture is not a linear, sequential process, it is still beneficial to have some sequential guidance to the process to increase your performance and odds of success.

Having an easy-to-understand summary also provides a communication tool for your team to understand the progress being made and what is coming next—and what holes need to be filled in. I have repeatedly seen the value of having this concise visual to provide a team with feedback on their progress. This is because it is short and sweet so that it can be easily digested even in the midst of the battle and acted on. If the venture is still in the planning stage, it is also useful before the battle has started to decide if it is worth engaging.

It is also a very efficient way to communicate with external mentors on where your venture creation process is at any time in a way they can easily process. Good mentors and advisors will want to hear the big picture first and then zero in on specific areas for questions. This tool gives you that big picture capability in a structured manner but when the questions come, you will have to dive into the work you have done in the 24 Steps.

The DE Canvas will allow you to quickly assess the big picture to know where you stand, and where your strengths and weaknesses are, so you can make adjustments.

Why Is the DE Canvas Not a Perfect Map to the 24 Steps?

I have found that the 24 Steps is an excellent process to get the essential information you need to make a successful new venture. It is an excellent way to get to strong "product-market fit" (PMF, as it is commonly known) initially and then "channel-market-fit" (CMF). Once you have this knowledge, it is pure gold, but you will not have everything you need to create a new venture. A product and a go-to-market strategy are absolutely essential but a company is more.

A scalable new venture starts with initial assets, a direction, values, and a compelling reason for existence. This is the first box we have added in front of the 24 Steps. It is the genesis and original DNA of your company.

Having a product that makes money at the individual unit economics level (i.e., Lifetime Value relative to Cost of Customer Acquisition) is likewise a necessary but not sufficient condition for a sustainable business. Marketing and sales (M&S) expenses are usually the biggest and most difficult investments in any startup to get in order, and that is what unit economics takes into consideration and why we prioritized it in the 24 Steps. However, you must account for all the costs of a business beyond this, particularly in research and development (R&D) and general and administration (G&A), which can equal or even exceed the M&S costs. This secondary consideration has been prioritized behind unit economics in the 24 Steps but it must ultimately be taken into consideration and the DE Canvas does this. This is covered in Box #8 and I have provided additional materials to help you with this in the Additional Materials section of this chapter. But do not worry about this now. Focus on filling out the other nine boxes from your disciplined execution of the 24 Steps and then come back to this at the end.

How to Approach the DE Canvas

It is important to set expectations on what the DE Canvas is and is not. The simple summary provided by the DE Canvas does not capture the full richness of your situation and, as such, it is not a perfect indicator of your success. Nor does the simple summary tell you why things have happened and how to fix things. So, while it has its limitations, I have seen its usefulness, in large part because of the benefit of simplicity mentioned earlier.

I have based the DE Canvas off the Six Themes of the 24 Steps from *Disciplined Entrepreneurship*, expanding two of the themes and adding the two sections mentioned earlier. The resulting canvas maintains the specificity, logic, and rigor of the 24 Steps.

More so than other canvases, this canvas has a suggested initial sequential nature to it. You should start with Section 1 and then follow the arrows to move through the canvas. You will move through the sections in an iterative manner, updating previous sections as you learn more over time, but providing a prescriptive initial flow is helpful and an important part of the Disciplined Entrepreneurship approach.

Each section maps quite well to specific steps:

- **Section 1, Raison d'Être (aka Reason for Existing):** Step 0
- **Section 2, Initial Market:** Steps 1, 2, 3, 4, 5, and 9
- **Section 3, Value Creation:** Steps 6, 7, and 8
- **Section 4, Competitive Advantage:** Steps 10 and 11
- **Section 5, Customer Acquisition:** Step 12 and 13
- **Section 6, Product Unit Economics:** Steps 15, 16, 17, 18, and 19
- **Section 7, Revenue:** Step 18 and 19 (for iterating and execution guidance)
- **Section 8, Overall Economics:** Parts of Step 19
- **Section 9, Design and Build:** Steps 20, 21, 22, and 23
- **Section 10, Scaling:** Steps 14 and 24

A note: I would encourage you to think of the Disciplined Entrepreneurship Canvas not as a fixed edict, but rather as a framework that can be customized as appropriate. If it does not quite fit, that is okay. Go ahead and customize it, but it should at least give you a good start.

Disciplined Entrepreneurship Canvas

PRODUCT: **REVISION:**   **DATE:**

Raison d'Être ①	Competitive Advantage ④	Customer Acquisition ⑤	Overall Economics ⑧	Design & Build ⑨
Why are you in business?	*Why you?*	*How does your customer acquire your product?*	*Does your product make money at a company level?*	*How do you produce the product?*
Mission:	Moats:	DMU:	Est. R&D Exp.:	ID Key Assumptions:
Passions:				
	Core:	DMP:	Est. G&A Exp.:	Test Key Assumptions:
Values:				
Initial Assets:	Competitive Positioning:	WoOs:	LTV/CoCA Ratio High Enough:	MVBP:
Initial Idea:				
		Possible Triggers:		Tracking Metrics:

Initial Market ②	Value Creation ③	Product Unit Economics ⑥	Revenue ⑦	Scaling ⑩
Who is your customer?	*What can you do for your customer?*	*Can you make money at the product level?*	*How do you drive and capture revenue for your product?*	*How do you scale your business?*
BHM:	Use Case:	Biz Model:	Preferred Sales Motion:	Prod. Plan for BHM:
End User Profile:		Est. Pricing:		Next Market:
	Problem Being Solved:		Sales Funnel:	
TAM:		Short Term – LTV:		
	Prod. Description:	Short Term – CoCA:	Short Term Mix:	Prod. Plan beyond BHM:
Persona:		Medium Term – LTV:		
		Medium Term – CoCA:	Medium Term Mix:	
1st 10 Customers:	Quant. Value Prop.:	Long Term – LTV:		Follow-on TAM:
		Long Term – CoCA:	Long Term Mix:	

Example of Using the Disciplined Entrepreneurship Canvas with Feedback

Old friend and master illustrator of this book, Marius Ursache, offered to test-drive the canvas for his project, the Disciplined Entrepreneurship Toolbox (www.detoolbox.com). I should note that the 24-step framework has been used not just for startups but for projects/product design and development in large corporations, government organizations, investment situations, community organizations, educational institutions, religious groups, student clubs, and even creative arts groups. Once it was used to organize a piano concert (thanks for letting us know, Amanda von Goetz!).

Below is Marius's first pass of his canvas, as well as my comments on it so that you can see what you should be considering when you fill out your canvas. Marius's draft is quite good, so I will focus my comments on where it could be improved, as well as how the canvas will help Marius discover where he should focus his attention next. You can see that the canvas makes it really easy to see which parts of Marius's plan are solid, and which parts he should consider revisiting. Marius first filled out this canvas several years ago, so he has made big improvements over time in some of the areas I'm highlighting in my comments. You can also see how he has customized it to his situation and to have his personal signature in terms of his style.

Here is Marius's initial Disciplined Entrepreneurship Canvas filled out:

The Disciplined Entrepreneurship Canvas

PRODUCT: DE Toolbox   **REVISION:** 3.1   **DATE:** September 4, 2023

1 Raison d'Etre
Why are you in business?

Mission
Give founders tools to improve success chances and early stage / angel investors access to good startups.

Founder passions
Innovation, teaching, smart conversations.

Values
Transparent, competitive, fair-play.

Initial Assets
Team (Marius & Vlad),
Connections (Bill Aulet, MIT, accelerators),
Current users (5,000+ for current product).

Initial Idea
Online tool to help startups get funded.

BHAG
Create jobs. Improve people's lives.

4 Competitive Advantage
Why you?

Moats
Network effect (both startups/ accelerators use it).

Core
We match the best startups with the best accelerators/investors, and help them work smarter together.

Competitive Positioning
Highly efficient process for startups
Progress driven investment for investors (better productivity than AngelList, F6S. Focused on process more than Visible, FounderSuite, Gust.)

5 Customer Acquisition
How does your customer acquire your product?

Decision Making Unit
A. Founders & Chief Product Officers
B. Sponsor: CIO/CTO or Managing Director of accelerator. Decision: managing team

Decision Making Process
A. Start trial, share with team, add data, discuss with team before trial expiration.
B. Analyze features & cost for tools, contact suppliers, negotiate & sign (4-6 mo).

Windows of Opportunity
A. Apply to accelerator, prepare for fundraising
B. New generation/new fund (twice per year) or change in leadership

Possible Triggers
B. Discounts, sales rep meetings or events.

8 Overall Economics
Does your product make money at a company level?

Est R&D Expenses
$50,000

Est G&A Expenses
$24,000

LTV/CoCA Ratio
8.5:1 / 7.8:1

9 Design & Build
How do you produce your product?

Key Assumptions
1. Startups will use the tool recurrently.
2. Accelerators need a better tool to source startups (than F6S/AngelList/Google Forms) and manage the acceleration process (than Google Docs/Slack/Email).

Assumption Tests
1. Simplify tool (not linear, iterative/depth)
2. Try selling a prototype/slideware.

MVBP
1. Current product with subscription
2. Presentation/prototype for accelerator features

Tracking Metrics
1. Retention for startups
2. Number of paying startups
3. Number of paying accelerators

2 Initial Market
Who is your customer?

Beachhead Market
A. Early-stage founders who want to improve their chances to fundraise.
B. Accelerators outside Silicon Valley who want to improve their process/outcomes.

End User Profile
A. Tech founders with an idea or product but no revenue.
B. Smaller accelerators who need deals.

TAM
1M tech founders outside US ($100M).
5,000 smaller accelerators ($30M).

Persona
Tech founder/Accelerator manager

First 10 Customers
NUMA (FR), MITEF Poland (PL), IncubatecUfro (CL), UDD Ventures (CL), etc.

3 Value Creation
What can you do for your customer?

Use Case
A. Learn about the biz side of your startup, apply it using a vetted process (DE24) & online tools.
B. Recruit better startups, engage more mentors, accelerate startups faster, get them funded.

Problem
A. Founders lack guidance and tools to help them be more disciplined/business-wise.
B. Accelerators' "spray and pray" strategy does not yield many successful startups.

Product Description
Process & toolbox for founders & accelerators + marketplace.

Quantified Value Proposition
A. Move faster. Get funded faster.
B. Get better pre-seed deals.

6 Product Unit Economics
Can you make money at the product level?

Business Model
Subscription model for both startups & accelerators.

Pricing
$15/mo per startup
$500/mo for accelerators

LTV
Short term: $200 / $15,000
Medium term: $250 / $17,200
Long term: $275 / $19,500

CoCA
Short term: $58 / $4,200
Medium term: $49 / $3,750
Long term: $32 / $2,500

7 Revenue
How do you drive & capture revenue for your product?

Preferred Sales Channel
A. Website
B. Direct sales

Sales Funnel
A. Search online →Read features & testimonials →Create trial →Add data in app →Receive trial end email →Discuss with team →Buy.
B. Outreach for interview to open door / Search tools/get referrals →Analyze features →Discuss with sales reps →Discuss with team →Negotiate →Sign contract →Buy.

Short Term Mix
Email newsletter, event presentations, inbound, direct sales.

Medium/Long Term Mix
Event presentations, inbound, direct sales.

10 Scaling
How do you scale your business?

Product Plan for BHM
Attached

Next Market
Universities, Angel groups,

Product plan beyond BHM
Investment marketplace

Follow-on TAM
100,000 angels ($1B).

After a quick review of this DE Canvas, a few things stand out to me that will direct our discussion, guidance, and actions going forward. On the positive side, this team/project seems to be getting off to a good start as the foundation in the first few boxes is strong. The raison d'être is strong, as are the original assets, and there is clearly a strong understanding of the marketplace. The team is also demonstrating discipline in narrowing the scope of the market they will serve initially, but as with almost all projects I see, I would like to see an even more focused Market Segmentation. This is now version 3.1 and it has improved considerably, so I am less troubled but in the early versions it stuck out and drew my attention immediately. There is compelling evidence that the problem and opportunity is well understood. Looking at the team's background, there is little concern about being able to build the product.

I am less confident but not too worried about the long-term competitive advantage. While the team describes a logical plan (i.e., network effects), achieving it will be a real challenge especially when we discuss some of the parts I am concerned about. As we look across the canvas, my confidence with the scaling dimension of this business is not high based on current information.

The biggest concerns[1] that jump out are regarding the product unit economics and revenue (Boxes #6 and #7). Executing to make that plan a reality is the question. It starts when I see the pricing of $15 per month per startup. This leads to an LTV in the $200–$300 range, which sets off red flags for me. This is a consumer-level LTV for a product this is really a B2B (Business to Business) proposition. Even when selling to accelerators, the LTV was in the low thousands of dollars in early versions, which got my attention as an area of great concern. As you can see, those numbers have moved up to $15,000 to $19,500, which is much better but still in a danger zone, because you can't afford direct salespeople in this LTV zone long term but you have to create the market and that usually requires direct missionary salespeople I also know entrepreneurial organizations are notoriously cheap for something like this, so our discussion focused in this area as well. I am concerned it is going to take time to achieve these LTV levels, and even then they are optimistic. As I now direct my focus to Boxes #6 and #7, I see genuine efforts to try to address this using digital marketing tools to keep the CoCA low, but the team has to acknowledge it will take some direct sales to be successful. Across the whole canvas, I have now zeroed in on the biggest challenge for this business and it is not building the product.

Without the unit economics working, there is no way the overall economics (Box #8) will work. It is not even worth worrying about them because the unit economics is a necessary condition for the overall economics to work. It is the first test. Without this as well, it will probably be impossible to achieve network effects the team is looking to achieve.

---

[1] Getting to be good with the DE Canvas just takes repetitions using it. I am able to diagnose quickly because I have literally looked at thousands of these canvases, but you will get good at it surprising quickly after you have built and/or reviewed others' DE Canvases multiple times. It is definitely an acquirable skill. And it feels great because you look so smart when you can do it!

It is very hard to scale a business that has not conquered its Beachhead Market. Some might say that it's okay to lose money in the Beachhead Market (this assumes you can find investors to take this risk, which is certainly not a given, especially if you live outside of Silicon Valley) if there is a clear path to an extremely scalable business. But again, Box #10, Scaling, does not give me that comfort even if that was a path we wanted to pursue.

The larger point from this example is to show how the DE Canvas works and its power. Napoleon Bonaparte was renowned for his ability to quickly assess a battlefield and determine an effective strategy. This talent, combined with his comprehensive understanding of the discipline of warfare, made him one of the most formidable military leaders in history. We are not fighting military battles but the DE Canvas gives you the ability to quickly scan the landscape for your proposed or existing business and figure out rapidly if it has the potential to be an attractively scalable venture/product.

It also gives you the ability to focus on the areas of highest concern, as well as the areas where you have the strongest position. This is very helpful. Its limitation is that it does not give you the richness of detail that you will want as you ask more questions, but that is fine. It is but one page, and your overall plan will be much more robust and able to handle the follow-on questions (or if not, you just got some great advice).

ADDITIONAL RESOURCES

There are additional resources for this step at www.d-eship.com/stepDECanvas. These materials include:

- Digital Version of DE Canvas
- Videos: DE Canvas Explainers by Bill Aulet
- Videos: Dollar Shave Club, Peloton examples described and explained by Bill Aulet
- Example: More detailed description of using the DE Canvas to evaluate Marius Ursache's DE Toolbox project
- Worksheet: Charlie Tillett model
- Online Course on Overall Financials: edX with Bill Aulet, Matthew Rhodes-Kropf, and Antoinette Schoar

Additional resources will be added as new and updated examples and information become available.

Summary

The DE Canvas tracks your progress and can also be used as a diagnostic tool for a business to find its strengths and weaknesses. Its value and its flaws are based on its ability to simply convey the current status of a business on one page. When it is understood that the boxes are dependent in a cumulative manner, the DE Canvas gives valuable insights in yet another dimension of the interrelationship of the different elements of your business and its ongoing sustainability.

At this point in the book, you will not be able to fill out the canvas or even probably understand all of the elements in sufficient depth, but it is something that you will be able to come back to as you progress through the book. It will then be a valuable tool for monitoring the ongoing strength of your plan. Note that the canvas, like your plan, will be continually updated as you learn more throughout the 24 Steps.

If you did not follow everything in this chapter the first time through, do not worry as that is normal. This chapter will make a lot more sense after you have finished the full book. You will come back then and revisit and find it very hepful. But for now ... enough of the warm up, let's get started!!!

Getting Started

START HERE

Three Most Common Ways to Start a New Venture

When I listen to my students, I hear a diverse range of reasons as to why they are interested in entrepreneurship. Some students have worked in industry for years and want a change. Some want to be their own boss. Some hold patents and are interested in the different ways they can commercialize them. Some have an idea about how their own life could be improved, and they wonder if that idea is interesting to others. And there are many more.

All of these reasons can be synthesized into three distinct categories (Figure 0.1):

- **Idea:** You have thought of something new that can change the world—or some small part of it—in a positive way.

- **Technology:** There is a technological breakthrough and you want to capitalize on it, or simply expedite its deployment to have a positive effect on society.

- **Passion:** You are confident and comfortable pushing for change in the world, and you believe that being an entrepreneur is the way to have the biggest impact. You may simply want to work for yourself but you don't have an idea or technology yet. Read on to learn how to find a good idea or technology aligned with your passion. I don't mean to scare you, but you will need more than passion. However, let's start with "passion" and develop it into something you can carry with you into the subsequent steps.

What does it sound like to have an idea versus a technology versus a passion?

You should be able to sum up your idea, technology, or passion in one succinct sentence.

Idea:	Technology:	Passion:
"I want to start a company in Africa that will create a sustainable business model to improve life for the people there and empower them with jobs."	*"I have a robot that allows the user to feel objects rendered by a computer."*	*"I have a master's in mechanical engineering and I can quickly prototype almost any technological gadget. Now I want to put my skills to use in the most impactful way possible, and be my own boss."*
Here, the idea is that a sustainable business model will reduce poverty in Africa more effectively than charitable contributions to the poor. This sentence is enough to move on to the first of the 24 steps, Market Segmentation, though as you will see, you will have to be much more specific before you can turn the idea into a business.	This statement radiates with potential. How could someone benefit from being able to have a three-dimensional object on their computer screen and still be able to feel it, in some way, in physical space? I co-founded a company, SensAble Technologies, around this very technology, and throughout the book, I share the SensAble story.	This person has identified a personal competitive advantage, the ability to prototype gadgets quickly, which can help a business go through product iterations faster. The person may want to consider a hardware-based business because it would line up well with the competitive advantage.

Figure 0.1: Three most common catalysts for a new venture.

I am frequently told that an entrepreneur cannot start without knowing a "customer pain," a problem that bothers someone enough that they would be willing to pay to alleviate the problem. That approach is one very good way to enter into entrepreneurship but it is not the only way. It can discourage some who would otherwise be interested in entrepreneurship. Furthermore, it discounts the importance of something even more essential. Starting a new venture is very, very hard—whatever it is that you are going to do—but gets you very excited. Accepting that fact is every bit as important as finding a problem to solve.

Raison d'Être: Internal Motivations Must Be at a Higher Level

Please don't try to start a company because you simply have an idea or technology. That is choosing to run in a marathon because you thought it was a nice idea to go for a run on a sunny day. You won't last.

You must have a driving passion and commitment for what you are thinking about doing. Entrepreneurial thought leader Brad Feld says that it is more than passion, it is "obsession."

This is what I refer to as the raison d'être (French for "reason for existence") for your new venture. If the response to the question "Why are you starting this company?" is "to make money," I reject this as not being an acceptable answer. That is profiteering, not entrepreneurship. You will not build a great company, nor will you and your team last through the inevitable ups and downs any new venture is destined to go through. To me, entrepreneurship is an ethical activity to make the world a better place, which is *not* simply profiteering. The raison d'être is fundamental to this.

Figure 0.2: You need a raison d'être for starting a new company that is more than profiteering.

As you can see from Figure 0.2, there needs to be a higher calling than simply making money or solving a problem, and more commitment than just passion. This will be a long, hard journey and you must have a high level of motivation to sustain it through these trying times and to recruit and retain others to do the same.

To be clear, making a profit on what you do is not inherently bad; in fact, producing positive cash flow from operations is necessary to create a sustainable organization. But it *supports* the primary mission; profit itself is not the primary mission.

Figure 0.3 is a simple test to see if you are actually ready to start a new company.

Passion => Commitment Checklist

	I understand that . . .	Yes	No
1	. . . founding a company will be really, really hard and I still want to do it.		
2	. . . it will be a lengthy process loaded with humiliating failures along the way, and I must learn from them and not take them personally.		
3	. . . I cannot do it alone.		
4	. . . the path to success is not an algorithm with set rules to follow, but an iterative process where I can only increase or decrease the odds of success. I cannot guarantee anything. Even if I achieve success, it is only temporary and I must keep iterating to continue succeeding.		
5	. . . as such, the goal is to make an "anti-fragile" organization—one that gets stronger over time when faced with problems, failures, uncertainty, and surprises.		
6	. . . when others provide advice, I will listen, but I will also recognize that it is up to me to choose which advice to implement, and how to implement it, since only I own the final results and accountability.		
7	. . . I will have to leave my comfort zone every day to grow and continue to be successful.		
8	. . . I am doing this for more than the money. I believe in my cause and my team.		

Figure 0.3: Gut check and setting expectations questions before starting a company.

You want to be clear on the nature of the journey you are about to go on before you start. The goal is to gauge whether you meet the minimal level of "informed passion/obsession" that is required to start a company.

If you did not answer "Yes" to all of these questions, it is certainly not the end of the world. You are being honest! Answering "No" to some of those questions does not disqualify you from being an entrepreneur at some point, and this book will still be useful to you. On the other hand, to give you honest advice, don't start a new company today. The time is not right.

And that's okay. I estimate that over half of my students fall into the category of what I call the "curious/exploratory entrepreneur." These are people who are interested in learning about how to start a company, but they're not ready to quit their job tomorrow and pour their lives into a fledgling company with high levels of uncertainty and chaos. Some of these students end up being very interested in corporate entrepreneurship, or in being an "entrepreneurship amplifier," where they work to increase interest in entrepreneurship and build up resources that will support startups.[1]

All of these people benefit from going through the 24 Steps with some idea or technology so that they better understand the level of detail that goes into starting a company. And someday if they become ready to start a company, they will have a much stronger set of skills and knowledge ready to apply to the challenge. Even if you are not ready to start a new venture, I think you should still be very interested in developing an entrepreneurial mindset, skill set, and way of operating for your own personal development. I encourage you to go through this book and the online resources and think about the principles involved in making your existing organizations better. You'll learn a lot that will benefit you in any sort of new product development, even if it is not at a startup. Also, who knows what could happen by the end of this book? You might even find that you have developed the passion necessary for success.

But if you don't have the requisite passion today, you won't be ready for the short-term and long-term challenges that starting a new company will bring you. If you want to do this in a corporate environment, you need to have a lot of passion, but it just won't be at the obsessive level you need to do a startup. And that's okay! We need entrepreneurs everywhere, as I talked about in the introduction.

No matter how you have become interested in entrepreneurship, you need to start by first answering the following question: *What can I do well that I would love to do for an extended period of time?* This means you will be motivated for the good days as well as the bad days, and there will be a lot of both.

Once you have answered this question, you will be prepared to narrow your focus down to an idea or a technology.

---

[1] I discussed different levels of interest in entrepreneurship, and their resulting personas, as part of my keynote speech to the United States Association for Small Business and Enterprise 2016 Conference. You can view slides from the speech at http://www.slideshare.net/billaulet/past-present-and-future-of-entrepreneurship-education-presentation-at-usasbe-conference-jan-10-2016

How to Go From "I Have a Passion" to "I Have an Idea or Technology" Good Enough to Start the 24 Steps

If you don't have something to start with, then you should find a problem that needs to be solved that you are especially passionate about solving. But what does this mean? Let's drill down and make this advice more actionable.

The best type of starting point for a new venture in terms of initial success is a "market pull" where you identify an unfilled yet meaningful need to fix some "customer pain," something for which there exists some group of people who are willing to pay money for a solution. It is called "market pull" because you are being pulled by the customer to satisfy an already defined general market demand.

The most common way to come up with an idea is from personal experience. For what problem have you seen a clever solution or workaround (i.e., hack) that impressed you? What problem have you experienced firsthand that you feel is significant and could be solved to great benefit for you and others like you? Often these problems are all around you if you look. Many entrepreneurs make an idea journal and fill it with ideas like this.

The most important thing for now is to be open to the ideation process (see below) and come up with ideas that your team thinks are worth pursuing. Step 1, Market Segmentation, is where you will start to rigorously test your idea against the market.

Another valid starting point can be a "technology push" based on some new-to-the-world concept that has the potential to create new market opportunities. It could be a technological breakthrough out of a lab. Or it could be taking a technology-enabled business model or process to a new market. Think of an Uber-like business model that builds a platform between underutilized assets (cars) and disaggregated demand (rides) to create more efficient markets—such a business is much more viable when every customer has a smartphone in their pocket. Generative AI, robotics, Software as a Service (SaaS), blockchain, or data analytics are other good examples. In this approach, your team has a competitive advantage or early passion about an exciting invention and is searching for a market to apply it to in order to create value and impact. It is a solution looking for a problem.

It can be challenging to take a technology and apply it to a true customer pain. Some teams get too enamored with the technology and they don't focus on understanding how to get paying customers.

Regardless of whether you choose a market pull or technology push, there is a lot you won't yet know about this initial identified customer problem. How urgent is the problem? How many people have this problem? How much will the customer pay for a solution? What does the competitive landscape look like? What will be your unfair (to your competitors) competitive advantage? How profitable a business can be built solving this problem?

You will explore those questions, and many more, throughout the 24 Steps, starting with Step 1, Market Segmentation. For now, your goal is to come up with *general* ideas that could be the basis of a scalable business that you will be excited about.

There are entire books, courses, conferences, and even companies focused on the "ideation" process,[2] so I will not try to comprehensively summarize it here. But I have a few key points related in general to brainstorming based on my research and experience:

1. **Diverse Perspectives:** Brainstorming is best done as a team with diverse perspectives. Without the whole team involved, some members may feel less invested in your success. Without diverse perspectives, your ideas may not be broad enough to find a truly great market opportunity.

2. **Use of Improv Mindset:** Use improv (improvisation) training techniques with your team. It's effective at getting people to think in the "Yes, and . . . " mindset that fosters effective brainstorming.[3] In this mindset you don't look for weaknesses; rather, you build on each other's ideas. Only after you've come up with a lot of ideas do you start a critical analysis.

3. **Early Test of Team:** Brainstorming and the subsequent filtering of ideas is also an excellent way to determine who should be and shouldn't be part of your founding team. While not the express purpose of this exercise, this is extremely valuable and not to be overlooked. It is an easy way to see if you have a coherent and cohesive team that works well together.

4. **Take It Seriously but Realize the Idea Will Change:** Take brainstorming seriously, but understand that this is a small part of the overall process. An idea is necessary to start with, and it gets your team moving in the right general direction. Having an original idea is the single most overrated thing in entrepreneurship. The quality of your team, having a clear target market, and having a sound process for execution (like the 24 Steps) are much more important factors in ultimate success than your initial idea, which often changes dramatically over time.

---

[2] Readers are encouraged to view the video about the IDEO development process released on February 9, 1999, on ABC's *Nightline* called "The Deep Dive." This video is available in many places, including YouTube. While this video is now dated and the product is not important but rather a means to demonstrate a process, it provides good insights into a good brainstorming process.

[3] My favorite and most efficient way to implement this step is to show the excellent video of a TED Talk given by David Morris in January 2012 for TEDxVictoria called "The Way of Improv," https://www.youtube.com/watch?v=MUO-pWJ0riQ. Show the 11-minute video to the group and then talk about it for 5 minutes to get people in a good mood to brainstorm constructively. It works extremely well.

Which Comes First, the Idea or the Team?

The answer to this very relevant question is tricky. Both the idea and the team evolve in parallel and there is a connection between the two. That being said, in my experience, there has to be some general direction or idea to rally an initial team. The initial idea should not be fully formed, and no matter what, it will be flawed in so many dimensions to almost make it laughable.[4] All this being said, the general theme of a problem is a way to catalyze like-minded people together to create a common vision. In that sense, the idea comes before the team, but they really develop together. That being said, people who join the team for the general initial idea and do not love the team, or people who join only for the team, will most likely create a team destined for mediocrity at best. It has to be a combination of the idea and the team, especially in the early stages.

What does not come first is the product. You should fall in love with the problem and the team but definitively not the product. That will evolve from the process and is not the starting point.

Finding a Founding Team: Entrepreneurship Is Not a Solo Sport

Once people are starting the process, one of the toughest questions I am asked is "How do I find a co-founder?" It is not easy and there is no simple formula. Finding your entrepreneurial soulmate is like finding your significant other in life. You have to get out there and hustle and use all means necessary. There is no algorithm or special site that will solve this challenge for you.

In the foundational entrepreneurship course I teach with other faculty at MIT, 15.390 New Enterprises, students who go through the 24 Steps must form teams in two weeks or less due to the time constraints of the academic semester. This process is not an optimal way to form teams, but it is enough for the student teams to gain experience in team formation and then have a team to proceed over the semester to implement (in an accelerated manner) the 24 Steps. From the ideas from the class that turn into businesses, some teams stay intact, but far more often teams undergo a healthy reconfiguration of their membership at the end of the semester to create a stronger, more unified team that is better suited to capture the business opportunity on a longer-term basis. This is an important evolutionary process.

Your choice of co-founders is extremely important. Research from MIT shows that businesses with multiple founders are more successful than those founded by an individual.[5]

---

[4] See one of my favorite books on entrepreneurship, *That Will Never Work* by Marc Randolph, for a brilliant description of this phenomenon.

[5] Roberts, Edward B, *Entrepreneurs in High Technology: Lessons from MIT and Beyond*, Oxford University Press, New York, 1991, p. 258.

Many resources go into more depth about finding good co-founders, as listed in the additional resources section at the end of this chapter. Probably the single best and most rigorous book for this topic is former Harvard Business School Professor Noam Wasserman's book *The Founder's Dilemmas*, where Noam covers this topic and more.

Ways to increase your odds of finding your entrepreneurial soulmate include:

1. **Get Out in the Entrepreneurial Community:** Attend entrepreneurial events and networking opportunities to meet potential co-founders, but understand the limitations of this approach. If you do not work with people in an intense way, it is hard to tell if you would be compatible co-founders. Simply attending events such as startup conferences and having casual conversations is really just the beginning. The more you can see of them in action, from pitch competitions to something even more challenging and chaotic like a hackathon, the more confidence you can have in your assessment.

2. **Co-Founder Matchmaking Platforms:** There are several online platforms that connect entrepreneurs with potential co-founders. These should only be the starting point; you have to really work together with deadlines and other pressure to know whether this is your true entrepreneurial soulmate or not.

3. **Business Incubators and Accelerators:** Business incubators and accelerators are a better place because you can see people in action with deadlines and find out about their reputations.

4. **Social Media:** Social media platforms such as LinkedIn, Twitter (now X), and Facebook can be useful tools to find potential co-founders. You can join groups or communities related to your industry and connect with other entrepreneurs. This just gives you leads, however, and you need to work together under some pressure to really know.

5. **Referrals and Personal Networks:** Don't overlook the power of personal networks when searching for a co-founder. Ask friends, family members, and colleagues if they know anyone who might be a good fit for your startup. Especially powerful would be alumni from your college or previous companies where you worked. These individuals will be able to give you an unvarnished perspective about the person, speak to their work, and attest to their values.

In the end, know that the decision of who your co-founders will be is one of the most important decisions you will make. You have to put the effort in and keep the bar high. If you want to build a great company, settling for good enough is never good enough. Interviews are overrated. There is a body of work on all of us out there if you dig enough. Find a situation where you can have a trial period before you buy. You shouldn't rush into a marriage, nor should you with a co-founder commitment.

Even if you make the most extensive, diligent efforts in the world to test out your co-founders beforehand, you should also understand that it still might not work out. Circumstances and people change. Stuff happens. My experience shows that even with a rigorous upfront process and the best intentions, it is the case that if you have four co-founders, the odds of all of them working out for the long haul is extremely low. Doesn't mean you shouldn't try to get the best co-founding team you can, but you should just understand that even then it doesn't always work out.

You have to do your best but also be able to have tough conversations to keep your team strong, because if you start cutting corners on your core team and settling, you are destined to mediocrity at best, and probably worse.

The Next Step

Let's assume now you have an idea or technology and enough of a founding team to get started. Again, to set expectations, you will not have a perfect idea/technology, but it is enough to get going. And you certainly don't have a perfect team, but you have one that is strong enough to give you confidence and excitement to head into the process. Let the 24 Steps begin!

The 24 Steps are not about generalities but rather it will be "The Search for the Holy Grail of Specificity" (Figure 0.4). This is one of my favorite illustrations because entrepreneurship is not abstract; it is very real. It is all about the specificity you can achieve. Winners get the specifics right.

ADDITIONAL RESOURCES

There are additional resources for this step at www.d-eship.com/step0, including:

- Worksheets:
  - Worksheet 0.1: Framework for Ideating
  - Worksheet 0.2: Market Pull Mini-Canvas
  - Worksheet 0.3: Technology Push Mini-Canvas
  - Worksheet 0.4: Hybrid Mini-Canvas
  - Worksheet 0.5: Framework for Building a Well-Balanced Team
- Bonus Topic: Hybrid Market Pull and Technology Push
- Bonus Topic: Building a Founding Team

Additional resources will be added as new and updated examples and information become available.

Two books will be useful to reference throughout the 24 Steps that were written specifically for the Disciplined Entrepreneurship process:

1. Paul Cheek's *Disciplined Entrepreneurship Startup Tactics*: the most current and up to date, with invaluable tools, templates, scripts, and more to help you implement each step.

2. The *Disciplined Entrepreneurship Workbook* was released in 2018, and this new revised and expanded edition incorporates many elements of this book, but not all. This can be a valuable additional reference.

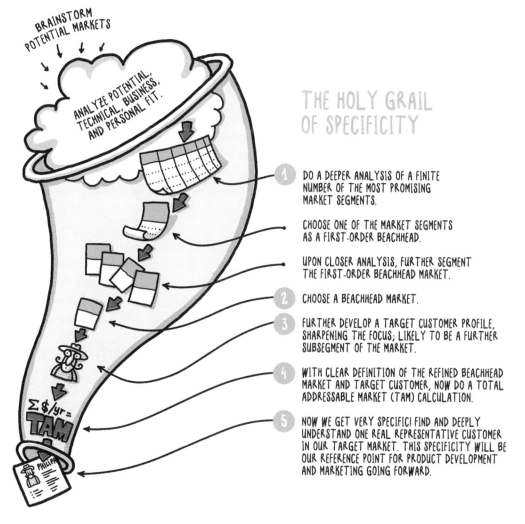

Figure 0.4: The Holy Grail of specificity.

 **STEP 1**

Market Segmentation

In This Step, You Will:

- Launch the structured DE (Disciplined Entrepreneurship) process.
- Brainstorm a wide array of potential customers and markets for your business.
- Narrow down your list to your top 4–10 markets.

SEEING THE WORLD
THROUGH THE EYES
OF THE CUSTOMER

SEEING THE WORLD
THROUGH THE EYES
OF THE COMPANY

For success in entrepreneurship, there are some glasses that are better than others.

Why This Step, and Why Now?

It is crucial to start the process with a focus on a target customer. Everything else about your business will be based on that focus. This step will provide you with a clear framework to direct your primary market research in the steps that follow.

Let's Get Started

Once you have completed Step 0, Getting Started, you should have an idea or technology that answers the question "Is this something the world could benefit from, and is it something I do well and would love to do for an extended period?" and an initial team excited to start the journey to make this happen. (Note: Throughout the 24 Steps, I will use "you" to refer collectively to your team.)

Now you will begin the 24 Steps by taking that idea or technology and brainstorming a wide array of potential customers who might be interested in some application of it. Then you will choose a manageable subset (depending on time and other circumstances, I suggest 4–10) of top opportunities and do in-depth primary market research (PMR), where you directly interact with potential customers, to learn more about them.

The First Commandment: The Single Necessary and Sufficient Condition for a Business

In every one of my courses, I start the same way: emphasizing the most foundational first principle of entrepreneurship. I ask, "What is the single necessary and sufficient condition for a business?" Many say "a new idea," which is not correct because many people have new ideas but don't have a business. Neither is it a product, a technology, a customer need, a business plan, a vision, a strong team, a CEO, money, investors, a strategy, competitive advantage, or company values. While all of those are great things for a business to have, none of them is the right answer.

The single necessary and sufficient condition for a business is **a paying customer.** This is the first and most fundamental commandment of entrepreneurship (Figure 1.1).

Figure 1.1: The first commandment of entrepreneurship.

The day someone pays you money for your product or service, you have a business, and not a day before. This simple but powerful truth will keep you focused on what is important. You should not define a business as a product, because if nobody buys your product, you simply do not have a business. The marketplace is always the final arbiter of success.

Now, just because you have a paying customer does not mean you have a *good* business. To have a good, sustainable business, you will need to gain enough customers paying enough money within a relatively short period of time to more than cover your costs and become economically sustainable.

There are some temporary circumstances where exuberant investors might fund you for a while, but they want a very clear line of sight to paying customers and validation that those paying customers are real and will make the business profitable. Understand that such investors are taking great risks and they will expect outsized returns, so you will pay dearly for taking such investment. Depending on your venture, that might work well for you, or it might not.

In any case, entrepreneurs need to be focused on paying customers because paying customers will provide the lifeline of cash to keep the new venture going. The nature of a startup is that you have few resources, so every action you take must be hyper-efficient and focused.

Therefore, you will not start by building a product or recruiting salespeople to sell your as-of-yet unproven product. Instead, you will take a customer-driven approach by finding an unmet need and building your business around it.

Three Key Criteria to Be Met If You Are to Create a New Market That You Will Dominate

Creating an innovative product where no market currently exists is essential to the success of an innovation-driven startup. Creating new markets is a very hard thing to do, so if you do it, you should be appropriately rewarded with a high, if not dominant, market share that you can use as a basis for future expansion. Being a "me-too" company in an existing market is not the goal, and you have to be careful about slipping into that state given your limited resources.

To create a scalable company in a newly defined market space requires not just hard work but also for you to work smart. You will have to be relentlessly focused on a well-defined, winnable, and appropriately sized initial target customer (i.e., not too big and not too small) that you can grow your business from. A target customer or "market segment" is a group of potential customers who share three fundamental characteristics:

1. They buy the same product.
2. They buy it in the same way (i.e., same use case, value proposition, channel).
3. There is word of mouth (WOM) of some sort between them; that is to say, that they significantly influence each other.

A market segment should have all three characteristics and not just the first one. This is the beginning of building deep focus and discipline into your process. Focus is an absolutely critical skill for an entrepreneur, and as you will find throughout these steps, focus is difficult. You must work hard to identify and understand market segments through initial brainstorming and then, even more importantly, PMR. Relying on gut feel, anecdotes, or third-party analysis is basically guesswork and is insufficient if you are creating new markets in a disciplined manner that optimizes your odds of success. You must base your decisions on firsthand experience and be more evidence-based and systematic.

WHEN "PAYING CUSTOMERS" LEAD YOU ASTRAY (I.E., BEING UNINTENTIONALLY UNDISCIPLINED)

While paying customers ultimately determine whether your product is successful, you may encounter two common pitfalls if you do not focus enough on creating a new carefully defined market.

The first is "selling to everyone," which is the idea that you, as a fledgling startup with little to no resources, can make products that fit the needs of anyone you run across. While it is true that without a paying customer, you do not have a business, that does not mean you take any paying customer! The disciplined entrepreneur has a plan and takes the right customer because they have a market segment focus, rather than an individual customer focus.

Here is an example. Let's say you have invented a new fabric technology (i.e., polymer) that gives you the ability to waterproof fabrics better than anything on the market. You first hear from your friend Sally, who read in the newspaper that camping equipment is a lucrative market, so she suggests you sell tents. Your cousin Joe chimes in; he wants waterproof underwear. A neighbor asks you to make easy-to-clean stuffed animals for their children.

To design and execute any of these products will take more time and resources than you probably have. If you start production on one product and find there aren't enough customers to make your venture profitable, you almost certainly will not have the resources to keep making products until you find a profitable market. Instead, you will find the right opportunity by intelligently and ruthlessly defining market segments at as granular a level as possible, while keeping them just big enough to be meaningful. To be successful, you will have to select a market to focus on and also deselect other markets that you will ignore, at least for now. I will show you how in Step 2.

The second common pitfall is the abstract paying customer scenario. If you are simply basing your Market Segmentation on secondary research you find on the Internet and then making calculations and conclusions on this, you are not being disciplined enough; you are simply having fun with spreadsheets. This may seem productive but falls under the category of "never confuse activity with progress" (Figure 1.2). In this scenario, the entrepreneur reads a report that someone else has written about a large market, but the entrepreneur has done little to deeply understand this market firsthand. This can be represented in this painfully simple fictional scenario as follows:

The Internet says China has 1.5 billion people. They all have teeth, so the market size is 1.5 billion customers. I'll build a toothbrush for the Chinese market, and because we have a great toothbrush, we will easily get 0.1 percent market share in the first year (what a conservative number that is!). If each person buys three toothbrushes a year, we could sell 4.5 million toothbrushes per year, and if we sell them for $1 each, we have $4.5 million in sales the first year with these conservative assumptions. And we have only just begun, because look at how much room we have to grow in terms of market share!

Figure 1.2: You need to directly interact with real live customers before making any decisions. Hence the need for Step 1A, Primary Market Research, to complete this process.

As mentioned, I call such a high-level market analysis "fun with spreadsheets," because you have not demonstrated in a compelling manner why people would buy your product or why your market share would increase over time. As I discussed in Step 0, you are at a general level and not a level of sufficient specificity at all. You also have not validated any of your assumptions by learning directly from customers—you probably haven't even been to China. After all, if entrepreneurship were this easy, wouldn't everyone sell toothbrushes to China?

(Continued)

Big companies with lots of resources can afford to work hard to gain incremental market share, but entrepreneurs don't have the luxury of resources. Don't get ensnared by small percentage of a big market syndrome.

Again, to reemphasize the key point here, take your resources and apply them to a narrow, carefully defined new market that you can dominate. Focus, focus, focus.

Complex Paying Customers: Primary versus Secondary Customers and Multi-Sided Markets

Thus far, I have used "customer" to refer to the entity—such as a household, organization, or individual—who pays for, acquires, and uses your product. Breaking this down to be more precise, within the broad definition of a customer, there is the end user, who ultimately uses your product, and the economic buyer, who makes the final decision about whether to acquire the product. The end user and economic buyer can be the same person, depending on the situation. You will dive into this in greater detail in Step 12, Determine the Customer's Decision-Making Unit (DMU), but for now I want to briefly mention a couple of more complex cases where a customer is not simply a singular entity.

This first of the two more complicated cases is when your business model calls for separate primary customers (end users, i.e., the one who directly uses the product) and secondary customers (economic buyers, i.e., the one who pays the person who produces the product) in order to make money. Often, these businesses are structured where the end user pays below cost, or gets a product for free, and an economic buyer pays for access to the end user and/or the end user's information. For instance, Google's search engine is free to use, but Google sells advertisements on search result pages to make money. Google's ability to provide advertisers with keyword-targeted ad placement and demographic information about search users further enhances Google's value proposition to advertisers.

To simplify things and to keep the process moving, you should note but not worry about this primary/secondary customer delineation and simply focus on the end user. If the end user does not gain value from the product, there will be no economic buyer. Again, you will dig into the nuances of the difference between the end user and economic buyer customers in Step 12 and thereafter. But for now, just focus on the end user and keep moving.

The second case is called a two-sided or multi-sided market (it can be more than two), where you need multiple target customers for your business to exist. Rideshare company Uber is a good example, because it needs both drivers and riders (supply and demand) to participate to be successful.

If you have a multi-sided market, you will complete each step of the 24 Steps once for each side of the market. But you will likely find through your PMR that one side of the market is harder to establish and therefore more critical to win for your business to succeed. I recommend that you start by focusing your efforts on the more difficult side first. It is usually on the demand side, but not always. For instance, when Uber started, there were lots of drivers (supply) but not enough riders (demand). In another case, in my classroom, there was a team building a new venture providing online one-on-one training of upper-middle-class, middle school-aged (10–14 years old) students by professional artists from places like Paris and Barcelona. In that case, it was easy to get the demand (students and parents) but they had a much bigger problem getting the artists, so it was the supply in this case.

How to Do a Market Segmentation

Step 1A: Brainstorm

"I already have my idea. Why do I need to brainstorm again?"

You probably have brainstormed many ideas (or technologies) and settled on the one you are now pursuing. You have not brainstormed the many potential end users who would benefit from your idea (or technology). You may think there is one obvious end user, but I have never seen an idea or a technology where it is not possible to brainstorm a multitude of end users, nor one that would not benefit from this process. The Market Segmentation's brainstorming stage is designed to sharpen your understanding of who might benefit from your idea.

Do not focus on viability or the solution at this point; rather, focus on getting as long a list as possible of potential people who would benefit from your idea. More is better at this stage. Let a thousand flowers bloom! You will narrow it down later in the process.

Often some of the most interesting initial or what you will call Beachhead Markets in Step 2 exist on the fringe of the spectrum and are overlooked by others, so think broadly. Wild ideas are welcome and encouraged at this point. Start by brainstorming a wide array of market opportunities. Include even the "crazy ideas" that you think are longshots, because they are helpful in expanding the boundaries of possibilities to where some of the most interesting opportunities might exist.

Even if you think you know the best initial solution, just note it and keep brainstorming. Don't get fixated on it. If it is the best one, it will rise to the top in the end. You need lots of other options to do a comparison at this point. This is an exercise you should do with your team. No idea is a bad idea. I encourage my students to use improvisation techniques where the first tenet is always to say "yes" to any idea. Being open-minded and creative at this stage is essential.

I make it a friendly competition in my classroom where whoever can come up with the most ideas wins a prize. And the person with the craziest idea gets a prize too.

While you will do much more of this later, talking about your idea or technology with potential customers even at this early stage will give you clear and accurate feedback for your brainstorming of possible Market Segmentation. In general, forget the unenlightened idea of "stealth mode." Stealthy is unhealthy, as HubSpot co-founder Dharmesh Shah famously told our students. Socialize your idea as much as possible.

Remember, the goal in this stage is to open the aperture as far as possible and let the sunshine of all the potential markets shine in. And make sure to do this as a team with everyone's engagement and input.

Step 1B: Narrow

You have by now identified numerous potential end users and applications for your idea or technology. It is not possible to analyze all of them, so you will have to narrow down the field to what you believe are the best 4–10 candidates so you can do a deeper dive to compare them and determine your potential first market.

How do you narrow the field down? My suggestion is that you start by voting ideas "off the island," to evoke the long-running reality TV show *Survivor*. Look at the ideas you have with a critical eye, based on a set of filters, to eliminate the ones you feel are not a good fit.

What filters should you use? People usually start with analytical market analysis filters (e.g., How big is the market? How strong is the competition? How strong is our value proposition? What is the ability of the customer to pay? How long will it take? What types of resources will I need?). While all of these are good questions, none of them are the *first* question you should ask. The first question you should ask is a personal filter question: Is this market segment one I could get really, really excited about and dedicate the next six years of my life to serving? Will I be proud to be associated with serving this marketplace? If not, don't do it. You will not last. Going back to a point in the previous chapter, you are simply seeking to be a profiteer and that will not last.

Once you have eliminated the markets you would not be excited about serving, now use the analytic lenses to determine your priorities and filter down the field to 4–10 candidates.

Figure 1.3 highlights that after the personal filter, you can apply the business filter, which is focused on the competitive and strategic considerations of the markets. In the next filter, which I call the external filter, you will consider how many additional resources you will need to achieve your goal in the marketplace and whether it is attainable. This includes teammates, partners, and capital. The final filter I list is the execution filter, which is a risk assessment of the market. How many things need to go right for you to win this market segment, and what are the odds of all of them being successful?

Figure 1.3: Filters for prioritizing and filtering out Market Segments.

In this section, you will not be as rigorous as you will be in Step 2 when you narrow the field of 4–10 down to one. But it is helpful now to see the criteria that you will use going forward, because they might be helpful to provide more specific structure to your filtering discussion.

In *Inside the Tornado*, Geoffrey Moore identifies five criteria that the company Documentum used to narrow down its list of 80 potential markets. I have expanded this number to eight by splitting the first criterion into two parts, and adding two of my own to incorporate the passions of your founding team into the discussion.

1. **Is the target customer well-funded?** If the customer does not have money, the market is not attractive because it will not be sustainable and provide positive cash flow for the new venture to grow.

2. **Is the target customer readily accessible to your sales force?** You want to deal directly with customers when starting out, rather than rely on third parties to market and sell your product, because your product will go through iterations of improvement rapidly, and direct customer feedback is an essential part of that process. Also, since your product is substantially new and never seen before (and potentially disruptive), third parties may not know how to be effective at creating demand for your product.

3. **Does the target customer have a compelling reason to buy?** Would the customer buy your product instead of another similar solution? Or is the customer content with whatever solution is already being used? Remember that on many occasions, your primary competition will be the customer doing nothing.

4. **Can you today, with the help of partners, deliver a whole product?** The example that I often use in class is that no one wants to buy a new alternator and install it in their car, even if the alternator is much better than what they currently have. They want to buy a car. That is, they want to buy a whole functional solution, not assemble one themselves. You will likely need to work with other vendors to deliver a solution that incorporates your product, which means that you will need to convince other manufacturers and distributors that your product is worth integrating into their workflows.

5. **Is there entrenched competition that could block you?** Rare is the case where no other competitors are vying to convince a customer to spend their budget on some product to meet the identified need. How strong are those competitors, from the customer's viewpoint (not your viewpoint or from a technical standpoint)? Can the competition block you from starting a business relationship with a customer? And how do you stand out from what your customer perceives as alternatives?

6. **If you win this segment, can you leverage it to enter additional segments?** If you dominate this market opportunity, are there adjacent opportunities where you can sell your product

with only slight modifications to your product or your sales strategy? Or will you have to radically revise your product or sales strategy to take advantage of additional market opportunities? While you want to stay focused on your Beachhead Market, you do not want to choose a starting market from which you will have a hard time scaling your business. Geoffrey Moore uses the metaphor of a bowling alley, where the Beachhead Market is the lead pin, and dominating the Beachhead Market knocks down the lead pin, which crashes into other pins that represent either adjacent market opportunities or different applications to sell to the customer from your Beachhead Market.

7. **Is the market consistent with the values, passions, and goals of the founding team?** You want to make sure that the founders' personal goals do not take a back seat to the other criteria presented here. In the case of a company I co-founded, SensAble Technologies, we wanted to "get liquid" (go public or get bought) within four to five years, a relatively short time horizon for the type of technology we created, because co-founders Thomas and Rhonda Massie wanted to move back to Kentucky, where they were from. Therefore, an important factor for us was whether we could show results in an acceptable time frame in whichever market we chose.

8. **How quickly can you win this market?** You have to find markets that you can win in a reasonable time frame consistent with your personal timelines. You do not want to get stuck in a market that could take years to win.

Start by asking these questions at an industry level but don't spend too much time at that level. What really matters is the end user and the specific job they are doing.

Your limiting factor is time—you will research each of these markets in depth, and you do not have time to consider an unlimited number of options. Four to 10 good market segment opportunities are sufficient (10 is too many in most cases and usually 4 to 6 is a good range).

That being said, don't rush the process and lose the benefits of full team engagement. Each time, before you eliminate a market segment, allow time for the group to discuss to make sure the group has all the information before making such a decision. This discussion can be a powerful learning and alignment process. Lastly, once the obvious candidates are removed, have the group vote on the remaining market segments to get a prioritized list.

Step 1C: Build a Market Segmentation Matrix

Now that you have narrowed your market opportunities, build a framework to analyze the top market segments in order to organize your research. Balance comprehensiveness with the benefits of simplicity. Figure 1.4 outlines several dimensions to consider for each market segment, and provides a sample template to organize the information. As with all the templates in this book, a digital copy of this is available at www.d-eship.com.

Market Segmentation Matrix Starter Template

Market Segment Name					
End User					
Task					
Benefit					
Urgency of Need					
Example End Users					
Lead Customers					
Willingness to Change					
Frequency of Buying					
Concentration of Buyers					
Other Relevant Market Segment Considerations					
Size of Market (# of End Users)					
Est. Value of End User ($1, $10, $100, $1K, etc.)					
Competition/Alternatives					
Other Components Needed for a Full Solution					
Important Partners					
Other Relevant Personal Considerations					

Figure 1.4: Market Segmentation Matrix with definitions.

Market Segmentation Matrix Row Definitions

1	**Market Segment Name**	Carefully name the market segment so it appropriately and precisely captures the group you want and no more; it is okay to be general at first, but you will have to narrow this down in time to make real progress.
2	**End User**	This is the person who is actually using the product, not the economic buyer or the champion (more on this in Step 12)—even if you are selling to a company or a general organization, you want to list here the people in that company who will be using your product.
3	**Task**	What exactly is it that the end users do that you will significantly affect or allow them to do that they could not do before?
4	**Benefit**	What is the benefit that you believe the end users will get?
5	**Urgency of Need**	What is the level of urgency to solve the problem or capture the new opportunity for the end user?
6	**Example End Users**	Who are examples of end users that you can, have, or will talk to, so as to validate your perceptions of this market segment?
7	**Lead Customers**	Who are the influential customers (i.e., lighthouse customers) where, if they buy the product, others will take note and likely follow?
8	**Willingness to Change**	How conservative is this market segment? How open are they to change? Is there something to force change (e.g., impending crisis)?
9	**Frequency of Buying**	How often do they buy new products? What does their buying cycle look like at a high level?
10	**Concentration of Buyers**	How many different buyers are there in this market segment? Is it a monopoly? Oligopoly (a small number of buyers)? Or many competitive buyers?
11	**Other Relevant Market Considerations**	This allows for customization of your segment for relevant considerations such as "high employee turnover," "very low margins/commodity," "high-growth industry," "high virality effect" (i.e., word of mouth), etc.
12	**Size of Market (# of End Users)**	Estimation of the number of end users to a relevant range (10s, 100s, 1Ks, 10Ks, 100Ks, 1Ms, etc.).

Figure 1.4: (Continued)

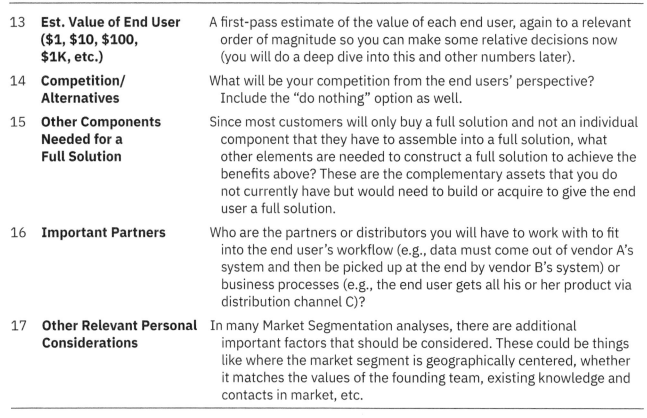

13	**Est. Value of End User ($1, $10, $100, $1K, etc.)**	A first-pass estimate of the value of each end user, again to a relevant order of magnitude so you can make some relative decisions now (you will do a deep dive into this and other numbers later).
14	**Competition/ Alternatives**	What will be your competition from the end users' perspective? Include the "do nothing" option as well.
15	**Other Components Needed for a Full Solution**	Since most customers will only buy a full solution and not an individual component that they have to assemble into a full solution, what other elements are needed to construct a full solution to achieve the benefits above? These are the complementary assets that you do not currently have but would need to build or acquire to give the end user a full solution.
16	**Important Partners**	Who are the partners or distributors you will have to work with to fit into the end user's workflow (e.g., data must come out of vendor A's system and then be picked up at the end by vendor B's system) or business processes (e.g., the end user gets all his or her product via distribution channel C)?
17	**Other Relevant Personal Considerations**	In many Market Segmentation analyses, there are additional important factors that should be considered. These could be things like where the market segment is geographically centered, whether it matches the values of the founding team, existing knowledge and contacts in market, etc.

Figure 1.4: (Continued)

Step 1C: Fill Out a Market Segmentation Matrix with Primary Market Research

Now that you have narrowed your market opportunities and built out a framework to analyze the top market segments so as to organize your research, you now have to fill in that matrix. Balance comprehensiveness of your research with the benefits of simplicity.

Figure 1.4 outlines several dimensions to consider for each market segment, and provides a sample template to organize the information. While I have found this to be comprehensive, you may want to add additional rows for special considerations like regulatory environment, special resource requirements or constraints, or macro-trends.

Once you have a basic structure, it is time to do primary market research (PMR), a fundamental skill of great entrepreneurs. PMR is when you directly interact with your potential market segment, the end user, but also the other stakeholders in that ecosystem. Interacting directly with customers will help you get a better sense of which market opportunity is best in a way that you never can get through secondary market research. Secondary market research is where others have done PMR and you simply read summaries of what they have discovered.

This is especially true for innovation-driven entrepreneurs because you are identifying a new market opportunity for a product that does not yet exist, so you will not be able to rely on Internet searches or on reports from research firms. If there is already a market research report out there with all the information you need, it is probably too late for your new venture. If that is the case, you have probably missed the window of opportunity—someone else has beaten you to the market. You only get unique understanding and insights from PMR.

Unfortunately, there are few shortcuts in this process. While you should find out what you can about customers and markets via secondary market research before you talk to potential customers, it is impossible to overstate the importance of doing direct customer research.

How to Talk with Potential Customers   I have found this whole topic so important to entrepreneurs and so poorly understood by them that I will dive deeply into more specifically how to do PMR in Step 1A. But I first want to provide some guidance that is specific to these early steps when you are learning from potential customers.

When you talk with potential customers, you are in full empathetic listening mode. You should encourage the flow of ideas; don't restrain them, steer them in any direction, or try to gain a commitment. You must be in "inquiry mode," not "advocacy mode"—although the latter will come later in the process. If the potential customer senses you are trying to sell them something, they will change their behavior; they will either say little or give you biased feedback rather than providing you with new, innovative ideas for markets. You must focus on identifying the problem and opportunity at this point and not falling in love with your idea or your product.

In this vein, you should not count on your customer to design your product or tell you the answer to their problems. The goal of this research is to understand their pain points, and later design a solution that will be of great value to them. To do so, you will need to thoroughly understand the underlying issues and sources of opportunity, whether by speaking with them (i.e., interviewing), watching them as they work (i.e., primary observational research), doing the job yourself (i.e., immersion), seeing their responses to carefully designed tests (i.e., A/B testing), or following their digital dust (i.e., tracking what they are clicking on when they visit your website, i.e., "click stream," which can also be a form of A/B testing). Actions are more important than words, because people sometimes say things that are contrary to what they actually will do.

You will want to talk with as many end users as possible, but individuals who are not end users may also give you valuable advice or may point you in the right direction. You may even find that you misidentified the end user in your segmentation.

There are a few key factors that are integral to collecting accurate information:

- You must have a high level of intellectual curiosity.
- You must be fearless about getting on the phone, in the car, or on a plane to pursue this information.
- You must listen and get people to talk.
- You must be open-minded and unbiased, and never presuppose a solution (inquiry, not advocacy).
- You must have the ability to explain what the essence of your proposed offering might look like while also being flexible.
- You must have the time and patience to devote to this important step.

There are three important caveats when conducting your PMR:

1. You do not have "the answer" for your potential customers and their needs.
2. Your potential customers do not have "the answer" for you.
3. Talk with potential customers in "inquiry" mode, not "advocacy/sales" mode. Listen to what they have to say, and don't try to get them to buy anything.

Again, I have included a more in-depth PMR guide in Step 1A that will help you practice focused, productive PMR.

How Long Should I Spend on Market Segmentation?

Give your full attention to this research for at least a few weeks (and maybe much longer if your situation permits) but certainly long enough so you and your team feel you have been able to make valid comparisons of different segments and you are confident, but not certain, about moving forward. The amount of time you spend will depend on a number of variables but most importantly on how effective your team is at getting PMR. You should spend enough time so that you can fill out the matrix for all your top segments with some accuracy. Don't just search the Internet and debate this in your office.

You will not find a singular perfect market segment—this is not a math problem with a deterministic singular answer. There will almost surely be multiple paths to success and none will be perfect to start with.[1] Fill out the matrix enough so your team is comfortable and then start moving forward, iteratively updating it. Remember, the 24 Steps is a sequential but not a linear process.

---

[1] I highly recommend reading or listening to the book *That Will Never Work* by Marc Randolph. No original idea or plan in entrepreneurship is completely correct. You just hope it is correct enough to jump-start the process.

Most of all, you learn nothing without action in entrepreneurship. Do not let yourself fall into "analysis paralysis." Make the best assumptions you can and then test them. Do not let the Market Segmentation be a never-ending process. After all, this is Step 1—you have 23 more steps to go! You will revisit this step as you get more information from the rest of the steps.

Other factors that will affect the time you have to spend on Market Segmentation:

1. The speed at which your target market is moving. If there has been a dramatic disruption in your target market and others are swarming in, you will have to move quickly.
2. If you have a strong competitive advantage, you will have more time. In the example below, we had a strong competitive advantage at SensAble Technologies, which gave us more time and space to do this step.
3. The personal needs of your team.

What Should I Come Out of Step 1 With?

You should come out of this step with three major achievements. While the first one is more tangible, the second two are even more important as they will pay dividends over and over again throughout the whole process. Here are those achievements:

1. **A solid analysis.** The matrix you fill out will give you fundamental information to move forward in an evidence-based manner, providing the foundation for the overall process.
2. **A mindset change.** Humans tend to focus on tangible things in front of them. It is absolutely human nature to want to focus on a tangible product as opposed to a more abstract customer and their needs and use case, but that is not the right mindset. Seeing the world through the eyes of the customer—as you saw in the initial illustration in this chapter—should correct this and give you the perspective of building your new venture from the customer back and not from your product out. This is incredibly important. Remember, fall in love with solving the problem and not with your product.
3. **The beginnings of a coherent and cohesive team.** This process is only as good as the team who will execute it. In this relatively fun and easy step to do Market Segmentation, you will be gently stress-testing your team to see if you can work together and debate issues and then ultimately come together in a unified fashion. If you cannot, then you should seriously think about adjusting your team. It is going to get a lot harder going forward. If this step is to be successful, you should have built a coherent vision for where you are going and also built cohesion within your team. Team is paramount above all else.

EXAMPLES

This book has various examples from class projects and early-stage ventures that highlight different aspects of each of the 24 Steps. In this revised and expanded edition, alongside these examples, you will also get to follow the progress of Bloom, a project from the foundational New Enterprises class at MIT, as the team goes through the 24 Steps for the first time. You will see how a new idea goes through the formulation stage all the way to the end of the 24 Steps, and I will add commentary to highlight aspects of their plans that I think are comprehensive, as well as aspects that I think they can improve as they do a second or third pass. You will see just how hard it is to get everything right on the first try, and how iterating and going back to work from previous steps is essential as you build out your new venture.

Bloom

In one of my classes, I had three talented women who identified a large and growing problem that they had a burning desire to solve. Anisha Quadir, Madeleine Cooney, and Sarah Malek shared a common experience of being young professionals who had to move around for their jobs. They had witnessed firsthand what some were calling "the loneliness epidemic." After a quick search on the Internet, they found out that what they were seeing was not unusual. One survey found that 45% of adults are eager to make new friends but found it difficult. Remedying the loneliness epidemic was their "raison d'être."

The first exercise was to think about all the potential customers who could benefit from this general idea. They were forced to think about different market segments with different needs beyond just theirs. This led them to spend a good deal of time doing PMR to learn more.

Through their PMR, they found that there were many causes of loneliness across a wide spectrum of women.

They found that increased remote working was removing traditional social interactions that were a source of friendship, and a rise in the gig economy allowing for more flexible work with less socialization. These factors, coupled with the traditional life transition from college to a post-college lifestyle, resulted in an epidemic of loneliness, or at least something that had lots of room for improvement.

This PMR helped them better understand what they were reading in secondary market research, which said that people reported barriers to making friends included feeling too shy, not knowing where to meet potential new friends in a healthy way, and feeling that other friend groups had already been formed.

With this in mind, the three women fearlessly threw themselves into solving this problem. They named their project for class "Bloom" with the purpose of allowing women to build and sustain relationships more easily. What would start out as a class project turned out to have a much longer life. It would go on to exist with a different name after the class. But for this book I will focus on the process they followed to take this general idea and make a concrete business out of it.

As you can imagine, after they had started to do their PMR, their Market Segmentation led to a broad spectrum of potential markets even beyond women. It ranged from youth to elderly across many demographics. They quickly realized that while some of the other markets might be even bigger, their passion and, frankly, competitive advantage was with women, which cut the market in half to start. Then they narrowed the market down further to women who had graduated from college. At this point they did more focused PMR, interviewing dozens of women in their potential target market segments (Figure 1.5).

PMR Lessons Learned

Initial Market: PMR Lessons

Hypothesis	Validated	Finding	Next Step
Friendship is a sensitive topic	Validated	Women don't want to look desperate for friends, this created a stigma against BumbleBFF / FB groups for some.	Brand the product for social discovery rather than for those who do not have friends
Women need social friends in the same phase of life and/or location as them	Validated	Women wanted others to socialize with in their area / stage of life, not a replacement for existing friends. Also often filter based on perceived similarities. e.g. school as a proxy for ambition / interest.	Enable users to filter or identify friends based on certain criteria
Scheduling is a big pain point	Validated	Women with non-traditional jobs or demanding jobs need to find friends with similar schedules.	Pressure test ways for Bloom to support scheduling of events to alleviate user pain points
Type of event is important and selects attendees	Validated	Money is a big barrier for women – either want more expensive places or inexpensive (both extremes exist). Investigated activity meetups and found workouts to be oversaturated for initial launch.	Enable users to indicate financial constraints without exposing to end user; enable that to support filtering
New grads are the best beachhead market	Validated with hesitancy	Strong opportunity for HENRY's, want friends with: 1) High ambition 2) Similar schedules given demanding jobs 3) High willingness to pay (e.g. prefer nice restaurants / "elite" activities). Prior to graduation, students are not thinking ahead on how to make friends in new cities.	Continue to conduct user interviews to validate the beachhead market and pressure test concerns
Some would enjoy being the "planner of events" for their assigned Bloom	Invalidated	Majority of women interviewed did not want to make the plan for a new group.	Identify ways to alleviate the overhead associated with planning events and validate those ideas via speaking with users
Big cities will be easier to launch the product	Invalidated	Smaller cities have fewer options; some cities such as NYC are oversaturated with solutions.	Continue to conduct interviews to understand which areas are best to launch and what changes would need to be made accordingly

Figure 1.5: Bloom's initial PMR summary.

Female Friendships are Unique and Critical to Success & Wellbeing
Yet, currently 60% of Women report feeling lonely

1 According to a study featured in HBR, women need larger friend groups than men, and they prioritize different attributes in their friends:

 Female friends have similarity in education, sense of humor and happiness

 Male friendships have similarity in shared activity, finances and social connections

2 Women depend on their social networks for professional success more than men:

 Women who had a female-dominated inner circle of 1-3 women landed leadership positions that were 2.5 times higher in authority and pay

 Men do not benefit from the size of their social network as much, and gender composition of males' inner circles was not related to job placement.

3 Women with larger groups of friends had better health outcomes:

Socially isolated women were **64% more likely** to die from cancer, and **43% more likely** to have a cancer recurrence

As we are in a loneliness epidemic, Female Friendships can offer the best medicine

1

Figure 1.6: Secondary market research to complement the initial PMR the Bloom team had done.

The team then did some more secondary market research to externally validate what they were seeing and found compelling evidence that they were on the right path (Figure 1.6). The most relevant article came from *Harvard Business Review* and it reaffirmed and sharpened their focus on the college graduate professional market. Combining their PMR with this secondary research, they had unique insights they would not have gotten from either alone. The team now was more determined, more motivated, and more focused.

With this in mind the team now built their Market Segmentation Matrix. After much discussion, they narrowed down the markets to seven market segments (Figure 1.7). Once they had the matrix structure with the market segments and rows, it took dozens of interviews and research online to collect the relevant information to fill it out.

Market Segmentation Matrix

Market Segment Name	Fresh Grads	The "Floker"	New Moms	H.E.N.R.Y Women - High Earning Not Rich Yet
End User	- Young women aged 21-25 who are new entrants in the city, having just graduated college	- Young women aged 24-27 who have relocated and thus need to expand their social circles	- Young mothers who do not already have a group of established "mom" friends	- Young women aged 24-30 who are generally high achieving - Have invested significant time into education and their careers
Task	Meet more people in the area so they can make friends and develop supporting relationships	Find like minded individuals to complete activities with them in a new city	Meet other young mothers who she can relate to and who can serve as a support system	Find other ambitious women looking to connect with other young, ambitious women
Benefit	Grow their social and emotional network in the area that they are living	Grow their social and emotional network in the area that they are living	Creating a safe space for mothers to meet other parents in the same stage of life	Find others who have similar schedules, ambitions, high-end interests
Urgency of Need	High	High	Medium	High
Example End User	University of Oregon 2021 grad who just moved to Austin TX for a new job	Moving to Boston from LA to start a new job as Manager at a Bank	First time mom, age 28, who does not have any existing friends with kids	30 year old investment banker living in NYC
Lead Customers	Social Media Influencers	Social Media Influencers	Social Media Influencers, Moms	High-end luxury apartment buildings
Willingness to Change	High	Medium	Medium	Medium
Frequency of Buying	High	High	Low	Medium
Concentration of Buyers	High	Medium	High	Low
Other relevant market segment Considerations	High Virality effect "word of mouth"	High Virality effect "word of mouth", feel embarassed about not having local friends	Peanut already exists as a strong competitor in this niche market	May be more interested in a platform that is "exclusive" in some way
Size of Market (# of end users)	2 million	2 million	1 million	500,000
Est. value of end user ($1, 19, $100, $1K ect.)	$10 - $20 ARPU	$20 - $30 ARPU	$20 - $30 ARPU	$30 - $40 ARPU
Competition/ Alternatives	Bumble BFF, Meetup, Facebook groups, dating apps	Bumble BFF, Meetup, Facebook groups, co-working spaces, Junior League	Bumble BFF, Meetup, Facebook Groups, Nextdoor, Peanut	Co-working spaces, Chief, Junior League, Charity organizations
Other components needed for a full solution	App needs to be free, and need to partner with local restaurants/activities/services for advertisement	Network effects and enough users to be matched in different groups every two weeks	Ability to filter by or find other new moms on the platform; App needs to be free to compete with Peanut	Activities offered need to be a certain level of caliber or to appeal to this segment
Important Partners	Lobbies of buildings/ HR departments to promote apps for "new to the city"	Advertisement platform with relevant restaurants, beauty services, female health services, event platforms	Relevant brands to new mothers; local businesses surrounding motherhood	Brands and businesses that are seen as "high-end" or exclusive; managed luxury apartment buildings
Other relevant personal considerations	Regional cultures/attitudes in different US cities. The types of events /activities women enjoy	Regional cultures/attitudes in different US cities. The types of events /activities women enjoy	Ability to host events that include children. Factoring in the age of children to the app	Expectations of a HENRY vs. other segments may be higher because network and time value of money may be more important

Figure 1.7: Market Segmentation results for Bloom.
(Note: A more robust version is available in Additional Resources with seven market segments.)

SensAble Technologies (Technology Push)

SensAble Technologies was my second startup and it is a wonderful example of how to do Market Segmentation in a successful manner. SensAble started its life as a powerful but raw technology that enables people to feel three-dimensional (3D) objects rendered by a computer. Based in the MIT Artificial Intelligence Laboratory and specifically in the Robotics Laboratory supervised by the legendary Professor Rodney Brooks, then-MIT undergraduate Thomas Massie—working with Professor Ken Salisbury—created a new device that would give its user the sense of touching virtual objects using a stylus-like interface. The device, named the PHANToM, would simulate shapes, motion, weight, and many other physical properties by increasing or decreasing the resistance or force felt by a user when moving a finger or stylus (Figure 1.8).

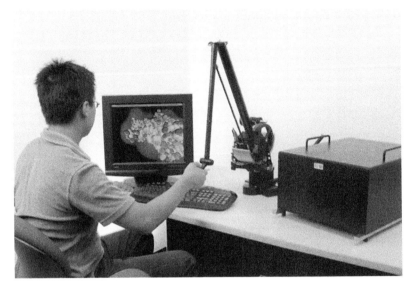

Figure 1.8: The SensAble PHANToM.

As others heard about this breakthrough idea and subsequent technological implementation, Massie received queries from all over the world about potential uses for the technology. Thomas and MIT smartly filed a patent for the fundamental concept of the PHANToM that made it a breakthrough. He started to sell versions of the lab product. However, his "early adopters" consisted mainly of universities and research labs—"technological enthusiasts" who will buy almost any innovative product. (Geoffrey Moore's book *Crossing the Chasm* goes into greater detail about technological enthusiasts, and says that these customers can be a first bridge to the ultimately most desirable broader market called the "early majority.")

When I first met Thomas, he was selling these devices to researchers under the company name SensAble Devices. He was interested in building a much more commercially oriented business that could have a bigger impact on the world, so we joined forces to create SensAble Technologies.

We worked hard to find a scalable market opportunity that would allow our business to reach the goals we had set out to achieve: being a company worth tens of millions of dollars in the relatively short time horizon of five years or less. I worked with our business development manager, John Ranta, who had experience in previous startups identifying such market opportunities and doing the hard work of PMR with customers to discover their real needs. We spent weeks building out a list of potential markets, using our current customers, trade show feedback, incoming product inquiries, and our own imaginations as sources of ideas.

No idea was too crazy at this point: a boxing channel, fixing space stations, computer mice that vibrated, helping to perform medical surgery, pornography, new computer games, educational opportunities, data analysis, flight simulators, virtual worlds, museums, sports training, computers for the blind. We did not prejudge any idea; rather, we wanted to open the aperture as wide as possible.

We discussed ideas weekly, sometimes nightly, and we discussed our core values and personal passions, which made certain markets unattractive (e.g., pornography). Another outcome of our brainstorming was that we saw where our product's real value was—applications that used 3D data, not those using two-dimensional (2D) data.

Once we had a comprehensive list of possibilities, we then systematically narrowed the field down to eight industries, and made the outline for a Market Segmentation chart (Figure 1.9).

Each of these market segments was a legitimate candidate for our initial market, and each was distinctive with different sets of customers, end users, and applications. For example, "Entertainment" was chosen as a potential market because of the strong interest we received from computer animators making 3D movies like the original *Toy Story*. Our tool would make it easier for them to design on the computer without their design intent being compromised. They could also do it in a much more productive manner than was available at that time.

Similar to what we learned in the digital entertainment industry from an application stand-point, the "Industrial Design" industry was selected based on feedback that product designers wanted to create 3D shapes on the computer in a way that was as easy as working with physical clay.

Likewise in each group—Medical Visualization (of 3D data), Surgical Simulation (and training), Micro Surgery (robotic-controlled operating room procedures), Geophysical Visualization (analysis of 3D seismic data), Non Visual C.H.I. (Computer Human Interface for the blind to use computers), and Prototyping (virtual prototyping of CAD/CAM files to see how they worked together; for example, to check to see assembly feasibility)—we had enough evidence to know that the market satisfied well the seven key questions presented earlier in this step.

For each of these segments, we then had to do PMR to fill out the matrix. Somewhere around 90% of the data in the chart came from direct interaction and talking with real potential customers in these industries about their situations, pain points, opportunities, and market characteristics. Very little data came from reports by well-known research firms or by finding data on the Internet.

This was a time-consuming but absolutely essential part of the process. Fortunately, because we had strong intellectual property through our MIT patent filing, we had the luxury of being able to take more time. Another factor that gave us more time was that we were already selling to tech-nological enthusiasts, which gave us enough of a revenue stream that we could spend over three months on the Market Segmentation analysis. You will want to spend at least a few weeks, but you are unlikely to have the good fortune to be able to spend as much time as we did.

Industry	Entertainment	Industrial Design	Medical Visualization	Surgical Simulation	Micro Surgery	Geophysical Visualization	Non Visual C.H.I.	Prototyping
End User	• Animator • Designer	• Stylist • Designer	• Radiologist • Surgeon	• Med Student • Surgeon	• Surgeon	• Geophysicist	• Blind Person	• Engineer
Application	• Sculpt • Animation • Paint	• Sculpt • Paint • Modeling	• Segment-ation • Navigation • Surgical planning • Diagnosis	• Training • Surgical planning	• Opthalm. Surgery • Neurosurgery	• View enhancement • Drill plan	• H.U.I.	• Design review • Model evaluation
Benefits	• Ease of use • Reduce cycle	• Reduce cycle • Increase accuracy	• Ease of use • Increase accuracy	• Increase use of new tech. • Increase accuracy	• Reduce cycle • Increase accuracy	• Reduce errors • Increase yields	• Increase access, "mainstream"	• Reduce cycle • Improve designs
Lead Customers	• Disney • ILM • Dreamworks	• Toyota • Ford • Rollerblade	• Brigham & Women's • German Cancer Rsrch	• U of Colorado • Penn • BDI	• Dr. Ohgami • Ottawa Eye	• BHP • WMC/CSIRO	• Certec • U Delaware	• Volkswagen • Stratasys • Toyota
Market Character-istics	• Early adopt • High-priced talent • High growth	• Dislike CAD & computers • High-priced talent	• Mainstream • High-priced talent • HMO	• Mainstream • High-priced talent • HMO	• Early adopt • High-priced talent • HMO • Not computer automated	• Late main • Oligopoly	• Late main • No money • Gov't sponsor	• Mainstream • Pressure to reduce prod. cycle
Partners/ Players	• Alias • Soft Image • Discrete Logic	• PTC • Alias • Imageware	• GE • Siemens • Picker	• Smith & Neph • Heartport • Ethicon • US Surgical	• Toshiba • Hitachi	• Landmark • Fractal Graphics	• IBM • Apple • SUN • HP • Microsoft	• PTC • Solid Works
Size of Market	40,000	X00,000	X0,000	X0,000	X,000	X,000	X,000,000	X,00,000
Competition	Watcom	None yet	None yet	Immersion	None yet	None yet		None yet
Platform	• SGI • Windows	• SGI • SUN	• SGI • SUN	?	None	• SGI • SUN	• Windows	• SUN, HF
Needs	• NURBS • Stylus • Dynamics	• NURBS • Stylus	• Voxels • Stylus • VRML	• 6 DOF • Custom devices	• 3 Finger scaling	• Voxels • Stylus	• Windows I/F • P300	• NURBS • VRML • Dynamics

Figure 1.9: SensAble Market Segmentation Matrix.

Our matrix included a line for "platform," which referred to the computer operating system and hardware that our technology would require for it to be adopted by that particular market segment. This may or may not be relevant to you, but it was to us at the time because there was a big difference in computer platforms.

Our row labeled "Needs" depended on which industry we would target. For the animator in the entertainment market segment, we included a NURBS (Non-Uniform Rational B-Splines) geometry engine so it could output the data files to the Alias Wavefront visual rendering animation suite. This software program was used by animators worldwide to create the three-dimensional animated images you see in animated movies today. The device would also have to include a stylus because the animators loved to sketch in 2D and were very accustomed to this. The last piece that we needed to include was a dynamics engine so that the figure could move in a realistic manner. All three of these items were generally available through other vendors so they were not critical parts. Still, it was important to have a very specific understanding of what our end users were using, to know what else was needed to make our system functional enough to meet their needs.

Gradeable (Market Pull)

SensAble Technologies is a classic technology push example (i.e., a new technology looking for a market). The question I often get after I explain that example is "Does this work for a situation where I don't have a technology but rather see a problem that needs to be solved?" This is the definition of the reverse situation, called "market pull," where you have a problem and you need to find a solution. The answer to the question is "Absolutely yes!" I have never seen a situation where Market Segmentation was not only possible but helpful. The Bloom example is one of a market pull. Let me give you another market pull example.

Gradeable was conceived by former students Parul Singh and Dante Cassanego based on their direct experience with teachers in public schools. They were an outstanding team with a shared vision and complementary skills. They were obsessed with making education better by empowering teachers with technology so they could focus on what they do best: teach students. They quickly learned that grading was one of the most productivity-zapping and energy-draining parts of their job. The current state was that when a teacher finished their school day (which was long) and went home to relax, they had to often spend hours doing the generally rote process of grading.

Both Parul and Dante were technology savvy and so they envisioned a way that teachers would be in large part relieved of this burden by using technology. They had no proprietary technology but they understood that by simply building a stand and putting a tablet computer (like an iPad) on the top, and then putting the students' submitted work underneath it and taking a picture of it, software could be written that could automatically generate grades.

In summary, the teachers would save enormous amounts of time from a low-value-add task as well as one that drained their energy and took away time from doing what they loved and where they contributed the most value—interacting with their students in a customized and thoughtful manner. Seems great, so how do Parul and Dante start the Market Segmentation?

Easy. What are the different market segments? You can start with segmenting in many different dimensions and there is no singular order that is correct. Let's start with the subject manner. Is it math, science, social studies, language arts, art, or something else? Other important segmentations would be grade level and type of school. Another key segmentation would be geography, which could quickly get down to regions such as U.S. states because of the state-specific regulations and decision-making process. A very important segmentation would be the demographics and psychographics (lots more on this in later steps) of the teachers. Are they new teachers with 0–5 years of experience, or 5–10 years, or more? How tech-savvy are they? See Figure 1.10 for a summary. Note that they customized the various dimensions greatly to better reflect the data that would help them segment their markets.

Market Segmentation Example for Teachers

Dimension	Option #1	Option #2	Option #3	Option #4	Option #5
Subject	Math	Science	Language Arts	Social Studies	Other
Level	Pre-K	Elementary	Middle	High School	Other
Type of School	Public	Independent	Religious	Vocational	Other
Geography #1	Massachusetts	New York	Connecticut	New Hampshire	Other
Geography #2	Urban	Suburban	Exurban	Rural	Other
Experience of Teacher	0–5 years	5–10 year	10–15 years	15 years+	Other
Receptivity to Technology	Technological Enthusiast	Early Adopter	Early Majority	Late Majority	Laggard
More to the specific situation . . .					

Figure 1.10: *Market Segmentation options for a market pull example, Gradeable.*

As you can see, the target customer segment is not just "teachers" but many different types of teachers, and it is extremely important to differentiate between them so the team can get focus. Even if some might have similar needs and want exactly the same product, they will have different circumstances and how they have to sell to them will vary, and that will make all the difference.

ADDITIONAL RESOURCES

There are additional resources for this step at www.d-eship.com/step1. These materials include:

- Video: Market Segmentation Explainers by Bill Aulet and Erdin Beshimov
- Video: Example described and explained in an interview with FINsix founder Vanessa Green Coleman
- Worksheet 1.1: Structure for Brainstorming Market Segments
- Worksheet 1.2: Market Segmentation Matrix (digital copy of what's in this book)
- Bloom Market Segmentation example: More detailed matrix with 7 market segments
- More Details on Prioritizing Market Segments

Additional resources will be added as new and updated examples and information become available.

Summary

The Market Segmentation process identifies multiple potential market opportunities. Once you have a list of potential markets, PMR on a finite number of market segments will help you determine which markets are best for your idea or technology. The goal of the research is not to provide a perfect solution, but to present a wide spectrum of market opportunities as you start to think about where you will focus your business. PMR, which involves talking directly with customers and observing them, is by far the best way to identify good market opportunities. This research will help you select a Beachhead Market in the next step.

I can say now after having seen thousands of plans, problems that arise later are most often the result of the entrepreneur not doing a rigorous job of Market Segmentation up front, so invest your time and effort here and it will pay many dividends later.

STEP 1A

Primary Market Research (PMR)

In This Step, You Will:

- Learn how to perform efficient and effective original research to better understand your customer.
- Learn the importance of doing this right and doing this continuously to feed the Disciplined Entrepreneurship process.

The process of the 24 Steps only works if you do high-quality primary market research (PMR). PMR is the essential fuel that keeps the process going in the right direction.

Why This Step, and Why Now?

When you first start down the entrepreneurship path, you brainstorm with the knowledge and expertise you have to determine an idea and potential markets. Your knowledge will soon run out and is biased by your own perspectives, so you will have to learn how to study your customer to obtain the critical information to grow your business. While PMR (primary market research) can and should start even before you settle on an idea, it will definitely be essential to fill out your Market Segmentation Matrix from Step 1 (Figure 1.4 and Worksheet 1.2). Getting good PMR is essential to your work because it is the input to each of the 24 Steps. If you put garbage into it, you will get garbage out. If you give it high-quality input, the process definitely works, and you will continue to feed the process for the rest of these steps (and beyond).

Let's Get Started

When you look back at the history of successful tech companies, especially in Silicon Valley, alumni from one surprising company keep coming up over and over again as leaders. That company is Procter & Gamble. This is actually not surprising when you analyze the situation further. Procter & Gamble employees are taught the importance of primary market research (PMR) and how to do it. While they are not the only ones who do PMR, nor did they invent it, they refined it and brought it to the mainstream. Often called "ethnographic research" and today frequently referred to as "customer discovery," it is something academics and businesses have been studying for a long time. As such, there is a good body of knowledge you can build off to be more successful—and then customize this for an entrepreneurial environment.

This is the purpose of this chapter—to distill, customize, and make actionable the fundamentals of PMR both to help you fill in the Market Segmentation Matrix you built in the previous chapter, and to do the important research throughout the 24 Steps and beyond. Markets are always changing and success has an expiration date on it even for the best products. As a result, doing PMR (and the 24 Steps) never ends. The day your company stops doing PMR is the day it starts dying.

Another key point on PMR is that it does not usually generate a singular right answer or even a small number of them. What you get from PMR is a portfolio of insights into our customer (end user, economic buyer, and champion as I will discuss more in Step 12) that will guide you to make informed hypotheses that you will test as you progress forward. It is not always clear what insight or combination of insights will be the most important for future scenarios where you will have to make a decision. As such, PMR is the gift that keeps on giving.

Consequently, it is a bad idea to outsource PMR to people outside your founding or core team, especially at the beginning. PMR is a bag of golden insights that you need to access over and over again in unpredictable ways, and very quickly. As such, it should always be treated as some of the most valuable information that your company has (i.e., proprietary) and protected as such. Likely it is every bit as valuable as any patent you might hold, and potentially more so.

A Practical Guide to PMR

I want to express my thanks to my colleague Elaine Chen, formerly at the Martin Trust Center for MIT Entrepreneurship and now the director of the Derby Entrepreneurship Center at Tufts University, as well as the entire marketing group at the MIT Sloan School of Management, specifically Professors Catherine Tucker, Duncan Simester, and Drazen Prelec, who provided important intellectual contributions and consultations with regard to this chapter. The good ideas are theirs, and I take full responsibility for interpretations or extrapolations to the entrepreneurial environment that might be more controversial.

A key design point of this book is not to create new, untested material, but rather to start from material that already exists and has been proven to work, and then make it accessible and integrate it together to make you a better entrepreneur. There have been decades of work on this topic, so let's take advantage of it rather than reinvent the wheel.

What Is PMR?

PMR is direct interaction with customers to understand their situation. The skills required to do effective PMR are required to complete almost every step of the 24 Steps. Step 1, Market Segmentation, is the first step that is heavily fueled by PMR, but, as mentioned above, you never stop doing PMR when you want paying customers.

Customer-focused companies, led by Procter & Gamble and including leading product design firms such as IDEO and Continuum Innovation, have long practiced PMR in their user-centered design processes.

More recently, a positive result of the Lean Startup movement, with terms like Steve Blank's "customer discovery," is that PMR is becoming more widespread and valued. But it is important also to understand that PMR has deeper roots as well, and this chapter explores the depth and breadth of academic and practitioner insights on the topic.

Entire books have been written on this topic, so I am going to try to synthesize it into what entrepreneurs really need to know to be successful. As Dharmesh Shah says, one of the key things you must do to be successful in a startup is to start. It is right there in the name. So don't get overwhelmed by the magnitude of this task; just get started. You will get better the more you do, I promise.

Definitions

- **Primary Market Research (PMR):** This is when you directly interact with potential customers to gain knowledge specific to your potential new venture. I will often call this "bottom-up" market information. Depending on where you are in the 24 Steps, you may be interacting with the end user or with other individuals within the company, such as the people who make spending decisions (the "economic buyers"), the people who will advocate for the purchase of your product (the "champions"), or others who influence or control the procurement process (collectively, the entire group is called the "Decision-Making Unit," about which I will get into much more detail in Step 12).

- **Secondary Research:** This is material you get from sources other than the potential customer. It is indirect. It is generally not specific to your business. These are the industry and government reports that you can find on the Internet or buy from a source that has already done them. I will refer to this as "top-down" market information.

- **Qualitative versus Quantitative Research:** Qualitative research is exploratory research that helps you generally understand a topic, and is often conducted through a small number of open-ended in-person interviews. Quantitative research uses a much more structured approach and focuses on gathering specific data to prove or disprove the hypotheses created in the qualitative phase.

- **Ethnographic Research:** This is technically defined as the systematic study of people and cultures. In PMR, it turns out that customer psyche plays an important role in decision-making. Sometimes it is even more important than a rational or economic perspective. However, you can't ask people directly why they do what they do, because people are bad at explaining their habits. And yet it is essential for you to understand this behavior. Anthropologists have been doing ethnographic research for a long time. They embed themselves in the cultures they are studying and observe closely to gain this information.

The Goal of PMR

The goal of good primary market research is to understand your customer in all dimensions: rationally, emotionally, economically, socially, culturally, habits, and more. After you have done this, not only have you walked a mile in your customer's shoes, but in some ways you understand them better than they understand themselves. Good primary market research is not just numbers. In fact, it is important to emphasize that it does not start with numbers, but rather that holistic understanding of the customer—the person, their environment, their journey, their job to be done. Only then can you solve significant problems or otherwise motivate and provide value to the customer.

It is not the customer's job to design your new product. As Henry Ford, the person who created the automobile industry, is reputed to have said, "If you asked people what they wanted, they would have said faster horses." Designing the new product is your job. As Elaine Chen says, "The customer is the expert of their problem, and you are the expert in finding a solution to that problem." It is your responsibility to systematically get enough unbiased information to design and then refine a new product that will create significant value for the customer, and many others just like them.

Good PMR is a continuous process of generating new insights and then converting them into testable hypotheses. You will then continue to use PMR skills to validate or invalidate these and new hypotheses going forward. You may go through the 24 Steps to launch your product based off of PMR, but in reality, the process never ends. Customers and markets change over time, so what is true one year may be invalid the next. PMR is an essential skill set for a great entrepreneurial team to have, and it makes being an entrepreneur a lot more fun too.

The Five Biggest Obstacles to Good PMR

The fundamental concept of primary market research is quite simple—go out and observe, listen, interact with potential customers and other associated stakeholders, do the job yourself, try competitive products, get on discussion boards—do whatever you can to understand the landscape you are entering. That can seem very hard for some people (i.e., engineers) and very easy for others. Even if it sounds easy, it is not. Here are some of the pitfalls that you have to be aware of before you start:

1. **Lack of Structured Process:** While there needs to be flexibility in how you obtain information, you have to have a process and know the process—and know that it is a process! I will walk you through that process here, and I will reference many other available resources at the end of this chapter.

2. **Not Properly Executing the Designed Process:** No process will work if it is not used, and this is no exception. You cannot come up with the right answers without interacting with others. You must get out and talk, observe, and test hypotheses with real potential customers, which often results in answers you would not have gotten on your own. You must dig and get good initial sources to talk to and then grow your sources. You have to learn the process

and execute it with good technique. Good technique has a lot to do with avoiding the biases I cover in the next three points.

3. **Confirmation Bias:** Extremely common for all people during research, confirmation bias is when you only see the information that confirms your worldview. You ignore or block out any information that runs counter to your hypothesis. A good way to counter this tendency is to set up criteria beforehand that will confirm or disprove your hypothesis so that you don't change the metrics for success once you start. Even then, bias can still creep in based on how you structure your questions and surveys, inadvertently prompting the customer to provide the answers you want to hear. You must be neutral and not "lead the witness."

4. **Selection Bias:** The people you interview, whether during qualitative or quantitative research, may not be a good representation of the opinions of the group as a whole. Think about Internet polls that allow everyone to vote without controlling for demographics. The type of people who vote do so in percentages that far exceed their true representation of the broader population. As such, they produce wildly inaccurate projections. This discrepancy was notably evident in the 2008 and 2012 US presidential runs of US congressman Ron Paul. His passionate base would vote him to the top of various Internet polls, but he did not gain traction in general elections. You need to really understand what your sample should look like to produce meaningful results, and control for variations between people that will affect your results. Sometimes selection bias can be exacerbated by not clearly defining who your customer is. If your end user is "women" and you are at the mall interviewing or observing potential end users, will a 15-year-old affluent urban female have similar opinions to a 40-year-old middle-class suburban mother of three kids? Think about whether your definition of end user is too broad to achieve reliable research results.[1]

5. **Social Acceptability Bias:** If you engage with family or friends, they will most likely not give you accurate answers because they don't want to offend you by not liking your ideas. They will be polite rather than brutally honest because they want to keep their social relationship strong. You need brutally honest feedback from unbiased people, so it is best to interact with people who do not have a social connection with you. Similarly, on sensitive topics like race or sexuality, you may have trouble getting honest answers from anyone, particularly with in-person or phone interviews as compared to anonymous surveys.

---

[1] As Elaine Chen points out, selection bias is especially pernicious in qualitative research because it is by nature anecdotal with a low number of sample points. Imagine talking to five people who seem to validate your hypothesis and you stop there, and it turns out that there exists nobody else on Earth who agrees with them. You have a lot less of this problem when running a survey with 500 respondents, assuming you have randomly chosen who you survey, and you controlled for the right variables by incorporating demographic or other questions into the survey and weighting the responses.

There are other biases such as the IKEA effect[2] (once you build a product, your confirmation bias gets much stronger), giving the more entertaining interview more weight, giving the last interview more consideration (recency bias), and so on. It is good to realize your biases and always be on the lookout for them. Being data-driven is good, but the data can be made to mislead as well, so that is not a sufficient answer. A great way to minimize biases is to have multiple people conducting the research who have been trained on the biases inherent in research, so that multiple perspectives will keep things honest.

Process and Techniques

This is the streamlined process I have used and encouraged others to use. It is not as comprehensive as those used in big companies, especially those market research powerhouses like Procter & Gamble, but you don't have the resources or time to be able to do it that way. You have to get the biggest bang for the buck, so this is an efficient, simplified process guide.

1. **Make a Plan:** Many of you will do what I did the first time I learned about PMR, which was just to go out and start talking to potential customers without a plan. This is not disciplined. Develop a plan. This may sound obvious, but it was not to me at first, and it may not be to you. Without a plan, your potential customers will get frustrated after they talk to you once and then you come back with more questions that could have been addressed up front. This customer, a valuable and precious source of information, will then write you off as disorganized and wasting their time. Please save yourself a lot of suffering and losing some potential great sources by having a thoughtful plan.

   A general plan will look much like the following from Elaine Chen's Primary Market Research Primer Guide[3]:

   1. Write out the goals and objectives of the research, and a detailed description of the research technique.

   2. Define recruitment criteria for interviewees.

   3. Develop a recruitment questionnaire.

   4. Develop supporting content (e.g., discussion guide, landing page, online survey).

---

[2] See "The IKEA Effect: When Labor Leads to Love," by Michael I. Norton, Daniel Mochon and Dan Ariely, July 2012, *Journal of Consumer Psychology,* https://www.hbs.edu/faculty/Pages/item.aspx?num=41121

[3] Elaine Chen's Primary Market Research Primer presentation can be found at http://www.slideshare.net/chenelaine/primary-market-research-an-overview-on-qualitative-and-quantitative-research-techniques

5. Recruit subjects.

6. Run the research program.

7. Digest results, and proceed to the next steps.

Of these items, the supporting content is often the most overlooked for its value, particularly the discussion guide. In any in-person or phone interview, a discussion guide is crucial so that you know the key questions you should ask each person, in part for consistency but also to make sure each interview yields all the information you need. It will allow you to have a structured dialogue with the person you are engaging with while maintaining flexibility. Likely you will constantly update this discussion guide at the beginning, but once you have done sufficient interviews, the changes become much less frequent.

2. **Start with Secondary Research, But Not Too Much:** Before you go out and start to do PMR, do some homework so you know at least the basics of the industry. Don't do so much that you think you are an expert of any kind, but don't be totally naïve. You will be wasting the time of those you engage with if you don't know the basics. On the other hand, don't assume all your secondary research is accurate, because sometimes the most interesting opportunities are where conventional wisdom hasn't kept up with the reality in the marketplace, or never matched it at all.

3. **Start Qualitative Before Quantitative:** The most common mistake is to start with a survey. You have to figure out the right questions to ask in a survey, so surveys are useful later but not up front. And while you'll start by asking specific questions to make sure the respondent's demographic (age, gender, etc.) and psychographic (personality, opinions, lifestyles) characteristics match your target customer group, your research questions should be very open-ended, such as "Please describe a good day for you. Now describe a bad day." Another question that some experienced PMR experts prefer is "Tell me about the last time you did X." Always follow up with "Why?" "Why not?" or "You said X. Can you say more?" Get them to tell you real and specific examples. These examples or stories are generally powerful and easy for the customer to tell you about. Don't add friction by asking for data or too many facts right now. You are probing for those big pain points, the biggest fears and motivators, in their lives. While your interview will be loosely scripted, let the customer take the conversation wherever they want it to go.

4. **Source Candidates to Engage with, and Use Them to Find More Candidates:** The best places to find candidates are at the "watering holes" for your target customer. Watering holes are those places where your target customer congregates physically or digitally. For many who are religious, it is their place of worship. For fitness enthusiasts, it is probably their high-end gym. For women about to get married, it is Pinterest. For others, it might well be an industry group or conference. For baby-boomer health-conscious consumers, it might well

be Whole Foods. Find out what the watering holes are for your target customer because that will be a highly efficient place to begin engaging them. The sourcing process requires some creativity, as do all the parts of the process, but here are some ideas to help you source leads and make initial contact:

- **Physical Watering Holes:** While digital watering holes can be convenient, you need to be comfortable physically getting out of your workplace and interacting directly with your target customer.

- **Digital Watering Holes:** You can usually find a group that is tied to your target customer and may even be arranged around the problem you are looking to solve. Today this could be a LinkedIn, Reddit, or Facebook group, but it could well be someplace else online. Other examples for your target customer might be TikTok, Instagram, Snapchat, or Twitter, and there are many more. This will also change over time as new virtual discussion forums become popular and the existing ones fall out of favor.

- **Blogs or Online Discussions:** Similar to LinkedIn or Facebook groups, these digital meeting places are efficient ways of finding candidates, but be sure to respect the rules of the blog or forum or you might get banned from the website.

- **Industry Groups and Membership Lists:** This is another form of a watering hole. Depending on the list, you may get a lower response rate than with some of the above methods.

- **Ads:** You can advertise on Google or Facebook, targeted at specific demographics, for as little as $20 to get the names of interested people and then follow up. And if no one responds, that's important information as well. To be most effective, you should carefully craft the wording of your ads, or you may spend a lot of money getting a lot of responses from people who are not truly in your target customer group.

- **Read Publicly Available Information:** When you do your secondary research, you will likely run across some names linked to your market. They might be names of people who write online reviews. Write those names down and find contact information for them. There are various tools to help you find someone's e-mail address (one I know of is email-hunter.co, but there are many others as well). When you contact them, you should be ready for rejection or, more likely, no response, but it only takes one to respond and then you are in. Like the camel's nose in the tent, you can expand from there. You may also want to try engaging with key people on social media like Twitter and build up a relationship that way.

- **The Last Question:** Once you get going, the best way to get candidates is from others in the target customer group. As such, your last question at the end of each successful interview should be "Who else do you know who has a challenge or opportunity similar to yours that I should speak to? Would you be willing to make an introduction?" Once you find one lead, your goal is to have your list grow by getting multiple new leads from every interview.

5. **Initial Contact:** Now that you have your initial list of people to contact (a list that should continually be growing as you do your research), things get real. You have to persuade your contact to give you at least 15 minutes of their time, depending on how many questions you have, and that is not easy if you are working with a "cold lead" where you are making first contact. When you initially contact the candidate, it is good to reference someone they know. That is easier than ever with LinkedIn, which shows you mutual connections for each person you look up. Start with short e-mails or dialogue to build credibility and rapport. Explain that you are doing research on their industry to try to help make it better, including their job. Be *completely* in inquiry mode and not one bit in sales or advocacy mode at this point. You are not really a company yet, nor do you have a product. If you think you are a company, then that is a problem. Be empathetic about making their job better, because that will show in your interactions. Still, be steeled for lots of rejection. There is copious research about little tips and techniques for interacting with cold leads. For instance, Stanford Professor Tina Seelig found that if you are physically approaching strangers, it is better to have a woman make the interaction rather than a man.[4] At first, you will probably feel as if making these initial contacts will never work, but you have to stay at it and then it will get much better. It is never easy, but it gets much easier the more you do it.

6. **Act Like a Great Journalist:** I have not been a journalist but have been so impressed when I have interacted with and observed great journalists in action. They have great active listening techniques to get people to talk. The great ones listen with 150% of their attention. They have a positive voice and physical stance when engaging. They are incredibly interested and empathetic. They shake their head and say "yes" a lot and are nonjudgmental. They lean forward and listen intently, and visibly so. They make the person being interviewed feel like the most important person in the world. Oh yes, and make sure to smile and be enthusiastic. Humor can help, but sarcasm is not good. The person must like you before they will open up. A couple of ways to verbally engage are using the person's name a lot and repeating back to the person the words they've said.

7. **If You Can, Have Two People Conduct the Interview:** Having two people conduct the interview allows one person to concentrate completely on engaging the interviewee while the other is taking detailed notes and observing the interviewee's nonverbal signals from another angle. Make sure to write down not just what the person says, but the nonverbal reactions as well. Having two people in the room also allows you more perspectives when reviewing notes afterward.

---

[4] Seelig, Tina, *What I Wish I Knew When I Was 20*, Chapter 1, HarperOne, 2009.

8. **Constantly Make Sure You Are Interviewing the Right People:** If you interview people who are not in your target customer group, you will get spurious information that will not help you understand your target customer, and in fact may confuse you or lead you astray. Make sure you put together a short recruitment questionnaire (it doesn't have to be longer than five questions) as part of your research plan that screens out people not in your target customer group. This helps you avoid the aforementioned and ever-present selection bias.

9. **As You Get to Forming Hypotheses, Small "n" Might Well Be Better Than Big "n":** After you have done some qualitative research, you will begin to form hypotheses about ways you might be able to benefit the target customer. But you don't want to spend forever on qualitative research to test it out, because you don't have the time. MIT Professor Drazen Prelec expresses it as small "n" (number of candidates) and big "n," where small "n" is a small-enough group size that you can go deep in each interview to understand what is causing the phenomenon you feel is important. A bigger "n" gives you more candidates but less in-depth understanding. In the qualitative stage, the smaller "n" is better; then, in the quantitative stage, the larger "n" becomes more relevant to test it out more broadly once you understand the hypothesis in a robust manner.

10. **You Should Be Surprised:** As Catherine Tucker points out, the goal of qualitative PMR is to develop new hypotheses; so if you are not surprised, you are probably not learning anything. That defeats the purpose of the process. It would also be a pretty clear sign of confirmation bias if you never learn anything, and that is not a positive thing.

11. **Moving to Quantitative:** Once you have developed credible hypotheses for the small "n" sample through your qualitative methods, then you should start to test them more systematically. The scripts and the surveys now get more structured, and will start to produce numbers, points on a cluster map, and the like. You will now get the data to validate, invalidate, somewhat validate, somewhat invalidate, or leave in the TBD column your hypotheses.

12. **Perceived Value Compared to Real Value:** Often, as Duncan Simester has shown in his research, there is a gap between real and perceived value. Both matter, as does the gap. In both your qualitative and quantitative research, understand the difference. Look to understand each of these and then quantify at the end as much as possible.

13. **Don't Always Believe What Is Said:** Often people say things with the best of intent but then do different things in reality. What they do matters more than what they say. One way to get at this discrepancy is A/B testing, where customers are randomly divided into groups and are treated differently to see how the difference in treatment affects the customer's response. You get to see what the customer actually does, instead of what the customer says they will do. Likewise, well-designed behavioral economics experiments are good ways to see what customers will really do regardless of what they say. You will explore this topic in more detail in Step 21, Test Key Assumptions.

Results

How do you know when PMR is complete? It never is. Entrepreneurs and good businesspeople are constantly talking with customers and seeing new opportunities and refining their offerings. That said, there are times when you have enough PMR to continue to the next step in the 24 Steps. You'll generally know you are at this point when your hypotheses are being validated and new customer contacts are providing little new information. If your hypotheses are being only somewhat validated, you'll have to decide whether to keep iterating on hypotheses before moving on to the next step, or to proceed while continuing PMR in parallel to develop better hypotheses.

As you go through the steps, you will be continually refining your hypotheses for greater specificity, and you will keep learning about the target customer, so do not think you must have the "perfect" answer before moving on. There are no perfect answers, and forward progress through the 24 Steps is the only way you will be able to rigorously test your assumptions. Sometimes you reach a limit on PMR where you have to take more concrete steps like a prototype or even a Minimum Viable Business Product (MVBP) like in Step 22.

As I mentioned before, people can say one thing—and really mean it—but then do something completely different, so do not expect that your interviews will accurately reflect the person's willingness to become a paying customer. Trust but verify the results. When money changes hands, the credibility of your results increases dramatically.

Toward the end, in Step 23, you will be setting up a unified full systems test for the MVBP, which will be the ultimate test for your product. It is likely you will find many surprises (or as I call them, learning opportunities!) when you build and test the MVBP. But your goal is to find as many of these surprises as possible earlier, especially ones that can be fatal if caught too late in the process. That is why throughout the 24 Steps, you formulate and test hypotheses at almost every step. Good PMR is essential to validating or invalidating hypotheses quickly so you spend more time building products that customers want.

Tools of PMR

The tools of PMR may seem like a longer list than it actually is. At the end of the day, an entrepreneur has limited time and resources. No one is as invested in a product's design and success as the core team is, so at the start, virtually all of the PMR has to be done by the founding team. It is difficult and dangerous to outsource primary market research. You would never outsource your eyes, ears, and brain to someone else, and certainly not in an innovation-driven startup like you envision creating.

The real gold in many cases is not your product, but rather the knowledge you have gained working with the new customers in this emerging market opportunity, since you will know their needs, wants, and context better than anyone else. This is why it is so crucial, when starting your company, that you deal directly with your customers. See firsthand how they like, use, dislike, and misuse your product.

I learned a very important lesson from IBM when I got trained there at the start of my career. They said, "Whoever owns the customer owns everything." That is especially sage advice for a new product in an emerging market.

Here are several methods that entrepreneurs have used for PMR:

1. **Customer Interviews:** As noted above, this is the most common. Essential for qualitative and also good for quantitative.

2. **Observational Research:** Watch customers do their work. Potentially, you would videorecord them or record their mouse and keyboard activity. You would ride with them in the passenger seat (in reality or metaphorically) as they do their job, carefully observing and asking questions at the right time while making sure not to change their behavior through your actions or questions.

3. **Immersion:** Do the customer's work and fully experience all the dimensions of the job in a way that will give you an understanding that may not come from observation.

4. **User Tests:** Landing pages and the like don't just draw in candidates but also give important insights into their behavior and preferences. A/B testing is another form of this and can be very effective, especially if it can be done digitally.

5. **Focus Groups:** This is another traditional tool but has become less and less enthusiastically embraced by entrepreneurs. It can be useful, especially if done very carefully, but it can also have lots of biases and is expensive.

6. **User-Driven Innovation:** This is a technique described and validated through research by MIT Professor Eric von Hippel. It encourages you to look for the end user with the most acute pain from the problem and see how they are finding or developing a workaround solution.

7. **Outcome-Driven Innovation:** This framework is also known as "Jobs to Be Done," created by Anthony Ulwick and popularized by Harvard Business School Professor Clayton Christensen. Outcome-driven innovation is based on the concept that customers have measurable outcomes they are trying to achieve in their day-to-day (aka when they are doing a job), and a company should link its innovation to those customer outcomes because customers buy products to get jobs done.

In the end, because entrepreneurs don't have much time or money, they focus on tools 1–4. They might do some other creative things, like a "mystery shop"[5] of the closest product. (I want to encourage this and other creative ideas.) For sure, focus groups are falling out of favor with entrepreneurs, and with reason because they are very expensive, hard to run, and can fall victim to groupthink or too much sway from the loudest person in the group. The methodologies tools of methods 6 and 7 offer interesting alternatives to creative entrepreneurs, and understanding them to make tools 1–4 better designed and more effective is time well spent.

PMR is an imperfect process and can be messy, but it is critically important.

ADDITIONAL RESOURCES

There are additional resources for this step at www.d-eship.com/step1A. These materials include:

- Videos: How-To: Interviewing Prospective Customers with Erdin Beshimov
- Videos: How-To: Organizing Your Customer Interview Data with Erdin Beshimov
- Worksheets:
  - Worksheet 1A.1: PMR Preparation Worksheet
  - Worksheet 1A.2: PMR Execution Worksheet
- Elaine Chen's Portfolio of Primary Market Research Materials
- Recommended additional books and online course

Additional resources will be added as new and updated examples and information become available.

Summary

PMR is the fuel that will drive the process of the 24 Steps. It is a crucial skill for every entrepreneur to have. It is not easy, especially at first, and you will only get better by doing it. But also know there is a large body of work that can provide guidance on how to do PMR well. Never stop doing PMR, because the day you stop doing it is the day your company starts to die.

---

[5] A "mystery shop" is when you go and buy the nearest similar product without identifying yourself as an entrepreneur considering entering the market. You learn how they create awareness, who they are targeting as their customer, what they see as their value proposition, and how well they support their customers throughout the full customer journey. It is amazing how many entrepreneurs don't do this but the smart ones do. You can learn a lot.

Select a Beachhead Market

In This Step, You Will:

- Analyze your top 4–10 market opportunities and choose *one* to pursue.
- Further segment that market to determine your Beachhead Market.

PERSON WHO CHASES TWO RABBITS CATCHES NEITHER

ROMANIAN PROVERB

HUNGRY DOGS HUNT BEST

Selecting a Beachhead Market is part of the critical process of narrowing your focus and attention to one critical area of attack.

Why This Step, and Why Now?

It is crucial to start the process with a focus on a singular target customer. You do not have a lot of resources or time, so you must focus your efforts to gain early victories and then build off this progress. By choosing a well-defined Beachhead Market, it will make all of the steps that follow much more efficient and effective because you will have great focus.

Let's Get Started

In Step 1, *Market Segmentation*, you built a matrix based on your PMR on your top 4–10 market segments. Now, select just one market opportunity from the matrix to pursue as your Beachhead Market; ignore the other markets.

Almost all first-time entrepreneurs find that, ignoring market opportunities is difficult and even painful. They doggedly hold on to the idea that more markets increase their odds of success and that they are best off hedging their bets until one market takes off.

In fact, the opposite is true. Such thinking will decrease your odds of success because you and your new enterprise will lack the necessary focus required to succeed. A key determinant of success for entrepreneurs is their ability both to select a market and to stay disciplined by deselecting the other markets.

Focus can be difficult, especially for entrepreneurs. People keep options open even when it is not in their best interest, according to Duke Professor Dan Ariely, who discusses the topic in his 2008 book, *Predictably Irrational*.[1] According to his research, when people are given what appear to be multiple paths to success, they will try to retain all the paths as options, even though selecting one specific path would have guaranteed them the most success. By choosing a single market to excel in, your startup can more easily establish a strong market position, and hopefully a state of positive cash flow, before it runs out of resources. By focusing in this way, you will position yourself to most quickly achieve the all-important positive word of mouth (WOM) that can be the source of success or failure for entrepreneurs.

---

[1] There is also a short and excellent summary of this topic in a February 26, 2008 article from *The New York Times*, "The Advantages of Closing a Few Doors," by John Tierney https://www.nytimes.com/2008/02/26/science/26tier.html

How to Choose Your Beachhead Market

In military operations, if an army wants to invade enemy territory with water access, the army may employ a beachhead strategy, where the army lands a force on a beach in enemy territory, controlling that area as their base to land more troops and supplies, and to attack other enemy areas. The 1944 invasion of Nazi-controlled Europe by the Allied forces is one of the most famous examples of a beachhead strategy. The Allied forces established beachheads on the shores of Normandy, which allowed them to gradually capture all Nazi-controlled territory on the European mainland. Without conquering the beachheads, they would have had no starting point for their invasion.

Likewise, your Beachhead Market is where, once you gain a dominant market share, you will have the strength to attack adjacent markets.

The most famous example of this is the strategy that Jeff Bezos deployed for Amazon by starting with books and then systematically expanding from there.[2] In almost all cases, there are multiple paths to success, so it is not imperative to choose the singular best market.

SensAble, from the previous chapter, is a good example of a technology that could have been successful in any number of market segments. Therefore, get started making some assumptions and testing them in the real world (i.e., doing), rather than getting stuck in "analysis paralysis." Your goal is to start a company, not become a professional market analyst. Action will produce real data that will tell you quickly if the market will or will not be viable. If the one you have selected is a viable market, great. If not, you will—if you are decisive and quick—still have time and resources to allow you to return to your matrix and attempt a second market.

The eight criteria I mentioned in Step 1, Market Segmentation, for narrowing your market opportunities are also useful in choosing your Beachhead Market:

1. Is the target customer well-funded?
2. Is the target customer readily accessible to your sales force?
3. Does the target customer have a compelling reason to buy?
4. Can you today, with the help of partners, deliver a whole product?
5. Is there entrenched competition that could block you?
6. If you win this segment, can you leverage it to enter additional segments?
7. Is the market consistent with the values, passions, and goals of the founding team?
8. How quickly can you win this market?

[2] For more details, see https://www.d-eship.com/articles/bezos-focus-on-books-greatest-execution-of-beachhead-marketing/

Choose a relatively small Beachhead Market; but it should also be big enough to prove your value proposition and get sufficient critical skills, credibility, and mass to move to the next market. For example, if you live in a small geographic region, start there before trying to launch in a larger region. A friendlier and more forgiving market is one where you can make adjustments quickly and easily, and you will always have to make adjustments in some key ways. Better to do this on your home turf with a smaller audience than in the biggest market and hurt your reputation in a key long-term strategic market. As the old saying goes, "You get one chance to make a first impression." Large companies do the same thing; they test-market new products in lower-exposure countries and regions before rolling them out worldwide.

Your Beachhead Market Still Needs to Be Segmented Further

As you begin to focus on your Beachhead Market, you will quickly recognize that it almost surely can be further segmented into smaller markets. Don't be discouraged, be encouraged. This is a good sign. This is a standard and good practice.

In general, you should not worry about being focused on too small a market (you will check the Total Addressable Market size in a later step). I have yet to see an entrepreneur focus too much—it is always the other way around, where the entrepreneur doesn't focus enough. You want to start in a market where you have a golden opportunity to dominate in a relatively short time period; a narrow, focused market is the best way to do so.

Investors, especially ones who have not been entrepreneurial operators, might well encourage you to think bigger and be more ambitious. Listen politely and incorporate that into your follow-on markets (Step 14, Calculate the Total Addressable Market Size for Follow-on Markets) but for now, you don't win the World Cup unless you qualify for the tournament and win in the first round. You have to win the first game to play another.

How do you tell if your market is targeted enough? You want to continue segmenting until your market opportunity matches the three conditions that define a market. This definition expands on one that Geoffrey Moore presents in *Inside the Tornado,* as explained below.

Three Conditions That Define a Market

1. The customers within the market all buy similar products.
2. The customers within the market have a similar sales cycle and expect products to provide value in similar ways. As you go through the 24 Steps, you will see that this means that not only is it the same use case (Step 6, Full Life Cycle Use Case) and the same value proposition (Step 8, Quantify the Value Proposition) but it is also going to be the same demographic and

psychographic (Step 3, Build an End User Profile), messaging, pricing (Step 15, Design a Business Model, and Step 16, Set Your Pricing Framework), decision-making unit (Step 12, Determine the Customer's Decision-Making Unit [DMU]), sales process (Step 13, Map the Process to Acquire a Paying Customer, and Step 18, Design a Scalable Revenue Engine), and influencers. Don't worry that you don't know the later steps yet (that is still to come), but understand the general idea. Your sales organization can shift from selling to one customer to selling to a different customer and still be very effective with little or no loss of productivity.

3. There is word of mouth (WOM) between customers in the market, meaning they can serve as compelling and high-value references for one another in making purchases. For example, they may belong to the same professional organizations or operate in the same region. This is referred to as "watering holes" (i.e., where they congregate physically or virtually; see Step 1A, Primary Market Research). If you find a potential market opportunity where the customers do not talk to each other, you will find it difficult for your startup to gain traction.

These three criteria for defining a market mean that you will get efficiencies of scale in the market and you have a good chance to do that magical thing that all startups want, "to go viral."

EXAMPLES

Bloom Continued

In the first step, you were introduced to Anisha, Madeleine, and Sarah, who had an idea for a problem they wanted to solve and so they started the Disciplined Entrepreneurship process for a new venture they called Bloom. As you recall from Step 1, they had built a Market Segmentation Matrix and filled it in after doing extensive PMR.

Now for this step, the team utilized the output of Step 1 and dug in deeper with the goal of choosing one singular market segment to focus on first.

As the team did more PMR (remember, it never stops!), the market segments evolved and simplified down to four. One market segment was urban women in their early to mid-20s, a group the team affectionately called "Bloomer" women as a pun on the name of the baby boomer generation. Their PMR suggested this segment is actually two subsegments—recent college graduates were one, and women in their mid-20s was another. The team narrowed down to two other market segments—female expatriates in the US, and HENRY (high-earning, not rich yet) women.

Having done this systematic analysis, grounded in PMR throughout the whole process, the team determined that their Beachhead Market was recent female college graduates in urban settings. They also prioritized the markets they intended to expand to after winning the Beachhead Market (Figure 2.1), which will be helpful and which will set them up well when they explore follow-on markets in Step 14, Calculate the Total Addressable Market Size for Follow-on Markets.

Initial Market: Beachhead Market Selection

	Beachhead	Description	Reasoning
Chosen Market	Fresh women graduates in urban settings	Young women (22 - 24) new to a specific city who are interested in making friends and experiencing the area with others	This is a further segmentation of our initial new graduate segment based on PMR. From our discussions, we found that for GenZ impacted by COVID, many were struggling to adapt to new cities and wanted to have greater support. They were also more open than older interviewees to make friends via a phone app.
Secondary Market	"Bloomer" women	Young women (25-27) new to a specific urban ara interested in making friends and experiencing the area with others	This is a further segmentation of our initial "Bloomer" segment based on PMR. We found that women who are in the phase of life where their friends are transitioning (e.g. friends getting married but they are single) are more likely to want to be involved. Although this market is promising, it was not chosen as the group tends to be more transient. Additionally, at an older age, the desire to socialize frequently decreases.
Tertiary Market	Female expats in the US	Young women moving to the US from a foreign country who most likely do not have a strong network where they are moving to make friends	Based on interviews, this segment was further divided into female expats in the US and US expats elsewhere as both are very interested in making female friends in areas. They also are more focused on those friendships being female due to safety concerns and like the idea of group initiation to reduce pressure. This market is promising but was not chosen as it introduces additional complexities logistically.
Quaternary Market	HENRY women	Young women who are very ambitious and interested in meeting / interacting with other ambitious women	Based on interviews, it became clear that this group highly values exclusivity. This is a great feature for building hype in the app and can lead to growth but also limits the ability for the product to scale and impacts the number of people that we can help support via this innovation. As such, we will not be moving forward on this segment.

Figure 2.1: Bloom's Beachhead Market selection, and prioritized list of subsequent market segments to address after they win the initial market.

SensAble Technologies

After much deliberation, we chose the industrial design industry as our Beachhead Market based on the seven criteria above, but we had not segmented the market any further, so after choosing the market, we discovered that industrial designers could and should have been further segmented into three distinct groups. One group handles rectangular shapes with sharp edges, incorporating a lot of simple geometry. A second group handles highly stylized shapes with smooth surfaces, best represented by mathematical equations. A third group works with highly organic and sculpted forms, often designing with clay. This was a group that was called "sculptors and model makers."

Our product was most appropriately suited for free-form designing, so the third group was the optimum market for us to focus on. Even within this group there were many different industries and use cases. When doing our PMR, we learned there were a lot of them in jewelry, furniture, fine arts, architecture, medical, footwear, and advertising companies. While all of these were interesting, we would need to do more research when we were ready and prepared to scale. So we were most drawn to the toy industry by our analysis. It was big enough but not too big and had a compelling need and consistency of use case. Plus, we had Hasbro in our backyard in New England. With this focus, we found that toy companies had extensive clay studios and many sculptors among their designers (Figure 2.2).

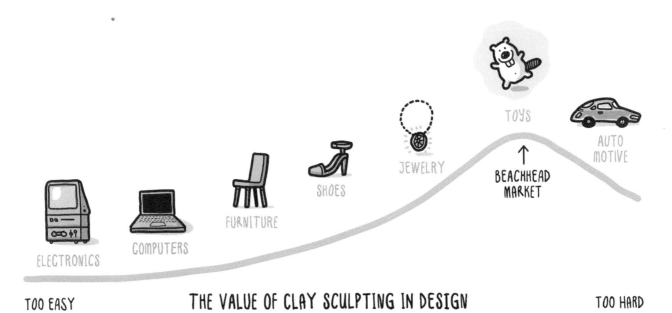

THE VALUE OF CLAY SCULPTING IN DESIGN

TOO EASY   TOO HARD

Figure 2.2: After further segmentation, the toy designer market was our initial primary focus for the Beachhead Market.

Tighter market segmentation here dramatically improved our odds of success because it made us much more efficient and focused downstream. Another example of disciplined segmentation leading to greater focus was that once we focused on designers in the toy industry, we started to get interest globally, but we said we would not take international orders to start. We would initially be focused on only US-based designers until we had experienced success in our home market. This decision disappointed our sales team, who wanted to take all orders, but we benefitted from this geographic focus. There are many issues you need to work out early on in a product's life cycle and it is good to have them localized so you can solve them quickly. It also reduces many other variables, including time zone differences, languages, cultural nuances, and even currency exchange.

Much to our surprise, after we had experienced success in the toy industry, we were able to group toy and footwear companies as one market, because industrial designers in the toy and footwear industries acted so similarly that they completely met the three conditions of a market presented earlier in this step. They both used lots of clay to sculpt highly organic, 3D art shapes that were shipped to China on a tight schedule. They would buy the same design products and use them in the same way. The pressures they faced were the same. The sales processes and value propositions were identical. Further, in a very telling sign, designers frequently moved between toy and shoe companies to advance their careers; they even belonged to the same subgroup in the Industrial Design Society of America.

ADDITIONAL RESOURCES

There are additional resources for this step at www.d-eship.com/step2. These materials include:

- Video: Selecting a Beachhead Market Explainers by Bill Aulet and Erdin Beshimov
- Video: Example described and explained in interviews with NVBots founder AJ Perez
- Process Guidance
- Worksheet 2.1: Market Segmentation Certification
- Worksheet 2.2: Beachhead Market Selection Framework

Additional resources will be added as new and updated examples and information become available.

Summary

Choose a single market segment to pursue, then keep segmenting until you have a well-defined and homogenous market opportunity that meets the three conditions of a market. Focus is your ally.

Build an End User Profile

In This Step, You Will:

- Continue to use primary market research to begin to build out a more detailed initial demographic and psychographic profile of the typical end user within your Beachhead Market segment.

Start by beginning to define your customer with a target customer profile.

Why This Step, and Why Now?

1. To keep the focus on the customer.

2. To validate (or invalidate) your selection of Beachhead Market by deepening your understanding of the end user.

3. To provide the necessary information to estimate the Beachhead Market Total Addressable Market (TAM) in the next step.

Let's Get Started

Now that you have identified a specific Beachhead Market, you will need to learn as much as possible about your target customer; more is better, even if it does not seem to matter right now.

It is critically important you recognize that, to be successful, you must build your business based on the customer you are serving, rather than pushing onto the market the product or service you want to sell.

Each customer actually consists of an *end user* and a broader *decision-making unit* that decides whether to acquire the product, as you will see in Step 12, Determine the Customer's Decision-Making Unit (DMU). You will start by learning as much as you can about end users because if nobody uses your product, there will be no value created and there is no sustainable business.

In this step, you will build a demographic and psychographic profile of this End User. The End User Profile must be specific enough that it allows you to calculate, in Step 4, the Total Addressable Market size of your Beachhead Market.[1] Later, you will add much more specificity by identifying one end user who fits the End User Profile to serve as your Persona (Step 5, Profile the Persona for the Beachhead Market).

You may think that after choosing a Beachhead Market, the End User Profile will be easy. However, it typically requires a lot of time, thought, and further research. This exercise will help you sharpen the focus of your Beachhead Market. You will quickly find that even though you think you have a narrow Beachhead Market, all submarket segments within it are not alike, and further segmentation will get you an even more precise definition of your Beachhead Market. Remember, the 24 Steps provide a sequential map to guide you but not a linear one. Looping back and updating your work from previous steps is a very good thing.

---

[1] It is important to clarify the Beachhead Market TAM from the overall TAM. Investors often ask, "What is your TAM?" and they most likely want an overall TAM number, which as you will see in Step 14, Calculate the Total Addressable Market Size for Follow-on Markets, includes follow-on markets as well as the beachhead.

Why Target a Specific Demographic?

Demographics are statistical characteristics of groups of people. Demographics are any tangible characteristics, such as age, race, and sex, and also income, job, income, geography, and so on.

Even though your Beachhead Market is narrow, you will find much variety among the demographics of potential end users.

Those differences will often correlate with their attitudes toward adopting your product, but ultimately people don't buy products based on their demographics. Instead, they buy based on their goals, habits, aspirations, fears, and other less tangible characteristics, called "psychographics."

Marketing professionals have historically found correlations between demographics and psychographics. Digital connectivity has weakened these correlations, but they still have some value.

Your goal is to create a description of a narrowly defined subset of end users with similar characteristics and with similar needs, using both demographics and psychographics. As a new venture, you need to focus on creating one product with one sales strategy, since you do not have the time or resources to pursue multiple products and multiple sales strategies.

This exercise really forces you to deeply understand who your customer is in all dimensions and who is not your customer. You do not want to spend your time and resources trying to be everything to everybody. That will surely fail.

As I will note throughout this book, you must continually talk, observe, and interact with your target customer to obtain this information and reconfirm it. Good, direct customer research (PMR) is paramount to this process; you will not be able to simply think through the profile on your own in a room with your team. You have to get out and interact directly with your potential customer.

How to Build an End User Profile

This book will describe the process for one-sided markets, where only one kind of end user is required for the product to work, so that you have a good grounding in the fundamental principles of building an End User Profile. Multisided markets, such as marketplace platforms like eBay that attract both buyers and sellers, use the same techniques described herein, but they require developing an End User Profile for each side of the market.

The fundamental concept of the End User Profile is that it must be a person and not an organization or department. In the end, it is a human being, or group of human beings, who will use your product, so you need to deeply understand this person.

Six items are the most common when building a useful End User Profile. You may want to expand or contract this list depending on the complexity and economics of your situation. I provide a sample worksheet to organize your research later on in this step (Worksheet 3.1).

1. **Demographics:** As mentioned above, demographics are quantifiable data that can be used to identify your target end user and also filter out those who are not your end user. These are things like gender, age, income, geographic location, level of education, school attended, and other relatively easily measurable factors. The good news is that these are pretty easy to figure out, but the bad news is that they might not all be useful in understanding your end user for your context. That is the art here. Knowing your end users are women in their 20s, even if you narrow the group down to a certain income group and geographic location, does not gain you much information if there exist wildly divergent attitudes, values, or fears in that group. Analyze the demographics, but then decide how much emphasis to put on the different elements as you move forward. Remember, more is better to start, within reason.

2. **Psychographics:** As discussed earlier, psychographics refers to the qualitative description of your target end users. What are their aspirations? What do they fear? What gets them promoted or makes them more money? Who are their heroes? Understand how and why they behave the way they do, rather than the general identifiable characteristics that demographics give you. Psychographics are immensely valuable but are much harder to get or analyze. Lots of government or industry database services or social media networks like Facebook can break down information by demographics, but far fewer can be searched by psychographics. This makes attributes below like proxy products and watering holes even more important because they may help you find end users with similar psychographics.

3. **Proxy Product:** What products do these end users also buy today? This information is valuable because it shows how the end users already behave, instead of how they might theoretically behave if your product were to exist. Sometimes, proxy products are complementary products. If someone owns a Lexus automobile (a high-end and expensive but high-quality car), they would likely buy an expensive but high-quality brand of tires like Michelin. Other times, proxy products demonstrate similar demographic and psychographic characteristics. If someone buys a Toyota Prius, a hybrid gas-electric car that is more expensive than Toyota's Camry sedan, they are indicating that they are likely interested in mitigating their environmental impact and that they have enough money to act on that passion. They are likely a good candidate to also own, or at least be very interested in, solar panels on their home.

4. **Watering Holes:** Watering holes are the places where your end users congregate and exchange information. They are reliable places for information about your product to be spread by word of mouth, which is far more effective than advertising. They also provide some corroboration for your demographic and psychographic information because you can infer things about people by the company they keep. The forms that watering holes take can be physical in nature, such as industry conferences, Saturday morning soccer fields, bars

(literal watering holes), and the like. More and more, these watering holes are digital in nature, such as Facebook, LinkedIn, Reddit, or specific industry group forums, which is fortunate for entrepreneurs because online platforms can be a much more efficient and rapid way to reach potential end users than hanging around physical watering holes.

5. **Day in the Life:** Tell the story of what it is like to walk in your end user's shoes for a typical day. In this step, the "day in the life" will be a composite—but make it a composite of end users whom you have actually spent a day observing and talking with. The resulting story sets aside abstract studies and statistics and brings it all home to your team by helping them understand what happens in real life. It also reinforces and helps you refine the rest of your End User Profile.

6. **Biggest Fears and Motivators:** What keeps your end users awake at night more than anything else? What are your customers' top priorities—their fears and motivators? I don't mean with relation to the product you're hoping they will buy; I mean in general. When you do your PMR, sit with end users and make a comprehensive list of all their concerns. Then ask them to weight their priorities by giving more points to higher priorities, with a total of 100 points across all the priorities. This exercise forces prioritization, giving you an even clearer sense of your end user. As part of the End User Profile, you'll want a weighted list of your end user's top five or so priorities. Confirm this list with the end users you talk to as much as possible. This list will be extremely useful going forward.

To reemphasize a critical point from earlier in this chapter, your PMR from previous steps will be useful here, but you will almost always need to do additional PMR to complete your End User Profile. Don't start taking shortcuts at this critical time. Specifically, don't guess or make stereotypical judgments about what your End User Profile "should" look like in an attempt to save time. In the end, you want information about real people, because it's real people who will use your product, not fictional characters in a marketing document.

Does Your Founding Team Include Someone in the End User Profile?

It is typically a huge advantage if someone who fits the End User Profile is on your team at the beginning, because the resulting depth of understanding you will have about your customer will be a critical factor in your success. Because an end user is on your team, you will not have to rely on assumptions, which are often inaccurate about who your end user is and what they want. If you don't have someone from the demographic already on your founding team, you should hire a target end user for your executive team.

However, over time you should move beyond a member of your team being the voice of the customer. First of all, you need multiple perspectives so that you ensure you can sell to a group of users. Second of all, the market will change and the member of your team may no longer be fully representative of the market you are trying to sell to. Third, once they start to express an opinion and it is accepted, they fall subject to the IKEA effect, where they value opinions they've made more highly than others' opinions,[2] or other biases that will make them less open to change as the market changes. Finally, social acceptability bias will inevitably start to creep in, and they will start telling you what you want to hear and not what is true to their experience as an end user. Domain expertise on the team is good as long as it is humble and will defer to the market data as the final arbiter. Best to realize that while this is a good way to get started, it is also good to mix this with strong PMR at arm's length as you grow so you can change more quickly and avoid biases.

EXAMPLES

Bloom Continued

In the previous step, Bloom chose their Beachhead Market of women who have just graduated college and now live in urban settings. As you can see from their work in Step 1, Market Segmentation, and Step 2, Select a Beachhead Market, they already had a good focus. Now they analyzed the PMR that had already been done, and they did a lot more PMR to gather information around the six key items for the End User Profile. They then talked among themselves about the key takeaways from their research and analysis, which is summarized in Figures 3.1 and 3.2.

End User Profile (1 / 2)

Overview:
Our end user is a young woman originally from the Midwest who has just graduated from a small college and has moved to a city in the Northeast for work. She is employed as a Marketing Associate making $40 - $50k per year.

Demographics:
- Female, aged 22-24
- Gen-Z
- Currently single but actively dating

Day in the Life:
Our end user wakes up at 8:00 am and eats a quick breakfast before heading to work at 8:30. She takes the subway to work, brings her own lunch, and is finished promptly by 5:00 pm. After work, she typically works out and completes any errands before settling in to watch *The Bachelor* with her roomates. On the weekends, she likes to be fully booked with social plans.

Psychographic Profile:
- Aspirations: adjusting to "adult life" in her new city; performing well in her first corporate job; making friendships & building active social life
- Personality: outgoing, adventurous, amiable

- Hobbies / Interests: bar nights, reality tv, improv and workout classes
- Fears: loneliness, moving back to her small hometown, failing in "adulting"
- Values: openness, humor, spontaneity

Figure 3.1: Bloom End User Profile (part 1).

[2] See https://thedecisionlab.com/biases/ikea-effect for a more thorough explanation of this cognitive bias named for the popular Swedish furniture chain.

End User Profile (2 / 2)

Proxy Products:
- Active on social media like Instagram & TikTok. She enjoys the visual components of these platforms and showcasing her personality
- Uses Hinge for dating platform. She values the ease in making digital connections

Watering Holes:
- Works at local coffee shops because she lives in a small, shared apartment
- Frequents small dive bar with her roommates
- Buys most of her clothing online and primarily grocery shops at Trader Joe's

Priorities:

Social Life	Career Success	Romantic Relationship	Health & Wellness	Money / Finances	Hobbies / Experiences
30%	20%	20%	10%	10%	10%

Figure 3.2: Bloom End User Profile (part 2).

In the end, not only did they have an understanding on paper of who their target customer was, but they also had all members of their team fully aligned on this critical guiding information.

SensAble Technologies

In the End User Profile for SensAble (Figure 3.3), we were starting to understand our target customer in a much more specific way. There is demographic information to help us build a market size in the next step, but there is also the rich context that was so important as we moved forward to make this real and was one of the key defining factors in our success.

SensABle End User Profile

Industrial Designer in Toy Companies

Gender	Male (90%), Female (10%)
Age	24–35, estimating that the average is close to 31
Level	Individual contributor and not a manager
Income	$50K–$60K per year, depending on the region
Education	Rhode Island School of Design, Pasadena School of the Arts, Savannah College of Art and Design—or more likely, they wished they had gone to these schools or some other high-end arts school
History	This is not their first job in the industry, so they have some experience. However, this is not their end job either. This is something they will do as long as it is interesting and fulfilling. The industry is tough and they realize they can be laid off if things don't go well. This also leads to a lack of strong attachment to their job, so if another job comes up, they will move on without reservation.
Context	The designers see themselves as artists, not business people. While they might want to be doing great art outside of the commercial world, they have realized that they need a paycheck to survive and have made that compromise. They also are serious about wanting to create products that show off their artistic skills, and they are frustrated with products that don't properly convey their specific design intent. They have not given up using clay studios, which convey design intent much better than the new digital tools that are being forced on them. The new tools are engineering tools that have been modified for designers but make it very difficult to convey design intent. While the designers are tech-competent and even savvy when it comes to creative tools, that is not at their core. It is a means to an end. There might be an Apple computer somewhere in their department, but at the office, they are primarily working on their Windows-based PC.
Personality	The designers like to socialize but would never be confused with fraternity boys. They do not have much money and are careful not to waste it. They drink carefully and/or do light recreational drugs when they go out. They like to sit around and listen to technopop music (like Thomas Dolby) and talk about the arts. They generally wear all black and a good number of them have body piercings and maybe even artfully done tattoos. While they do like to socialize, they can also be quiet and introverted much of the time.

Figure 3.3: SensABle End User Profile's key components.

ADDITIONAL RESOURCES

There are additional resources for this step at www.d-eship.com/step3. These materials include:

- Video: Target Customer Profile Explainers by Bill Aulet and Erdin Beshimov
- Video: Example described and explained in an interview with E-One Timepieces founder Hyungsoo Kim
- Process Guidance
- Worksheet 3.1: Building an End User Profile for Beachhead Market

Additional resources will be added as new and updated examples and information become available.

Summary

Your analysis of your target customer is nowhere near complete, but the End User Profile points you in the right direction for future steps. The journey is only beginning, but you are starting off with the right focus—a well-defined target customer. This is a critical step in your search for specificity and in starting to make your customer concrete and very real. It is also a critical part of the process to help ingrain the mentality that you should build your company around your customer's needs, not based on *your* interests and capabilities. The latter does matter, but it is secondary to how you should think about your business.

Now that you know the profile of the end user, you can assess future interactions you have with potential customers to determine whether they are actually in your End User Profile and are worth your time. If they do not fit the profile, engaging with their needs will distract you from building a great product to meet a specific customer pain. And you can now estimate how many end users exist in your market, which leads you directly to Step 4, Calculate the Total Addressable Market (TAM) Size for the Beachhead Market.

Calculate the Total Addressable Market (TAM) Size for the Beachhead Market

---

In This Step, You Will:

- Estimate how large your Beachhead Market is—specifically the total revenue you could achieve in your Beachhead Market 100% market share (while unlikely, the number is still useful).

- Use this market size number to determine whether you need to further segment the market to have a more appropriately sized Beachhead Market.

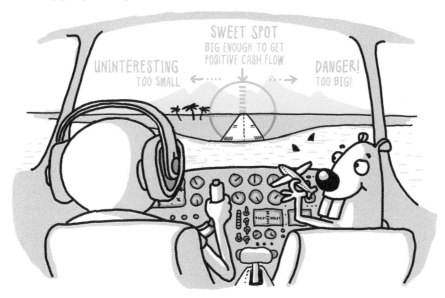

It is important to start to understand the size of the Beachhead Market you are targeting early; you will modify this as time goes on. This systematic estimate of market size reassures you are heading in the right direction.

Why This Step, and Why Now?

The TAM needs to be an appropriate size for your new venture. Too big and you won't be able to mobilize enough resources to compete; too small and your company won't have enough revenue to sustain itself. The exercise of calculating the TAM also increases your team's knowledge of the market. Beyond just a simple number, your team will exit this step understanding what makes the selected Beachhead Market attractive. This understanding may be more important than your specific TAM size and a simple "go/no go" decision. The data you gathered to create your End User Profile in the previous step will be essential in calculating your beachhead TAM.

Let's Get Started

To calculate the TAM, you will do the following:

- Estimate the number of end users in the Beachhead Market, using a combination of top-down and bottom-up analysis.
- Estimate the annual revenue that each end user is worth to your company.

The TAM will be helpful in determining whether your Beachhead Market is too big or too small, but remember that it is a general estimate. You should not present it as a precise number. It is extremely important to always show your assumptions so that others can understand your logic.

Start by estimating the number of end users in the Beachhead Market. You will use a combination of top-down analysis (based on secondary market research) and bottom-up analysis, what is called "counting noses" (i.e., counting the number of end users one by one). Since bottom-up analysis is more difficult, I have reserved that process guide for the "Advanced" section, which is in the online Additional Resources noted at the end of the chapter.

In a top-down analysis, you will use the criteria from your End User Profile from Step 3 to locate secondary research that helps you demonstrate how many end users exist. In particular, the criteria from the demographics, proxy products, and watering holes categories are the easiest to use for this analysis.

One way to start is by taking your biggest demographic or psychographic category where it is easy to use secondary research to find the number of people in this category. For instance, if one of your more general demographics is how many schoolteachers are in the United States, this number is easy to find on the US Department of Education's website—roughly 3.5 million around the year 2020.

Next, further segment that number based on the other criteria from your End User Profile. You will likely need to make assumptions to piece together the data you can find into a reasonable breakdown. You can use Worksheet 4.1, Top-Down Analysis: Visual Beachhead Market TAM Estimation, to structure your breakdown and clearly state your assumptions. The goal is to come out with a rough estimate for how many end users fit your End User Profile.

The Bloom and OnDemandKorea examples in this step illustrate how to do a top-down analysis.

You are unlikely to find one secondary source that matches all your criteria. Therefore, select a few key criteria (try to simplify to four or fewer) that help you narrow down the information the secondary sources give you.

Once you have determined the number of end users in your market, determine how much revenue each end user is worth to you each year. This part is tougher. Remember, you're not determining the price of your product (that starts in Step 16, Set Your Pricing Framework); you're making a first-pass estimate on the customer's willingness and ability to pay for a solution. Don't indicate precision that you clearly do not have, but instead focus on getting an order of magnitude.

Here are three good ways to start an estimate on the annualized revenue per end user:

1. **What the Customer Currently Spends:** The customer is likely spending money already to try to solve the customer pain, or spends money on a product that causes the customer pain and your product would replace. You'll want to know:

   - How much does each product cost?

   - How many of each product does the customer buy for the end user?

   - What is the average lifetime of the product before it's replaced?

     The annualized revenue is the total cost per end user of the product(s) the customer buys for the end user, divided by the lifetime. For instance, if each customer buys one automobile at $15,000 that lasts for five years, the annualized revenue is $15,000 / 5 = $3,000.

2. **The Customer's Available Budget:** Think about the following:

   - When you look at the market today, how much is being spent overall to solve the problem that you are looking to solve for a typical user?

   - How much money does the customer have (household income, business revenue, etc.)?

   - What fraction of that amount could you see being allocated to solve this problem?

3. **Comparables:** Comparables are similar products or data points in different markets that you can use to bolster your TAM analysis. There will be no exact comparable because you are doing something new, but often you can find companies that provide data points that are close enough to what you intend to do that they are very valuable. For instance, if you are creating a product whose revenue is supported by advertising, what are current advertising rates for similar demographics to your end user? Comparables require some creative thinking, but they can be extremely valuable to sanity-check your other TAM estimates. Worksheet 4.2, Beachhead Market TAM Estimation Calculation Table, is provided so you can use it to help structure your analysis.

   After you have come up with these various data points, triangulate against them and make a judgment call as to what you think is the appropriate range at this point. Remember, you will not get this precisely right, so the key is to spend enough time to make an informed guess at this point without investing a tremendous amount of time and effort (it is important to keep moving) and then revisit it later.

Limitations of a Singular TAM Number: Other Important Considerations

The single number of the TAM is a generally accepted simplification to give you a quick sense of the magnitude of your Beachhead Market. Before you draw a final conclusion from this number, there are some other important factors you should consider that will change how attractive the TAM is:

- **Profitability:** How profitable is the revenue? Is it software where the profitability is essentially over 99%? This will make your TAM size more attractive. Or is it a commodity like energy where your profitability on the revenue could be 10% or even less? That makes the number much less attractive. In most businesses, your goal in the Beachhead Market is to get to positive cash flow, if possible, prior to expanding to adjacent markets.

- **Time to Conquer Market:** How long will it take to succeed or fail in this market? Is it a mobile app that will likely succeed or not in six months? That makes the TAM more attractive. Or rather, is it more like a medical device or new drug where it will take years to learn your fate? For a new venture that is resource-constrained, that makes the TAM less attractive. Note that I am not saying a medical device company is a bad choice for a startup, but instead that the much longer time to conquer market will need to be offset by a higher TAM.

- **Compound Annual Growth Rate (CAGR) of Overall Revenue:** Is this a market that is just starting up and has great growth potential? That would be a positive factor. Or is it a mature market where users have set habits and the total market size is in decline? That would be a negative factor.

- **Anticipated Market Share:** Is this a winner-take-all market driven by networking effects? That could be a positive factor if you have a strong competitive position. Or is it a market that will have many players and no player will get more than a small fraction of the market? That would be a negative factor.

There are other considerations as well (such as how much investment will be required, what is the strength of the current entrenched "competitor"—a lot of that would have also come up in the Beachhead Market selection process in Step 2), but this is sufficient to have a good dialogue with your team. While the TAM size and the other considerations are important in determining whether a Beachhead Market is enough to proceed, do not forget the seven factors in Step 2 that led you to choose the initial market segment you did. The size of the market is just one dimension to evaluate when determining how confident you are in your selection of Beachhead Market. You are balancing the Beachhead Market TAM size with the odds of success and the strategic value of the market (i.e., how well this market will strengthen your long-term competitive advantage, which you will later call Core in Step 10, Define Your Core, and how well it positions you for follow-on markets).

Defining your Beachhead Market and End User Profile provides you with enough specificity to make a first-pass calculation of the Total Addressable Market (TAM) size for the Beachhead Market. Again, the TAM for your Beachhead Market is the amount of annual revenue, expressed in dollars per year, your business would earn if you achieved 100% market share in that market.

Entrepreneurs often tend to inflate the TAM with excessive optimism, but a big number is not necessarily better. The goal of this exercise is not to impress others, but to develop a conservative, defensible Beachhead Market TAM number that you have faith in.

What Should My TAM Be?

In the original version of this book, I wrote, "If your Beachhead Market TAM is less than $5 million per year, it is possible that your new venture has not identified a big enough Beachhead Market." I would like to clarify that the lower-end number was a very general guideline and was in the context of the United States. You should feel free to entertain smaller markets, but think carefully if you are being ambitious enough in the long term. Many have rightfully justified smaller markets to start, especially outside the United States. The reason you do not want the Beachhead Market

TAM to be too small is because entrepreneurs often inflate the size of their market and their expected market share. Usually, the market will be even smaller than you think, and you will not be able to achieve the level of market share that you think you will. Your advisors, partners, and investors know these things, so if your TAM is very low to start, they will assume it is actually even lower. In such a small market, it will likely be very difficult to get to cash-flow positive and achieve critical mass.

Generally, in the US, a Beachhead Market TAM that is between $20 million per year and $100 million per year is a good target. Anything above that, and especially if it is over $1 billion, will suggest that the market is too big for a startup to reasonably conquer, and further segmentation will be beneficial. It is possible that an initial TAM of $5 million per year could be a successful business, if you can capture the market quickly and convincingly. This would be even more so if the gross margins on your product would be very high (e.g., 90%, as it would be for software, mobile apps, information-based business models) and you do not need a lot of employees to do it. This could create positive cash flow from the market, which would be a significant accomplishment and a good Beachhead Market.

As you learn more in the later steps, you will likely come back and revisit this calculation and modify it to make it more credible. Remember that it is not just the number; you should also have a clear understanding of your market when presenting your idea or technology to others, such as advisors and investors, because they will expect you to present a TAM figure and explain your logic behind it. However, do not spend an inordinate amount of time on making the TAM calculation precise, because as mentioned above, there are limitations to a singular number and the other factors can make it significantly more or less attractive.

EXAMPLES

Bloom Continued

Building off the Bloom example from the previous chapters, Figure 4.1 shows how the team built off their End User Profile and outlined their assumptions to systematically come up with a Beachhead Market TAM estimate of $36M.

My feedback was that this Beachhead Market was still too broad and they should narrow it down to a specific geographic region to start.

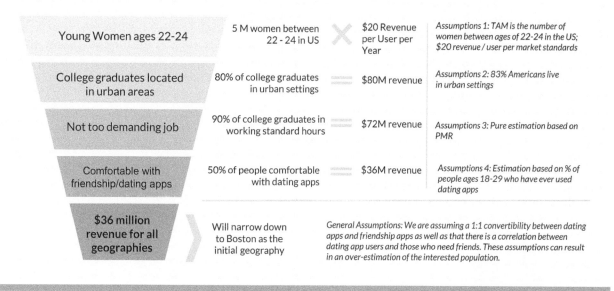

Figure 4.1: Bloom Beachhead Market TAM estimation.

OnDemandKorea (Mix of Top Down and Bottom Up Analyses)

A group of MIT students noticed a simple market opportunity. Quite a number of their classmates and friends who were born in Korea and living in the United States were particularly interested in staying current with news and shows in their homeland. One of the major ways to do this was to watch Korean soap operas. The students noticed that many of them visited websites where they could watch bootlegged, low-quality versions of these shows. With their background, technical skills, and connections, the students were confident they could build a site that would display much higher-quality video and do it legally. The analogy would be iTunes as compared to Kazaa or the original version of Napster.

So the team dutifully built their End User Profile, as you can see in Figure 4.2. They researched the number of Koreans in the United States. The first number they found was a census number of 1.7 million people, but this was a low number, as it is for many immigrant census numbers. These numbers do not include international students and others who do not register in the census.

Further digging and research online unearthed articles suggesting the number was 2.5 million, which was what businesses serving this community used as the more accurate number. While this number was good to know and valuable for the long term, the question that was more relevant to the team was "How many of these Koreans actually go to the websites that they had seen their Korean friends use?"

To solve this problem, the team worked to identify the 89 websites (including Joonmedia, Bada, and Dabdate) that illegally showed Korean dramas in the United States. Then they used the Internet service Compete to determine the amount of traffic each website received. The total traffic for these websites was 1.2 million unique users. They were validating that there was a market here already. But they were far from done!

Next, the team ran tests to see how much of the user base were women, as opposed to men, as their End User Profile was women aged 20–35. After they had run many tests, they started to become confident that the ratio was 60:40 (percentage of female to male users of these services). That narrowed the base down to 720,000 potential end users. Further tests found that about 55% of the user base were in the 20–35 age range. This resulted in 400,000 end users who fit the team's End User Profile.

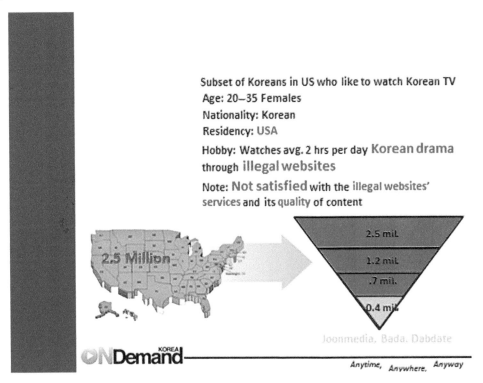

Figure 4.2: Beachhead Market TAM sizing example: OnDemandKorea.

While this was an excellent start to calculating the TAM, it did not end here. The TAM is not a number of customers, but rather dollars per year. So to complete the TAM calculation, the team needed to determine how much the 400,000 potential customers would pay in a year.

Toward this end, they assumed they would use an advertising model. This was such a well-defined and attractive customer base that when OnDemandKorea did the job they knew they could, the company would have a very loyal following, spending at least an hour per day on their site. With this information, they researched potential advertising rates and used $1.25 per user per month as a reasonable target. They assumed no other revenues so they could be on the conservative side. This translates to $15 per user per year. When this is multiplied by the 400,000 primary customers, they arrived at a beachhead TAM of $6 million per year.

While this might not seem a very exciting market for some, especially large companies, this was a sufficient Beachhead Market for this team to get them to cash-flow positive because of the company's low costs and high margins. It was also a way to build critical capabilities and critical mass in the company to get started. They were confident that once they won this market, they could expand and increase the revenue per customer with new offerings, or simply expand their market dramatically by adding subtitles in Chinese at very little cost. Once they had the Chinese subtitles, they had become confident from their research that Chinese people living in the US would readily adopt Korean soap operas as well. Once they had their beachhead, there were many ways to grow it, but the beachhead had to be big enough to get them to cash-flow positive and achieve critical mass.

Worksheets

Top-Down Estimate of Number of End Users in Beachhead Market

Number of people in your largest demographic or psychographic characteristic = _____

Based on End User Profile characteristic:_____

Assumption(s): _____

_____

Source(s): _____

_____

1st segmentation based on end user profile = _____

Based on End User Profile characteristic: _____

% of previous segment: _____ %

Assumption(s) for calculation:_____

Source(s): _____

_____

2nd segmentation based on end user profile = _____

Based on End User Profile characteristic: _____

% of previous segment: _____ %

Assumption(s) for calculation:_____

Source(s): _____

_____

3rd segmentation based on end user profile = _____

Based on End User Profile characteristic: _____

% of previous segment: _____ %

Assumption(s) for calculation:_____

Source(s): _____

_____

End users in beachhead market = _____

Based on End User Profile characteristic: _____

% of previous segment: _____ %

Assumption(s) for calculation:_____

Source(s): _____

_____

Worksheet 4.1: Top-Down Analysis: Visual Beachhead Market TAM Estimation.

Worksheet 4.2: Beachhead Market TAM Estimation Calculation Table.

1.	One-Time Charge Data Point	
1a	Estimation of price per unit	
1b	Number of units needed per end user	
1c	Average life of product in years	
1d	Annualized revenue (1a*1b)/1d (Data Point 1)	
2.	Budget Available Data Points	
2a	Current spending per end user (Data Point 2)	
2b	Total budget for the end user	
2c	What percentage of budget could go to this solution reasonably?	
2d	Annualize revenue (2b*2c) (Data Point 3)	
3.	Comparables	
3a	Who are the comparables for your business?	
3b	What are the comparable products?	
3c	What is the comparable converted to similar annualized revenue (Data Point 4 plus however many more you deem relevant)?	
4.	Interpreting the Results	
4a	Consensus on estimate of annualized revenue per end user, based on the four Data Points above (a range is fine)	
4b	How did you end up at this number/range?	

ADDITIONAL RESOURCES

There are additional resources for this step at www.d-eship.com/step4. These materials include:

- Video: Beachhead Market TAM Explainers by Bill Aulet and Erdin Beshimov
- Video: Example described and explained in an interview with Thyme Labs founders Amanda von Goetz, Andrew Radin, Daipan Lee, and Rohit Singh
- Process Guidance
- Worksheet 4.1: Top-Down Analysis: Visual Beachhead Market TAM Estimation (duplicate from this chapter but in digital format)
- Worksheet 4.2: Beachhead Market TAM Estimation Calculation Table (duplicate from this chapter but in digital format)
- Worksheet 4.3: Beachhead Market TAM Analysis Other Factors Summary
- Worksheet 4.4: Interpreting and reflecting on TAM calculation
- Worksheet 4.5: Bottom-Up TAM Analysis Worksheet
- Bonus Material: How to Do a Bottom-Up TAM Analysis
- Example of Bottom-Up Analysis: SensAble Technologies

Additional resources will be added as new and updated examples and information become available.

Summary

The TAM is how much annual revenue you would accumulate if you achieved 100% market share. This is calculated, for now, only for your first Beachhead Market. A bottom-up analysis, where you can show how many potential customers you have identified from your PMR and extrapolated to the broader market, will give a more accurate picture of your market. Complementary to this, but much less compelling on its own, is a top-down analysis where you are working with market analysis reports and extrapolating without direct interaction and validation. Often, very important subtleties are missed in top-down analyses, so if you are serious and you have the time and bandwidth, start with the top-down (much easier) but then supplement it with the bottom-up TAM calculation as well. You might not have that luxury now, so it is okay to keep moving and come back later.

Profile the Persona for the Beachhead Market

In This Step, You Will:

- Choose one actual real end user to be your Persona.
- Build a detailed description of that real person.
- Make the Persona visible to all in the new venture so that it gets referenced on an ongoing basis.

The Persona is a real person, so this allows you to get very specific in your description and also has the benefit of ensuring that everyone is unambiguously focused on the same target.

Why This Step, and Why Now?

The Persona creates a single real-world case that allows you to gain extreme clarity in all dimensions. This makes the job of creating a first draft of a Full Life Cycle Use Case (Step 6), a High-Level Product Specification (Step 7), and a Quantified Value Proposition (Step 8) much easier. The Persona will provide a very efficient and effective touchstone (i.e., "North Star") to you and your organization for all decisions going forward. Simply put, it accelerates a process that could otherwise be caught up in debating based on general target profiles.

Let's Get Started

This is one of the most fun and unifying steps of the 24 Steps. You will identify one real end user in your Beachhead Market who best represents your End User Profile and do a detailed profile on that specific individual. Unlike the End User Profile in Step 3, which is a composite of your target customer, the Persona is a singular person who best represents the primary customer for the Beachhead Market.

The process of defining a Persona for your Beachhead Market makes your target customer tangible so that all members of the founding team, and all employees, have absolute clarity and focus on the same goal of making your target customer successful and happy. Rather than guessing or arguing about what your potential customers might want, the Persona answers these questions definitively.

This is important for you on many levels. As a startup, your challenge is to motivate a brand-new team to focus on solving a customer problem/opportunity in a completely new way, and you don't have the resources to let the team spend valuable time squabbling about which direction to go. Not only will the Persona allow you to get to a workable answer quickly, but it also has the benefit of making your team more motivated. Behavioral economists have known for decades that real-world narratives are the most powerful way to motivate people.[1] The Persona is how your startup tells the story of who your customer is and why it matters that you are solving your customer's pain—and gains full alignment and buy-in from your team.

Those with a marketing background are likely familiar with the concept of a Persona, using a generic name like Mary Marketing or Ollie Owner as a composite of what the marketing team thinks the typical customer is like. This is what they did at HubSpot at the beginning and it was

---

[1] For more on the power of the narrative, see *Made to Stick* by Chip and Dan Heath and *Why David Sometimes Wins: Leadership, Organization, and Strategy in the California Farm Worker Movement* by Marshall Ganz.

extremely helpful for them. But while even a generic Persona can be helpful, it is best to push the process even further. The Persona should be a real person, not a composite.

By choosing an actual end user as your Persona, your Persona becomes concrete, leaving no room for second-guessing. Does your user have a dog, and what is their attitude toward owning pets? Who is their biggest hero? Where do they get information when they are trying to solve problems at work? All of these questions can be directly answered by asking the Personas detailed in the examples for this chapter. You can debate these questions internally, but if your Persona is a real person, it is not a debate. The answer comes from good PMR and then recording it.

No one end user represents 100% of the characteristics of every end user in your End User Profile. But as you work toward defining the Persona, you will be able to find someone who matches the profile quite well. You will then focus work going forward around this individual, rather than on the more-general End User Profile.

How to Choose and Profile Your Persona

The process of creating a Persona is important, so you should involve all the key members of your team, regardless of their role in the group. Team members who are involved in the process, even if they do not think they have a lot to contribute, will end up enjoying, embracing, and getting a lot of value out of the process of creating the Persona. They will feel ownership and understand the nuances of the Persona that might not get written down, and gain appreciation for the other members of the team and their perspectives.

If you already have sales, an analysis of the most successful customers to date would be a good starting point. If you have not sold any product yet, then look at the PMR you have already done, and analyze some of the customers who showed the most interest in your potential offering. Make sure they would actually pay for it and are not "just interested." There is a big difference.

You are looking to answer the question "If I had only one end user to represent our End User Profile, who would it be?" From your End User Profile, you have a good start. The Persona should conform very well with this profile, while also providing more specific details.

You and your team should take the PMR you have on some of these customers, as well as the End User Profile, and discuss the pros and cons of making each customer the Persona. After this analysis, you will choose one to be the Persona, knowing that you might change it later as you get more information. Don't spend too much time worrying about whether you have the perfect Persona; just make your best guess and get the process started.

Next, prepare a fact sheet like Worksheet 5.1 about the Persona, based on the information you already have. Include a drawing or photograph of the individual. You will typically want to include information about the person's life (born, raised, education, family, age, etc.) as well as the person's job (what company, how many years, training, managers, salary, performance metrics if a B2B case, etc.). All of this information should be specific—not just that they make a five-figure salary or live in the northeastern part of the country, but rather that they earn $65,000 a year and live in a specific town. By preparing a fact sheet, your team will also identify key facts specific to your business that you will want to include for the Persona to be useful to you.

In your fact sheet, you will use the end user's real name. It might seem a bit creepy to use a real name, so if you feel uncomfortable, you can use an alias instead. Typically, once people understand the purpose and role of the Persona, they are okay with using a real name, at least for internal use within the company.

Most importantly, you want to list the Persona's purchasing criteria in prioritized order, as these priorities will dictate what purchasing decisions the Persona makes. The top priority is the concern that keeps the Persona awake at night. It is the thing that they either fear the most or get most excited about. It is what will get them fired or promoted and often the most visible thing that could go right or wrong. It is crucial to understand how your customer prioritizes their needs and wants. You will build off of this list throughout the 24 Steps.

Now that you have identified what facts you have and don't have, interview the end user who is your Persona (you presumably have already met the individual at least once in the course of your PMR) again and fill in the gaps in what you know. Allow the conversation to be open-ended, because you will likely learn additional facts that are relevant to your Persona. Add this information to the fact sheet in another team meeting to make sure everyone is on the same page and that no crucial details have been omitted or overlooked. Also, go beyond what your Persona says and carefully notice all the details about her as well. Is her desk organized? Does she have pictures in her office? What kind of clothes does she wear? Are there particularly odd characteristics, such as in our Persona of Chuck Karroll (see Figure 5.5), where in the year 2011 he still had a pager instead of relying on a cell phone? These details are often the most telling of all.

For validating information like your Persona's purchasing criteria in prioritized order, a list provided by the Persona will get you started, but when interviewing your end users, you cannot necessarily believe everything they tell you; you should validate what they say. Revisit Step 1A, Primary Market Research (PMR), for techniques on interviewing and validating what you learn from your Persona.

Once you have finalized your fact sheet, summarize the key points somewhere visible to the whole team. You might start by taking a large sheet of paper and posting it on the wall. Some companies make a cardboard cutout of the Persona and keep it in the office. Other leading-edge companies pull up an electronic version of the Persona when making important decisions to discuss what the Persona's perspective would be on the subject. (See Figure 5.1 for an example summary.)

DEMOGRAPHICS

42, MALE, FRENCH, DIVORCED
LIVES IN BORDEAUX
MASTERS OF FINANCE
SMALL BUSINESS OWNER

PSYCHOGRAPHICS

STORY
BORN IN A WINEMAKERS FAMILY
STUDIED IN PARIS
WORKED IN CORPORATE FINANCE
CAME BACK FOR FAMILY
TAKING OVER FAMILY BUSINESS

MOTIVATION
PROVING THAT HE IS WORTHY
INNOVATING WINEMAKING
WINNING WINE AWARDS AGAIN

FEARS
LACK OF FINANCING
CONFLICT WITH FAMILY
FAILING TO CHANGE COMPANY

WATERING HOLES

WINEMAKING FORUMS
THE WINEMAKER'S ASSOCIATION
SCHOOL ALUMNI CLUB
TRADESHOWS & FAIRS

PROXY PRODUCTS

APPLE PHONE, LAPTOP, HEADSET
WINEMAKING TECH
BUSINESS INTELLIGENCE TOOLS

PRIORITIES

FINALIZE AUDIT OF BUSINESS
DISCUSS PLAN WITH FAMILY
ANALYZE WINE TECH SUPPLIERS
GET FINANCING FOR WINE TECH

PHILIPPE
POIROT

Figure 5.1: Making the Persona visual means everyone on your team will be more engaged in the process and will keep the Persona in the front of their minds.

The Persona Is More Than Just a One-Time Exercise

The value of the Persona persists well beyond the completion of this step. The Persona should become a touch point as you think about decisions going forward. What features should you prioritize? What should you drop? How should you allocate resources? Who should you hire to sell the product? What should your message be? Who should you partner with? Where do you go to meet your customers? Who is influencing your customer's mindset on your product?

The process of answering these questions starts to bring alignment among the team and resolves misunderstandings that are bound to occur from imprecise communications. Once the Persona is done, it is also useful to maintain this alignment going forward. If done effectively, it will help guide all kinds of decisions and create a consistent vision throughout the company.

You may find that you made errors while developing your Persona fact sheet, or that your Persona does not adequately represent the End User Profile, so you may need to go back and revise your Persona in an iterative fashion in later steps. This is not only okay, but highly recommended and a productive exercise.

The point is that building the Persona is not a one-time event but rather should be visible or at least accessible to all members of the team as you move forward with your business. It should be your North Star.

Should I Create Multiple Personas? If So, When?

As discussed in Step 1, Market Segmentation, when talking about how to define "customers," companies similar in nature to eBay and Google should actually start out with two Personas. This is not due to a lack of focus, but rather to the fact that their core businesses are two-sided markets, so they need one Persona for each market. For example, when eBay first started its auction site, it would have had one Persona for a buyer and a completely different Persona for a seller. Likewise, Google, at the beginning, should have had one Persona for its target search user and another Persona for its target buyer of advertisements.

Google and eBay are so large today that they have many Personas to match the many areas of their business, and entrepreneurs sometimes like to point to big companies like these two as reasons why startups too can have many Personas. However, large companies have the resources to cover many markets and use many Personas. You do not have this luxury, so don't be led astray by what large companies do with Personas. Focus on your one Persona; or, if you have a multisided market, one Persona for each side of the market.

The Persona Helps You Focus on What to Do—and What Not to Do

The Persona exercise can even be extended to make Personas who you explicitly decide not to serve. Such an exercise can help you to focus and not distract your precious resources. You can even talk about how you handle these customers and efficiently redirect them. It is hard and takes practice for entrepreneurs to turn away business, but it is exactly that type of focus that will allow you to build a scalable and profitable business. Often in entrepreneurship, your success is determined as much by what you do not do as by what you do.

Mitigating the Downside Risks of a Persona

The downside of orienting your team around a Persona is that no one person can fully represent your target end user in all dimensions. But starting with a focused Persona and adjusting when you think it is leading you astray from your End User Profile is better than not having focus at all. Entrepreneurs have limited resources and time, so you need action and a strong, unified team to fight the status quo and inertia. You can update the Persona later, especially in Step 9, Identify Your Next 10 Customers, so make your best guess now and keep the process moving because you don't learn without action.

A question I frequently get is whether a member of the founding team can be the Persona. Teams with members who come from the target customer group start the process with deep domain expertise, which is extremely valuable. In fact, this is often the case for many of my classes' most successful teams. If you don't have someone on your team with deep domain expertise and contacts in your target market, you will have to find someone like that soon and add them to your team. It is impossible to know who and what you don't know.

On the other hand, if you make a member of the founding team your Persona, you probably have not gotten someone in the middle of the bell curve (see Figure 5.2). I have seen it work well, but I've also seen it fail spectacularly. It can be hard for people to step back and realize they are not the best representation of the broader market. So, while it is helpful to have a founder who fits the broader End User Profile, I encourage you to use a Persona who is external to your company.

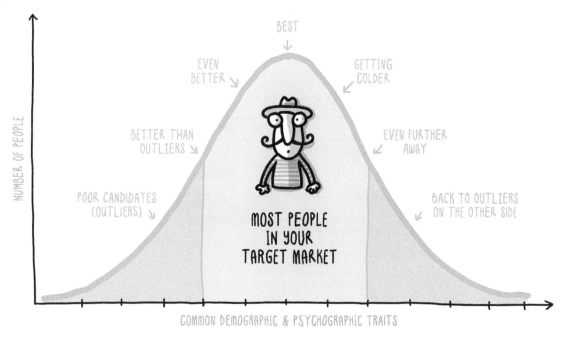

Figure 5.2: The Persona is the best representative of the broader target market segment in all dimensions.

EXAMPLES

Bloom Continued

Because Bloom had such a tightly defined Beachhead Market segment, finding their Persona of Katie L. was relatively easy, but the team still had to talk to dozens of potential end users before they settled on Katie.

Katie L. gives a very clear North Star that is invaluable for the many first-draft decisions they will be making rapidly going forward. You can see in Figure 5.3 that Bloom was able to ascertain many specific facts about Katie, and as a result they know her much more deeply than they knew their general End User Profile.

Initial Market: Persona

Persona – Meet Katie L.

Priorities

Social Life 40%   Career Success 20%
Love Life 20%   Health/Wellness 10%
Finances: 10%

Demographics:
- 23 year old Caucasion Female, Single
- Philadelphia, PA
- Marketing Coordinator, Brinker Capital: Income ~ $60K
- Registered Democrat

Story:
- Hometown: Raleigh, NC
- Lehigh University, Psychology
- 40 min reverse commute to work
- Was Active in her Sorority
- Doesn't like living alone. Social with groups, shy 1-on-1

Katie is the perfect Persona because she is new to the city, prioritizes her social life, enjoys exploring the city, and is eager to meet new people

Psychographic:
- Bubbly outgoing and just moved into Philly and is excited to make new friends
- Uses Classpass and enjoys new workouts
- Like to try new restaurants/bars
- Wine nights during the week and tequila during the weekend

- Dog mom to Gucci
- New TikTok user
- On way to Yelp Elite
- Watering Hole: Trader Joe's, Fado Irish Pub

Goals: Get promoted to HR Manager, plan trip to Turk & Caicos with College Friends, pass PHR Exam, find a boyfriend

Fears: not having plans on the weekend, disappointing her parents

Drink of choice: **Margaritas**
Food of choice: **Wings**
Favorite shows: Bachelor
Favorite Podcast: **Girl with No Job**

Figure 5.3: Bloom's Persona.

SensAble Technologies

At SensAble, we had a Persona, though it did not fit perfectly with our End User Profile. Let's call our Persona Ed Champ (the name has been changed to protect his real identity), who was actually the manager of the designers. He was 40 years old, approximately 10 years older than the target profile, but he understood and empathized with the designers. In this way, the psychographics mattered more than the demographics. He was young in spirit for his age, but he also had enough perspective and comfort in his job to give us meaningful answers when we asked questions. He not only had deep domain expertise, but he understood the rational, the emotional, and the social considerations of our end user, because he was from that group and still resided deeply in that territory. It was key, too, that we had a terrific relationship with him. When we had questions about product development (e.g., the priority and value of specific features) or sales and marketing (e.g., pricing, messaging, decision-making process), and we could not figure out the answers based on the description of our Persona, we would simply call and ask him.

The profile of Ed Champ is shown in Figure 5.4.

It is interesting that after all these years, I can still see this person and his white flowing hair and stocky build. In fact, when writing this book, I was able to write the description in Figure 5.4 off the top of my head, because he seemingly was part of our family at the time.

Name	Ed Champ
Title	Sculpting Manager, Boys' Toys R&D, Hasbro, Pawtucket, Rhode Island
Age	40 (He is about 10 years older than the developers he hangs out with, but he fits in well with the group and is thought to be one of the guys—they are almost all guys—even though he is their supervisor.)
Income	$73.5K (He is the highest paid in the group, by a good margin, due to his seniority; he has been at Hasbro in this location for 14 years and has been a top performer and promoted through the ranks.)
Schooling	Missouri State University—Bachelor of Fine Arts and Science: Sculpture and Anatomy (He secretly admires Rhode Island School of Design—RISD—graduates but that is not how he got here.)
Personal	Has a girlfriend, but no talk of marriage; he seems to be married to his job. He has a child from a previous relationship, but the child does not live with him; many of his friends are gay.

Figure 5.4: Ed Champ Persona for SensAble.

Career Promotion	It is very unlikely he will get further promoted as he does not like management and it is not his forte. He hopes to make more money to keep up with inflation, but mostly he just loves his job and living in Rhode Island with creative types—and at his age, the job security is good.
Industry Associations	A strong and active member of IDSA (Industrial Design Society of America) above all else. There are local meetings that he looks forward to. These can be epic, in part because of the relevant content, but even more so because he gets to hang out with people from RISD, Pasadena Arts Center College of Design, and others who wish they had gone to one of those schools, and talk into the night about the latest in art and design. There are national meetings as well, and he sometimes goes to the big SIGGRAPH conference (often held in Los Angeles), where there are some great parties.
Music	His group listens to technopop artists like Thomas Dolby; while he is not wild about it, he likes it.
Socializing	His social life often revolves around his work. He likes to hang out with designers but they don't have much money, so when they go to bars, they drink wine (but not beer) and sip whatever drink they get so that it lasts. They have little disposable income so they have to be very careful not to blow money. Interestingly, they are more likely to do designer drugs (e.g., ecstasy) than to lose control by getting drunk. At the bars they go to in Providence, he and his friends often wear all black. It is also common for them to have body piercings, to wear jewelry, and to have discreet tattoos. But always, their life revolves around art and talking about art.
Heroes	Milton Glaser, John Lasseter (Disney & Pixar), Steve Jobs
What Gets Him Motivated	Making great products and seeing them get to market with his design intent.
What He Fears Most	1. Having to leave Hasbro because it is acquired or something worse. This is not true for the other designers, but unique to him 2. Putting out a product that he feels is crap because he ran out of time to get it done right 3. Having his design intent ruined by the engineers after he sends it on to them
Priorities	1. Time to market 2. Being able to express his design intent 3. Being assured his design intent is not lost when engineers get ahold of it

Figure 5.4: (Continued)

Mechanical Water Filtration Systems Persona (B2B)

Another good example for Persona development comes from a team of students who had a technology for water purification. The team originally segmented markets and was focusing on potable water (i.e., drinking water) because of the high margins. After a Market Segmentation analysis (Step 1), they realized that there were better entry markets where the bar was not so high. They ultimately decided on a Beachhead Market (Step 2) of cooling data centers, specifically those at large companies or real estate entities that manage large data centers shared by multiple clients. The TAM was calculated to be $50 million per year, with a compound annual growth rate of 20%. Therefore, it was an attractive and properly sized market, but one that would rapidly attract competitors as well. As such, the team needed to be focused and conquer this market quickly.

They quickly realized they had a potential multidimensional value proposition. From a sustainability standpoint, this allowed the data centers to move from a model of taking cold clean water at one end of the data center and shooting out what was effectively dirtier and warmer water at the other end. This circular as opposed to one-time use of water would significantly decrease their impact on the local community. The cleaner water would also decrease their electricity consumption, thus decreasing their carbon emissions as well. The solution also has cost-saving benefits of reduced electricity costs. Finally, cleaner water would improve the reliability or the all-important "uptime" of the data center, which was already very good but it was important that at worst, it would not decrease data center availability. With what they believed to be a strong value proposition in mind, the team enthusiastically made data centers their Beachhead Market.

Initially they thought the end user would be the data center manager; but their PMR found that the actual end user was the facilities manager, who reports to the data center manager. The facilities manager had the budget to purchase a water filtration system but the facilities manager was a bit uncomfortable with financial things so left a lot of the budgeting decisions to the data center manager from whom he took his lead. After a half-dozen interviews with facilities managers at these data centers, the team started to get a clear picture of the end user.

The team eventually decided that one of the potential end users, Chuck Karroll, best represented the facilities manager they were trying to sell to. (I have changed his name and some of the details to protect his identity.) The team chose him because they had talked to many customers and they felt he represented the customer base very well. He was also someone to whom the team had ready access for ongoing questions. After talking to many customers, it just seemed like an organic and easy process because a pattern had emerged and Chuck fit very well into the recurring theme. When you read through Figure 5.5, notice how you can very much visualize Chuck from these details.

Chuck's background helps the team understand the social pressures and incentives he faces. (There was, in fact, a great deal more the team knew about Chuck, which provided a much deeper understanding of him and his psyche, but I summarized the key points here for the sake of brevity.) His career trajectory information helps them understand his performance incentives—promotions, wages, and recognition—and how established he is at the company. They also understand where he gets his information from, which is important because Chuck will be vetting everything that the team tells him against these sources.

These are not generalizations or assumptions based on stereotypes. These observations are based on researching and talking directly with Chuck. Not every facilities manager is a volunteer firefighter like Chuck, but most facilities managers in this Beachhead Market will have a similar mentality, even if they don't have a pager or aren't members of the volunteer fire department (although a surprising number of them do and are).

Chuck's priorities in making purchasing decisions are especially important to the team. When the team first started, they believed their unique selling proposition was being environmentally friendly, but their PMR showed that Chuck cared very little about this. In fact, at the time, facilities managers were much more likely to be climate skeptics. Chuck cared much, much more about reliability than reducing his carbon footprint.

Sure, there was a lot of talk about "green data centers," but that was a nice-to-have, not a need-to-have. It was very clear that Chuck's main priority was preventing data center downtime, because his customers (higher-ups in his own company) and his customers' customers (the actual paying end customers) expected the data center to be as reliable as an electric utility. If the system went down, Chuck's office phone and/or pager would immediately ring and it would not be pleasant. In fact, it could be the CEO of his business unit, who was generally nice, but irate when the system was down. This was Chuck's biggest fear in life and he would do whatever was necessary to make sure that there were no outages, and if there were, they were fixed ASAP. Now you see why he has a pager.

After preventing data center downtime, meeting the business unit's growth objectives was priority two since the general manager of the business unit was a very influential person who wanted to make his numbers and keep getting promoted. This could only be done if the data center continued to grow. If Chuck did not meet these growth goals, the pressure would come down from the data center manager. Maybe Chuck would be in jeopardy of being replaced, but it was a far less dire consequence than having the data center go down.

Chuck's third priority was not to exceed his budget, which would impact his performance review. He was much more likely to get fired for substandard reliability and less so for not meeting growth objectives, but staying within budget was something he was measured on as well. It should be noted, however, that if he did a great job with the first two priorities, he was given a bit of a pass on priority three.

Environmental issues ranked only fourth in his priorities, if at all. It was something he knew he had to talk about and he had to be conversant in green issues. As such, he would put together an annual e-mail to his manager (the data center manager) and the company's new "green guru" about environmentally friendly steps he was taking, but doing well on environmental issues was considered the way a student considers an extra-credit problem on a test—nice to have, but not the main thing.

Facilities Manager, IBM NE Data Center, in Littleton, MA	
Environment	• Now has just over 20K Blade servers today growing at 15% per quarter for the past two years and for the foreseeable future
Personal Information	• Second-generation American (parents from Ireland) • Born in Medford, Massachusetts • Medford High to Middlesex Community College • Moved to Winchester • Family with 2 kids (12, 15) • Just turned 40 this year
Career Context	• Mid-career, 18 years at IBM and not looking to leave. • He is technical in the technician sense, not the engineering development sense. • He is maintenance-focused and his vocational degree is relevant. • He has been in the current job for five years and has had three different managers already but hopes to keep this job for next five years at least. • Promotion path forward is to manage more facilities. • Makes $65K per year and has the potential for a 5% bonus at the end of the year, based on the unit's overall performance and his contribution as determined by his boss, the data center manager. • Eligible for salary increase each year, based on his appraisal (can be between 0 and 12%). • He has been consistently ranked a 1 or 2 (on a scale of 1–5 where 1 is the best) in his yearly performance review, with reliability and supporting the business unit's growth as two key metrics upon which he is rated.
Information Sources	• He prefers people to websites when he looks for information and answers to questions. • Belongs to AFCOM (association for data center management professionals) and gets a lot of information from them, and especially likes to go to the Data Center World conference in early October each year in Las Vegas. • Second-biggest influence is the Uptime Institute. • Has started to look at Green Grid but not impressed. • Also starting to get forwarded e-mail about a blog (Hamilton and Manos) that other influential facilities managers are starting to read, and he has recently bookmarked it himself.

Figure 5.5: Persona for Mechanical Water Filtration Company (Chuck Karroll).

Facilities Manager, IBM NE Data Center, in Littleton, MA	
Purchasing Criteria in Prioritized Order	1. Reliability (highest priority)
	2. Growth (high priority)
	3. Costs (medium priority)
	4. "Greenness" (low priority—extra credit)
Other Noteworthy Items	• Drives a Ford F-150 pickup truck and always buys American.
	• Wears a pager ("beeper") that is always on.
	• Listens to country music.
	• He used to be a volunteer fireman and is proud of it. He makes level-headed decisions when there is a crisis, calling in his training to act fast and put out fires.

Figure 5.5: (Continued)

Worksheet

Persona Profile for Beachhead Market

Add a visual image of the Persona here	
Name	
Address	
E-mail and phone	
Title (if appropriate)	
If business-to-business (B2B), where they exist in the overall org chart	
Demographics:	
Gender	
Age	
Income	

Worksheet 5.1: Details on Beachhead Market Persona.

Education level	
Education specifics (schools, majors, awards, etc.)	
Employment history (companies, jobs, awards, etc.)	
Marital status	
Kids and other family info	
Ethnicity	
Political affiliations	
Other demographic 1:	
Other demographic 2:	
Other demographic 3:	
Other demographic 4:	
Psychographics:	
Why do they do this job or live the life they do?	
Hobbies	
Heroes	
Aspirations in life	
Fears in life	
Personality traits	
Interesting habits	
Other psychographic 1:	
Other psychographic 2:	
Other psychographic 3:	
Other psychographic 4:	
Proxy Products (which products have the highest correlation with your Persona)	
Is there a product or products that the Persona needs to have to get benefit from yours?	

Worksheet 5.1: (Continued)

Are there products the Persona uses that embody the psychographics and demographics from the end user profile?	
Any other unusual or interesting products of note that the Persona has?	
Watering Holes (real or virtual places where the Persona interacts with others like them):	
Favorite sources for news (e.g., which newspapers, TV shows, websites, blogs)	
Places where Persona congregates with other similar people	
Associations Persona belongs to and the importance of each	
Where does the Persona go for expert advice and/ or to get questions answered?	
Day in the Life (describe a day in the life of the end user and what is going on in this person's head):	
What are the typical tasks the Persona does each day, with the amount of time associated with each?	
Which of these typical tasks are habits?	
Which require the most effort?	
Which does the Persona enjoy?	
Which does the Persona not enjoy?	
What makes it a good day for the Persona?	
What makes it a bad day?	
Who is the Persona trying to please the most?	
What is the top priority of the person/people the Persona is trying to please?	

Worksheet 5.1: (Continued)

Priorities:		
Priorities (what are your Persona's priorities— focus first on biggest fears, then biggest motivations—and assign a weighting to each so that it adds up to 100)	1. _____	Weighting: _____
	2. _____	Weighting: _____
	3. _____	Weighting: _____
	4. _____	Weighting: _____
	5. _____	Weighting: _____

Worksheet 5.1: (Continued)

ADDITIONAL RESOURCES

There are additional resources for this step at www.d-eship.com/step5. These materials include:

- Video: Persona Explainers by Bill Aulet and Erdin Beshimov
- Video: Example described and explained in an interview with Cannonball founder Raffaele Colella
- Process Guidance
- Advanced Topic: Persona Profiles for Multisided End User Market
- Worksheet 5.1: Details on Beachhead Market Persona (duplicate from this chapter but in digital format)
- Worksheet 5.2: General Information on Persona

Additional resources will be added as new and updated examples and information become available.

Summary

The process of developing a Persona provides specific details about the primary customer within your Beachhead Market. You are now selling not to some composite "end user profile," but to a specific individual. Your whole team should be involved in this process to ensure everyone is on the same page and truly understands the Persona, so they can maintain a customer-based focus. An important detail to understand about the Persona is their purchasing criteria in prioritized order. You should really understand your customer and what makes them tick, not just at a rational level, but at an emotional and social level as well. The better you understand your Persona's needs, behaviors, and motivations, the more successful you will be at making a product and a new venture to serve them. Once you have made a picture or visual of your Persona and fleshed out the fact sheet, make it all visible within your business so that everyone on your team works toward the same common goal.

Full Life Cycle Use Case

In This Step, You Will:

- Describe in detail how your Persona realizes they have a problem/opportunity, finds out about possible solutions, analyzes those solutions, acquires one, uses it, gets value from it, pays for it, buys more, and tells others about it.

- Start to understand the full context of the opportunity you are helping your customer realize.

Building a Full Life Cycle Use Case further focuses the discussion on what specifically your product will do for your customer—and what your customer will do with it.

Why This Step, and Why Now?

The Full Life Cycle Use Case provides rich context and perspective on what the opportunity is with your target customer. This valuable information will form the basis for future steps and also help the team understand potential barriers to adoption from a sales/customer acquisition perspective. You can do it now because you now have the Persona identified and developed. With the Persona, you can now efficiently and effectively do the PMR required to complete this step, which represents a first draft since you still have much to learn about the use case. You will iterate on it starting in Step 9, Identify Your Next 10 Customers.

Let's Get Started

Now that you have assembled great specificity about your end user, you will collect equally specific details about how this person does what they do today and how potentially they could use your to-be-designed product. You will construct a use case, but your use case will be more expansive than the traditional definition. What you will be doing is to understand and map the full workflow of your Persona. It is important to keep in mind that this is the customer's perspective, not yours.

The first thing you need to understand is what the problem is that your target customer needs to be solved. The problem is not better technology. The problem is not a solution or product. The problem is the objective your end user wants to achieve.

A great methodology for this is JTBD, which stands for "Jobs to be Done," a concept popularized by the late Clayton Christensen, a Harvard Business School professor and renowned innovation guru, as well as his colleagues who have carried it on, Bob Moesta and Tony Ulwick. The JTBD theory is a framework for better understanding customer behavior.

According to this theory, customers don't merely buy products or services, they "hire" them to do a job. In other words, customers are looking for a solution to a specific problem, and products or services are seen as a means to that end.

A famous example they use to illustrate this is that customers don't simply buy a drill; they hire the drill to create holes. This insight may lead a business to develop better drills, but it might also open up a more innovative approach, such as creating an entirely new way to create holes that doesn't involve drills at all.

This is why you don't ask customers to design the product and/or what product they want; you carefully ask them what problem they are trying to solve. Ultimately, by asking a lot of "Why?" questions, you will understand the customer's problem in such detail that you can design a product they may have never imagined that much better meets their actual need.

What to Include in a Full Life Cycle Use Case

The Full Life Cycle Use Case should first explain how the Persona determines their existing JTBD and how it is suboptimally being addressed by existing offerings. Then you have to understand what is the activation energy/pain/circumstances that will get this target customer to start to explore whether there is a better solution to what they are doing today (i.e., overcoming the inertia of the existing habits). Then you want to understand how the Persona would seek out information about options and ultimately (hopefully) find out about your product. Since you have been doing extensive PMR, your Persona likely found out about the product through the course of your research, so you should instead detail how your Persona would have heard about the product if they had been a completely new prospect.

It is helpful to outline this customer's current full life cycle workflow, because by knowing the customer's current process, it is easier to integrate your product into their operation. Customers who are generally satisfied with their overall workflow will rarely want to radically overhaul their process even if your product provides benefits over their current system.

Your goal is to spend enough time and effort to get a useful first draft, and then you will continually update this information as you move forward through the 24 Steps. With a grounding in PMR, you'll end up with a valuable set of information that will prove a competitive advantage.

The following factors are all essential parts of the Full Life Cycle Use Case:

1. How end users will determine they have a need and/or opportunity to do something different
2. How they will find out about your product
3. How they will analyze your product
4. How they will acquire your product
5. How they will install your product
6. How they will use your product (in detail; see the Satisfier example further on)
7. How they will determine the value gained from your product
8. How they will pay for your product
9. How they will receive support for your product
10. How they will buy more product and/or spread awareness (hopefully positive) about your product

The Full Life Cycle Use Case should be visual, using diagrams, flowcharts, or other methods that show sequence.

EXAMPLES

Bloom Continued

Continuing the Bloom example, the team's Full Life Cycle Use case is seen in Figure 6.1, derived directly from the conversations they had with their Persona.

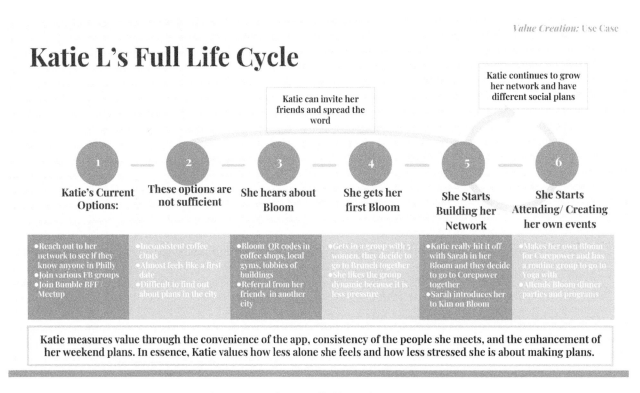

Figure 6.1: Bloom Full Life Cycle Use Case.

It is appropriate to note here as well that Bloom was a class project and meant to show how this process can be implemented quickly. Two of the three members of the team chose to pursue the project after class and make it into a real new venture called Livvy. In that process, they iterated on all of the materials like this Full Life Cycle Use Case to make it more detailed and in line with what the market feedback was.

Satisfier: Example of Incomplete Use Case

The hospitality industry lives and dies by the quality of their customer service. From hotels to restaurants to entertainment venues, the sales and profit of a location fall quickly if customers are not happy when they leave. Regional managers with many locations to oversee have their issues compounded because they need to guarantee the satisfaction of a large number of customers. Regional managers are constantly looking for tools to more accurately and rapidly measure customer satisfaction for their specific environments.

Toward this end, one student team had an idea to take advantage of the increasingly ubiquitous nature of smartphones to provide real-time survey feedback for businesses. After their PMR, they determined that the quickest and most capital-efficient way to get their company off the ground would be targeting a specific group of foodservice companies that served universities. The team's idea was to create posters with a picture of the food offerings available on that day and put them at the exit of the eating establishment. Under each picture were two QR (Quick Response) codes that allowed the consumer to easily register either their approval or disapproval of a food option. In such a scenario, the foodservice companies could get instant feedback on their menu. The student team prepared a mini-use case (Figure 6.2), detailing how the customer would use their product.

1) Management creates one or more surveys on Satisfier's website

2) Banner/flyer is placed on a key location

3) Customers rate their experience using smartphones

4) Results are immediately available on Satisfier's website

Figure 6.2: Satisfier use case.

This is an easily understood segment of the Full Life Cycle Use Case that can be presented to potential end customers for feedback. The team has thought through how its product would be used by the customer to create value. The example forced them to be specific about many things that can otherwise be glossed over. They incorporated not just what their product was (from Step 7, High-Level Product Specification) and who the Persona was (from Step 5, Profile the Persona for the Beachhead Market), but now they could detail how everything interacted and how the entire story would play out. They learned about key people and roles they needed to consider. It generated common understanding and alignment throughout the team regarding the problem being solved and how their product solved it.

Such a use case might seem obvious, but it is much harder than teams anticipate and it is always a valuable touch point as you go forward. This use case, while helpful, is incomplete in that it leaves out many of the early elements (how did your customer find out about your product and then decide to bring it in for a test?) and the later elements (how does the customer pay for your product, get service for it, and ultimately help generate a following for your business by buying more products and/or generating word of mouth for your company?). However, this is where most companies begin and then build out the front and back ends.

FillBee: A More Robust Example

Another student team was looking to revolutionize the furniture shopping experience by making it possible to see what any combination of furniture in your home would look like before you buy it. Through a sophisticated 3D rendering platform that took in the dimensions of your house or apartment, a 3D world would be created where the user could use a computer to try out different pieces of furniture before purchase. Conceptually it sounded great, but what often works conceptually does not work in reality, so a disciplined approach to mapping out the use case would help them gain confidence in their plan.

FillBee started its use case development by mapping the Persona's perspective on how they currently shop for furniture.

A primary pain point in the furniture acquisition process—that the furniture sometimes does not fit in the user's home and has to be returned—is shown in Figure 6.3. To arrive at this point, the team went through many visual iterations with a multidisciplinary team. Working backward, FillBee identified "research+plan" as the step where improvements can be made regarding measuring rooms and furniture. FillBee's product also condenses certain steps, such as condensing "research+plan," "browse," and "buy" into one online process rather than a combination in-person/online process.

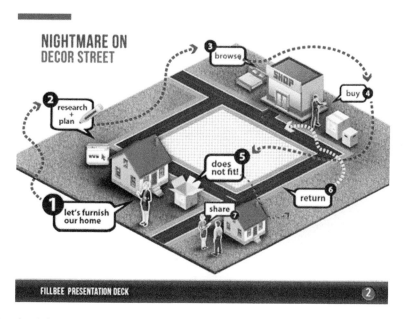

Figure 6.3: FillBee's nightmare on Decor Street (example of Full Life Cycle Use Case before new solution is implemented).

FillBee is also a good example of a product that has a two-sided market, where furniture buyers and furniture sellers are both FillBee customers. Therefore, the team created a Full Life Cycle Use Case for each side of the market. In its "how they will use your product" step for the buyer Persona, the team demonstrated how to tie in the Persona to each step of the process, using lots of detail to fully flesh out how their buyer Persona, Amanda Phillips, would use the product. The more detail provided, the easier it will be for you to find weaknesses or flaws in your plan, based on your knowledge of the Persona. The deeper your knowledge of the Persona, the better it will be for your analysis. This analysis should increase your confidence level and will be much more cost-effective than trying to fix the problems later on.

As you can see in Figure 6.4, FillBee's use case is rich in details. It is clear they have spent a good deal of time with their Persona. When Amanda says she would like to use the system and is willing to pay for it, she is not speaking in conceptual terms, but rather understands the specifics of what she is agreeing to sign up for.

Multiple Initial Set-Up Options Aimed at Ease of Use
To get started, Consumers can:
1.) Start with standardized room shape templates
2.) Enter the dimensions of their room
3.) Start with a pre-loaded room layout
4.) Upload 2 pictures of their room
5.) Upload a 360° video of their room

Furniture from Multiple Retailers
Consumers shouldn't be confined to one or two local retailers. With FillBee Marketplace, Consumers can:
• Select furniture by type
• Drag and drop the chosen item
• Repeat the previous steps until they've built the perfect room

Reduced Friction at Checkout
On FillBee, Consumers can:
• Use FillBee Diagnostics to optimize spend
• View discounts and coupons in an aggregated view
• Complete a purchase through one checkout process, rather than from multiple vendors

Design with the Crowd
FillBee's social and collaboration features let Consumers:
• Share in the decision-making and design process with their friends and families
• Keep up on the latest trends in design and decor
• Get help from a Pro Designer

Real-Time Feedback Feature Helps Consumers Make Better Informed Decisions
FillBee Diagnostics will perform an automated sanity check on the layout Consumers create, providing Consumers with:
• Tailored recommendations based on the Consumer's prior usage and purchase history
• Automated design-centric alerts such as spacing recommendations between two furniture items
• An automated ratings engine that provides ratings based on design and cost metrics

Figure 6.4: FillBee's Amanda Phillips Use Case: good but still missing some upfront and backend elements.

ADDITIONAL RESOURCES

There are additional resources for this step at www.d-eship.com/step6. These materials include:

- Videos: Full Life Cycle Use Case Explainers by Bill Aulet and Erdin Beshimov
- Videos: Example described and explained in an interview with TravelDoc founder Marcel Muenster
- Process Guidance
- Worksheet 6.1: Full Life Cycle Use Case

Additional resources will be added as new and updated examples and information become available.

Summary

The first part of this step is understanding the real problem to be solved. That will involve asking a lot of "Why?" questions to get to the real problem, not the surface-level feature or technology you think they need. The JTBD framework is very helpful in this regard. Once you understand the problem, you can start to intelligently map out the full life cycle use case. Creating a visual representation of the full life cycle of your product enables you to see how the product will fit into the customer's value chain and what barriers to adoption might arise. Just showing how the customer uses the product (the typical definition of "use case") is valuable and should be done, but it will not provide an accurate enough picture to fully understand what obstacles will come up when trying to have your customer adopt your product.

High-Level Product Specification

In This Step, You Will:

- Create a visual representation (e.g., brochure, landing page, storyboard) of your product for potential customers as well as your own team.
- Focus on the benefits of your product created by the features and not just the features.
- ***Not*** build the product.

Defining the High-Level Product Specification at this time gives you a starting point for the solution that will create value for your target customer and also makes sure everyone agrees on what "it" is.

Why This Step, and Why Now?

You can and should do this step now because you have a Persona to guide you in what they would like. You are also clear on what the problem you are solving is thanks to Step 6, Full Life Cycle Use Case. You will need this now to start to quantify our benefits (Step 8, Quantify the Value Proposition), so it logically falls here. Again, this will be a first draft that you continually refine and iterate on, but you need something to keep the process moving. It will also make sure your team has a common agreement on what the current vision of your product is, which will be essential going forward.

Let's Get Started

People are often surprised that they are already at Step 7 and only now beginning to outline what their product will look like. Is that really correct? Absolutely! Many companies build a product too soon and fall in love with their product or technology and stop listening to the customer with all their heart and soul. That is wrong. You should fall in love with solving the problem in the best way possible, not with your technology or product.

Numerous studies show that, once you build a product, you irrationally fall in love with it and stop listening as much as you should. This is called the IKEA effect,[1] and it is why you do not build a product at this point, as much as you might want to. At this point, you only build a High-Level Product Specification. It is imperative that you stay in inquiry mode at this time and not advocacy mode to push your product. You should not be confident that you know what the right solution is yet. That is what you will determine through the process.

So far, you have tightly defined your customer, what they need, and how they will go about acquiring and getting value from a solution from you, even though the actual details of the product are still rather fuzzy. That all starts to change now. You will start by creating a general definition of the product. You will continue to learn more and to refine this product definition over the remaining 24 Steps.

Create a High-Level Product Specification

At its core, a High-Level Product Specification is a drawing. It is a visual representation of what your product will be when it is finally developed, based on what you know at this point of the

---

[1] "IKEA Effect: When Labor Leads to Love," *Harvard Business Review* working paper, http://www.hbs.edu/faculty/Publication%20Files/11-091.pdf

process. It is something you draw without understanding all the underlying details, coding, building a supply chain, manufacturing, and other elements to bring a real product to market. The goal is to have enough of a description to put in front of your target customer to get feedback and also to gain consensus within your team on where you are going while maintaining flexibility.

To begin, take a blank piece of paper and make as simple a visual representation of your product as possible. This is a good starting point, and then slowly increase the level of detail but keep it simple. Only add what is essential. Key design considerations include:

1. **Visual:** If it is hardware, this is easy and surprisingly clarifying. For software, use a series of simulated screenshots to form a storyboard that shows how someone would use the product. The key here is that you have something concrete and specific enough that your team understands thoroughly.

2. **Focus on Benefits:** Focus on the benefits and not on the technology or the functionality. In particular, focus on the benefits that are related to the Persona's top three priorities, with special focus on the top priority. Benefits are what matters. Remember that the Persona's job is not to design the product for you, but to provide feedback on whether the benefits are useful.

3. **High Level:** Don't include too much detail! Just enough to show high-level functionality that will drive the benefits.

4. **Hits the Spot:** Make sure the product specification resonates deeply with the Persona. Conversely, ignore people outside your Beachhead Market. They don't matter.

5. **Flexible:** Make sure your product specification builds in the ability to iterate with the Persona about key features, functions, and benefits. A wise man once said, "Listening is the willingness to change." Actively listen to your Persona's feedback.

It is amazing how much this exercise of drawing a picture of what your product will be forces convergence on a team and removes misunderstandings. It sounds like it should be easy to do, but more often than not entrepreneurs find it harder to do than they initially thought as issues and disagreements arise within the team. Now is the time to resolve any issues, because the cost will be much higher and much time will be lost to inefficiencies.

This simple visual representation of your product can now also be shared with potential customers, immediately generating an unambiguous understanding of your product. You are not selling the product, but are merely iterating with customers so that you more thoroughly understand the strengths and weaknesses of your product spec. This is very important. There is still a lot left to learn before you are sure you have the right product and know how you will make it, price it, and distribute it.

This product specification will change over time and be refined, like all of the other steps in this book.

Next, Make a Product Brochure and/or Landing Page

Some have suggested creating a short, one-page press release about your product at this point. While that is a good idea, I think you should do more. Make a landing page, storyboard, or trifold brochure that more clearly outlines the benefits your product provides. Some people will wait to make a brochure until they have iterated the specification with other customers in Step 9, Identify Your Next 10 Customers, but others find a brochure useful at this stage.

Building a brochure helps you to see your product from the customer's point of view and provides you with a concrete "straw man" to test with your customer. It forces you to see your new venture from your customer's vantage point, in their words. It also allows you to validate your ideas and learn if you are on the right track. Often, when entrepreneurs begin to write down features, they become too inwardly focused. Creating a brochure helps to avoid that pitfall.

There will be a time for features, but focus relentlessly on benefits here. Features are only useful if they create new functionality, and functionality is only useful if it creates new benefits to your target customer.

A good brochure should have the following items:

1. First draft of company name and tagline.
2. Name of product and tagline.
3. Image or picture of product so it is clear what it is.
4. Clearly identified benefits aligned with the Persona's #1 priority (don't be subtle—it should come out in the taglines and maybe even the name of your product).
5. Two additional benefits (if appropriate) aligned with the second and third priorities of the Persona that don't dilute the impact of the first benefit.
6. A sense of the magnitude of the benefit to be expected by the end user. Use your work from Step 6, Full Life Cycle Use Case.

7. Some other information might be relevant, but always be diligent about not diluting your main message—if you say too much, you say nothing in particular.

8. Have a clear call to action.

9. Everything should be fully aligned with the customer's priorities and will resonate with the customer in all elements (e.g., names, taglines, pictures, benefits emphasized, fonts, colors, word choice, language, references, call to action).

There are great individuals and agencies you can hire to design your landing pages, brochures, or storyboard, but do not overpay. Focus on high-level content—not too many details—and make your product description look nice but not overdesigned. You are not expected to become an expert in design or user interface/experience. You want to think through the content carefully from a logical standpoint and be concise in how it addresses the Persona's priorities in compelling fashion. That way, if you choose to delegate or outsource the design, you can give them clear direction and not settle for an inferior brochure.

Historically, the brochure is the most commonly and widely given elevator pitch about your product because it can be done when you are not in the room and even when you are sleeping. It makes consistent messaging possible and scalable, so don't just downplay it as "marketing hype." It really matters.

You also have to back it up with a great product, but that is coming. First, you have to make sure you are building the right product for your customer, and this process really helps to communicate that to all sides.

Concept of Spiraling Innovation

Throughout this book, I have talked about pushing to have a first draft and then iterating on it. This step is a great example of this. Think of this as spiraling innovation. This means don't worry if you get it right the first time; just give it your best. It will surely not be 100% right but hopefully it will be at least 10% right, and then iterate to figure out (humbly) what is the 10% of your hypothesis that is right and keep that. Then start to build off that and fix the rest. This will happen in an incremental fashion.

A High-Level Product Specification is a great way to do this in a concrete way. From experience, I can tell you it works a lot better than just talking about the product. Having something visual and specific will jump-start the spiraling innovation process (Figure 7.1) and then you just keep working it until you get to a product definition you are happy with. Figure out what the customer wants and will pay for, keep that, and change the rest. Iterate to make it better over time.

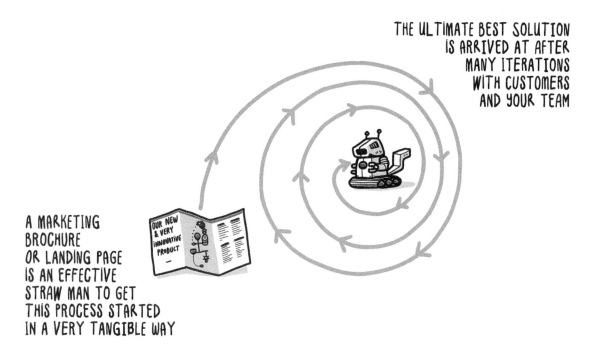

THE ULTIMATE BEST SOLUTION IS ARRIVED AT AFTER MANY ITERATIONS WITH CUSTOMERS AND YOUR TEAM

A MARKETING BROCHURE OR LANDING PAGE IS AN EFFECTIVE STRAW MAN TO GET THIS PROCESS STARTED IN A VERY TANGIBLE WAY

Figure 7.1: Put a first-draft brochure in front of your Persona. It will definitely be wrong in many ways, but will hopefully be right in some ways.

EXAMPLES

Bloom Continued

While a High-Level Product Specification might seem like an easy task before and after it is done, it is not easy while it is being done, as the Bloom team found out. The concept of helping women make friends more easily was pleasing, and the team's unstructured discussion about ideas for how to help was exciting, but when it came to making the storyboard of how this would happen, it was really hard.

The process of making this specification was at least as important as the output. It first got the team fully aligned on what it thought was initially correct based on the PMR it had done to date. While everyone had heard the same feedback from the potential customers, they were all processing it differently. Making the first draft of the spec and storyboards (Figure 7.2) resulted in a highly productive discussion of what features they were to prioritize and why. They also created some alternatives to test the priority of key functionality so they could do A/B testing with their Persona.

High Level Product Specification

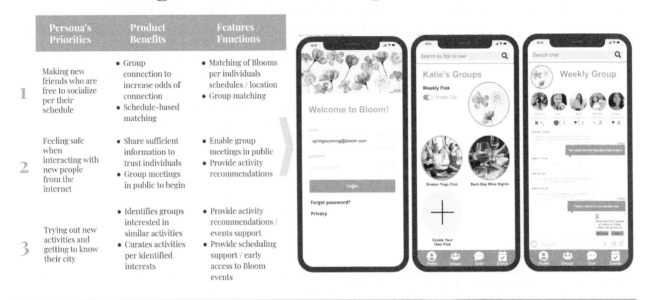

Figure 7.2: Bloom High-Level Product Specification storyboard.

The next stage in the process was for the team to review this with the Persona, and surprise, the Persona changed some of it.

The layout for their High-Level Product Specification is very well done. It makes sure that the top priorities of the Persona are addressed and the features and benefits are tightly tied to them.

This High-Level Product Specification is not locked in; it will be adjusted not just in Step 9 but also on an ongoing basis. But for now, the team has a common agreement of the best path forward with regard to the product—until they get more signals to the contrary.

Altaeros Energies

The students behind Altaeros, Ben Glass and Adam Rein, started with the idea of building a wind turbine in the sky, high enough to get consistent wind, and anchored to a platform in the ocean. Conceptually, it sounded simple, but when the team tried to explain it to potential customers, they encountered a lot of questions regarding what exactly they were proposing. It was hard to have a meaningful conversation. Finally, the team built an image of what the product would be, and found that even within the team they had some disagreement. Ultimately, they came up with the image you see in Figure 7.3. By the end of the process, the team had a common understanding of the product, and could easily use this High-Level Product Spec as a basis for more in-depth PMR.

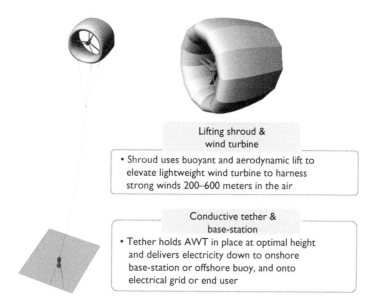

Figure 7.3: Altaeros High-Level Product Specification.

SensAble Technologies

Our "digital clay" solution, which we called FreeForm, included both hardware (the physical PHAN-ToM) and software. In the new digital clay molding bench, the hardware was the easier item to describe. It was easy to imagine the prototype hardware getting smaller and more stylish. The hard part was going to be designing the software, so that is what we focused on.

The message we got from our PMR was that customers wanted a product that would have the ease of use of clay, but also the benefits of having digital files so that designs could be saved, modified, and sent electronically around the world.

We started to develop the High-Level Product Specification as a set of PowerPoint slides. We showed the tools that designers used at the time and then we showed how that tool set would not only be replicated, but expanded with our digital clay molding bench (Figure 7.4).

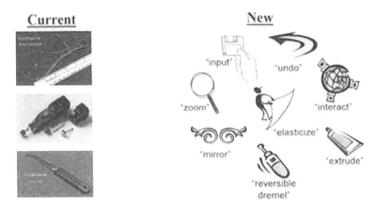

Figure 7.4: SensAble replaces and expands the current tool set.

There would also be drop-down menus that would allow the user to digitally select the materials, the tool, the end effector, and whether a template was to be used (Figure 7.5). This made it much easier for us to focus and test the viability of some concrete ideas with ourselves as well as potential customers.

Another screenshot showed a clay studio, with a hunk of clay in the center, and with drop-down menus above, to show designers the interface they would be using to mold their digital clay.

Our High-Level Product Specification allowed us to get good feedback on our product from our customers. Our final product looked much different, but the spec was still successful because we needed a starting point for the dialogue and this worked well.

User Selections

Materials:	Tools:	End Effector:
☐ Soft Clay	☐ Sculpt	✐ Point
☐ Medium Clay	☐ Hot Sword	● Ball
☐ Hard Clay	☐ Push/Pull	◆ Triangle
☐ Blue Foam	☐ Extrusion	■ Square
☐ Ren	☐ Dremel	◗ Half Elipse
☐ Metal	☐ Scribe	⋎ Hook
☐ Other	☐ Other	✕ Other

Template:
☐ Yes
☐ No

Figure 7.5: SensAble drop-down menu for user selections.

ADDITIONAL RESOURCES

There are additional resources for this step at www.d-eship.com/step7. These materials include:

- Video: High-Level Product Specification Explainers by Bill Aulet and Erdin Beshimov
- Video: Example described and explained in an interview with Changing Environments/ Soofa founders Sandra Richter and Jutta Friedrichs
- Process Guidance
- Worksheet 7.1: Visual Representation of High-Level Product Specification
- Worksheet 7.2: Alignment of High-Level Product Specification with Persona
- Advanced Topic: High-Level Landing Page, Product Brochure or Storyboard

Additional resources will be added as new and updated examples and information become available.

Summary

Visually sketching out your product will allow your team and your potential customers to converge around an understanding of what the product is and how it benefits customers. Staying at a high level, without too many details or a physical prototype, allows for rapid revision without investing too much time and resources this early in the process of creating your new venture. Building a visual representation of the product will likely be harder than you think, but will get everyone on the same page, which will prove extremely valuable going forward. Don't build the product yet.

Quantify the Value Proposition

In This Step, You Will:

- Determine how your product will benefit your target customer for what they care about most.
- Formulate a simple structure and calculate quantitative metrics (in most cases) to be able to communicate this value to the customer extremely efficiently and effectively.

The relentless march for specificity continues. The Quantified Value Proposition gives you a concrete understanding and a way to communicate the measurable benefits of your product.

Why This Step, and Why Now?

Customers will be much more likely to buy your product if the value it provides lines up with their highest priorities and is crystal clear. Now that you have defined the Persona's priorities (Step 5), and you have a Full Life Cycle Use Case (Step 6) and High-Level Product Specification (Step 7), quantifying your product's value proposition is the missing step to validate that you can create significant value for your target customer.

Let's Get Started

"When you can measure what you are speaking about, and express it in numbers, you know something about it; but when you cannot measure it . . . your knowledge is of a meager and unsatisfactory kind."

—*Lord Kelvin*

Your Quantified Value Proposition demonstrates the measurable benefits your Persona gets from your product. These benefits will be aligned with what you now understand is their top priority.

Products often have a large number of benefits. For instance, your product may help a customer simplify a process or reduce their environmental impact or help a business gain additional sales for their own products. In a simple view of the world, benefits fall into five categories: "better," "faster," "cheaper," "more reliably," and "more sustainably." While you might think all are important, your customer is more focused and you must be too. The goal of the Quantified Value Proposition is first to align with their top priority and then to clearly and concisely state how your product benefits your customer in this area. Again, focus and specificity are the key.

The Quantified Value Proposition focuses on what potential benefits are to be gained, rather than going into detail on technology, features, and functions.

Aligning Your Value Proposition with the Persona's Priorities

You've already identified the top priorities of the Persona. You have charted your Full Life Cycle Use Case, so you understand how your customer will use your product.

You will now create a value proposition focused on the criteria you identified as your Persona's top priority. If their top priority is time to market for producing goods, and your product's value is that it will lower the cost of production, then your value proposition will not activate your target customer to buy your product. If your product also lowers the time to market, you should focus on that and you will get the Persona's attention and activate them.

Keep It Simple: The "As-Is" State Compared to the "Possible" State with Your Product

Once you know the top priority of your Persona, simply focus all your efforts on this factor. Talk with the Persona about how to measure that priority quantitatively, and what units to measure it in. For instance, if your Persona's top priority is saving money, then your value proposition will likely be expressed as dollars, or dollars per time period (such as dollars saved over the course of a year). If it is reliability, your measurement might be percentage rate of failure, errors per thousand products, downtime per month, or a similar measurement.

Next, take that quantitative measurement and map out with the Persona what is the "as-is state" for how the Persona today solves, or tries to solve, the problem you defined in Step 6, the Full Life Cycle Use Case. Use the Persona's own words when describing the as-is state. Then visually break it down into concrete stages.

Next, define, with buy-in from your whole team, the "possible" state of how the user will solve this problem with your proposed new product. Explicitly show, in detail, how your proposed product will better satisfy the Persona's #1 priority. Express the possible state by using the same units with which you measured the Persona's top priority.

The difference in value between the "as-is" state and the "possible" state is your Quantified Value Proposition. It is that simple. See Figure 8.1 on how to structure this work.

Be sure to use the words of the customer in your diagram so they can understand that it is customized to them—or at least to their industry.

Define the "as-is" and "possible" states so clearly that any target customer will easily be able to understand, agree or disagree, and then comment on the assessment.

Be sure to make the numbers in the "possible" state ones that you are highly confident your product can attain. You do not want to be too aggressive and fall short of what you set as an expectation. Often, entrepreneurs are much too aggressive in claiming how beneficial their product is to customers. As a result, they fall short of expectations and lose credibility. Following the mantra of "under promise, overdeliver" is wise, especially for new B2B ventures.

Sometimes, the Persona has multiple top priorities that are intertwined. See the example for InTouch, where the Persona, a pregnant mother-to-be, wanted reassurance that her fetus was healthy and wanted to establish intimacy with her unborn child.

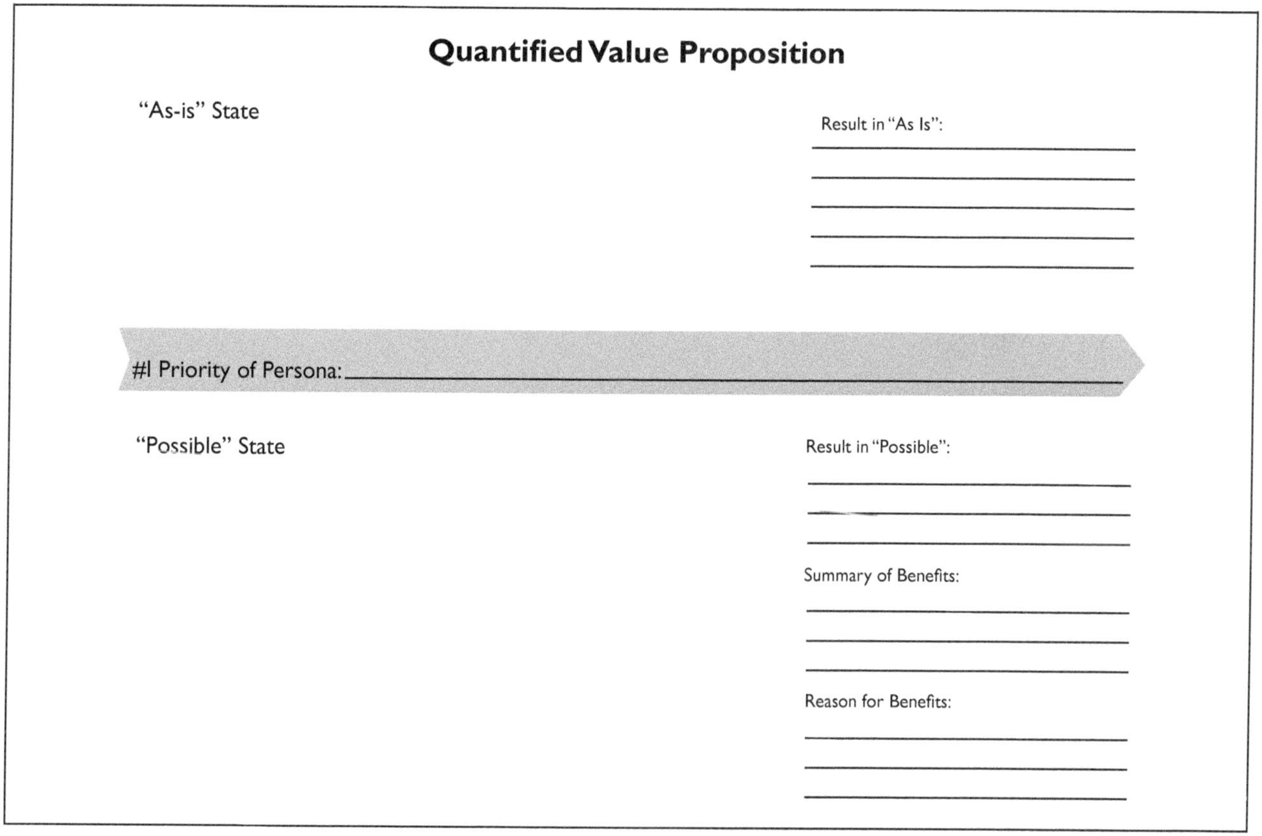

Quantified Value Proposition

"As-is" State

Result in "As Is":
_____
_____
_____
_____
_____

#1 Priority of Persona: _____

"Possible" State

Result in "Possible":
_____
_____
_____

Summary of Benefits:
_____
_____
_____

Reason for Benefits:
_____
_____
_____

Figure 8.1: How to visually represent your Quantified Value Proposition.

EXAMPLES

Bloom Continued

From Step 5, Profile the Persona for the Beachhead Market, you know the number-one priority of Bloom's Persona, Katie, is "social life." This translated to how many compatible friends she could meet and the strength of those relationships. This is a hard metric to measure, but when the team spoke with Katie, she confirmed that this was a good metric. Using this, the team determined that they wanted to focus on how many quality friends Katie would be able to get with Bloom as compared to the current "as-is" state that exists for a given time period.

Quantifying Value Proposition

"As is " State					Results
Moved to Philly after graduating. She does not know the city well and does not have anyone to explore with	Try to find friends via Facebook Groups/Bumble BFF. Time Spent 3 hours a week searching	Katie attends coffee date with one woman. Becca on Saturday Morning	Follow up with Becca to see if she has plans later. There are new to the city parties but Katie does not want to go alone	Katie hears about the Junior League through her coworkers. The women's club costs about $300 plus event tickets	In 1 Week Katie spent 3 hours looking for ways to meet new people, she had 1 organized coffee date is potentially thinking about paying $300 for membership to Women's Club

"Possible " State					Results
Moved to Philly after graduating. She does not know the city well and does not have anyone to explore with	Joins Bloom for free and is instantly matched with group of 5 women who will meet up for Brunch this Saturday through a Bloom event. Katie chatted with the woman for 30 min. this week	At brunch, Katie hit it off with ⅗ women really well and they planned to do CorePower together. Another women invited the woman over to her house for wine night that night	At CorePower, Katie sees Bloom QR Code. She "checks in" on the app, and sees a public Bloom for Corepower of 10 women. One of the women is organizing an after yoga drinks through Bloom and Katie signs up	Katie starts building her own Blooms. She adds a total of 5 women from Brunch and CorePower, and they decide to have Bachelor Nights. They create a Public Bloom inviting more women.	In 1 Week. Katie spent 30 minutes initially in her weekly Bloom, met 5 women at brunch, made additional plans with 3 of them to do Yoga, gained a network of 10 women who enjoy the same studio as she does and now has weekly recurring plans with at least 5 women for bachelor night.

Figure 8.2: Bloom initial value proposition example.

Katie filled in the "as-is" state (pretty grim) and the team then made sure to confirm with her that it was correct: one new friend despite all the effort and expense. Then they pivoted to the possible state where they felt comfortable that with Bloom (backed up by an experiment they ran), Katie would meet five quality new friends. In Figure 8.2, you can see this laid out on one slide. The value proposition is that Katie is frustrated and is looking at expensive alternatives to solve her problem, and is pleased to see the potential new Bloom option.

One piece of feedback I had is that I worried Bloom was overpromising with these results and I encouraged them to manage expectations. It should be noted that for this example, the team was on a short time frame for a semester-long course. so you can understand they were pressed for time. As a point of comparison, you can see in Figure 8.3 an example of what the team did later on to refine this example after doing more PMR.

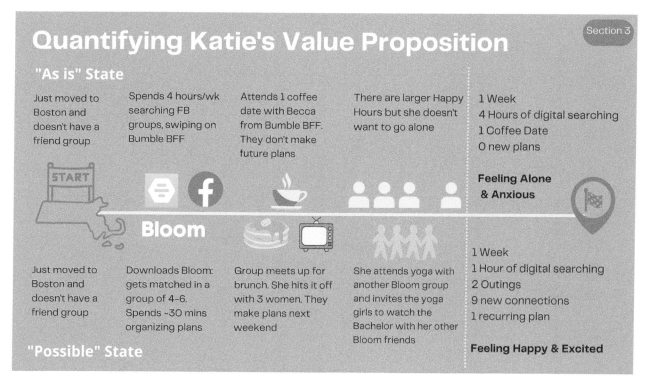

Figure 8.3: Refined Bloom Value Proposition after more PMR and iterations.

SensAble Technologies

As discussed in Step 5, the SensAble Persona was an industrial designer in the toy industry. The top priority for the Persona (particularly because it was a priority for the Persona's management, a critical part of the decision-making process for purchasing new products) was time to market for new toys. Faster time to market gave them flexibility to better read market signals, which directly tied to their profits. This was a constant mantra in their design department—faster time to market.

With this insight, we first determined the average time to market for a new toy using the current software, processes, and other tools available. We were careful to see the development process the way the customer does—in this case the toy manufacturer—using the customer's own words to describe the process. We iterated with one toy manufacturer until they confirmed we had it right. We then went to another toy manufacturer to see if their process was similar and it was, with some small tweaks. After a while, we became very confident we had an excellent detailed description of the "as-is" state. Then we mapped how long each stage of the process would take using our product (Figure 8.4).

This simple chart was one of the most valuable and powerful slides we ever created at SensAble. This resonated immediately with our Persona and all of our target customers. The 50% reduction

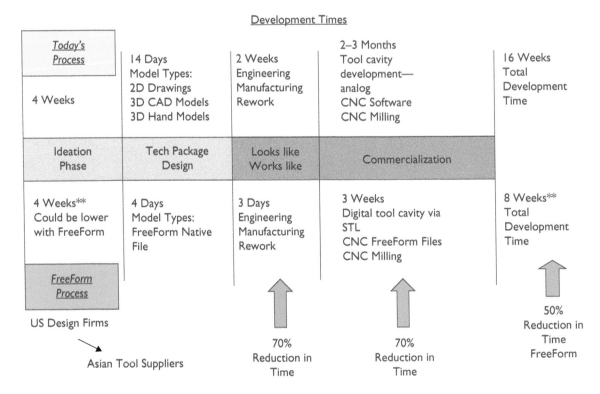

Figure 8.4: SensAble Quantified Value Proposition.

in time to market our offered product could mean increased profits of hundreds of thousands to millions of dollars per toy. We did not have to express our value proposition in dollars because the actual dollar amount would vary widely. Also, manufacturers were fluent enough in their process to know what a 50% reduction in time meant for them. Our advocates could communicate this to anyone in the company and they would immediately understand the great value. This is an excellent example of a Quantified Value Proposition.

InTouch (Intangible Benefits)

Not every value proposition is a clear-cut number. One example is InTouch, a hardware/software product for first-time mothers-to-be who want a higher level of intimacy with their unborn child. The system would be a patch or belt the pregnant mother wears, with sensors near the fetus that would read the heartbeat and other vital signs of the unborn baby. The system would then take all of the data it had collected and put it through their proprietary algorithm and indicate whether the baby was healthy, stimulated, and happy. For instance, the mother could read to the unborn baby and then see if this made the fetus more or less "happy." Or it could be used simply to check the baby's heartbeat and general health.

You might consider this an unconventional idea (and you would be in the majority), but that does not matter as long as there is a large-enough target market that finds this concept attractive and compelling and, most of all, is excited enough about it to motivate them to pay for such a product.

The team knew the Persona's top priorities were to have reassurance that the fetus was okay and to establish intimacy with the unborn child. The team determined the "as-is" state to include expensive and cumbersome heart-rate monitors, imprecise and unpredictable intuition, costly and inconvenient professional ultrasounds, and the haphazard and uncomfortable consultation with "Dr. Google" online (Figure 8.5).

The "possible" state was using the InTouch product—which only existed as a High-Level Product Specification at this point—and gaining deep intimacy rapidly. They did not have to quantify the intimacy gain because their visual representation of the "as-is" versus "possible" states resonated with the first-time mothers, who validated it for them.

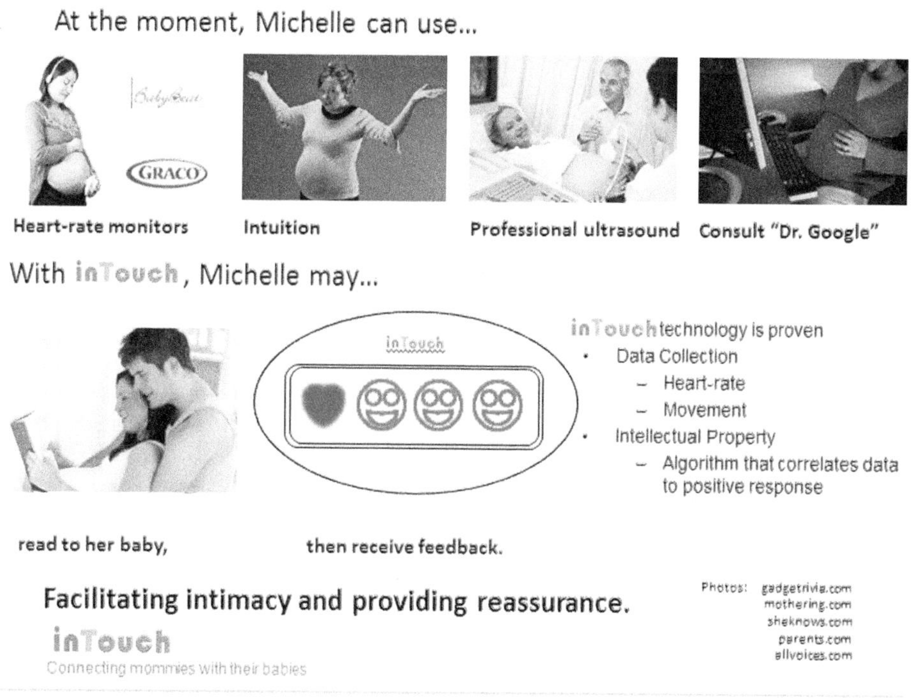

Figure 8.5: InTouch value proposition example.
Credit: (c) Monkey Business/Adobe Stock; (e) WavebreakMediaMicro / Adobe Stock.

Meater

This team started with biosensor technology that was significantly better than what was currently available in the market at the time in terms of size, efficiency, and pricing. They went through the process to determine an appropriate Beachhead Market and settled on the cattle ranching industry. The proposed solution was a biosensor that could be affixed to a cow's ear, much like the way cows are currently tagged, to detect disease earlier. Sick cows identified earlier can be separated from the herd, reducing infection rates, and allowing more effective treatment of diseases due to earlier detection than current methods.

The Persona, a rancher, was primarily driven by money. The Persona had no personal attachment to the cattle; making as much money as possible was by far the rancher's top priority.

First, the team determined the current economics for a typical herd of cattle (the "as-is" state), verifying it with numerous ranchers and refining it until it was clearly valid and credible. The team then determined the "possible" state from using their product, making some conservative assumptions they could support with compelling validity evidence, and then showing how much money a rancher would save by using their product (Figure 8.6). The difference between these was their

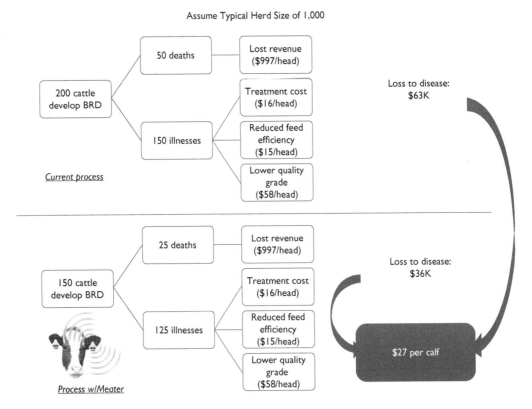

Figure 8.6: Meater loss-to-disease comparison.

Quantified Value Proposition. This could easily be quantified because the Persona's top priority was something very measurable—money.

This was a compelling and highly specific Quantified Value Proposition that made it much easier to engage and quickly close their target customer on acquiring the product. It will also be of great help in later steps when the team looks to determine its Business Model (Step 15) and Pricing Framework (Step 16).

ADDITIONAL RESOURCES

There are additional resources for this step at www.d-eship.com/step8. These materials include:

- Videos: Quantified Value Proposition Explainers by Bill Aulet and Erdin Beshimov
- Videos: Example described and explained in an interview with Native Mind founder Ning Shirakawa
- Process Guidance
- Worksheets:
  - Worksheet 8.1: Units to Measure Quantified Value Proposition In
  - Worksheet 8.2: Verbal Description of the "As Is" and "Possible States"
  - Worksheet 8.3: Quantified Value Proposition visual summary

Additional resources will be added as new and updated examples and information become available.

Summary

At this stage in the process, you should now be feeling pretty good. You know who your customer is, and you have an overview of what product you'd like to build and what value it will deliver. You have made great progress, but you will need to refine all of this a great deal more to develop competitive advantage as well as a go-to-market strategy to build and launch your product. Regardless, completing this step is still an important milestone—congratulations!

Identify Your Next 10 Customers

In This Step, You Will:

- Create a list of the next 10 potential end user customers in your Beachhead Market after the Persona who closely fit the End User Profile.

- Engage them in a dialogue on your plans and validate or invalidate the work you have done so far.

Explicitly identifying the Next 10 Customers after the Persona increases your level of confidence that you are on the right path and they will be invaluable to refining the steps completed so far.

Why This Step, and Why Now?

To date, you will have made a first draft of three crucial elements of your plan (Full Life Cycle Use Case, High-Level Product Specification, Quantified Value Proposition) based on the input of one person, the Persona. This step follows those steps because you will now do a deeper dive to refine those steps with 10 more real target customers, grounded in your work in the market realities—and you will dramatically reduce the risk of building a product that no one wants.

Let's Get Started

One danger of focusing solely on your Persona is that you could build your business to be too specific, thus limiting your ability to sell to others in your target market. If the Persona is done correctly, this will not happen, but your Persona will not be perfect.

This step is a checkpoint to guard against the potential exposure of hyper-focus on a Persona and also to make valuable refinements of your work to date. The output of this step will be highly beneficial to stay firmly grounded in the realities of your Beachhead Market.

Three Criteria to Make the List of Your Next 10 Customers

In the final list you produce in this step, you are looking for homogeneity (i.e., they are all the same) as opposed to heterogeneity (i.e., they are different) in the following three key criteria which were first discussed in Step 1, Market Segmentation:

1. **Same Product:** They will buy the same product, without any alterations.
2. **Same Sales Process:** The 10 names on the list will buy it in the same way, with the same value proposition, same distribution model, same messaging, and basically the same pricing. If not the same demographic, they are the same psychographic in that they are buying your product for the same reason. In other words, it is a highly replicable sales process to go from one to the next. Same slides, same discussion, same references, same use case, same brochure, same pricing discussions, same watering holes, same proxy products. The only thing that really changes are the names.
3. **Word of Mouth:** If you sell to one of them, it will be a positive reference at a minimum to the others. Even better, they will go to the watering holes and tell others about your product.

In summary, all 10 on the list are very clearly from your well-defined Beachhead Market segment.

How to Find Your Next 10 Customers

This step may sound easy and you may think in your case it will be easy, but I can assure you that if you do it correctly, it will not be nearly as easy as you think. It is important to have a systematic process to do it.

1. **Make as Long a List as Possible to Start and Keep Adding to It:** It will take more than 10 candidates to find your Next 10 Customers, because you will not be able to contact some of them, and others you will find do not fit your End User Profile as well as you had hoped. You will have to be creative to make your candidate list. Start by asking your Persona who else they know similar to them and where you might find more people like them (i.e., watering holes). Go back to your target End User Profile and look at the watering holes and proxy products for tips. Ask you family and friends; this can come with some biases, as I have discussed earlier, but you have to start somewhere. Comb back through your PMR from previous steps. Realize that this will be hard work but extremely valuable when done.

2. **Initiate Contact and Stay in Inquiry Mode:** Contact each of the potential customers on your list and present your Full Life Cycle Use Case, High-Level Product Specification, and Quantified Value Proposition (Steps 6–8). While having these conversations, be sure that you are operating in "inquiry" mode, not "advocacy/sales" mode, because the latter approach will diminish the quality of your interactions. Determine whether the customer's needs are in line with what you've established thus far from Steps 3-8. Also validate with these customers the hypothesis regarding top purchasing priorities.

3. **Keep Building Your List with Each Good Interview:** If a customer validates your hypotheses from the previous steps, now is a good time to ask the customer if they would consider providing a letter of interest or even intent to buy your solution, if it becomes available. You are still in "inquiry" mode, so you are asking, "If a company were to offer this product, would you be interested in purchasing it?" rather than "Will you buy this product?" If they are extremely enthusiastic, you can even ask them if they would be willing to prepay for the product, which is a fantastic level of commitment. Before you take their money, however, make sure you can deliver what they want and also make sure there are no special conditions in their purchase order that you cannot or do not want to be expected to meet.

4. **You Will Need to Kiss a Lot of Frogs to Find Your 10 Princes/Princesses:** If a customer's feedback is not aligned exactly with your assumptions, take good notes and think how this affects your analysis. Do not overreact to each new interview, even if there is a major disconnect, unless you see a pattern. You will know intuitively if there is a major disconnect after a few interviews. Don't get discouraged if it takes a lot more than 10 or 20 candidates to find your list of 10 next homogeneous customers. That is normal.

5. **Don't Get Distracted by People Who Are Outside Your Target Profile:** If someone gives you strong feedback, before you take it to heart, make sure they are your target customer. If not, ignore it. The only ones who matter are your target customers.

6. **Update Your Assumptions Based on This New PMR:** Now that you have contacted each customer, you may have new data. At this point, you can go back and modify your earlier assumptions and determine whether to contact additional customers. Your end goal is a homogenous list of 10 customers who are truly interested and aligned with your Persona and other assumptions.

7. **What Is the Market Telling You? Maybe It's Time to Fold and Find a New Beachhead Market:** If you find that you cannot create a list of 10 customers who are excited about your High-Level Product Specification with the same Full Life Cycle Use Case and Value Proposition, then you may need to reconsider your Beachhead Market.

8. **This Information Is Gold to Be Protected:** While this step is conceptually simple, contacting customers and getting information from them will require a good amount of work, but will be invaluable as you move forward. Do not share this list of customers or the information you gather with others outside your company.

Is the Current Persona Valid?

In the process of determining the Next 10 Customers, you are testing to ensure that your Persona is truly a useful and credible representation of the target customer. If the Persona is a statistical outlier relative to the target customer group, it will not only be a poor source of information, but it will lead you to develop a product your target customer might not want. While validating the Persona, you may also uncover other interesting traits that customers share with the Persona, which will allow you to revise the description of the Persona to make it stronger. Often in this step, you find an even better Persona than you started with, which is a good thing. Your Persona is so important as a North Star that if you find a new candidate who is a 5% or more better representative of your Beachhead Market, strongly consider changing your Persona.

DEALING WITH NEGATIVE FEEDBACK

Throughout the 24 Steps, your purpose is not to complete each step with 100% accuracy, but rather to test hypotheses and to learn from your potential customers. Getting negative results will happen and that is helpful. No matter how smart you are, most of what you initially believe is wrong and you must be humble and willing to acknowledge this or you will definitely fail. The key is how your entrepreneurial team responds to this new information and that will be a fundamental factor in your team's success. Therefore, if any step returns negative feedback, meaning feedback that does not support your hypotheses, you have received valuable information that there may be an error in the assumptions you have been using up to this point. You must listen, but it may just be noise—your fundamental hypotheses may still be true and there may still be a big market out there. It is a very careful balance. Don't be arrogant. Negative results at one step are not the end of the venture in most cases, but moving forward with a faulty plan that was based on hope and not facts is a recipe for failure.

"But why should I listen to the naysayers?" you may ask, pointing to Steve Jobs or other entrepreneurs who achieved success through seemingly ignoring customers. True entrepreneurs see possibilities that others do not and overcome obstacles that others cannot. But you cannot will a market to exist any more than you can change the laws of thermodynamics. Even the most powerful personalities with extreme "reality distortion zone" powers cannot do so, as history has shown with Dean Kamen and the Segway, or even Steve Jobs at NeXT Computer. This is where this customer-centered process comes into play. The market ultimately wins and will be the final arbiter of your success or failure, so listen carefully.

EXAMPLES

Bloom Continued

As I continue the Bloom example, I think it is important to state again that this was a project in a one-semester class, so don't look at it as a case of perfection. It does give a great example of how you get started, but not necessarily the ideal end state. In my class you only have three months to cover all the steps, so the students don't have as much time as they like to complete each step—but in some ways, this is actually good training for the real world.

Still, as you look at the Bloom example below, you can see many positive indicators. They have found 10 customers showing strong interest in their product who have the same or similar use cases and value propositions (Figure 9.1). They have also found ways to source good leads for new customers.

Then what worries me? The source column is where I look first to gauge the bias in the data in the matrix. My first reaction is concern when 4 of the 10 candidates are sources via "Friend of a friend." My concern is regarding "social acceptability bias" with such data—are these four candidates saying they are interested just to be nice to their friend, or do they actually have a genuine interest in the product? In this case, however, that concern is less when you realize that Madeleine, Anisha, and Sarah come from the target market, so it is more likely that friends of friends would truly be interested in the value proposition. Still, it is imperfect, and you would like more of an arm's-length relationship. But sometimes you have to start with what you can get and keep moving . . . and then come back and fix it later.

My bigger concern is with entries 2, 3, and 9, where the lack of a tight use case and/or value proposition makes me more uncomfortable. I would not launch a real company or product with this analysis, but again in their defense, they did not have much time and did a great job within the constraints. And as they worked to take this out of the classroom and into a real startup, they greatly refined this step along with others. All of this said, this is still encouraging, and while you might want to do more work, this looks promising, so let's move to the next step.

The Next 10 Customers...

	Name	Relevant Info	Demographic	Psychographic	Use Case	Value Prop	Overall	Contacted	Interest Level	Source
1	Ola	Recent Grad Suburbs	A	A	A	A	A	Yes	Medium – desires social activities but worries about critical mass	Friend of a friend
2	Gracie	Graduating in May	B	A	B	A	B	Yes	High – desires new friends now	Friend of a friend
3	Leigh	Recent Grad in NJ	A	A	A	B	A	Yes	Medium – ok with social life being boyfriend, but would try	Recommended
4	Mia	Graduating in May	B	A	A	A	A	Yes	High (needs it immediately)	
5	Dominique	Recent Grad Boston	A	A	A	A	A	Yes	High – in various friend finding groups on FB	Facebook Group (New to Boston) Proxy Product
6	Jenny	Recent Grad NYC	A	A	A	A	A	Yes	Medium – wants "new social life"	Friend of a Friend
7	Monica	Moved to Boston	B	A	A	A	A	Yes	High (needs it immediately)	Facebook Group (New to Boston) Proxy Product
8	Lily	Recent Grad in Boston	A	A	A	A	A	Yes	Medium – would use but planning to go to Law school next year	Friend of a Friend
9	Katherine	Graduating in May	A	A	B	B	B	Yes	Medium – has lots of friends moving to NYC with her	Recommended
10	Camilla	Recent Grad in Boston	A	A	A	A	A	Yes	High – has not had success on Bumble BFF	Bumble BFF Proxy Product

General Info. / Fit / Interaction

Figure 9.1: Bloom's Next 10 Customers.

Methane Capture of Landfill Sites

A very energetic and savvy student team was building a plan for a new venture that included creating a sophisticated technology to monitor and capture methane from landfill sites, thereby reducing the harmful emissions from these sites and converting them instead into valuable fuel to produce electricity.

They did all of the steps, including the Market Segmentation (Step 1), Persona (Step 3), Full Life Cycle Use Case (Step 6), and Quantified Value Proposition (Step 8). They felt like it all made sense, but they had to verify this in the real world.

The team made a list of the 10 most promising landfill sites, considering their location, size, ownership structure, and other factors. They then proceeded to contact the appropriate person at each site and found an extremely positive response from 8 of the 10. In fact, they got letters of intent at the end of the meeting from more than half of them, giving the team an incredible boost of confidence that they were on the right path (Figure 9.2).

	Project Owner—Location *(names changed for this book)*	Total Megawatts Installed	Name/Contact Info *(names changed for this book)*	Contacted?
1	Waste Management—City Name, State	9.8	Site owner	Y
2	Smith Waste Systems—City Name, State	4.8	Site owner	Y
3	Energy Systems, Inc.—City Name, State	18.4	Third-party operator	N
4	Waste Management—City Name, State	16.8	Site owner	Y
5	Waste Management—City Name, State	16.5	Site owner	Y
6	Energy Systems, Inc.—City Name, State	12	Third-party operator	N
7	Waste Management—City Name, State	9.8	Site owner	Y
8	Waste Management—City Name, State	7.9	Site owner	Y
9	Smith Methane Group—City Name, State	7.34	Third-party operator	Y
10	Smith Waste Management—City Name, State	6.9	Third-party operator/ Site owner	Y

Figure 9.2: Methane capture Next 10 Customers.

ADDITIONAL RESOURCES

There are additional resources for this step at www.d-eship.com/step9. These materials include:

- Video: DMU Explainers by Bill Aulet and Erdin Beshimov
- Video: Example described and explained in an interview with Eterni.me founder Marius Ursache
- Process Guidance
- Worksheet 9.1: List of Potential Contacts
- Worksheet 9.2: List of 10 Next Customers
- Worksheet 9.3: Summary of Information Gained from Each Interview
- Worksheet 9.4: Overall Lessons Learned from Interviews

Additional resources will be added as new and updated examples and information become available.

In this case, the process worked flawlessly and the results were extremely comforting and validated the team's plans.

Summary

This step injects a huge dose of reality into the process in a very constructive way. Make sure your team is open to the hard work and hard feedback you will get because, if done with balance, it will be an invaluable course correction for your team and get you headed in the right direction with a tremendous amount of momentum and confidence. Remember, listening is the willingness to change your mind. Do so intelligently and based on data and real evidence as well as logic.

Define Your Core

In This Step, You Will:

- Determine the single thing that you will do better than anyone else that will be very difficult for others to copy. This may be a capability or set of assets that you may or may not yet have today but you will develop for the future.

- Identify other things (i.e., moats) that provide you with competitive advantage and likely buy you time to develop and reinforce your Core.

You need to figure out something that you do that will make you better than anyone else at producing a solution for your customers. This will be the new venture's eventual crown jewels.

Why This Step, and Why Now?

Having a clear definition of your Core will allow you to focus your limited resources to build and reinforce it. It will also ensure you do not do all the work to create a market and then have someone come in and steal it away from you because you did not think strategically. You do this analysis now because you now have sufficient context to understand the real driver of your value creation, as well as the general market dynamics.

Let's Get Started

Alert: This is usually the hardest step of the 24 Steps. So far, you have focused almost exclusively on meeting the needs of a well-defined target customer. Now you will start looking to the future by determining what about your business makes you unique, what your "secret sauce" is.

I like to describe the Core as the crown jewels of your business. The analogy to crown jewels refers to the precious gems, crowns, scepters, and other ceremonial objects that are owned by a monarch or a royal family. It has enormous symbolic (if not always functional) value: if the royal family was in possession of the crown jewels, the kingdom still existed and the royal family still ruled. If the crown jewels were lost, there was no kingdom and the royal family lost their power. As such, the crown jewels were carefully protected in fortified castles with moats around them. If someone wanted to threaten the kingdom, they had to first go through the moats, but even then they had not conquered the kingdom until they got the crown jewels.

Carrying this analogy forward to new venture creation, the Core is something that allows you to deliver the benefits your customers value with much greater effectiveness (or maybe even exclusively) than any other competitor. It is what protects you from losing your business kingdom. It is that single thing that will make it very difficult, if not impossible, for the next company that tries to do what you do to be as successful as you. It could be a very small part of the overall solution, but without it, your competitors don't have a comparable solution.

The Core provides you protection, ensuring that you don't go through the hard work to create a new market or product category only to see someone else come in and reap the rewards from your work by copying it.

In this step, you will look to identify one thing. In reality, it might be a combination of things you have (i.e., moats) that are advantages that will slow competitors down, but ideally you should strive and be able to develop some singular key capability (i.e., Core) that your competitors don't and won't have that will allow you and your shareholders to sleep well at night knowing your kingdom will not be taken from you.

General and Specific Examples of Core

Determining your Core is a very situation-specific exercise. It requires great thought and there may be multiple options for a Core. Rather than prescribe how to determine your Core, I will give you some examples from categories that could inspire (or become) your Core.

- **Network Effect:** If this is your Core, you become the standard by achieving so much critical mass in the marketplace that it does not make sense for potential customers to use another product. The value to the user of this product falls under Metcalfe's Law, which essentially says that the value of the network to any individual on that network is exponentially related[1] to the number of users on the network. The company with the most users is the most valuable; hence it is logical for new users to choose that network. As a result, the network becomes even more powerful; it is a positive feedback loop. Examples of businesses that achieved this are eBay (for both buyers and sellers), LinkedIn, Facebook, and Google for Advertisers.

- **Deep Technical Capabilities and Assets That Are Virtually Impossible to Replicate:** This is a scenario where you are determined to accumulate and continually grow an expertise in a specific area by assembling a portfolio that could include patents, trade secrets, human capital, codebase, processes, supplier relationships, ongoing R&D, and so on that is proprietary for you and virtually impossible for others to duplicate. Honda has essentially achieved this in the area of motor capability and expertise. From weed whackers to lawn mowers, scooters, motorcycles, cars, airplanes, power tools, and robots, its products are considered extremely dependable and reliable because of Honda's deep, focused expertise in this area. It is then clear to Honda's management that they must invest in keeping their capabilities in this area at the highest levels on a continual basis, otherwise they would be subject to losing their market share. There is a risk with this strategy for a Core that if there is a dramatic technology shift, the advantage of your Core becomes neutralized. ChatGPT has done that to companies who rely on their codebase and the capability of software engineers because it seems that ChatGPT can now generate code much faster than humans in many situations.

- **Global Logistics and Supply Chain Coupled with an Unwavering Deep Investment in Purchasing Expertise and Systems Over Decades:** This is where you get your unique competitive advantage by building out some capability in the supply chain that is virtually impossible to replicate. A great example of this strategy is Walmart. While the value proposition the customer sees is "low price," what allows them to do this is a relentlessly strong and capable purchasing department that has global supply chains, processes, and management training

---

[1] Technically Metcalfe's Law is $V \sim n^2$, which means that the value of the network to any user on the network is directly related to the number of nodes on the network to the second power.

to find the low cost for any item they carry. This is reinforced by the process and systems as well as management training, incentives, culture, and expectations that have built up and been reinforced over many years.

- **Distribution Monopoly (Real or Virtual):** The previous bullet point focused on the supply chain to develop a Core, but you can also do the same on the distribution side. If you can lock up the channel and have a real or virtual monopoly on distributing your product to your target customer, this can be a Core too. A highly visible example of this is Gillette razors. They have come to dominate the shelf space in stores for high-end razors, and going back to the 1990s and early 2000s, they held a virtual monopoly on this. Things changed with Dollar Shave Club and Harry's and the direct-to-consumer revolution, which loosened Gillette's monopoly on the default distribution channel up until that point—brick-and-mortar stores— that had given them a powerful Core.

- **Proprietary Data:** At the time this book was first published, this was becoming a prevalent source of Core for new ventures—if not the most prevalent. This can be data on your customers that you accumulate such that you can provide them high value by microtargeting them with recommendations (purchasing, healthcare, educational, etc.). It could also be proprietary data that you acquire to train your machine learning system so it provides better insights. A great example of this is Spotify, where the more you use the system and tell it what you like, the better it can produce a personalized playlist that you are likely to value—and if you don't, it will figure that out and get better as it accumulates more data. Historically, competitive advantage in the 1960s to 1990s was gained most often through hardware. From the 1990s to the 2010s it was software as the hardware became commoditized. Today, software has become ubiquitous and commoditized at an increasing rate by generative AI (e.g., ChatGPT), and therefore competitive advantage will be more often in the data. So, don't overlook this area.

These are just a few examples of defining a Core. The key is that the Core be clearly defined, and your founding team aligned so that the Core is what the business will continually work to develop, and will always put first when planning and executing any strategy. The Core is your business's last defense against the competition.

Core Is Not Your Quantified Value Proposition Restated

Your value proposition is a benefit to the customer. Your Core is not a benefit. Your Core is the capability, asset or set of assets, or something else that allows you to uniquely produce your value proposition superior to anyone else.

How to Define Your Core

Of all the steps thus far, defining your Core is more inward-looking and less PMR-based than any other step. You will rely on internal introspection combined with external data gathering and analysis. While the process may seem broad and general at first, your resulting definition of your Core should be concrete and specific.

Defining your Core is not easy. It cannot stay an abstract intellectual exercise, but must integrate many different considerations, including what the customer wants, what assets you have, what you really like to do, what is the capability and assets of competitors, and what the personal and financial goals of the founders are. At the same time, defining your Core must be done efficiently (i.e., not take too long) and you must arrive at an answer that you are highly confident is accurate. You should not be changing your Core over time like other elements in the 24 Steps; it is most powerful and effective if it remains fixed over time. Once you lock in on it, you can really start to develop it. You may have to change it sometimes, but do so reluctantly, unlike the highly iterative process you are doing in the rest of the 24 Steps. If you change it, you do so at your peril, because you will often lose whatever advantages you have built. That being said, it does happen that sometimes a Core changes as you learn more about your market, your customers, and your own company assets. Google is a great example—they thought their Core was the technological excellence of their search engine algorithm, but in the end, it was their ability to embrace a new business model around keyword-based text ads in search, and to achieve network effects before anyone else.

Your Core does not have to be fully formed when you start, but you should develop a plan to strengthen your Core. For example, Honda's Core is the capability to build great motors, but they developed this Core over time, and entered markets such as the United States primarily on the strength of being a low-cost provider of weed whackers, scooters, motorcycles, lawnmowers, and cars. Eventually as they strengthened their Core, they no longer needed to be the low-cost provider to compete.

Do Not Disclose Your Core to the Public

Once you have identified your Core, there is no need to put that information up on your website or share it on social media. You are trying to develop a competitive advantage, so treat this like a trade secret. You don't want your competitors to know what it is as you are developing it until it is too late for them to catch up. This can be a little tricky because internally, you want at least your leadership team to know what it is and be aligned, but not your competitors.

What About Patents?

One common starting point when entrepreneurs try to define their Core for the first time is to say that their Core is a patent. Let's discuss this a bit now.

A patent is an insight that presumably no one has ever had before or at least brought forward. Technically, a patent is an exclusive right granted for an invention, which the World Intellectual Property Organization states is a product or a process that provides, in general, a new way of doing something, or offers a new technical solution to a problem. However, to get a patent, you must fully document and disclose all the technical information about the invention to the public in a patent application. And if the patent is approved, you will get protection for only 20 years to block others from implementing that idea.

While patents can be a great source of value to a company, it is important to know their limitations. By fully disclosing all the details of your idea, that is a recipe for others to duplicate it, or to use it as a guideline for how to implement the underlying idea while not violating your specific patent. The mystery is gone. Secondly, the onus is on you to enforce your patent, which can be very costly and take lots of time with no guarantee of success in the end. You will spend your time hiring lawyers to litigate and stop competitors, instead of spending time making your company's fundamentals stronger, and you may ultimately fail due to subtleties that arise in the process of litigating the patent protection. Finally, this protection lasts for only 20 years from the filing date, so its value decreases over time as the end date gets closer. Something that decreases in value over time, instead of increasing in value, does not fit the definition of a Core.

Patents can be a valuable asset to your company, as a moat around the castle, but they are not a Core. It is important to realize there has never been a great company created solely because they won in the patent office. Great companies are created in the marketplace.

The value of patents depends heavily on your industry. In the medical industry, especially the biotech industry, patents are incredibly important in ensuring the success of a product or a new company. In other industries, there may be some value, but often patents are insufficient for ensuring business success. They tend to be static and markets are dynamic. Developing your company's capabilities is generally better than a patent—but it is best to have both for sure. For instance, teams with high levels of capability in an area will continually produce innovative goods, over time overwhelming a company that is built around one or a small number of patents (except in such specific cases as biotech).

What About Culture?

Some companies find an advantage in the marketplace by creating a process and culture that innovates incredibly fast. They stay close to the customer and then use strong product management and agile development to translate their initial head start into a sustained and growing advantage as time goes on. But is this really a Core? The answer is almost surely no.

This strategy is difficult to sustain, as hard as you try (and you should try!), as your organization gets bigger and smaller companies enter the market and begin competing with you. Those new, smaller companies will likely have advantages that allow them to be nimble as well, perhaps surpassing your pace of innovation once your business is large. Most companies wisely do not rely solely on their speed of innovation as their Core, but rather use it as a motivator and a moat around the castle before they finally settle on a Core. To put it simply, all businesses should aim to innovate quickly, regardless of their definition of Core, but few businesses will find lasting success in rapid innovation without something else as a Core.

Core Is Different Than Competitive Position

Your customers will not see your Core as the reason they buy from you. They will instead look at your Competitive Position, which you will map in Step 11. Your Core will drive your ability to deliver certain benefits to the customer, which has to translate into value for the customer (based on the customer's top priorities), which then leads to a better Competitive Position. The Core is how you are building a capability to differentiate yourself from your competitors, and it cannot be easily replicated by others. It is the most concentrated way to gain differentiation from your current and potential competitors so you can really focus your limited resources to gain maximum value for your new venture.

First-Mover Advantage Is Not a Core Unless . . .

One of the most overused and incorrect terms used when defining a Core is "first-mover advantage." The term refers to a company being successful solely by being the first in the market. However, most companies that are first to market end up losing the market to a later entrant that outperforms the first company (so-called "fast followers," see Facebook, Google, every product ever made by Apple), so first-mover advantage by itself cannot translate into a sustainable Core and could be seen as a disadvantage. First-mover advantage can help a company with a well-defined Core, but it cannot win the market simply by being first; this must be translated into something else like locking in key customers or suppliers or distributors, achieving positive networking effects for your company, proprietary data, recruiting the best talent in a certain area, and so on.

Locking Up Suppliers Is Typically a Moat, Not a Core

One way to gain a competitive advantage is to anticipate the key elements of your solution and lock in vendors on an exclusive or a functionally exclusive arrangement. You can generally request exclusivity in return for meeting agreed-upon milestones and minimum order quantities, especially if the supplier sells its product to a much different market than yours, or if you are buying large volumes from a relatively small supplier. Apple has employed this strategy effectively, using it to maintain high profit margins that give the company lots of resources and flexibility, but its Core is actually different.

Like intellectual property, unless you can do something extraordinary in the supply chain like Walmart has done, locking up key suppliers is probably a good moat strategy to slow down your potential competitors while developing a more robust Core. It should be aggressively used when appropriate and buy you time to find a Core, but it is not your ultimate Core. The Core is the crown jewel, the fundamental barrier to market entry that competitors should not be able to break through.

EXAMPLES

Bloom Continued

Bloom is a good example where they did not have technical expertise, a patent, or any initial advantages on the supply or distribution side. They essentially had to build a plan to develop a Core from thin air. But they were not deterred. That being said, this is very difficult. You can see in Figures 10.1 and 10.2 the first draft of their Core.

Competitive Advantage: Assets & Moats

We Value Inclusion, Diversity & Collaboration

Assets	Moats
Strong ... **Weak**	**Strong** ... **Weak**
1. **Diverse Team**: Our team comes from differing backgrounds of Finance, Consulting and Tech and has expertise spanning a wide range of industries and functional work	1. **Unique Algorithm Inputs:** Our algorithm includes unique inputs including availability to meet and sense of humor to match women with greater success
2. **MVP**: Easy to build via no-code and/or test via Facebook groups. Ease of integration with Resy, EventBrite through open APIs	2. **Free for Users:** We reduce the barrier to entry for many women by offering the application for free. Instead, monetization through advertising and partnerships. This will create stronger network effects as more women enter the Bloom platform ecosystem
3. **Family Support & Learnings**: Entrepreneurial family backgrounds	3. **Design / Artistic Background:** All founding members have artistic backgrounds that they have used to build out the design as well as UI/UX of the Bloom application
4. **Research Backed**: Strong data on psychological impact of friendships on women **"2nd Mover"**: Ability to learn from the successes and failures of similar products	4. **Network Effects:** All founding members have strong undergraduate and graduate networks of students and young professionals to leverage upon launching the app to gain critical mass
5. **Technical Talent**: Ability to leverage the MIT network for technical expertise	

Figure 10.1: Identifying and prioritizing Bloom's assets.

Our Strong Core

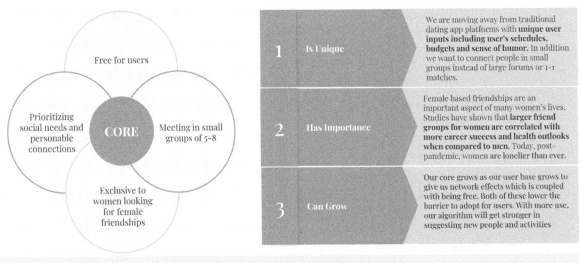

1	**Is Unique**	We are moving away from traditional dating app platforms with **unique user inputs including user's schedules, budgets and sense of humor.** In addition we want to connect people in small groups instead of large forums or 1-1 matches.
2	**Has Importance**	Female based friendships are an important aspect of many women's lives. Studies have shown that **larger friend groups for women are correlated with more career success and health outlooks when compared to men.** Today, post-pandemic, women are lonelier than ever.
3	**Can Grow**	Our core grows as our user base grows to give us network effects which is coupled with being free. Both of these lower the barrier to adopt for users. With more use, our algorithm will get stronger in suggesting new people and activities

Value Proposition: A convenient and easy way to help women enhance their social lives through new female friendships

Figure 10.2: Bloom first-draft plan for a Core.

First, they started by identifying all their valuable assets in a list and then prioritizing them from strongest to weakest. This is the first step in trying to crack the riddle of what your Core can and should be. The team then translated those assets and moats into a first-draft Core. This proposal for a Core is not compelling. They have rightly identified the value proposition but they need something unique to give them an unfair advantage in delivering this. "Meeting in small groups of 5–8," "exclusive to women looking for female companionship," "prioritizing social need and personable connections," and making it "free for users" are good ideas to make a unique value proposition, but if they work, they can be quickly adopted by a competitor. As you can see, this is not easy!

As the team refined its plan beyond a first draft, the Core evolved into one related to network effects supported by proprietary data. Their plan was to get a jump start on this market and achieve popularity via the innovative initial design followed up with strong customer support that would give them high customer satisfaction and positive word of mouth. Once this got started, they would ensure that systems were in place to capture user data in strategic ways to generate value to the users. They would collect this data with careful and strict safeguards on protecting the privacy of their users, so they could then obtain large amounts of proprietary data that would allow them to make matches for women that no one else could.

SensAble Technologies

When we thought about what the Core for SensAble would be, it seemed obvious to some. We had a unique hardware robotic device called the PHANToM, a device that was renowned for its clever design. In addition, we had an extremely fundamental patent for "force reflecting haptic interface" (U.S. patent #5,625,576), which was one of the most referenced patents of all time.[2] We also had Thomas Massie, the driving intellect behind the technology, and a rising engineering star at MIT, fully invested in the company. Surely that was the Core, right?

However, when we stepped back and thought about our priorities as founders, we realized that we were looking to achieve a high level of success in a relatively short period of time. Co-founders Thomas and Rhonda Massie wanted to return to Kentucky in four to five years, and I wanted to do something big that could scale quickly and be of interest to venture capitalists, which would be a five-year timetable.

If our focus were intellectual property, we would become dependent on others, with an unpredictable time frame, and would need to become legal experts to ensure others did not ignore or circumvent our patents (i.e., patent trolls), which was not interesting to us and not aligned with our personal goals and passions. This was not an attractive scenario for us, and so while we aggressively pursued building our intellectual property portfolio with our IP lawyer Steve Bauer and MIT, it was one of the outside moats of our castle, not the crown jewels (Core) that we would protect in the centermost part of the castle.

If our focus were hardware, it would take a lot of time and money to achieve success, and hardware companies were not as attractive to investors as software companies. Robotics in particular was extremely out of favor during the mid-1990s. After some thinking, it became clear we should not be a robotics company at all. In fact, aligned with this thinking, our beachhead market was not about robotics, but about design. So as with intellectual property, we aggressively protected and developed our PHANToM hardware with a patent through MIT, even though we knew it was a moat and not the Core.

We had been able to lock up the supply of a key component (the high-fidelity motors) that made our hardware far superior to what other companies were offering, presenting a substantial barrier

---

[2] Gregory T. Huang, "From MIT Entrepreneur to Tea Party Leader: The Thomas Massie Story," Xconomy, May 17, 2012, www .xconomy.com/boston/2012/05/17/from-mit-entrepreneur-to-tea-party-leader-the-thomas-massie-story/2.

to entry. But if market conditions had been right, our competitors would have found a way to produce the key component themselves. We instead defined our Core as revolving around software, which was more scalable and would be more valuable. In talking with Thomas, we realized the software behind the PHANToM was very complicated (the hand is truly faster than the eye—we had to achieve update rates of 1,000 frames per second to simulate touch, as opposed to the 20–30 frames per second that displays visual images on televisions and movie screens). It was not just the interface software but also how we represented weight, shapes, texture, deformations, and many other physical properties of the objects we rendered for touching in the computer and then how they interacted with them. We ended up defining our Core as "the physics of three-dimensional touch." This Core was to be embodied in a software engine that rendered 3D objects on the computer, not for visual representations but for touching them.

With a formalized definition of our Core, we needed to translate it into a sustainable advantage that would grow over time. So, we quickly identified the key people on our team who had the skills to support the Core. We then identified the people outside the company who were leaders in this field and moved quickly to build strong relationships with them and lock them in with us. We also identified the organizations and institutions where these people would be found (specific departments at MIT, the late Randy Pausch's group at Carnegie Mellon, the late Fred Brooks's group at the University of North Carolina at Chapel Hill, Andries Van Dam's group at Brown University, and multiple groups at Stanford University[3]) and developed our visibility, reputation, and relationships there to recruit the best and the brightest future stars. This became a top priority of Thomas Massie as the CTO and he reviewed it at least quarterly in his technical strategy discussions. We made sure to have a strong skills development plan in this area and our incentive system reflected this as a priority with strong compensation and large stock option grants. And, oh yes, they got the most powerful and expensive computers of anyone in the company to develop their code.

In this way, we determined a Core that would protect us and give us a huge competitive advantage as we successfully developed the market. It was certainly not obvious in the beginning, and the obvious answer would have been a far less optimal Core, so the extra attention paid to determining a Core was well worth the effort in the end. It paid dividends many times over going forward. While others violated our patent and reverse-engineered the hardware or brought to market alternatives, no one ever broke the code for our software physic operating system engine, GHOST.

---

[3] We knew all of these groups very well because to work on this problem, they needed to have a PHANToM and they all had questions about how it worked that they needed answered to develop their software.

ADDITIONAL RESOURCES

There are additional resources for this step at www.d-eship.com/step10. These materials include:

- Video: Define Your Core by Bill Aulet and Erdin Beshimov
- Video: Example described and explained in an interview with ThriveHive founders Max Faingezicht and Adam Blake
- Process Guidance
- Worksheet 10.1: Guide to Systematically Defining Your Core

Additional resources will be added as new and updated examples and information become available.

Summary

Defining the Core is the first step where you spend a lot of time looking internally, in contrast to the strong customer focus of many of the other steps. The decision on the Core can take a while and may seem a bit frustrating as you want to move ahead and continue to make progress.

But you must understand that making sales without a Core is not sustainable if you want to be a high-growth company, because your success will only draw attention to the opportunity you have identified, and then competitors will rush in. At that point, your wonderful new venture will turn out to have been built on a foundation of sand and it will come sliding down when the first big wave hits it.

So even if you aren't sure what is the best selection for Core, pick a few candidates for the Core and realize you have to make a decision soon. Some of your potential Cores may end up as strong moats, but the most important thing is that you are thinking ahead and protecting yourself, and it is also highly relevant as you proceed to Step 11, Chart Your Competitive Position.

STEP 11

Chart Your Competitive Position

In This Step, You Will:

- Show visually how well your product meets the Persona's top two priorities, as compared to existing products, and is therefore better positioned for success with your target customer.
- Analyze whether the market opportunity you have chosen fits well with both your Core and your Persona's priorities.

The Competitive Position is where you take your Core and make sure it translates into real and unique value for the customer.

Why This Step, and Why Now?

Customers don't really care about your Core. What they care about are the unique benefits you will provide to them in the areas they are most concerned about. Now that you have identified your Core in Step 10, you need to make sure that the benefit you provide to the customer is compelling. This keeps you focused on what is important, and also gives you and others a clear sense of how you compare to the customer's alternatives.

Let's Get Started

A common question you will get is "How does your product compare to your competitors'?" The wrong answer is a technical description of your product and the features it possesses. The right answer is how it helps your customer make more money, or save more lives, or reduce their carbon footprint, or sleep better at night, or have a faster time to market, or increase reliability . . . and how you do this better than any other alternative. This focus on the customer realizing benefits from your product will be far more compelling to a customer than any list of features.

It is important that when you are looking to create a new market, you build from the customer back with a clean slate, rather than picking an existing product and making a better version of it. In their book, *Blue Ocean Strategy*, W. Chan Kim and Renée Mauborgne provide a framework to help in this regard. They describe how if you focus on an underserved customer and make a product for that customer that truly meets that customer's need, there is no need to focus on the competition because your unwavering focus makes the competition irrelevant. While I applaud this mindset, it is not completely true because the reality is that you will get questions about competition.

Most customers usually make purchasing decisions on a comparative basis, considering all options and determining which solution best fits their priorities. The chart you will produce in this step shows how much better you are than your competition; it can also highlight areas of weakness. Taken together with the Quantified Value Proposition from Step 8, it shows the superiority of your product for their situation.

While there is some flexibility with your Core, it is usually limited. Inability to translate your Core into benefits for your customer does not necessarily mean your Core is wrong, because the Core is a reflection of your team's assets and capabilities; instead, there may be a better market opportunity where your Core is more suited. The Competitive Position is the link between your Core and your Persona's priorities, and shows that there is alignment between your Core and your target market.

NO FAN OF FEATURE WARS

The most common way I see first-time entrepreneurs represent their product versus competition is by a matrix of what features they have as compared to the alternatives. It looks something like Figure 11.1.

Competitive Comparison

Description of Feature/Technology	Our Company	Competitor #1	Competitor #2	Competitor #3
Feature A – Block Chain	✓	✗	✓	✗
Feature B – Generative AI	✓	✗	✗	✗
Feature C – Robotics	✓	✗	✗	✓
Feature D	✓	✓	✓	✗
Feature E	✓	✗	✗	✓
Feature F	✓	✓	✓	✗

Figure 11.1: Avoid the feature war matrices; focus on benefits, not features.

Don't do this! This gets you into the wrong mindset and just leads you deeper and deeper into the quagmire of feature wars. "The more features I have, the better!" is a wildly unproductive mindset and most often leads to failure. You get into feature creep and a technology mindset starts to take over, as compared to a customer-oriented one. Fewer features is often much better, especially if they are ones that are smartly designed and thoughtfully integrated in a way to fit the customer's workflow. Customers want benefits, not features.

This reminds me of a memorable interview I heard with then-CEO Steve Walske of Parametric Technologies (PTC), a very successful CAD/CAM (Computer-Aided Design/ Computer-Aided Manufacturing) company. PTC had extremely sophisticated technology but had distinguished itself in the market by making that technology accessible to customers in a way that made them one of the most successful software companies of their time.

The interviewer kept asking questions about the technology and Steve answered them patiently, but after repeated questions about it, he stopped and reset the conversation. He said that he was happy to talk about the technology, but he wanted all those listening to understand it only mattered if it helped their customers' businesses be more successful. He said, "I want everyone to leave this conversation knowing that we are really a very simple business. Our customers give us $2 and then they make $10 or more as a result. The technology supports this and that is the only reason we develop and sell the sophisticated technology we do."

The Toughest Competitor of All: The Customer's Status Quo

Often, your largest obstacle will be convincing customers to make a change from their status quo. This is the "do nothing" option. People and organizations have an enormous amount of inertia when it comes to change. They already have habits and breaking them is very hard.

Your Quantified Value Proposition (Step 8) should have picked up any problems with your product versus your Persona's top priority, but comparing your product to the status quo here ensures that you have a valid real market and not a conceptual, fictitious one. Don't assume your customers will change. You have to give them a compelling reason to do so.

Related to this is another often made mistake. Often when my students come up with an idea only to find another company doing something similar, they fear they are too late. Then their competitive mindset kicks in and they believe they can and must crush the other small startup company. They invest a lot of energy in beating what they believe to be their direct competitor, rather than delivering a product that meets the customer's needs. Yet they and the perceived competition combined have an infinitesimally small market share. The much bigger share of the TAM comes from getting people to change what they are doing today, overcoming natural human and organizational inertia. It is far better to address the untapped market of "customer doing nothing" than focusing on some other brand-new startup.

In the end, if you have a good Core and people convert from the status quo to a new solution, the market will take off and both you and the other small competitor will win big. In such an outcome, it is likely that the two of you will merge, both get bought by bigger firms, or both go public. The beauty of having a strong plan for a Core is that you can focus even more on the customer. Once you have your Core and Competitive Position, don't focus too much precious time on competitors; rather, spend most of it working with customers, developing your Core, and getting products out the door.

How to Chart Your Competitive Position

As with the other steps, this is a pretty simple logical step—the key is getting the right information from your PMR.

Charting your Competitive Position starts by identifying the top two priorities of your Persona. That is a simplification that has tradeoffs but making things simple and being able to communicate them effectively usually offsets the value of nuances. Keep it simple is your best strategy here.

Your Core is probably inspirational and thoughtful, and your product's features are great, but they do not dictate the customer's priorities. Stay locked in on your customer.

For this step, you will also need to deeply understand your competition, including the customer's do nothing/status quo option. This calls for significant in-depth PMR where you don't just analyze the alternatives online, but you actually go and immerse yourself in the alternatives the customer has available. It is important when evaluating competitive options to follow them through their full life cycle. Read reviews. Go to customer meetups. If your product is tech-based, remember to fully evaluate the less tech-based options as well.

Once you have all this information, create a simple matrix/graph as follows:

1. Divide both the x-axis and y-axis into two halves.

2. On the x-axis, write the number-one priority of your Persona.

3. On the half of the x-axis closer to the origin, write the "bad state" of this priority (e.g., if the priority is "reliability" then write "low" here).

4. On the other half of the x-axis, write the "good" state of this priority (e.g., "high" for "reliability").

5. On the y-axis, place the number-two priority of your Persona. Write the "bad state" on the half of the y-axis closer to the origin, and the "good state" on the other half of the y-axis.

6. Plot your business on the graph, along with those of your competitors (current and future). Also include the customer's "do nothing" or "status quo" option.

Figure 11.2 shows this in colorful illustration where the Core is represented by a troll preventing others from getting to the upper right corner. The chart in Figure 11.3 is more systematic and shows the results of this process. It lists the Persona's status quo, as well as other companies whose products potentially address one or both of the Persona's top two priorities.

Figure 11.2: The Competitive Position shows your customer how you are different than the other options and why your team will be a long-term success.

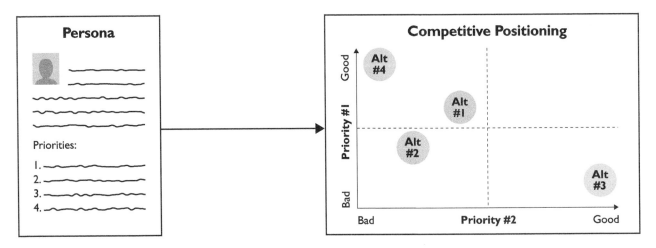

Figure 11.3: Competitive Positioning chart (assume on this chart that "Alt #1" is the customer's status quo).

If you have done good PMR, your business should be positioned in the top-right quadrant of this graph, at the high end of the "good" states of each priority. The bottom-left quadrant is where you absolutely do not want to be. Other locations on the chart are not necessarily bad but not as good as the upper right. If you find yourself somewhere other than the top-right of the chart, you should reevaluate your product compared to your competition.

Next, review this chart with your target customers for feedback; refine it as needed until the chart accurately describes your product and the competition relative to the Persona's top two priorities.

EXAMPLES

Bloom Continued

Bloom started with deep PMR to understand the alternatives that women have to make connections and friendships. The team actually spent a good deal of time using the current alternative products (e.g., Bumble, Facebook groups, and Hey! VINA) to fully understand the benefits their competition provides users. What is also interesting is that the team did not just focus on tech products as competitors, but also looked at old-fashioned non-tech organizations like the Junior League and went to those organizations' meetings to understand the benefits and drawbacks of these options firsthand. Figure 11.4 shows Bloom's Competitive Positioning chart.

Charting Our Competitive Positioning

Competitive Positioning

- The two most commonly used applications today are Bumble BFF and Facebook Groups. However, both have clear weaknesses.
- BumbleBFF has barriers to adoption that include pricing as well as association with the dating world. Premium costs $20 per month
- Facebook Groups are free but ineffective due to the overwhelming sizes of the groups and manual effort required due to lack of matching of women
- The Junior League and The Wing are both exclusive organizations that require application and certain standards of admission. JL membership ranges from $300–$700 per year excluding event tickets. The Wing costs $185 per month
- Hey! Vina matches women 1:1 through algorithmic matching, but at $6 a week is not a realistic option for many women

Figure 11.4: Bloom's Competitive Position.

SensAble Technologies

For SensAble, there were some who believed our Competitive Position was based on the PHANToM hardware device or, more generally, the ability to feel things that were seen on the computer screen. These, however, were the features of the product that technical people were interested in; it was not the reason our target customer would buy our product, FreeForm. Our PMR with our Persona made clear that their first priority was speed to market; second was ability to convey design intent.

The designers wanted a solution that had the ease of use and ability to convey design intent like clay, but had the benefits of flexibility and communications of a digital asset like the digital CAD/CAM software tools. The CAD/CAM tools that management was pushing were not being successfully adopted by the designers. We were able to take advantage of this because those tools were not built with the priorities of the designers in mind. The CAD/CAM and Alias/Wavefront CAID (Computer-Aided Industrial Design software) tools had impressive underlying technology, but they limited what could be done and were very nonintuitive for the designer. Despite impressive theoretical arguments, as I will talk more about later in Step 23, Show That "The Dogs Will Eat the Dog Food," we could see the "dogs were not eating the dog food."

The chart in Figure 11.5 visually and succinctly captures the difference between the status quo of clay as well as the competitive offerings from CAD/CAM and CAID companies as compared to our product. It also was only possible because of our Core. Because of this, we could make a compelling case to the customer as well as our stakeholders that no one else could legitimately make the claim that they could address the customer's priorities as well as SensAble's FreeForm product.

In summary, we were the only ones who had the benefits of a physical interface to make it possible for designers to accurately capture design intent with the benefits of having a digital asset to dramatically decrease time to market. It was a clear and winning formula.

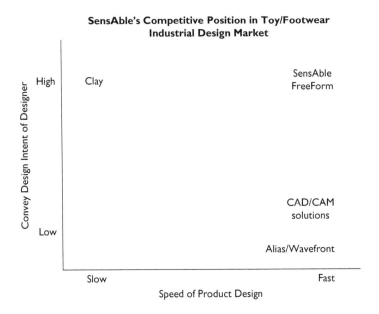

Figure 11.5: SensAble's Competitive Position.

SunSpring

This team of MIT and Harvard students from my Energy Ventures course had access to a unique technology that used solar energy to filter water. They had identified a Beachhead Market of filtering drinking water for military teams stationed in places that were off the grid or lacked access to reliable electricity.

In this case, cost was not a top priority for the military. Rather, the key elements were reliability and efficiency because teams needed to carry the product on remote missions where there were no opportunities for repair or for procuring additional sources of water. Any product fulfilling the military's priorities had to work all the time, and had to deliver as much filtered water as possible. These priorities fit well with the team's Core, which was its technological capability, but their Competitive Position is expressed by how the product met the customer's needs (Figure 11.6).

- SunSpring's value proposition is increased efficiency, flexibility, mobility, reliability, and operation simplicity vis-à-vis its competitors

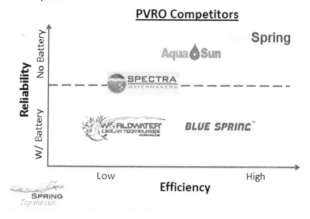

Figure 11.6: SunSpring's Competitive Position.

ADDITIONAL RESOURCES

There are additional resources for this step at www.d-eship.com/step11. These materials include:

- Video: Charting Your Competitive Position Explainers by Bill Aulet and Erdin Beshimov
- Video: Example described and explained in an interview with Demeter founder Vimala Palaniswamy
- Process Guidance
- Worksheet 11.1: Defining Your Competitive Positioning

Additional resources will be added as new and updated examples and information become available.

Summary

Defining your Competitive Position is a quick way to validate your product against your competition, including the customer's status quo, based on the top two priorities of the Persona. If you are not in the top right of the resulting chart, you should reevaluate your product. This will also be a very effective vehicle to communicate your qualitative (not quantitative) value proposition to the target customer audience. This keeps you focused on what is most important, creating value for your customer.

Determine the Customer's Decision-Making Unit (DMU)

In This Step, You Will:

- Build a fundamental and systematic understanding of who makes the decision to acquire your product—including influencers.

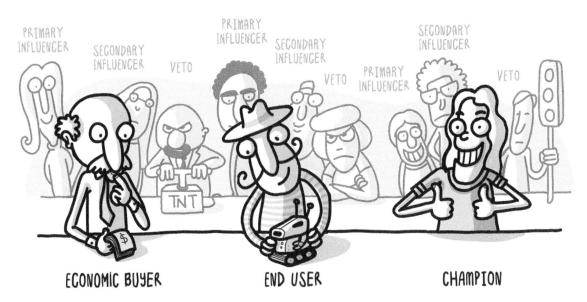

ECONOMIC BUYER   END USER   CHAMPION

Your target customer comprises three elements. They may be all in one person but more often it is more than one person. Understanding this situation is crucial.

Why This Step, and Why Now?

You are now getting confident that you can uniquely create value for our target customer. The question now is, can you get paid for this? This step starts that analysis. You begin with getting the foundational knowledge about the acquisition process. In later steps, you build on this to determine if you can make enough money to have a sustainable business (Steps 15–19).

Let's Get Started

At this point, you should have a good idea of who your target end user customer is and how you can uniquely create value for them. That being said, there will be no value created unless the customer acquires the product and uses it. As such, you turn your attention to the sales or customer acquisition process. Rarely is the sales process simple. In fact, it might be the most complicated part of the whole process discussed in this book.

When almost any product of significance is acquired and adopted for use, whether in a B2B or even in a lot of B2C businesses, multiple people will have to be convinced that your product is worth purchasing.

Your target customer is composed of three elements. They may be all in one person but more often it is more than one person. Understanding this situation and explicitly mapping it out carefully, with the role, interests, and influencers of each, is critical. It is not just important for the sale, but also much earlier in the process when you are developing the product and all of its attributes.

But for now, let us focus on the aspect of how to sell your product successfully and efficiently. To do so, you will need to identify all the people who will be involved in the decision to acquire the product—the Decision-Making Unit (DMU). Some people will actively approve or block the acquisition, while others will be more passive.

This process, or some variant of it, has been presented in sales training programs for decades. I will use a simple common language to describe this process and integrate it into the 24 Steps. This process works for both B2B cases and B2C cases, though B2C cases often involve fewer people.

Primary Roles in the DMU

There are three primary roles in the DMU:

- **Champion:** The champion is the person who advocates or pushes hard from within the trusted circle of the customer to purchase the product. This may or may not be the end user or economic buyer. The champion is the "straw that stirs the drink." The champion may also be referred to as the "advocate."

- **End User:** This is the person who will actually use the product to create the value that is described in Step 8, Quantify the Value Proposition.

- **Primary Economic Buyer:** This is who will pay you as a result of the end user using the product. This person controls the budget. Sometimes, the primary economic buyer is also the champion and/or the end user—especially in B2C situations. There may be multiple economic buyers as well.

Additional Roles in the DMU

There are three additional roles within the DMU:

- **Primary and Secondary Influencers:** These individuals often have a depth of experience in the subject matter, and can influence someone in the DMU, including the champion and end user. Typically, influencers can be sorted into primary (plays a major role in the decision-making process) and secondary players (plays some part in the decision-making process but less than the primary). Sometimes the influencer is trusted enough that their word acts as a de facto veto. Other influencers in the decision-making process may include industry groups, media publications, individual journalists, outside contractors, friends and family, websites, blogs, social media, and anyone else who people in the DMU turn to for information and feedback.

- **Person with Veto Power:** These individuals have the ability to stop a purchase.

  - In a consumer market, an individual rarely has veto power; rather, the primary influencer(s) may have the authority or be well-respected enough to exert a de facto veto. One example of true veto power in a consumer situation would be a homeowner's association or town zoning law that requires your customer to obtain a special variance from the association or town before being able to install or use your product. In that case, the association or town would be part of the DMU. In a corporation, the IT department often has veto power over acquisition of computer hardware and software if it does not comply with corporate standards.

  - Unions and collective bargaining agreements may also block a purchase because of certain provisions that essentially have become regulations.

- Corporate standards are another area of veto power.
- **Purchasing Department:** This department handles the logistics of the purchase. They can be another obstacle, as this department primarily looks to drive prices down, even after the decision to purchase has been made by the primary economic buyer. They can try to disqualify you based on certain purchasing rules. In general, you should neutralize but not sell to, and the less time spent doing this, the better.

Understanding the DMU of your customer is integral in determining how you will position and sell your product. It will give you great insight into what your odds of success are and, importantly, how much resource, skill, and time it will take for a new customer to acquire your product.

How to Determine the DMU

Once again, doing primary market research, operating in "inquiry" mode rather than "advocacy/sales" mode, is how you get helpful information about the DMU. If the customer truly believes that your product uniquely provides a strong value proposition, the conversation will flow naturally. They should want to help you at this point!

This is an excellent time to ask the end user, "Assuming we could produce the product we have described, what would need to be done to bring a product in to pilot it? Who besides you (make sure you make them feel good!) would be involved in the decision to bring our product in? Who will have the most influence? Who could stop this from happening? Assuming the product does what we believe it will do, whose budget will the money come from to pay for it? Does this person need anyone else to sign off on this budget? What levels can they sign off on without getting further approval? Who will feel threatened by this and how do you think they will react?" Those are a lot of questions and you don't ask them all at once, but getting this information will help you start to understand the DMU. In a B2B setting, make sure to ask a number of different end users in the organization, since one end user may not have all the information you are looking for.

If the champion or primary economic buyer is not the same as your End User Persona you will want to build a Persona fact sheet for the individuals in each role. You will have to think about how you will appeal to them, so you get a "yes" or at least a "neutral" response. In the case of your champion, a neutral response is not enough. They have to be significantly and positively activated. They are your engine to get this moving.

Once you have gathered this information, plot it out visually so the information is unambiguous. You can then show this map to your Persona and Next 10 Customers to get feedback quickly, helping you revise the map until it accurately reflects the DMU for your first set of customers. The DMU for each customer should be similar, and you should see patterns start to emerge. If you do not, either your customers do not match the Persona or you have not segmented the market enough.

EXAMPLES

Bloom Continued (B2B2C Example)

With Bloom, the team has a choice of who will be the champion and primary economic buyer, which will make a big difference in how they approach their go-to-market plan in later steps. As you probably recall from Step 5, Profile the Persona for the Beachhead Market, Katie L. was their End User Persona (Figure 12.1). You might well assume that Katie L. would also be the primary economic buyer, and either she or one of her friends would be the champion. That is a viable strategy.

What Bloom did was have Katie L. be the primary economic buyer and focus on getting a champion who would give the team exposure to many end users. With this strategy, they would very likely be able to have a lower cost of customer acquisition (CoCA—Step 19, Calculate the Cost of Customer Acquisition) with regard to the end users.

Bloom proposed selling B2B to human resources (HR) directors who would view Bloom as a benefit they could offer to their female employees. Attracting and retaining female employees is a priority for them. Bloom will help their employee retention goals.

While you could try to make the employer the primary economic buyer as well, it gets a little complicated because HR cannot pay directly for this benefit, as it is only available to a subsegment of their employees (i.e., only to women). One approach is to have the end user purchase the product, and the company could reimburse them as part of a larger wellness program, similar to reimbursing a gym membership. The company may in fact become the ultimate economic buyer but it will initially have to flow through the end user's bank account.

To make this work, Bloom would need a dual champion structure because while the HR director will advocate for it, Bloom's offering also needs to be approved by a benefits provider, such as a health insurance company, to get listed as a benefit to the employees. The benefits provider would be considered a champion in this case. Bloom found that at least one benefits provider has identified "loneliness" as a health problem affecting their costs and the value they provide to their customer, which is the employer. As such, the provider and the HR director could become a powerful champion team. Over time, the benefits provider could even become the primary economic buyer. If the end user no longer has to pay for the product upfront, that would accelerate adoption of Bloom's product by the end user.

This example demonstrates how there can be nuanced decisions to make with regard to the DMU that can dramatically affect other elements of the 24 Steps, resulting in increased odds of success, impact, revenues, and profits.

Decision-Making Unit

End User/Economic Buyer: Katie	Champion A: HR Director at Katie's Employer	Champion B: VP Partnerships at Named Insurance Company
Key Demographics - 23 year old Caucasian Female, Single - Philadelphia, PA - Marketing, $60k / Remote Work **Key Psychographics:** - Just moved to Philly, doesn't know anyone - Bubbly/outgoing - Like to try new restaurants/bars - Wine nights during the week and tequila during the weekend	**Key Demographics** - 40 year old Caucasian Female - HR /Onboarding job - Salary $120K **Key Psychographics:** - People Pleaser; pandemic isolation has made job harder - Travels to recruit diverse candidates, focused on recruiting more women to work at Citadel in Philly	**Key Demographics** - 45 year old Latino Male - 2 children; lives in CT - Salary: $300k **Key Psychographics:** - Focused on health and wellness trends / solutions for Cigna offerings - Eager to find digital resources for Cigna clients to improve the "loneliness epidemic"
Watering Holes: Happy Hour @ Mission Taqueria, CorePower Yoga Class, Facebook Group "20's in Philly" **Priorities:** Meeting new people, feeling less lonely, health/wellness, saving 10% of income	**Watering Holes:** Women's networking conferences, College career fairs, LinkedIn **Priorities:** Recruiting more women, maintaining health/wellness of new employees	**Watering Holes:** Health Care Professional Conferences, LinkedIn Groups, Client Offices **Priorities:** Meeting company goal on improving loneliness, finding new mental health partnerships
Influencers: Instagram/TikTok influencers, mental health experts on social media, college friends in other cities	**Influencers:** HR professionals at competitive firms, Cigna coworkers, Female Citadel employees	**Influencers:** Competitive insurance firms (Aetna), his wife, Cigna mental health experts

Figure 12.1: Bloom DMU first draft.

Mechanical Water Filtration Systems (B2B Example)

Previously you looked at the Mechanical Water Filtration Systems venture (Step 5, Profile the Persona for the Beachhead Market), which chose to focus on producing a water purification solution for data centers and ended up with the End User Persona of Chuck Karroll.

While determining the DMU for their Persona, and validating that DMU with their Next 10 Customers, the team behind Mechanical Water Filtration confirmed that Chuck was the end user, but there were a number of other key players to consider.

Determining secondary influencers of the end user was straightforward; this group included the Hamilton and Manos blog, the AFCOM meetings Chuck attended, and the occasional Uptime Institute events that he was involved with (including their newsletter). The DMU within the company, however, turned out to be rather complex.

First, the team explored the relationship between the facilities manager, the data center manager, and the chief information officer (CIO), both for the Persona's company and the Next 10 Customers. The team found out that the typical data center manager was a much different profile than the facilities manager. The data center manager was typically a man or a woman who had a four-year college degree and was likely pursuing or already had a graduate degree. They were much more ambitious than Chuck, usually staying in their job for three to four years before getting promoted, which was much shorter than Chuck's typical facilities manager colleagues, who stayed in their jobs 10 or more years. The data center manager was dependent on the facilities manager because they did not want the data center to go down, which would impact their own career progression, but they also had many other things to focus on. They were much more financially savvy than the facilities manager and, as such, handled the budget, and they were the primary economic buyer.

The CIO of the organization was involved in a tangential way. The CIO would never drive the decision, but if a purchase ran counter to his goals or he saw the purchase as risky, he would veto it. He would ask questions to test the proposal but had little influence. He was also very unlikely to block a decision jointly supported by the facilities manager and the data center manager.

The challenge now was that while the end user and primary economic buyer were now understood, the team also learned that neither person on their own would push for the acquisition of this system; they were both risk averse. The team was missing a champion.

After more work, the team determined that a newly installed VP of Sustainability (or some such title) was their best bet to advocate for their solution from the inside. They developed a demographic and psychographic profile for this person: most often female, graduate degree in environmental management or some related field, much more liberal than the facilities manager. She was also very politically savvy, most often reporting in to the CEO and getting lots of face time with the CEO to help prepare the annual or quarterly ESG (environmental, social, and governance) report to the board of directors. She had gone through a rigorous interview process to be hired directly into the executive team, and had not been in her job too long but presented very well in meetings.

Understanding this DMU breakdown really helped the team dramatically. They would start with their champion and make sure she was on board with the positive ESG impacts that their solution could have (i.e., reduction of tons of CO_2 put into the environment due to reduced electrical consumption, plus reusing water instead of outputting dirtier water into the community) while also increasing reliability (not that much, but enough to address the objection that would come from the facilities manager), all while reducing costs (e.g., decrease electric expenses). This was a relatively easy sell to her but she had to be well-prepared. The team's job was to give the champion the evidence that she needed to fight the battle internally for them.

While this worked well to activate the process and the champion had sufficient gravitas in the organization to advocate for the company (in large part because she reported to and had the ear of the CEO), there was still friction in the process with the facilities manager. To win over the facilities manager, the company had to work with the internal corporate engineering group, which had a long and trusted relationship with the facilities manager and advised him on the latest technology trends in the industry. This internal corporate engineering group was often heavily influenced by external engineering firms that specialized in building and upgrading data centers.

Other players you see on the map in Figure 12.2 had to be kept in mind as well, despite not being primary players in the process. The mechanical contractor did not have a lot of influence, but the team was wise to touch base with him to make sure that he did not propose replacing their

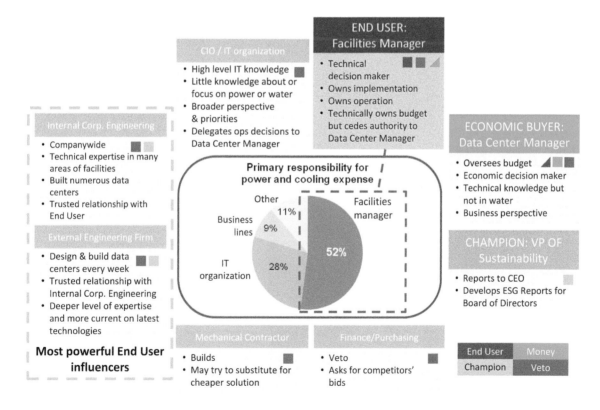

Figure 12.2: DMU for B2B Mechanical Water Filtration Systems example.

solution with a cheaper one. The purchasing department did not have much influence, either. It was at the end of the chain, but the team had to be aware of their procedures and policies, and make sure not to make mistakes at that point in the process. You can see how this process works. It is like a jury where you have to win over everyone.

Not understanding all of these constituencies could lead to mystifying delays in the sales process; offending them or proposing something counter to their interests would likely kill the proposed acquisition.

All of this is shown in the DMU map in Figure 12.2.

ADDITIONAL RESOURCES

There are additional resources for this step at www.d-eship.com/step12. These materials include:

- Video: DMU Explainers by Bill Aulet and Erdin Beshimov
- Video: Example described and explained in an interview with TVision founder Yan Liu
- Process Guidance
- Worksheet 12.1: Determining and defining the DMU

Additional resources will be added as new and updated examples and information become available.

Summary

To successfully sell the product to the customer, you will need to understand who makes the ultimate decision to purchase, as well as who influences that decision. The champion, the end user, and the primary economic buyer are most important, but those holding veto power, as well as Primary Influencers, cannot be ignored. Doing this in a systematic way can be a source of competitive advantage.

Map the Process to Acquire a Paying Customer

In This Step, You Will:

- Map out the decision-making process (DMP) or, more precisely, the process by which your customer acquires your product.
- Build a first-draft sales funnel.
- Estimate the sales cycle for your product.

After knowing who will make the decision, it is critical to know how they will make the decision.

Why This Step, and Why Now?

In Step 12, Determine the Customer's Decision-Making Unit (DMU), you built a structure to make clear *who* makes the decision to acquire your product. Now you have to build a similar structure to make clear *how* they make a decision to acquire your product. The how is the process by which you convert a potential customer into a paying customer, and from initial contact to final payment. This is much more complicated than asking your champion to pressure your primary economic buyer.

This information will be a prerequisite to analyzing and choosing the appropriate business model to capture some of the value you are providing (Step 15, Design a Business Model), setting the Pricing Framework (Step 16), and estimating the value of a new customer (Step 17, Lifetime Value). In this step you will also determine the key factors in the sales cycle such that you have the information you need to intelligently map out your sales channel strategy (Step 18, Design a Scalable Revenue Engine), which in turn will allow you to estimate the Cost of Customer Acquisition in Step 19. All of this will give you an understanding of your unit economics.

Let's Get Started

The following items from the Full Life Cycle Use Case (Step 6) will be the basis for initial information you need to start the work on this step. Specifically, this involves:

- How customers will determine they have a need and/or opportunity to move away from their status quo and how to activate customers to feel they have to do something different (i.e., purchase your product)
- How customers will find out about your product
- How customers will analyze your product
- How customers will acquire your product
- How customers will install your product
- How customers will pay for your product

You will add more information to your previous work from Step 6 but don't recreate it unnecessarily. What you add should build on your previous work.

By mapping the process to acquire a paying customer, you will capture more detail about each of these items especially now considering the DMU, and better understand the internal purchasing mechanisms of your target customer. A seasoned entrepreneur with extensive industry experience may be able to build a map of the process relatively quickly; but the first-time entrepreneur will find the task tougher, with lots of educational moments on how the real world works. Don't short-circuit this educational process. The information you learn in this step is critical for the new entrepreneur to learn and appreciate. It can make or break a business. It is always good to find someone with deep experience from your target customer group to mentor you, but you need to understand the information yourself and internalize it.

Some elements in your map will vary depending on the industry, but the basic components of the process will be the same. The common elements include lead generation, access to influencers, prepurchase planning, purchasing, and installation—followed by what you will do to make sure the customers successfully use the product and gain value from it. Many of these elements will also have multiple subcomponents.

Be sure to factor in any regulations from governmental or quasi-governmental organizations that would potentially impact your ability to sell your product. You should have uncovered in the DMU (Step 12) whether any governmental officials hold veto power over a project—such as when a regulator must approve an element or milestone in the process. By mapping this process, you will also outline what regulations you and your customer are required to fulfill for the product to be sold. One good example of regulations proving too onerous for a business idea is presented later in this chapter (PayPal for Kids). Similarly, there could be internal standards for your target customer's company that must be complied with, but the process is still the same.

For each phase in the process, include:

- Who are the key players from the DMU who will be involved?

- What is their influence on the process? Again, this is hopefully information you have already obtained in Step 12 when you built the DMU, but now you are putting it in temporal order and developing educated estimates on how long each component will take.

- What is their budget authority (amount and type)?

- How long will it take to complete each phase you identify? List them in temporal sequence, noting any that can run in parallel. (Be diligent. You need to have at least 80% certainty in each step. Make conservative estimates because entrepreneurs almost always underestimate the time to complete each phase.)

- What are the inputs and outputs of this phase?

Through this process, you will better understand the customer's business as it relates to your product. You may well even go back and update the Full Life Cycle Use Case. Mapping out this process is important because you will need to navigate the same process over and over to sell to more customers. As such, understanding this process will pay dividends later, when you can more easily acquire new customers in a repeatable fashion.

Budgeting/Purchasing Authority

A key factor in each component of this step is to identify the budgeting/purchasing authority of each individual involved in that phase of the process as appropriate. One common limit you will find is that an individual can only purchase items up to a certain dollar amount, such as $5,000, without approval from a more senior person. What this means is that if you can keep your price below $5,000, purchasing approval comes directly from one decision maker as opposed to multiple. If it is above this price point, it will surely be a longer and more involved process, which will drive up your sales cycle time and ultimately your cost of customer acquisition. Identifying these limits will help with your Pricing Framework analysis and decision (Step 16). Getting the pricing points right could dramatically reduce your sales cycle, which could be the difference between success and failure for your new venture.

Another important consideration is whether payment will come from the yearly operating budget or the longer-term capital budget. Identify which budget your customer would use to pay for your item, and what that budgeting process is. In some companies, it may be much easier and faster to get approval to include an expense in the operating budget than in the capital budget; but with other industries and companies it may be exactly the opposite. While seemingly a small item, this could mean the difference between a three-month sales cycle and a minimum one-year sales cycle, which could mean the success or failure of your new venture, especially if you are not aware of it a priori.

Time Is of the Essence

Make sure you take into consideration the time it takes to move through each phase in the process. Once you have made all your time estimates, go back and validate whether the estimates are reasonable. Are you accounting for delays? Are you being aggressive or conservative in your estimates? You should be conservatively realistic.

Optimizing Your Process Map

In many cases, you will have a choice between a simpler sales process and a more complicated one, as the Bloom team started to discover when they defined their DMU. For instance, if Bloom chooses a simpler direct-to-consumer approach, its cost of customer acquisition is likely smaller because the tools used to market to consumers are cheaper than the tools needed to persuade large companies. However, a more complicated sales cycle that involves the end user's employer, and that employer's benefits provider, may greatly increase the lifetime value of a customer because the end user's employer is paying for the product, disincentivizing the end user from cancelling their subscription. The drawback is that a longer sales cycle also increases the risk that a competitor will copy the product, or that the environment changes unfavorably before closing the sale (for instance, the champion could change jobs), or investor and/or employee fatigue.

If, in the first scenario, you had a simple map and sold one unit of your product per month, and in the second scenario the process map is more complicated but you can sell 1,000 units of product in a year from now, I would seriously consider the second option.

You should also understand how your competitors are selling to your customer. By your analysis, you might find there is a different way to sell into the customer that gives you an advantage or an entirely new market opportunity that your competitors are not currently capitalizing on. This happened for one of my students, Dominik Guber, when he launched the home beer brewing kit BrewBarrel. Initially, he saw the end user—the well-educated 25- to 30-year-old ambitious professional German man—as also the primary economic buyer and champion. But when he started mapping out the sales cycle, he realized that while his competitors focused on selling directly to the end user, he could target his product as a gifting opportunity for the end user's relationship partner, and so he changed the DMU to include the relationship partner as the primary economic buyer and champion.

So, in summary, when you have decisions about what paths you can take for choosing your DMU and customer acquisition process map, you are optimizing and balancing in four dimensions:

1. Cost of Customer Acquisition (CoCA)
2. Lifetime Value (LTV) of new customers
3. Risk involved, usually directly related to the length of your sales cycle
4. Competitive Position

Operationalizing Your Process: First-Draft Sales Funnel

The customer acquisition process is not something you will do once and then not have to do it again. It is also something that is not theoretical; it must be very grounded in the real world and actionable on an ongoing basis. As will be discussed in Step 18, Design a Scalable Revenue Engine, this element of your business is becoming increasingly critical to your new venture's success.

Therefore, in this step, you will translate this map of the customer acquisition process into something that successful businesses have been using for a long time, a "sales funnel." It will be a first draft that you will enhance and iterate on over time. This will become an important tool you will use to effectively manage your business going forward.

I must note here that entrepreneurs have learned a lot from history about the effectiveness of sales funnels, but the very name itself carries some unfortunate baggage with it. Historically it has been the sales department, and to a lesser degree the marketing department, in organizations that has driven and managed this business measurement/tool. As will be highlighted in Step 18, this has changed a great deal recently.

Today it is a much healthier model to think of revenue as opposed to sales. To many, this might seem like a trivial difference but it is not and will be less so going forward.

Sales has connotations of a sales department with direct and maybe indirect sales resources but most often run by a direct sales leader. Direct sales can be appropriate for your startup at times but is very expensive, whereas revenue is rapidly being driven more by other sources than direct sales, because these sources are often better suited for an early-stage venture. In Step 18, you will dive into the many other sources that you must be at a minimum aware of and probably activated to use to make your business scalable and successful in the long term. This could include creative marketing, Product-Led Growth (PLG), customer success, Generative AI revenue tools, and more. This is today one of the most prolific areas of innovation in the entire entrepreneurship space.

Even the concept of a funnel has some misdirection today, as it should be seen more as a revenue loop where successful customers provide a positive feedback loop to feed the funnel back at the top the best leads that can possibly have. I always say that the best salespeople you can have are not those you hire but your own customers.

For these reasons, I would prefer to call this a "revenue loop" rather than a "sales funnel," but since the term "sales funnel" is so entrenched already, I will just modify it to fit the needs of the 24 Steps. It will still prove a very valuable framework to design, monitor, and optimize our customer acquisition process.

Figure 13.1 is a general sales funnel.[1] Stage 1, "Identification → Leads," is how the customer acquisition process starts by getting the names of potential customers. This can come from anywhere and there are no assurances that they are real potential customers or even real people. These leads then progress to Stage 2, "Consideration → Suspects" where there is confidence that they are real people and there is a reasonable chance they could be customers, but there are still lots of questions.

---

[1] There are different methodologies and companies often have their own customized versions of this with different names and more or less stages, but they all have this same basic concept. So if you understand this general sales funnel, you can understand the more customized versions you will see elsewhere.

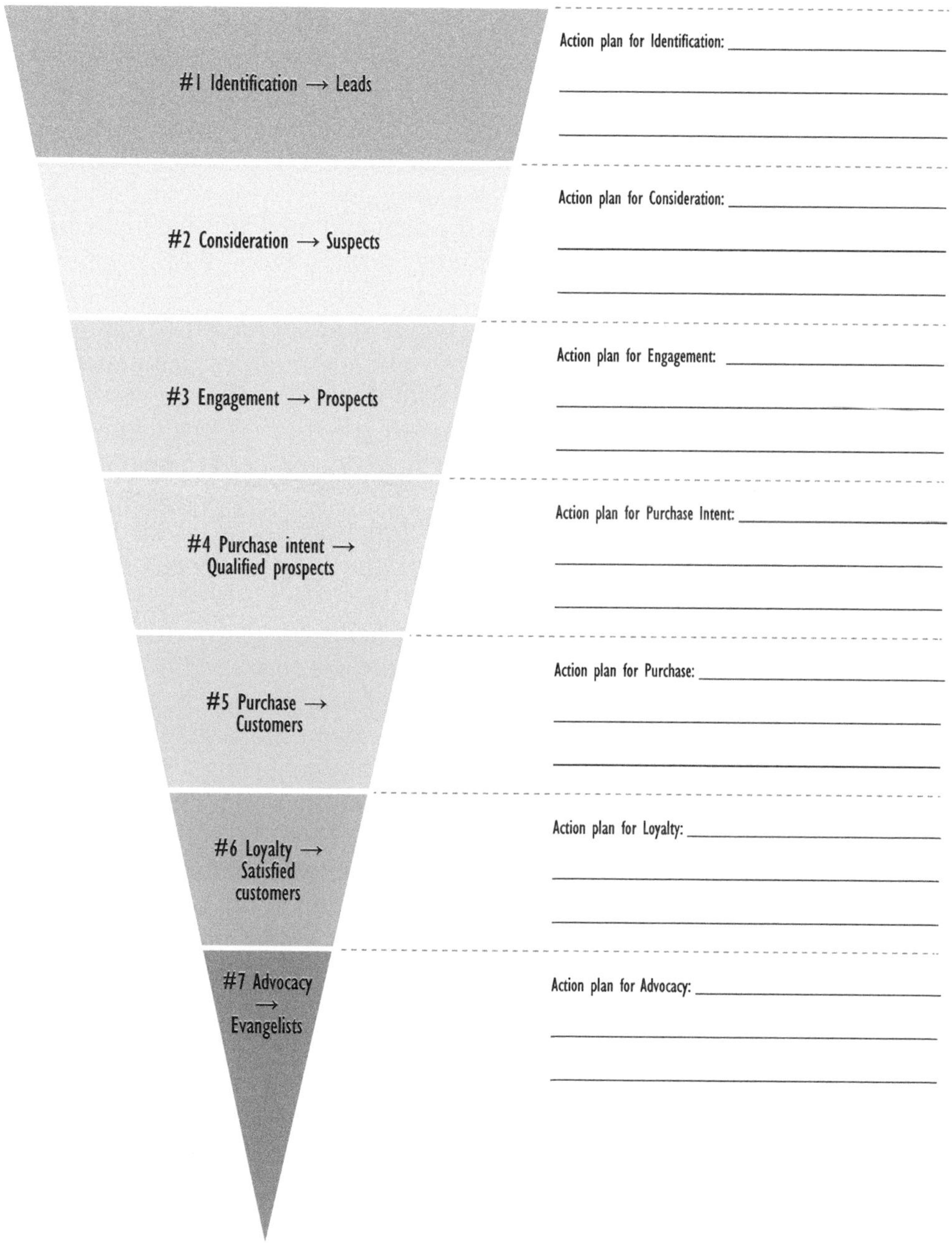

#1 Identification → Leads

Action plan for Identification: _____

_____

_____

#2 Consideration → Suspects

Action plan for Consideration: _____

_____

_____

#3 Engagement → Prospects

Action plan for Engagement: _____

_____

_____

#4 Purchase intent → Qualified prospects

Action plan for Purchase Intent: _____

_____

_____

#5 Purchase → Customers

Action plan for Purchase: _____

_____

_____

#6 Loyalty → Satisfied customers

Action plan for Loyalty: _____

_____

_____

#7 Advocacy → Evangelists

Action plan for Advocacy: _____

_____

_____

Figure 13.1: First-draft sales funnel.

In Stage 3, "Engagement → Prospects," some of these questions are answered and it becomes clear that they fit your target customer profile and the odds are now increasing that they are potential customers from an early engagement you have with them.

In Stage 4, "Purchase intent → Qualified prospect," there has been more engagement and they have indicated that they are interested and have funds to buy your product. This is very interesting now. You are far from done, but things are very encouraging.

In Stage 5, "Purchase → Customer," you close the deal and they become a paying customer for your business. Congratulations, and historically many "sales funnels" have stopped here. That would almost surely be a big mistake.

In Stage 6, "Loyalty → Satisfied Customer," you begin what is called the "Customer Success" process. You make sure that they not just pay for your product but they install it and start to get value from it, and then get value on an ongoing basis. In this stage, you invest to make your customers very happy with your offering. There is a big difference between satisfied and very satisfied, as researchers have shown,[2] and it is almost surely worth the investment to be on the very satisfied side of this equation.

The last stage is also part of the Customer Success function, Stage 7, "Advocacy → Evangelist." In this stage, you intentionally invest to encourage your now very happy customer to advocate for you at the watering holes for your target customer.

Your investment in the last two stages will be repaid handsomely by creating a strong feedback loop from Stage 7 back to Stage 1, turning your funnel into a loop. In addition, the leads that are produced by this feedback loop will be the highest quality you can have because they will already be well qualified, and as a result will move down through the funnel with great velocity and high yield rates (i.e., percentage that move between the stages as you go down the funnel). So, they will give you the shortest sales cycle with the lowest Cost of Customer Acquisition (more on this in Step 19) and will probably push you the least on discounts. Why? Because they don't see you as risky because your product is already working for one of their colleagues.

The framework that starts in this step will be a crucial tool to understand and improve your ability to achieve profitably and in a sustainable way, the first commandment of business, to get paying customers.

There are significant additional materials on this topic in the online Additional Resources described in the section at the end of this chapter.

---

[2] Jones, Thomas O,. and W. Earl Sasser, Jr., "Why Satisfied Customers Defect," *Harvard Business Review,* November-December 1995, https://hbr.org/1995/11/why-satisfied-customers-defect

WHEN REGULATIONS MAKE A MARKET DIFFICULT TO ENTER: "PAYPAL FOR KIDS"

One of my star MBA students, Frederic "Freddy" Kerrest, who also had a computer science degree from Stanford, entered MIT with the determination to found a major new venture upon graduation. He aggressively pursued opportunities to build his knowledge and experience in how to create new ventures. He even ran the legendary MIT $100K Entrepreneurship Competition.

He methodically evaluated ideas to start his company in his second year and settled on an idea that I will simply call "PayPal for Kids." The market opportunity centered around online commerce opportunities for children, an area that was constrained by the need for a parent to approve every transaction, no matter how small, because the parent's credit card was needed to make transactions.

Freddy's premise was that he could create a service expressly for kids where parents would place a set amount of money—say $50—in an account that kids could use to purchase items online, anywhere that credit cards are accepted, without parents needing to preapprove every purchase.

Parents could prevent money from being spent on sites and purchasing categories they did not approve of, and they would be able to see after the fact what their child had spent money on. Part of the value proposition to the primary economic buyer (the parents) in this case was the ability to teach their children about personal budgeting and financial discipline.

From the excellent primary market research that had been done, it appeared that this was a great business opportunity. Then it came time to outline the Process to Acquire a Paying Customer. It was at that point that things began to change.

Freddy aimed his venture to serve parents and children throughout the United States. But he discovered that to collect money and distribute it as his model dictated, with his company getting a percentage of each transaction as revenue for his business, he needed to be registered as a bank or financial institution in any US state he wanted to do business in. For his venture to be successful, he would therefore have to register as a financial institution in dozens of different states. The cost, time, and bureaucratic mentality needed to properly do this killed the idea, because Freddy did not want to start a business that needed to deal heavily with government regulations.

Here, the key hang-up in the Process to Acquire a Paying Customer was not the length of the sales cycle but rather the complexity of it and certain requirements that had been overlooked previously.

(Continued)

Freddy quickly used his newfound knowledge to continue to pursue ideas and opportunities with more wisdom. Based on his prior experience in enterprise software (deep market knowledge is always a great place to start as an entrepreneur), Freddy co-founded a company called Okta, an identity and access management company based in San Francisco, which became an iconic company in the tech industry. Okta has been publicly traded since April 2017 and has a market value of tens of billions of dollars. This is an example of the maxim that most often, your first idea is not your best idea and even if it was, you get better at executing the more times you try. In the end, success in entrepreneurship is much, much more about execution than it is about ideas.

EXAMPLES

Bloom Continued

As discussed with Bloom in the last step, they started to make some decisions regarding the DMU that make an already two-sided market even more complicated because now their champions will be business organizations. This means that they will really need a customer acquisition road map for both the end users (who are in this case the initial economic buyers) as well as the champion. This makes the problem at least twice as challenging but, as I said before, could pay off very well for the team.

Understanding their customer acquisition process will involve capturing both businesses and end user consumers, so they will not focus only on the consumer side; understanding the process will have to be duplicated on the business side as well. Regarding this consumer end user and economic buyer, their customer acquisition plan is very simple (Figure 13.2).

Decision-Making Process

1. Determine Need: New Stage of Life (Moving)

Young women who are moving to a new city are very aware of their lack of a friend group, and need to find new social circles. This consideration is often top of mind. Identify these customers by targeting women who are searching for apartments, using moving services, recently graduated.

2. Find Options: B2C Ads

Women will take to a Google search or social media to find groups & events that will allow them to socialize. We will use Google AdWords and advertise on TikTok, Instagram and in tandem with moving companies and managed apartments.

 Budget: High   Time: < 1 day

3. Analyze Options

We plan for Bloom to initially be championed through influencers on TikTok, and soon after spread through word of mouth among young college graduates who are very digitally savvy.

 Budget: Low   Time: < 1 day

4. Download Bloom

The app will be free to download for users to remove friction from the purchase decision. This is especially important at first to attract critical mass that will make the app worthwhile for users.

 Budget: Low   Time: <5 mins

5. Use & Get Value

Users create a profile and get matched into a group of women for immediate socialization. The initial match will be highly important for retention - it must be strong and effective.

 Budget: Medium   Time: 1 week - 1 month

6. Refer Other Users

Bloom will allow users to refer their friends and create custom groups, facilitating a growing network of women. To encourage referrals, there will be a bonus that allows women to have first priority for events.

 Budget: Medium   Time: 1 - 2 months

Figure 13.2: Bloom end user and economic buyer decision-making process.

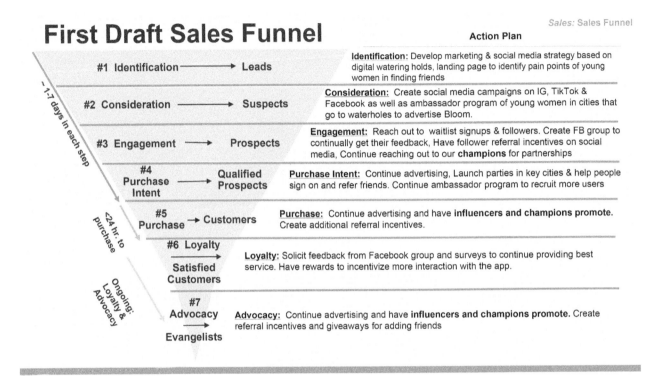

Figure 13.3: Bloom's first-draft sales funnel.

Once Bloom had the high-level flow of the decision-making process, the next phase was to convert this into a first-draft sales funnel (Figure 13.3).

This is an excellent start on one side of the market that will be refined as they go on. You would do a similar process and analysis for the champion or B2B side of the market to complete Bloom's work for Step 13.

One final part of Step 13 is to look at the length of your sales cycle. Bloom has a very nice summary of this in Figure 13.4.

Sales Cycle Length

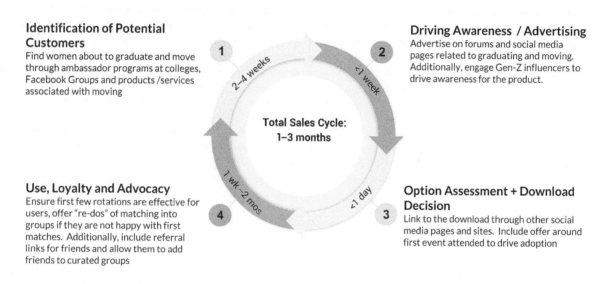

Identification of Potential Customers
Find women about to graduate and move through ambassador programs at colleges, Facebook Groups and products /services associated with moving

Driving Awareness / Advertising
Advertise on forums and social media pages related to graduating and moving. Additionally, engage Gen-Z influencers to drive awareness for the product.

Use, Loyalty and Advocacy
Ensure first few rotations are effective for users, offer "re-dos" of matching into groups if they are not happy with first matches. Additionally, include referral links for friends and allow them to add friends to curated groups

Option Assessment + Download Decision
Link to the download through other social media pages and sites. Include offer around first event attended to drive adoption

Total Sales Cycle: 1–3 months

2–4 weeks | <1 week | <1 day | 1 wk – 2 mos

Figure 13.4: Bloom sales cycle summarized and quantified for length of time.

Mechanical Water Filtration Systems

Continuing this example from Step 12, Determine the Customer's Decision-Making Unit (DMU), this new venture team had narrowed down the DMU but still had options. Even after they focused on selling their systems to the DMU consisting of the facilities managers as the end users, the data center managers as the economic buyer, and the VP of Sustainability as the champion, there were still more decisions to be made. Should they sell to brand-new data centers built from the ground up to be more energy efficient, or should they focus on retrofitting existing data centers? Did they have to choose?

They were initially planning to sell their system to new data center constructions because that would not involve having to replace an existing system or sell against a solution that already worked for the data center. Besides, they were getting more inquiries from new data center constructions as opposed to retrofit situations, so it seemed to make logical sense to pursue the new constructions market.

After extensive interviews, they mapped the Process to Acquire a Paying Customer at new data centers, as well as retrofitting existing centers. In the process, they uncovered something interesting that changed their focus from new centers to retrofit opportunities.

The team had secured its first pilot program in a new data center in less than nine months, so they could have assumed that this was the sales cycle. But upon performing an analysis of developing the map of the Process to Acquire a Paying Customer more generally, they realized that the way they had secured the pilot was an exceptional case and not repeatable for other customers. When they looked at the length of the acquisition process for new data centers after the pilot, they discovered that the sales cycle would take an average of 2.5 years and possibly more, which was a red flashing light (see Figure 13.5). This is very, very long for a startup to handle when it is often struggling to survive week-to-week, with the ups and downs of cash, employee morale, and product stability. What this analysis clearly showed was that this was a very risky market to focus on.

While the revenue from the pilot could help pay bills and minimize cash burn, the team then turned their analysis to retrofits as potentially a better way to enter the market due to its shorter sales cycle. While this was still a yearlong sales cycle, it was much better than the 2.5 years the first alternative offered.

Still the team was worried because they had not seen many inbound queries about retrofits, so they revisited their Persona and did brand-new primary market research on the retrofit market. They found that existing data centers received the idea well, but they were much less likely to be shopping for a solution because they already had one that worked. Still, they found some receptivity in some of the customer base once they spoke to the champion. While it was not without its challenges, this primary market research and analysis gave them the confidence to pursue this new strategy with full force.

Description of the Acquisition Process

NEW PROJECT
- Contact CIO to get approval and gain access to internal company specialist.
- Contact internal company specialist/green czar/corporate facilities manager to influence engineer.
- Contact design engineer to work together in definition of water system, give specifications, and have them prescribe MWFS.
- Contact general contractor and purchasing to ensure proper installation and purchase.

RETROFIT

- Contact facilities manager and help him sell to data center manager.
- If necessary, contact CIO to get approval and gain access to data center manager and internal company specialists.
- Contact facilities manager/data center manager/purchasing to ensure proper installation and purchase of our product.

NEW PROJECT

Lead Generation	Access to Influencers	Access to Design Engineers	Design Phase	Construction Phase: Actual Sale to Contractor	Installation
1–2 months	2–4 months	2–4 months	6–12 months	12–15 months	1 month

RETROFIT PROJECT

Lead Generation	Access to Facility Manager	Access to Influencers	Negotiation with Purchases and Budget Owners	Installation
1–2 months	4–6 months	2–4 months	2–3 months	1 month

Figure 13.5: Mechanical Water Filtration Systems sales cycle analysis.

In summary, after a systematic development of the DMP, the team decided to focus on retrofits to get going, but once cash-flow positive, they would begin selling to new data centers as well. This was an extremely important insight that came out of the analysis.

ADDITIONAL RESOURCES

There are additional resources for this step at www.d-eship.com/step13. For Step 13 you will find:

- Video: Business Model Explainers by Bill Aulet and Erdin Beshimov
- Video: Example described and explained in an interview with TVision founder Yan Liu
- Process Guidance
- Worksheet 13.1: Utilizing information gathered in Step 6 to jump-start Step 13
- Worksheet 13.2: Developing the details of your DMP
- Worksheet 13.3: Estimating Length of Sales Cycle
- Worksheet 13.4: First-Draft Sales Funnel (Digital version of Figure 13.1 in this chapter)
- Worksheet 13.5: Qualitative Summary of Step 13

Additional resources will be added as new and updated examples and information become available.

Summary

Determining the Process to Acquire a Paying Customer defines how the DMU decides to buy the product, and identifies other obstacles that may hinder your ability to sell your product. While this process may at first seem opaque, confusing, and random, it is not. You need to take a disciplined approach to breaking it down and defining it. Don't underestimate how important this is and how the sales funnel is the lifeblood of your organization, because without continually getting new paying customers, you cease to be an impactful or interesting business. Remember the first commandment: there is no business without paying customers.

Windows of Opportunity and Triggers

In This Step, You Will:

- Determine the optimal times when your customer will be open to acquiring your product.
- Learn how to choose one and best capitalize on that window of opportunity by designing programs to create positive progress.
- Understand the power of habits.

Know your Windows of Opportunity and take advantage of them with well-designed Triggers—timing is crucial!

Why This Step, and Why Now?

This step builds directly off Step 12, Determine the Customer's Decision-Making Unit (DMU), and Step 13, Map the Process to Acquire a Paying Customer, but adds a third and necessary dimension such that they can be put into action with the optimal odds of success. Since the original *Disciplined Entrepreneurship* book was published in 2013, I have refined many things. One very important thing is regarding the effect of timing in the customer acquisition process (Step 13). While you may do an excellent job on Steps 12 and 13, you might well not succeed if you do not understand the timing dimension of this challenge. In fact, you might get false signals that your analysis is wrong and your strategy is not working simply because you are not executing your plan at the right time.

Let's Get Started

One of the biggest challenges for any company, especially a startup, is getting their first customer. That initial customer adoption is especially tough, which is why you need to spend so much time dissecting that process and improving it. Getting the 1,001st customer after having 1,000 customers may not be easy, but I can assure you it is almost always much easier than getting the first real customer. In this case, by a "real" customer I mean someone who is not a relative or a friend or a technological enthusiast who will buy one of everything. Instead, a real customer is someone who has a business problem (not a technological one) and has no previous relationship to you. That customer found out about your product and chose to buy it to solve that customer pain/opportunity without special conditions.

    To get that first customer, you must overcome an enormous amount of inertia because it is significantly easier for the customer not to buy your product and to keep doing what they are currently doing. The status quo is an extremely powerful force to overcome, as discussed in Step 11, Chart Your Competitive Position, especially before a product is widely accepted and people change their purchasing habits accordingly. Habits of people and companies are very hard to break.

    There exists a great analogy from physics. Isaac Newton's first law of motion begins by stating that bodies at rest will remain at rest unless acted upon by an external force (Figure 13A.1). The potential customer is initially at rest and will stay so unless you find a way to start the process. Finding that catalyst to action is often the most important step in the Process to Acquire a Paying Customer—and often the most underrated.

NEWTON'S FIRST LAW OF MOTION
ADAPTED FOR STARTUPS

1   AN OBJECT AT REST WILL REMAIN AT REST...

2   UNLESS ACTED UPON BY AN UNBALANCED FORCE.

3   AN OBJECT IN MOTION WILL CONTINUE WITH CONSTANT SPEED AND DIRECTION...

4   UNLESS ACTED UPON BY AN UNBALANCED FORCE

Figure 13A.1: When you start, your customer is like an object at rest. Getting the customer to take the first step toward acquiring your product is the hardest step, so it requires special attention.

Great marketers, especially in consumer markets, have known for a long time about two concepts that will help you deal with this challenge. They are called Windows of Opportunity and Triggers.[1]

A Window of Opportunity is a time period in which your target end user, your economic buyer, and/or your champion will be particularly open to considering purchasing your product. Most important of all of these is when your champion is particularly receptive because it is your champion who is going to be the engine of propulsion to make sales happen for you. Examples of common Windows of Opportunity include:

- Seasonality (e.g., selling lemonade in summer and Christmas wreaths in winter in the Northern Hemisphere)
- Crisis (e.g., blackout, security breach) or impending potential crisis (e.g., forecast for a storm, the COVID-19 pandemic)

---

[1] Charles Duhigg discusses Windows of Opportunity and Triggers extensively (albeit with different names) in his book *The Power of Habits*, especially when he discusses the success that the superstore Target has had in using product purchase history to predict future purchases. Duhigg profiles one infamous case where Target began sending pregnancy-related advertisements to a teenage girl, prompting the girl's father to complain angrily to the store manager—only to take it back a few days later when he found out that his daughter was, in fact, pregnant, and Target had figured it out before he had.

- End of fiscal year (extremely relevant for business, but also for some consumers due to taxes)
- Budget planning cycle
- Life transitions (e.g., graduation, first job, first home, having a child)
- Change in leadership (e.g., company hires a new chief information officer)
- Change in regulation (e.g., enactment of the Affordable Care Act, a major governmental change to regulations on the American healthcare system)
- Searching online and finding your product (more on this later)

A Window of Opportunity only identifies a time period when you have a much better than normal chance to start the acquisition process, but it does not start the process for you (Figure 13A.2). Now you need to apply that external force to get the customer moving. That is a Trigger.

EXPIRING DISCOUNTS   **TIME-LIMITED OFFER**   **SCARCITY**   **FREE GIFT**   **SALES REP INTERACTION**

Figure 13A.2: Triggers are specific actions you take within the Window of Opportunity.

A Trigger is an action you take within the Window of Opportunity to create an urgency and/or strong incentive for the target end user, economic buyer, and/or champion to act, starting the Process to Acquire a Paying Customer. A well-designed Trigger also increases the odds that the customer will make it through your sales funnel and acquire your product. Examples of Triggers include:

1. A salesperson suddenly appearing in person, on the phone, or in an online chat to discuss the situation
2. Offering a discount that expires after a short period of time
3. Indications of scarcity of supply, which creates FOMO (fear of missing out)

4. Limited time availability to join a special community, another way to create FOMO
5. Special offer of additional value to reward quick decision
6. Clear action that will help you avoid a disaster—such as a security assessment to avoid a devastating cybersecurity breach that just hit a competitor and is making headlines today

These simple concepts apply to almost every product and are extremely well known to large corporations like Target, Google, Amazon, and Procter & Gamble. Ironically, they are less well-known but even more important to entrepreneurs, who face more inertia in the form of obstacles to customer adoption. I have often seen a well-defined Decision-Making Unit (DMU) and Process to Acquire a Paying Customer fail if the entrepreneur does not understand their Windows of Opportunity and does not set up effective Triggers against them.

A full picture of the sales process with the initiating role of the Windows of Opportunity and Triggers is summarized in Figure 13A.3.

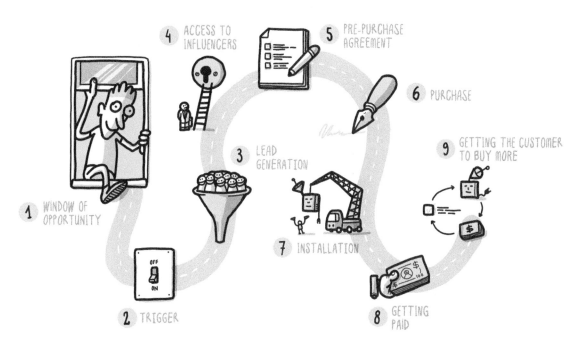

Figure 13A.3: Understanding and utilizing Windows of Opportunity and Triggers are vital in kicking off a successful sales process.

EXAMPLES

Bloom Continued

A good example of how to implement this in a new venture is from our team at Bloom. For our course, with the limited time the students have, I have them focus on the end user first, which makes sense because the end user will be the one to determine long-term success. As such, here is a summary of the potential Windows of Opportunity (Figure 13A.4) and the one they chose as well as the Trigger to capture them:

Customer Acquisition: Windows of Opportunity & Triggers

Windows of Opportunity and Triggers

Importance	What?	Why?	When?	Triggers
Very High (Our Focus)	Graduating College	New graduates are often moving into new phases of life where they need new friendships, either because of new job, new location or new priorities	Spring, May & June	Campus ambassadors, career offices, graduation events
High	Moving Cities	There is a high likelihood this young woman will need to build a social network in their new city	Throughout the Year	Moving companies, "New in Town" Facebook Groups, Managed apartment buildings
Medium	Starting a New Job	Bloom could be offered as part of an onboarding package or overall benefits package for new & existing employees to combat loneliness, improve mental health and help with relocation	Throughout the Year, heavier in Jan and Feb	Large companies with high turnover and/or relocation, HR departments, Insurance companies as part of "wellness" package
Medium	New Restaurant Opening	Engaging an influencer early to promote Bloom as a service for a new transitional period in life such as moving will drive great awareness and adoption	Throughout the Year	Opening events, websites, joint advertising
Low	Starting or ending relationship	Women who are in relationships or single often want friends who are in a similar stage in life, i.e. also in a relationship or single	Throughout the Year	Couples events or packaged bundles, dating apps

Figure 13A.4: First draft of Windows of Opportunity Options and Selection as well as Triggers for Bloom.

The other side of this involves the champion, which is also extremely important, and that is actually much easier. Bloom simply needs to understand when new benefits are announced to the employees and then work back the decision process to understand when those decisions are made and even further back, to when does the analysis start. This would be relatively easy information to get from your champion, because after all, she is your champion.

General High-Level Examples

Figure 13A.5 shows high-level examples to illustrate this concept and implementation.

	Company	Window of Opportunity	Trigger	Comment
1	Travel website	Users come to website and look for price on a specific route (e.g., Boston to London).	Highlighted text under the price says, "Only 2 seats available at this price."	Extremely effective; scarcity of supply incentivizes action now.
2	Computer company selling high-performance and/or bulk orders of computers and/or computer peripherals (e.g., IBM)	End of fiscal year (let's assume December 31 for this example) when business departments have unspent money in their budget for the year that is just about to end—if they don't spend the money, their bosses might think they don't need the money for future years and will cut their budget accordingly.	"If you let us know in early November, we will be able to schedule our people to ensure the equipment is installed, invoiced, and paid for well before the year end so you don't have to stick around over the holidays."	Gets customer to commit to you earlier, before others who would be competing for the same funds. There may still be smaller amounts of money left over right at year's end, so you could have another Trigger to capture that, but you have already gotten the lion's share of the available money.
3	College student supplies company/service	When students first arrive at school—in most places in the United States, this is late August or early September—and they form their buying habits for the academic year.	Flyers in dorms advertising giveaways and discounts that are especially attractive to new students.	Habits, once formed, are difficult to break, so smart marketers invest in the Window of Opportunity to get consumers' habits to favor them.

Figure 13A.5: Summary of multiple examples of Windows of Opportunities and Triggers.

	Company	Window of Opportunity	Trigger	Comment
4	Security company	A highly visible data breach is in all headlines.	Offer to top prospects a special audit team to assess how exposed the prospect is, and suggest immediate plans to address the exposures.	Combines urgency of a crisis with scarcity of resources.
5	Enterprise software company	New chief information officer is hired by a prospect.	Offer to review inventory of software and produce a report of where company could improve.	Regime change is a great Window of Opportunity because often everything gets rethought and new leaders want change.
6	New company that de-ices planes faster and cheaper	Right after a storm there is extreme pressure because of delays; executives want a plan so that delays don't happen again.	Salesperson calls and explains the new offering to airlines that had the most cancellations and delays.	Having experienced significant pain, customer wants to avoid it next time, so is especially open to new solutions.
7	HubSpot	A business owner visits HubSpot's website to learn about inbound marketing and HubSpot products, suggesting they are a good prospect for products that would improve the business owner's own website.	Free website grader tool that gives a numeric grade for the quality of the prospect's website with a report on what the website does well and areas to improve score—the grader also collects the prospect's contact information (e.g., e-mail address) to follow up.	With the prospect's contact information and the knowledge that the prospect is interested in improving their website, HubSpot can follow up and continue to engage with the interested party.

Figure 13A.5: (Continued)

	Company	Window of Opportunity	Trigger	Comment
8	Enterprise software company	One of your competitors is bought by a big company with a poor customer service and acquisitions track record. The new big company also has little history in the new market segment of the acquired company.	Offer a special one-time trade-in program so users of the competitor's software can acquire your software at a steep discount. Offer free technical support for the transition for the first 20 that sign up.	Highlights your stability in a world that just got disrupted and there are new levels of risk.

Figure 13A.5: (Continued)

ADDITIONAL RESOURCES

There are additional resources for this step at www.d-eship.com/step13a. For Step 13A, you will find:

- Worksheet 13A.1: Windows of Opportunities and Triggers Worksheet and Reflection

Additional resources will be added as new and updated examples and information become available.

Summary

Make sure to include an analysis of Windows of Opportunities and Triggers in your sales process. It makes a big difference.

Calculate the Total Addressable Market Size for Follow-on Markets

---

In This Step, You Will:

- Briefly consider which "follow-on" markets you will expand to after dominating your Beachhead Market.
- Calculate the size of these follow-on markets, and remember TAM is expressed in $/year in revenue if you had 100% market share, even acknowledging the limitations already mentioned in Step 4, Calculate the TAM Size for the Beachhead Market.

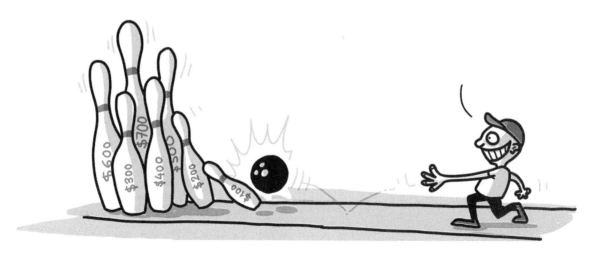

While maintaining a relentless daily focus on your Beachhead Market, you should also do some small amount of analysis on what happens if and when you win the Beachhead Market.

Why This Step, and Why Now?

At some point, you must look beyond the Beachhead Market. Up until this point in the process, you have been relentlessly focused on an increasingly well-defined initial market. The premise is that when you "land," you will then have an unfair advantage to be able to "expand." The goal from the beginning was not just to win the beachhead. Beachhead Market is an entry point for a bigger market with much broader impact. So now you will take a step back to make sure you have an attractive long-term game plan. While you could do this step at a different time, I recommend doing it now because you have more definition and confidence of what success in your Beachhead Market will look like and what unfair competitive advantage you can leverage to expand thereafter.

Let's Get Started

So far, you have focused on customers in your Beachhead Market, and rightly so. At this point in the process, you will take a step back and quickly validate the existence and size of other, similar markets ("follow-on markets") that you will target once you have dominated the Beachhead Market. This is a check to make sure you are heading in the right direction to build a scalable business and also a reminder of the size and nature of the bigger opportunity.

What good does this step do? It keeps you and your stakeholders cognizant of the long-term potential of your business as you begin to design your product and build capabilities. You will excite management, employees, and investors by showing that the business has the potential to be extremely impactful beyond just the Beachhead Market. You will also get a better sense of other potential markets if your Beachhead Market turns out to be much more problematic than you envisioned and you have to pivot.

However, it is very important that you do not let this broader market and subsequent TAM (reminder, TAM is Total Addressable Market) calculation distract you and your team from the Beachhead Market. The broader TAM calculation should galvanize the team to conquer the Beachhead Market first, while keeping the team thinking about the importance of developing and growing your Core. As the illustration at the beginning of this step illustrates, success in the follow-on markets only happens after you win your Beachhead Market.

This step will also give you a chance to answer the question of "How big can this be?" When people hear about your new venture and see you focused on a Beachhead Market, they may be impressed, but only if they feel it is the first step on a path to greatness. When investors or others ask in general, "What is your TAM?" they are almost always asking, "How big can this be?" They will not be satisfied with a $20M a year TAM.[1] They want to hear about a billion-dollar TAM. That TAM is the Beachhead Market TAM combined with all of the follow-on market TAMs, which you will estimate in this step. So if someone asks you what your TAM is, before you answer, make sure you clarify what it is they are asking about—which is most likely the overall TAM and not the Beachhead Market TAM.

Two Directions to Expand—and One Not To

There are two types of follow-on markets. One involves selling the same customer additional products or applications, which is often referred to as upselling. Since you already have a keen awareness of your target customer's needs and priorities from all of your research, this knowledge can be used to determine what additional products you could create for or even resell to the customer. One benefit is that you can use existing sales and distribution channels to sell the new products, leveraging the investment you have made to build a positive relationship with your target customer.

The second option to expand, and the path often taken by innovation-based startups with a product focus, is to sell the same basic or slightly modified product to "adjacent markets," which are markets that would benefit as well from the product you have developed. While selling to these new markets usually requires some product refinement, and/or different packaging, marketing communications, or pricing, you are leveraging the product success you have had in the Beachhead Market. The challenge is that you will have to establish new customer relationships in each adjacent market, which can be risky and expensive.

There is a third option that is represented by the upper-right box of Figure 14.1, which is selling a new product to a new market. This option does not make logical sense. You have spent so much time refining your understanding of your current market and your current product, so why would you choose an option that requires you to develop both a new product and a new market? You are leveraging none of the assets you worked so hard to build—and it is almost surely not the lowest-hanging fruit for you to capture. While avoiding this option may seem obvious now, it is worth noting and getting an agreement, because in the heat of the battle I have found many an entrepreneur who choose this path without realizing the folly of such a move.

---

[1] It is important to note that the TAM metric of revenue per year is used. If you are a social enterprise, you might well, and appropriately so, complement or even lead with other metrics like tons of carbon-dioxide taken out of the atmosphere, lives saved, people raised out of poverty, or the like. These may even be more important to you than dollars per year in revenue but as stated at the beginning of this book, this book's goal is to help you build economically sustainable entities and, as such, revenue is essential. Revenue per year is also usually a very good proxy for impact—but not always. Remember, your new venture is set up to first and foremost achieve its raison d'être and maximizing profit comes in second.

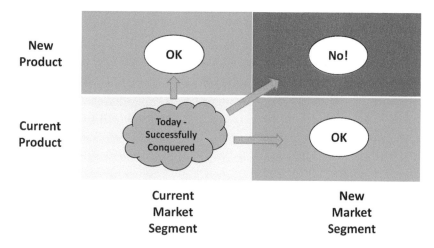

Figure 14.1: Follow-on market strategies, two of which are good and one which is bad.

How to Calculate Broader TAM

Think through the various adjacent markets and upselling opportunities that logically make sense with your product. You should be able to identify at least five or six follow-on markets, where each market is either selling additional products to the same customer or selling the same or similar product to adjacent markets.

Use the same general methodology to calculate the TAM for each follow-on market that you did for your beachhead TAM in Step 4, but for this step you really only need ballpark estimates. You need not and should not spend much time at all on this step right now—probably one-tenth or less of the effort and analysis you did for your Beachhead Market. Likely, much of the information you need for this step was already gathered when you did your initial Market Segmentation in Step 1.

If you want to attract venture capital and/or build a big business, the general rule is that the broader TAM (for 10 or fewer follow-on markets), plus your Beachhead Market TAM, should add up to over $1B.

EXAMPLES

Bloom Continued

Starting with a beachhead TAM of $6M per year, the Bloom team identified several follow-on markets, both using their initial product to sell to adjacent markets, and selling new products to their Beachhead customer. You can see in Figure 14.2 that for the adjacent market of "Bloomer" women, they also identified an opportunity to sell new products once they move into that adjacent market. Figure 14.3 gives more information about the adjacent markets they identified.

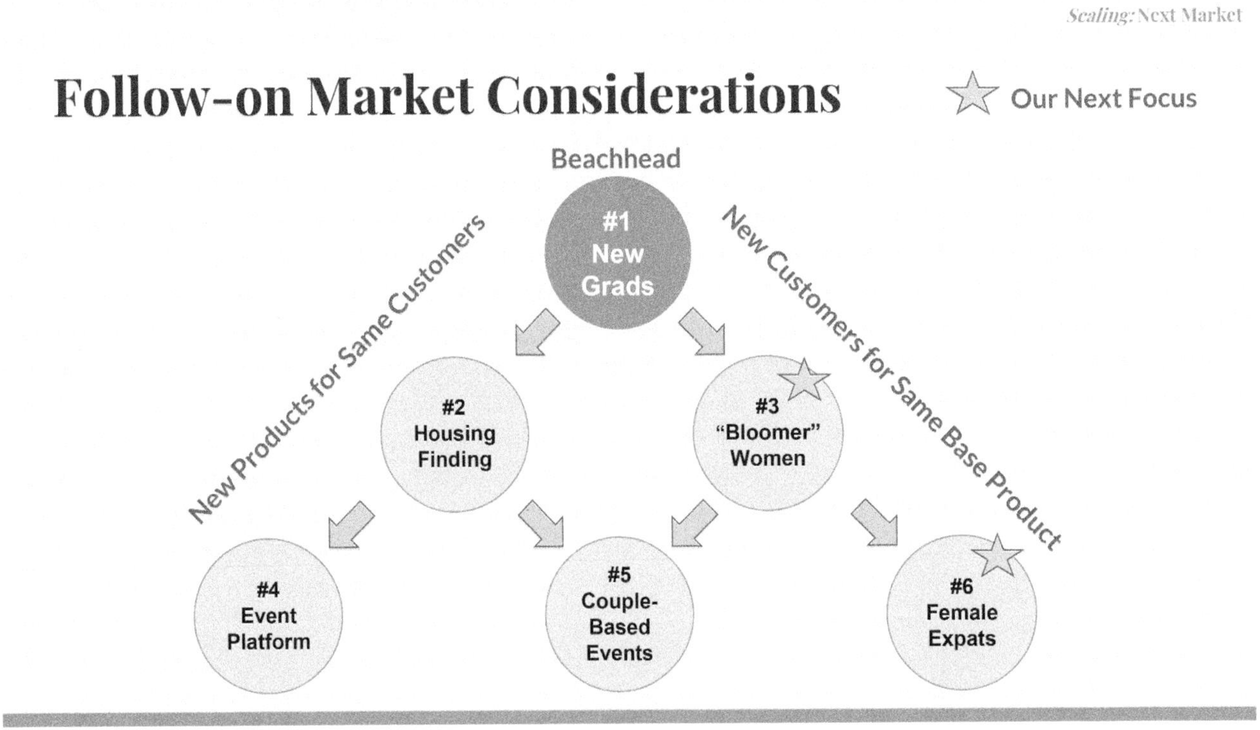

Scaling: Next Market

Follow-on Market Considerations ⭐ Our Next Focus

Figure 14.2: Summary of Bloom growth strategy.

Follow-on Markets for Acquisition

Beachhead Market

Core Product
- Match users into groups of 5-8 to enable connection.
- Rotate user groups to support further connections.
- Simple algorithm to support users to match to women they are most compatible with.

Core Product Expansion - Event Support
- Plan activities for users, facilitating their in-person connection via event planning / logistics.
- Support feedback from matches / events to better improve the experience.
- Improved machine learning algorithm for better matching women and learning from group rotations.

Follow-On Market

Expand to "Bloomer" Women (Estimated TAM ~$36M)
- Expand to the adjacent market of women who are slightly older than college age, who could be moving etc.
- Expand event functionality to ensure that there are events appropriate for this age demographic.
- Support age filtering / other relevant filters to let users dictate more control over who they're matched with.

Expand to Female Expats (Estimated TAM ~$7M)
- Expand event planning capabilities to be functional abroad.
- Automate and streamline event venue on-boarding to support faster international growth.
- Support "Bloom" creation across geographies to support women in more remote locations.

Figure 14.3: Bloom follow-on TAM calculations.

While their analysis is thoughtful and thorough, and was great for a classroom exercise, the total identified TAM is only about $50M per year. Sorry, that is simply not enough for this very talented team. I know they can and should have higher aspirations for bigger impact.

As the team started to go beyond the classroom and turn it into a real company, I pushed them hard to make the follow-on TAM much bigger—hundreds of millions of dollars bigger. That is how they will attract top talent and resources and build a company that is worth them making a long-term commitment to. If you are not able to show a path to high impact (or what we call "greatness"), you won't attract top talent and resources. This is a good start but more work needs to be done to show a potential path to greatness that is worthy of this founding team's long-term commitment.

Smart Skin Care

A student team was looking to commercialize a novel drug delivery technology that allowed for medication to be time-released on the skin of people. After a robust Market Segmentation and Beachhead Market selection process, they settled on an initial market of sunscreen for extreme athletes, with a $20M per year TAM. Considering that their gross margins would be very high, this was a good-sized market to get started in and build up some momentum to attract much bigger markets.

They looked at other follow-on markets as well to see where they could use the underlying technology to easily enter markets and gain a large market share. Each of the market opportunities in their simple flowchart (Figure 14.4) were $100M or more per year and the TAM for the follow-on markets added up to around $2B per year. You don't need to get into a lot more detail than a flowchart to understand there is a path to greatness here.

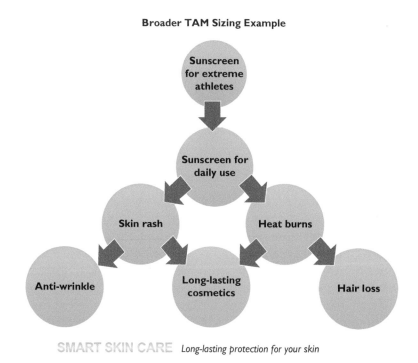

Figure 14.4: Broader TAM sizing for Smart Skin Care.

ADDITIONAL RESOURCES

There are additional resources for this step at www.d-eship.com/step14. For Step 14 you will find:

- The Process Guide to calculate the Total Addressable Market Size for Follow-on Markets, including:
  - Worksheet 14.1: Visual Representation of Follow-on Markets
  - Worksheet 14.2: Structure to Discussion Prioritizing Follow-on Markets
  - Worksheet 14.3: Follow-on Markets TAM Calculation and Other Considerations

Additional resources will be added as new and updated examples and information become available.

Summary

The calculation of the Broader TAM should be a quick validation that there is a bigger market and should reassure team members and investors that your business has great long-term potential.

STEP 15
Design a Business Model

In This Step, You Will:

- Understand the various existing Business Models across industries for capturing some of the value your product brings to your customer.
- Choose a Business Model that best aligns with both your customer and your venture's goals.

THE AMOUNT OF TIME
SPENT ON VALUE CREATION INNOVATION

THE AMOUNT OF TIME
SPENT ON VALUE CAPTURE INNOVATION

Entrepreneurs usually spend far too little time on analyzing and choosing a Business Model.

Why This Step, and Why Now?

Wise selection of a value extraction Business Model can dramatically reduce Cost of Customer Acquisition (CoCA), increase Lifetime Value of an Acquired Customer (LTV), and provide you with a competitive advantage. It may even be the difference between your product being adopted or not. You do this now because, thanks to the work you've done in the previous steps, you have for the first time all of the elements needed to make an informed decision.

Let's Get Started

Business Model is a term that is used extensively in entrepreneurial and business discussions where the definition is very general and not precise. In this situation, Business Model is specifically the method by which you extract rent (i.e., get paid) for the value you create. This could technically be called your value extraction model. Before you choose your Business Model, you should consider the different ways you could get paid for your product and choose the one best aligned with all of the stakeholders' interests. There may even be more than one or a hybrid way to extract rent as well.

Entrepreneurs often incorrectly spend a disproportionately small amount of time thinking about and choosing a Business Model. They invest a lot of time in developing the End User Profile, the product definition, and the value proposition, showing how they will create value for the customer, but barely any time analyzing and making a reasoned choice in this area. They are so excited to bring the product to market that they just default to adopting whatever Business Model is popular with their competitors. Then they jump right to the pricing, missing a potentially golden opportunity.

The track record shows that companies that spend time and effort on innovative Business Models can see enormous payback, more than spending more time incrementally improving their products.

Google's search product is an excellent example of an innovative Business Model. Prior to Google, the Business Model or "value capture framework" of search engines was to fit as many banner advertisements on a page as possible, and to charge as much as possible for them. Google, by contrast, used simple text ads and targeted them based on the keywords used in a particular search. Advertisers found this technique more attractive than banner ads, because they had better data on the effectiveness of individual ads, and could make more effective ads based on the data. This highly innovative Business Model, not the technical proficiency of its search algorithm, is what made Google the juggernaut it is today.

Ironically, this idea of commercially viable contextual search was not Google's but rather came from Overture, an Idealab company that was the first to bring to the commercial market a credible keyword-based advertising solution under the name of GoTo.com. Google simply embraced the idea more enthusiastically and executed a rollout plan that made it the de facto leader in online advertising. You don't have to come up with the idea yourself, but rather you have to recognize its value and implement it more effectively than everyone else. Steve Jobs was well known for this. It is called "lateral innovation," which is taking an idea and moving it laterally into your market and implementing it to fit your market. But back to Business Model innovation . . .

Business Model innovation is generally recognized as the number one factor in the success of the first online music store of significant magnitude, Apple's iTunes. Before iTunes, the standard method of capturing value for digital music was to charge a monthly subscription fee for access to a library of music, where failure to pay the fee meant access to the music was cut off. While this is popular today, at the time it was very unsuccessful and really held back the industry. For decades consumers had developed the habit of paying for music by buying records, CDs, or tapes. You buy it once and you own it forever. This subscription model at the time was not compatible with what consumers wanted. Habits are hard to break. Apple recognized this and successfully differentiated itself with a one-time $.99 per song charge, after which the user could keep the digital song forever. This approach fit perfectly with the consumer buying expectations of that time and iTunes took the whole market segment to a new level.

Interestingly, looking back now with the benefit of more time, you can see that the success of this Business Model turned out to have an expiration date. The free, ad-supported Pandora system and later Spotify changed consumer behavior again and the iTunes model fell out of favor for the majority of the market. Business models have to adapt to market conditions.

These are but two illustrations of why you should make sure to spend time on deciding what your Business Model for value capture will be and don't just default to the current standard in your industry.

As a new business, you will have many options for Business Models, but it is difficult (though not impossible) to change a Business Model once you have established a base of customers. This is one advantage you have over the current entrenched vendors in your industry area. Therefore, evaluate your Business Model through your customer's perspective when you launch and consider testing different options before you settle in on the Business Model you will use to capture value. It could be a source of competitive advantage.

A Business Model Is Not Pricing

A Business Model is a framework by which you extract from your customers some portion of the value your product creates for them. This should not be based simply on some percentage markup based on your costs. You should constantly be working toward achieving Business Models and pricing that are value-based even if you have to make temporary shifts along the way to get there (e.g., joint development contracts, government projects, pilot projects where the scope is unclear and the risk is high). Pricing will follow your Business Model choice and it is not the same thing.

Key Factors When Designing a Business Model

When thinking about an appropriate Business Model for your business, there is no one universally right answer, because it depends on your specific situation. There are four key factors (Figure 15.1) that I always make sure entrepreneurs consider:

1. **Customer:** Understand what your customer is willing to do. The knowledge you gained from mapping the Decision-Making Unit (DMU) and Process to Acquire a Paying Customer will be valuable here. Is there a Business Model that streamlines the DMU and the sales process without significantly adversely affecting your Lifetime Value (LTV) of a Customer? Be well aware of how much budget they have and what they are paying today.

2. **Value Creation and Capture:** Assess how much value your product provides to your customer and when. Then determine which ways of capturing value match up well. Your Quantified Value Proposition will help here.

3. **Competition:** Identify what Business Model your competition is executing.

4. **Distribution:** If you have to go through a distribution channel, make sure your Business Model does not create problems for them. Make sure you can also implement the right incentives for them to sell your product with the Business Model.

Figure 15.1: There are multiple considerations when designing a business model.

FREE IS NOT A BUSINESS MODEL

I often hear "Freemium," or offering your product for free while charging for additional features, referred to as a Business Model. It is not. It is a customer or data acquisition strategy. For something to be a Business Model, money has to come into your company. If you expand this and settle on "Freemium to Premium," then you have a plan for money to change hands and this is a viable or even smart customer acquisition and Business Model strategy. It also might be a way to acquire data that you can then monetize in other dimensions, which would be a viable business strategy.

Generalized Categories of Business Models

Thinking through some of the common types of Business Models will help you get a better sense of which is the best fit for you. You will likely decide on a hybrid Business Model that includes elements from multiple categories. It is a good idea to look at Business Models in industries other than your own; such lateral thinking often results in creative, effective Business Models. This list is designed to give you some exposure to the many options available, but you should also think beyond the list when designing your Business Model.

1. **One-time Up-Front Charge plus Maintenance:** This is the most common Business Model, where a customer pays a large up-front charge to obtain the product, with the option to secure ongoing upgrades or maintenance of the product for a recurring fee. The up-front charge may need to come out of the customer's capital budget, especially if the expense is large, and spending from the capital budget requires a potentially long and formal approval process. The ongoing maintenance charge would come out of the customer's operating budget. For your business, a large up-front infusion of cash is good because it helps offset your high cost of capital, but with this decision you will very likely minimize your ability to secure a recurring revenue stream.

2. **Cost Plus:** In this scenario, the customer pays a set percentage above the cost of producing the product. This is common in government contracts as well as situations where you and your customer want to share the risk of producing the product. The challenge with this model is that it requires agreement on the accounting assumptions, trusting that the numbers are correct and will continue to be correct. This model might also be attractive when your product

is immature and there will almost surely be scope creep, but in that case the offering should mature and you can then migrate to a different Business Model. It can also create incentives that reward activity rather than progress, which is bad for both you and your customer.

3. **Hourly Rates:** This model also tends to reward activity as opposed to progress, which can be the wrong incentive, but when a project is poorly defined or very dynamic, this might well be the preferred model. A common Business Model for services firms, it is similar to scenario 2, but the rates are set by the market demand rather than costs.

4. **Subscription or Leasing Model:** This is a set payment each month or another predetermined and agreed-upon time period. It is a great way to get a recurring revenue stream. There are a number of variations, including:

   • *Annual or Multiyear Commitment:* This locks the customer in and provides them with predictable lower payments as opposed to a one-time up-front payment. One type is a subscription prepayment such as what MIT senior lecturer Howard Anderson used when he founded Yankee Group. He charged an annual fee for a monthly newsletter that would be delivered over the course of the year; the resulting up-front cash flow created less need for capital. (Note: Getting prepayments, even if you have to provide discounts, is generally good for startups.)

   • *Month-to-Month Commitment:* This method gives the user great flexibility and you can often extract a much higher monthly payment for this arrangement, compared to an annual or multiyear agreement.

5. **Licensing:** Licensing your intellectual property to customers and receiving a royalty can result in a very high gross margin (gross margin is the difference between marginal revenue and marginal costs). In addition, if you are licensing your product, you do not have to make big investments in production and distribution capability for a whole product. However, there are many downsides to the strategy. Licensing generally only works when the IP is extremely strong. Even then, you tend to get into an adversarial relationship with your customer in time. I recommend against this option except in extreme cases.

6. **Consumables:** Another value capture framework that can be advantageous to both the customer and your business is the consumables model. For the customer, the benefit is a low up-front cost, with ongoing costs based on usage, which the customer can usually control. The customer might not have an easy way to pay for a large up-front cost but has much more capability to procure once usage has started. Once usage has started, they can justify the purchase of some consumable product the solution uses. The amount of consumable that

needs to be purchased is directly related to usage; in many cases, your customer can pass the cost on to their own customers. For your business, it might very well be a way to reduce the friction to capture new customers and thereby reduce the sales costs and also substantially increase the amount of money you will get from that customer over the long term. This is a very popular model for medical devices, but it is also used frequently in the consumer space. A highly visible and well-recognized example is the razor/razor blade model made famous by Gillette. HP is another example, where almost all, if not all, of their profit on printers comes from selling inkjet cartridges.

7. **Upsell with High-Margin Products:** Similar to the consumable Business Model, the central product is sold at a very low margin, but the overall margin is increased from the sale of very high-margin add-on products. This Business Model is often used in consumer electronics stores or websites and new car sales. A camera might be sold at just above cost, which attracts the customer, but then the customer buys add-ons that have a higher margin, like a warranty extension for one, two, or three years. Similarly, when buying a new car, the lion's share of the profits are made from the additional accessories and services.

8. **Advertising:** As with newspapers and magazines in their heyday and now with websites, the ability to attract and retain a desirable demographic can be monetized through third parties who want access to the customers you have attracted. When done properly and on a sufficient scale, this can be a very lucrative model, as Google and others have shown; but many startups have fallen substantially short when they attempt to rely solely on advertising. For businesses like LinkedIn, advertising is part of a broad portfolio of revenue streams.

9. **Reselling the Data Collected—or Much More Likely, Temporary Access to It:** Somewhat similar to the advertising model, reselling user data requires first attracting end users with a free product, then receiving money from third parties who pay for access to demographic and other information about your users. This is a major source of revenue for LinkedIn, which sells a special package for recruiters that gives access to a wide array of LinkedIn user data. The medical industry also resells access to user data for market research.

10. **Transaction Fee:** Online retailers often pay or receive a commission for referrals that lead to sales. One obvious example is eBay, which receives a fee from each successful auction, paid by the seller. The model is similar to how credit card companies work, where a percentage of each transaction goes to the credit card company.

11. **Usage-Based:** A usage-based model—similar to how electric utilities are metered—has been used across various other industries. Cloud computing products, such as Amazon's cloud service that hosts websites, charge by the amount used. This allows customers more control over their expenses because they only pay for the amount of bandwidth used, rather than paying for extra capacity they don't use.

12. **"Cell Phone" Plan:** This is a predictable, recurring base fee charged in exchange for a certain amount of committed usage, with additional charges, often at much higher marginal rates, if the customer uses more than their allotted amount. The base charge is generally far less per amount of usage than the overage charge. You get predictability from the base charge, as does the customer, because they know what they can use, but they also have flexibility if they need additional usage. MIT Senior Lecturer Jim Dougherty, when he was at IntraLinks, used this strategy to effectively monetize its principal product, an online interface for lawyers and investment bankers to securely share documents with clients, in a manner his customer base greatly favored.

13. **Parking Meter or Penalty Charges:** I always found it curious that cities had incredibly large and expensive parking meters that had to be put in the sidewalk extremely securely. And yet for a long time, the hourly parking rate was only 25 cents. It defied logic that a quarter per hour justified the significant purchase and installation costs of a meter, along with the expense of paying someone to collect the quarters. Of course, one day it occurred to me how they made money when I came back to my car and found a $25 parking ticket that became a $40 ticket if I did not pay it in 10 days. What a Business Model! No wonder they have so many parking enforcement people. But this is the same Business Model used by credit card companies and (for a while) Blockbuster by charging late fees. You have to be very careful if you use this model, because taking advantage of your customer's naïveté is an unstable Business Model.

14. **Microtransactions:** A new successful model that came into vogue with online computer games, and is now being tested to try to save newspapers, is microtransactions. In this model, the customer is asked to provide their credit card and then they make very small transactions (defined as less than $12; often they are $1 or less) for digital goods (which have virtually no marginal cost because they are electrons). There are many of them so they can add up.

15. **Shared Savings:** This Business Model is often brainstormed, but rarely used because of the complexities in implementing it, despite its conceptual elegance. In this scenario, the customer pays only once they have realized savings or benefits from the product. One area where this has been used with success is the Energy Efficiency Service Companies (ESCOs) such as Ameresco. It is generally not implemented because it is hard to determine how much savings to attribute to the product, especially over a multiyear time period. One area where this model works, because the accounting is clear, is venture capital, where the general partner gets around 20% of the profits from their investments (this is termed the "carry").

16. **Franchise:** If an entrepreneur comes up with a good idea and is able to implement but does not have the desire, skills, or money to roll it out, they can use the franchise model and get paid a percentage of sales and/or receive a large initial startup fee in return for providing the knowledge and brand that has been developed. You can also make money by selling your brand-name products to the franchises to be distributed.

17. **Operating and Maintenance:** A new business might not want to really sell a product but rather get paid for running a plant or other operation for a fee. While this is similar in some ways to a consulting agreement, the customer has more incentives to control or cut costs, because it will directly impact the customer's income. This model is common in the energy sector.

This is not an exhaustive list of Business Models, but it will help you think about different ways to capture value for your business.

Don't Be Afraid to Think Outside the Existing Categories

A Rhode Island company called Amie Street used an innovative Business Model to capture value from song downloads based on demand. The very first downloads of a song would be free, but as the number of downloads increased for that song, the company would increase the charge to the customer. Customers were incented to go and listen to music and see if they could pick songs before they became popular. If they recommended a song when it sold for a low dollar amount, and the song later gained popularity and increased its price, the recommender would be given 50 percent of the price difference.[1] Amie Street was bought by Amazon for an undisclosed price in September of 2010; what made Amie Street attractive to Amazon was the company's variable pricing and clever incentive schemes.

Be careful, though, not to spend so much time being clever with your Business Model that you lose focus on creating value. The two sides to a business, creating value and then capturing value through a Business Model, should be in balance.

---

[1] Michael Arrington, "Amie Street: Awesome New Music Model," TechCrunch, July 23, 2006, https://techcrunch.com/2006/07/23/amie-street-awesome-new-music-model/.

Bloom Continued

The Business Model discussion for Bloom is a great example of all of these concepts put into practice. As you can see in Figure 15.2, they systematically analyzed the four key factors before choosing an option.

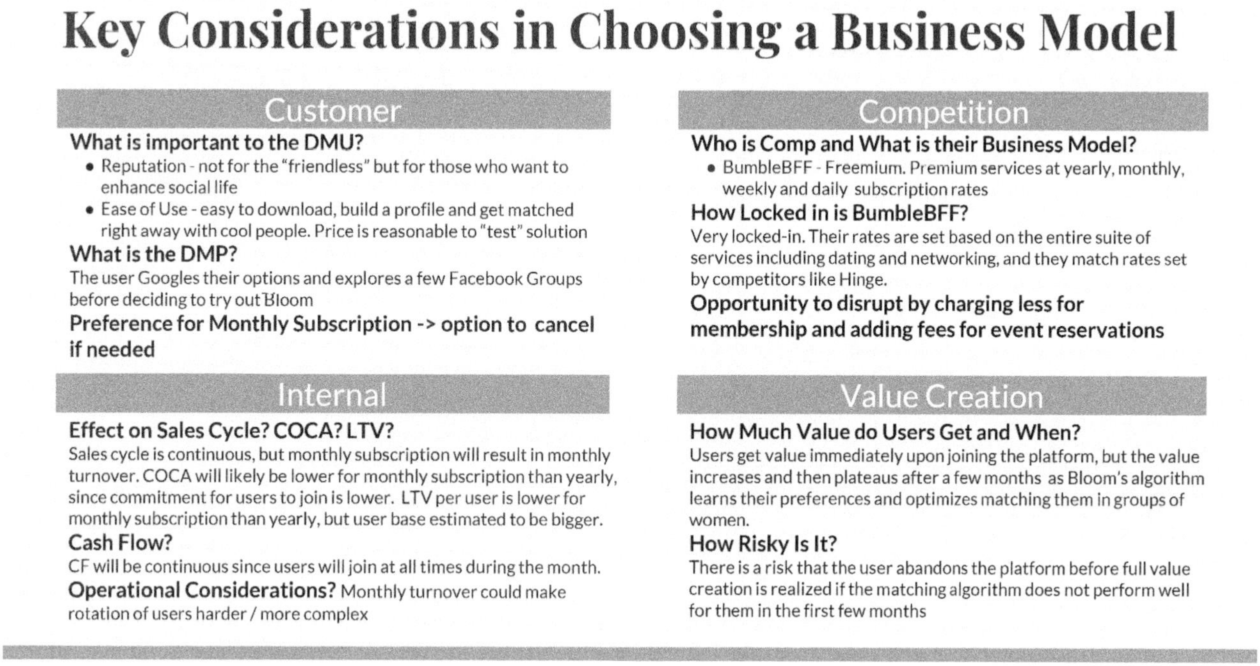

Key Considerations in Choosing a Business Model

Customer

What is important to the DMU?
- Reputation - not for the "friendless" but for those who want to enhance social life
- Ease of Use - easy to download, build a profile and get matched right away with cool people. Price is reasonable to "test" solution

What is the DMP?
The user Googles their options and explores a few Facebook Groups before deciding to try out Bloom

Preference for Monthly Subscription -> option to cancel if needed

Competition

Who is Comp and What is their Business Model?
- BumbleBFF - Freemium. Premium services at yearly, monthly, weekly and daily subscription rates

How Locked in is BumbleBFF?
Very locked-in. Their rates are set based on the entire suite of services including dating and networking, and they match rates set by competitors like Hinge.

Opportunity to disrupt by charging less for membership and adding fees for event reservations

Internal

Effect on Sales Cycle? COCA? LTV?
Sales cycle is continuous, but monthly subscription will result in monthly turnover. COCA will likely be lower for monthly subscription than yearly, since commitment for users to join is lower. LTV per user is lower for monthly subscription than yearly, but user base estimated to be bigger.

Cash Flow?
CF will be continuous since users will join at all times during the month.

Operational Considerations? Monthly turnover could make rotation of users harder / more complex

Value Creation

How Much Value do Users Get and When?
Users get value immediately upon joining the platform, but the value increases and then plateaus after a few months as Bloom's algorithm learns their preferences and optimizes matching them in groups of women.

How Risky Is It?
There is a risk that the user abandons the platform before full value creation is realized if the matching algorithm does not perform well for them in the first few months

Figure 15.2: Bloom key considerations in choosing a Business Model.

Once they had done this analysis, they then chose the top six options they wanted to evaluate to compare and contrast. You can see the summary of those options in Figure 15.3.

Product Unit Economics: Business Model Candidates

Summary of Business Model Candidates

#	Option	Unit	Customer Fit	Value Creation Fit	Competitor Fit	Internal Fit	Pros	Cons	Grade
☆1	Subscription: Monthly	# of users and/or per feature set	A	A	A	A	Recurring revenue, common, customers used to it, monthly is reasonable commitment	Not innovative, easy to discontinue, admin burden of monthly payments	A
2	Subscription: Yearly	# of users and/or per feature set	B	B	B	B	Recurring revenue, high up front cash	Harder to sell to customer, bigger commitment	B
3	Subscription: Weekly	# of users and/or per feature set	A	A	B	B	Constant cash flow, higher margin, weekly commitment flexible for customers	Easy to discontinue, admin burden of weekly payments	B
4	Usage-Based: Per Event	Per event attended	A	A	A	B	Customers have control, Margins configured per event, disincentivizes ghosting	Disincentives event attendance, admin burden of event coordination	A
5	Advertising	Per ad, per run time, per view	B	C	C	C	No cost for users, helps with customer acquisition	Annoying to customers, could hurt platform likeability	C
6	Reselling Data	Per record	C	C	C	C	No cost for users, helps with customer acquisition	Annoying to customers, data privacy and regulation, long lead times	C

Our chosen model is a monthly subscription per user that includes tokens that can be used to reserve a spot at group events. We believe a monthly subscription is long enough to incentivize participation, but short enough that it is a reasonable commitment for users vs. the big upfront cost of a yearly subscription model.

Figure 15.3: Bloom summary of top six Business Model candidates.

As you can see in Figure 15.3, the team chose a monthly subscription Business Model and in Figure 15.4 they describe why in more detail.

Chosen Business Model

Decided Model	Unit	Pros	Cons
Subscription: Monthly	# of users and/or per feature set	Recurring revenue, common, customers used to it, monthly is reasonable commitment	Not innovative, easy to discontinue, admin burden of monthly payments

Short-Term: Grow through Free Subscription

Initially, the product will be free for all users in order to:
- Reduce download friction so that user base will reach critical mass
- Allow for easier collection of feedback and interaction without alienating initial user base

Medium-Term: Segment Users through Freemium Model

Once we have data on user base and have proven our value, introduce tiered service levels with a price slightly less than BumbleBFF in order to:
- Capture greater value from users that have a higher willingness to pay
- Not alienate existing customers and maintaining critical mass by keeping the free tier

Long-Term: Introduce Add-Ons for Optimized Engagement

Once product has matured, retain the tiered pricing but consider introducing other paid features such as:

- Fee for extra rotation to a new group
- Access to exclusive events
- Compatibility metrics

Figure 15.4: Details and deeper dive on Bloom's chosen Business Model.

It is important that a decision the team made in their Business Model was to start with a low-cost monthly subscription model but they would also offer exclusive events for a separate fee. This is combining the subscription with a per usage model, which not only gives the customer more flexibility but also gives the company clear signals of what their customers value, which is not possible in an unlimited usage subscription model. This is an excellent example of a structure process to thoughtfully examine the different possibilities for a Business Model and, in the end, choosing one with the best odds of success. That being said, as they test this in the market, they will learn new information and have to be open to modifying the Business Model early on because new valuable market evidence will come to light as soon as they run experiments in the real world.

ADDITIONAL RESOURCES

There are additional resources for this step at www.d-eship.com/step15. There you will find:

- Video: Business Model Explainers by Bill Aulet and Erdin Beshimov
- Video: Interview with Tekuma founder Marwan Aboudib
- Design Your Business Model Process Guide
- Worksheet 15.1: Key Considerations in Choosing a Business Model
- Worksheet 15.2: Identification of Units to Charge For
- Worksheet 15.3: Framework for Analysis and Discussion of Different Business Models
- Worksheet 15.4: Reflection on Choice of Business Model

Additional resources will be added as new and updated examples and information become available.

Summary

The Business Model is an important decision that you should spend time focusing on. The decisions you make here will have a significant impact on your profitability, as measured by two key entrepreneurship variables: the Lifetime Value of an Acquired Customer (LTV) and Cost of Customer Acquisition (COCA). Do not focus on pricing in this step; that follows your decision of Business Model and will be addressed in Step 16, Set Your Pricing Framework.

Once you have established a Business Model, it is possible but generally not easy to change to a different model. Therefore, choose a Business Model that distinguishes you from competitors and gives you an advantage over them, because they cannot easily change their Business Model to match yours.

Set Your Pricing Framework

In This Step, You Will:

- Use your Quantified Value Proposition, Business Model, and other information you have gathered to determine an appropriate first draft price point and framework for pricing your product.

Even though it's impossible to know the right pricing for your new product just yet, you'll do some analysis now and make some decisions to get started, but also build a framework to intelligently adjust the pricing decision as you move forward.

Why This Step, and Why Now?

Pricing is something that is often talked about sooner than it should be. Now is the right time because you have the necessary information to have an intelligent conversation about pricing as a result of the work you have done in Step 8 (Quantify the Value Proposition), Steps 10 and 11 (Define Your Core and Chart Your Competitive Position), Steps 12 and 13 (the DMU and sales process) and Step 15 (Design a Business Model). Pricing will be necessary information to continue forward to Step 17 to determine the LTV (Lifetime Value) of a customer, which is the first critical component of the unit economics calculation.

Let's Get Started

With a Business Model in hand, you can now make a good first estimate on your Pricing Framework, understanding that it will almost surely change as you continue through the 24 steps. This step is the beginning of a pricing process, because you will likely end up with multiple price points and pricing strategies, and you will iterate as you experiment and get feedback from the market about price points. Whereas your Business Model is much less likely to change, price points are often subject to change. Some businesses even change pricing on a daily basis (e.g., gas stations) or, on a real-time basis (e.g., dynamic pricing of airline tickets).

Your goal for the moment is to create a first-pass strategy that will allow you to calculate the Lifetime Value of an Acquired Customer, which, along with the Cost of Customer Acquisition (CoCA), is an important variable that indicates the profitability of your business. You will find it easier to go back and change your Pricing Framework once you have gone through and made your other calculations, as opposed to trying to get everything right at first.

The process you are about to embark on is not just about getting to a number, but more importantly it is building the knowledge and critical skills that will help you adjust your price over time as you get more information.

The Pricing Framework is extremely important in influencing your profitability, so it is important you price your product correctly. In his book *The 1% Windfall*, Dr. Rafi Mohammed cites a McKinsey & Company study that shows that for companies in the Global 1200, a price that is 1% higher would lead to an 11% increase in overall profits, because once costs have been paid, the remaining revenue is all profit, as represented in Figure 16.1. Of course, there is always an upper limit to your price. Incorrect pricing might exclude your company from customers' consideration or put you at a competitive disadvantage (after all the hard work you have put in to date!). The Pricing Framework is a balance between attracting as much revenue as possible and attracting as many customers as possible.

Figure 16.1: Increasing pricing by even 1% can have a disproportionately high positive impact on your bottom line, but be patient until the market matures and you have enough data to make that more precise adjustment.

Basic Pricing Concepts

1. **Costs Shouldn't Be a Factor in Deciding Price.** Set your pricing based on the value the customer gets from your product, rather than on your costs. Cost-based strategies almost always leave money on the table. In software, for instance, the marginal cost (the cost of producing one more copy of the software) is virtually zero, so pricing based on cost would make it extremely difficult to make any money. Instead, use your Quantified Value Proposition, determine how much value your customer receives from your product, and charge some fraction of that. The exact fraction depends on the competition and the industry, but 20% tends to be a reasonable starting point, leaving 80% of the value for the customer, who is taking a risk by incorporating your product into their infrastructure. Some companies, like Microsoft and Intel, have been able to take advantage of monopolistic positions to price higher, but short-term gains through this strategy may create long-term problems for your business if your customers think you are gouging them.

   - The percentage of customer value that you can capture with your pricing depends on your Business Model and how much risk you are pushing onto your customer. A monthly subscription model, where a customer is paying over time but can also cancel at any time, will allow you to price higher than an up-front charge model, where the customer is taking additional risk by paying for the product in full before knowing how beneficial the product will be for them.

- If costs come up in conversations about your product, immediately turn the discussion around to how much *value* you create for the customer. As mentioned in Step 11, Chart Your Competitive Position, Steve Walske, the successful CEO of Parametric Technologies, simplified his business into the simple maxim that customers gave PTC two dollars and they got back ten. This type of approach frames the situation more appropriately and creates a value proposition that is very hard to argue with.

- Don't give out your cost numbers to anyone who does not have a real need to know. Do not tell your sales group, because any good salesperson will use any and all of their resources to make a sale, even if it means driving the price down to costs. This mentality is why you hired and love them. (If you doubt this, read about the behavior of real estate agents in *Freakonomics* by Steven Levitt and Stephen Dubner.) If you open yourself up to discussions about costs, it can lead back to inappropriate discussions about your pricing, which will lead to decreased morale, productivity, and profitability.

2. **Use the DMU and the Process to Acquire a Paying Customer to Identify Key Price Points.** Steps 12 and 13 provide invaluable information about how your customer's budget works. Knowing an individual's purchasing authority limits can help reduce friction in the sales process. One example of using this comes from Kinova of Montreal, Quebec. Kinova sells the Jaco assistive robotic arm for disabled people in wheelchairs (Figure 16.2). When Kinova entered the market in the Netherlands, their primary market research found that consumers could get reimbursed up to 28,000 euros from their health insurance for purchasing the product. If the price went above 28,000 euros, the consumer would need to pay the extra amount out of pocket, creating friction in Kinova's sales process. Despite an extremely strong value proposition that could have supported a higher price, Kinova priced its product at 28,000 euros, which dramatically decreased the company's sales cycle length and Cost of Customer Acquisition (Step 19). As a result, the company quickly ramped up sales and enjoyed a much larger market share than it would if it had priced the product at a higher amount. This was a tradeoff of forgoing slightly higher profits for a much faster sales cycle and market entry, one the company was very happy to make.

3. **Understand the Prices of the Customer's Alternatives.** It is imperative to understand, from the customer's perspective, the alternative products available, and how much the customer would pay for each, including the customer's status quo. Carefully research what other alternatives would achieve similar benefits for the customer, what the prices of those alternatives are, and how much better your solution is. Data collection and analysis is very critical in this step.

Figure 16.2: Kinova's Jaco assistive robotic arm.

4. **Different Types of Customers Will Pay Different Prices.** When I was getting one of my companies off the ground, I got some sage advice from the legendary entrepreneur Mitch Kapor. "The bad news," he said, "is you will sell half as many units as you think you will. But the good news is you will be able to sell to the first group of buyers at twice the price." He was spot-on. Geoffrey Moore explains why in *Crossing the Chasm*. Different types of customers will pay different amounts, so a differentiated pricing strategy and structure for these distinct customer segments will mean substantially higher profits for your business.

Moore breaks customers down into five waves:

- **Technological enthusiasts** are the first people to buy a product. They love technology and will buy one of anything. Some are consumers, while others work in corporate, university or government R&D labs. They will only buy one (hence half the number you expect) and also want to have it right away, so they are willing to pay a high price (hence twice the price).

- **Early adopters** are also price-inelastic but are very interested in feeling like they got a special deal and will require lots of attention and extra service, so make sure to build that into your pricing model.

- **The early majority (pragmatists)** is where you will make yourself a great and truly scalable company. That is the price point that most people think about when they are talking about and planning for a pricing strategy. This group is price sensitive.

- **The late majority (conservatives)** are later in the process and your pricing strategy will be very clear by then; they like well-defined, conservative plans.

- **Laggards/skeptics** come so late in the process that you may have already sold your company at this point.

5. **Be Flexible with Pricing for Early Testers and "Lighthouse Customers."** These two types of customers are beneficial to have early on. Early testers will collaborate with you to improve your product, and lighthouse customers strongly influence the purchasing decisions of others in the industry. Allow for flexibility on pricing with these two groups of customers, whether through discounting an up-front charge or through a free or low-cost trial period, as it is important to get them committed and satisfied. These customers may help you create case studies or do on-site seminars where you can promote your product, or otherwise be strong references in the market. However, do not give your product away to these customers, and do not discount any ongoing revenue streams, because that would signal your product has a very low value, setting a dangerous precedent. Have early customers sign an agreement where their pricing terms be kept confidential, and be firm with other, later customers who try to secure the same pricing terms, because you do not want your early one-time-only deals to define your general pricing strategy. Additionally, if you have the option to discount hardware, software, or data access, I much prefer to discount the hardware and hold the line on software pricing. Customers can more easily understand hardware value versus software or data value, and it will be easier to reestablish higher hardware pricing as opposed to reestablishing software pricing.

6. **It Is Always Easier to Drop the Price Than to Raise the Price.** It is best to price high and offer discounts initially, rather than price too low and find you need to raise the price later. Usually, your first customers will have larger budgets than your later customers, who are more likely to accept less-than-cutting-edge technology in exchange for a lower price. Also, you will find it difficult to convince customers to accept a higher price when they are used to paying a lower price. Sometimes, a price increase is necessary as you learn more about the market, but successful price increases do not happen frequently.

Avoid Analysis Paralysis—Make Your Best Guess and Keep Moving

No matter how much time you spend on this step running studies on willingness to pay and statistical analysis, you will not know for sure the right price. This analysis is valuable, but there is a limit. Until you put the product in the customer's hands and they realize the actual real-world value compared to their alternatives, you will not know the optimal pricing for sure. And the optimal pricing will always change over time.

So, do the analysis, understand the various inputs to determining an optimal price, give yourself flexibility to make changes later, and make your best guess. Throw it out there and see how the market responds, and adapt quickly. The worst thing you can do is get stuck in analysis paralysis and let your competitors start to iterate with customers. Then your competitors will get the invaluable real-world knowledge and data, and even more importantly, they will have the customer relationship. A key maxim I learned early on in my career at IBM is that "Whoever owns the customer relationship owns the gold." If you are talking to the customer, that is good. If your competitors are, that is bad.

EXAMPLES

Bloom Continued

As you saw in Step 15, Design a Business Model, the Bloom team did an excellent job of identifying the key considerations for choosing a Business Model, which makes this step much easier because of the overlap.

Bloom's analysis (Figure 16.3) focuses on comparisons to price points of competitors as well as the ability to pay of the target customer group. The team talks less about the value created, but they do take this into consideration in the pricing-driven incentives structure. Understanding that they will not have much pricing power at first due to the relative immaturity of their product, they will have to start out with a price that is slightly lower than the number one competitor, Bumble BFF. That would be the starting point to achieve quick market penetration, but is not where they want to be long term.

They settled on $20 per month and approximately $50 per event for their exclusive events. This is where they will start and then adjust as they get more feedback from the market. As their product develops, hopefully they will get more pricing power.

Considerations in Setting the Initial Pricing Framework

Factor	Considerations	Data
Competitor Pricing	Gaining critical ground against competitors and seeing the benefits of network effects is extremely important to Bloom's success. As such, it is especially important to price with competitors in mind, even though Bloom has other differentiating features.	**BumbleBFF:** free non-premium, lifetime premium ($149.99), 6 months premium ($99.99), 3 months premium ($59.99), 1 month premium ($29.99), 1 week premium ($13.99), 1 day premium ($3.49) **Hey, Vina!:** free non-premium, Lifetime VIP ($99.99), 6 months VIP ($47.99), 3 months VIP ($29.99), 1 month VIP ($14.99), 1 week VIP ($5.99)
Price Sensitivity of Beachhead Market	New Grads are typically making entry-level salaries and do not have a great deal of disposable income. Thus the price needs to be reasonable for them to join.	New-grad US women on average make $35K starting salaries, 81% of that of men due to the persisting gender gap, leaving limited disposable income [1].
Pricing driven incentives	Each pricing framework has implications on how the users will interact with the platform that should be considered when choosing a framework	Regular user interaction with the platforms crucial for Bloom's success. On average, users use 9 apps a day regularly, it is crucial for Bloom to become one of those apps and pricing structures / initiatives can help drive that adoption [2].

Figure 16.3: Considerations for Bloom's Pricing Framework.

Helios

This student team was working on developing an exciting new thin-film technology that captured solar energy and could release the energy on demand. The team's Beachhead Market was remotely deicing windows on corporate and government fleets of automobiles.

The team factored in that the primary alternatives to their product were drivers manually deicing their individual cars, or maintenance employees manually deicing a fleet. This is a very low-cost alternative that had worked for years. Union rules and desires also had to be included. To get to a good educated guess on pricing, the team had to clearly understand its Quantified Value Proposition, as well as the rational and emotional qualities of the Decision-Making Unit.

The team created a first-pass Pricing Framework, and then once they calculated their Lifetime Value of an Acquired Customer (Step 17) and Cost of Customer Acquisition (Step 19), they went back and revised their Pricing Framework based on those calculations. In the revised Pricing Framework, they set the price at $100 per unit, which would provide $100K in the first year of sales (based on the target customer's average vehicle fleet size of 1,000). With average 20% fleet turnover, they would net $20K per year afterward. As part of their framework, they compared their technology to window tinting, concluding that customers would judge their pricing against what they were used to paying for tinting. The strategy also discussed a discounting strategy for pilot customers to jump-start positive word of mouth.

This case is a good reminder that different steps depend on each other, and you should continually revisit and revise your assumptions based on work done in later steps.

ADDITIONAL RESOURCES

There are additional resources for this step at www.d-eship.com/step16. There you will find:

- Video: Pricing Explainers by Bill Aulet and Erdin Beshimov
- Video: Example described and explained in an interview with Ministry of Supply founders Aman Advani and Kit Hickey
- Pricing Framework Process Guide
- Worksheet 16.1: Consideration in Setting an Initial Pricing Framework
- Worksheet 16.2: Summary of decision on Initial Pricing Framework with assumptions and testing plan going forward

Additional resources will be added as new and updated examples and information become available.

Summary

Pricing is primarily about determining how much value your customer gets from your product, and capturing a fraction of that value back for your business. Costs are irrelevant (except for setting a floor) in determining your pricing structure. You will be able to charge a higher price to early customers as opposed to later customers, but be flexible in offering special, one-time-only discounts to select early testers and lighthouse customers, as they will be far more beneficial to your product's success. Unlike your Business Model, pricing will continually change, both as a result of information you gather and as you progress throughout the 24 Steps, as well as in response to market conditions.

Calculate the Lifetime Value (LTV) of an Acquired Customer

In This Step, You Will:

- Estimate the revenue you can expect to receive from each additional customer.
- Estimate gross profit over time from that revenue estimate, taking into account the net present value.

LTV and CoCA are really just educated estimates that will help you understand the critical drivers behind your company's financial success. Understand the high-level concepts and key assumptions, remember that these numbers are ranges and not precise, and don't get lost in the details.

Why This Step, and Why Now?

So far you have zeroed in on a very well-defined Beachhead Market that you can provide unique value for. You should have high confidence of this from Steps 1–11. Since those steps, you have turned your focus to how the customer acquires the product. The effort and resources to get the customer to acquire the product is the biggest unknown in almost every new venture. For most new companies, marketing and sales expenses are well over 50% of their total expenses and the one that carries the most risk.

To address this in a systematic fashion, you started in Steps 12 and 13 (the DMU and customer acquisition process) to understand this process in much more detail so you could make educated decisions regarding the marketing and sales investment required. In Steps 15 and 16 (Design a Business Model and Set Your Pricing Framework), you analyzed what the best method and general amount would be for value extraction (i.e., how and what rent you should receive). You are now in a position to estimate what the value of an average customer will be. That is what is called LTV (Lifetime Value). This is the first of the two key elements you need to understand to do a first check on the viability of this business. The other is CoCA, or Cost of Customer Acquisition. These two elements make up the critical numbers that summarize your "unit economics."

Let's Get Started

Calculating the average LTV, along with the average CoCA, will help you determine how profitable your business will be in the Beachhead Market.

A very expensive case study regarding the importance of LTV, CoCA, and unit economics can be seen in Pets.com. The company was founded in August 1998 to sell products over the Internet to consumers for their pets. The concept was that people spent a lot of money on their pets and this new company had a new business model that sold directly to consumers, eliminating the costs of maintaining physical retail stores.

The concept and the strength of the management team, as well as, frankly, an overexuberant venture capital market, allowed the company to easily raise millions of dollars from investors. In their drive to build a brand and acquire customers, they aggressively advertised their website, including a high-profile Super Bowl commercial in 2000. They were acquiring customers but had not rigorously analyzed the unit economics.

When they went public in February 2000 and analysts started to scrutinize their unit economics, the walls came crashing down. The math did not lie and investors realized that because of the low margin on the products they were selling and the very high costs of customer acquisition, which had stayed relatively constant rather than decreasing as they should, the company was losing money with each new customer it captured. The company was bleeding cash, but management doubled down and said it was simply a matter of volume, that when the customer base was large enough, the company would be cash-flow positive. This was wishful thinking rather than genuine economic analysis because management had not developed a clear path to increase the LTV, nor had they developed a clear path to significantly reduce the CoCA. So the bleeding of cash just increased as they got more customers.

In November 2000, less than a year after it went public, the company was shut down and assets were liquidated. Three hundred million dollars of investor money had been vaporized, but, to put a positive spin on it, it can be viewed as a $300 million educational lesson to make sure people are disciplined and intellectually honest about their unit economics analysis before they invest too much time, money, or energy into a new venture.

One would think that this education would prevent future mistakes along this line, but this has not been the case. Groupon was a billion-dollar disappointment in the 2010 era and even more recently there was another reminder. In April 2020, to much fanfare and backed with $1.75 billion in funding, Quibi, a short-form streaming platform for mobile devices, was launched with a rock star CEO, Meg Whitman, and a line of blue-chip investors, partners, and supporters.

A *Wall Street Journal* report in July 2020 suggested that Quibi was paying more than $100 to acquire each subscriber, given their massive marketing spend. If these figures are accurate, Quibi's CoCA was incredibly high. On the LTV side, Quibi struggled with low retention rates after the end of the free trial period, which suggests that their LTV was likely low. Nine months later, Quibi was sold in a fire sale for $100M. The math of unit economics is not to be ignored, even if you have a legendary leadership team and blue-chip investors.

In this step, you will focus on LTV, and then, armed with this information, work your way into CoCA in the two steps that follow.

LTV and Unit Economics in Full Perspective

If your LTV is greater than your CoCA, that means an average new customer pays for the marketing and sales expenses it took to acquire that customer. If your LTV is less than your CoCA, then you are losing money on each new customer. And that's before considering the other significant costs of the business. Research and Development (R&D) is everything you do to make the product—generally in the range of 20–35% of overall business expense, but there is great variance by industry. General and Administration (G&A) is everything else you need to run the business like legal, information technology (IT), human resources (HR), facilities, and the like—generally in the 10–20% range but again there will be great variance by industry. Sometimes entrepreneurs think they live in a different world where they can ignore these unit economics, but they do not. Let me be clear: *If there is no path to make your LTV exceed your CoCA at some point, your business is not viable long term.*

Since your business has more expenses than just marketing and sales (as mentioned above) and you want to have profits to reinvest in the business, LTV should not just equal or slightly exceed the CoCA. Entrepreneur and venture capitalist David Skok's rule of thumb for Software as a Service (SaaS) businesses is that LTV should be at least three times or greater than the CoCA.[1] This factor varies wildly from industry to industry—lower for service business, which have lower R&D costs, and much higher for pharmaceutical companies, which have very high R&D and regulatory costs.

There are a couple of other reasons why it's important for the LTV to be a multiple of CoCA. First, there is usually some over-optimism built into the LTV and CoCA calculations despite your greatest efforts to make it real; so a 3:1 ratio ensures there is plenty of room for error. Second, a new venture is a highly variable system, so having a high ratio of 3:1 or greater will ensure that you have the ability to manage through the tough times when the unexpected happens (e.g., product delays, competitive reaction, recession).

You should know the general range of your LTV as well as what drives LTV. Knowing what drives LTV is equally important as, if not more important than, the number itself.

The LTV will help you make smart decisions about your new venture going forward. This is the area that trips up most novice and even experienced entrepreneurs and, as such, gets the most scrutiny from smart investors.

Key Inputs to Calculate the LTV

Here are the key inputs that you will need to estimate the LTV:

1. **One-Time Revenue Stream, If Any.** Typically, if there is an up-front charge for your product, it is a one-time source of revenue.

2. **Recurring Revenue Streams, If Any.** Subscription and maintenance fees, as well as repeated purchases of consumables, are all recurring revenues.

3. **Additional Revenue Opportunities.** If there are opportunities to "upsell" the customer, where the customer purchases additional products with minimal additional effort from your sales team, include these as revenue streams. Remember to consider the DMU and the sales cycle you mapped out in Steps 12–13. Underestimating either of these could lead you to a distorted view.

4. **Gross Margin for Each of Your Revenue Streams.** The gross margin is the price of your product minus the production cost of making an individual product. Cost does not include sales and marketing costs (which is factored into the CoCA) or overhead costs like R&D or administrative expenses.

---

[1] "Startup Killer: the Cost of Customer Acquisition," ForEntrepreneurs, https://www.forentrepreneurs.com/startup-killer/

5. **Retention Rate.** For each recurring revenue stream, this rate is the percentage of customers who continue to pay the recurring fee for the product. This usually is expressed as a monthly rate or a yearly rate. (The opposite of retention rate is "churn rate," which is the percentage of customers you lose.) Assume, for simplicity, that once the customer has stopped paying a recurring fee, the customer will no longer be receptive to upselling. Do not assume that on a multiyear or multi-month contract customers will make all of their payments. Early termination of a contract by the customer should be incorporated into the retention rate.

6. **Life of Product.** For each one-time revenue stream, this is the length of time you expect the product to last before the customer will need to either purchase a replacement or discontinue use of the product.

7. **Next Product Purchase Rate.** For each one-time revenue stream, this rate is the percentage of customers who will buy a replacement product from you when the current product has reached the end of its life.

8. **Cost of Capital Rate for Your Business.** Expressed as a yearly rate, this is how much it costs you, in debt or equity, to get money from investors for your business. For a new entrepreneur who lacks a track record and is just getting started, the appropriate number is most likely 35–75% per year.[2] This number is so high because an investor gives you money they cannot get back for years at a time (an illiquid investment). The investor is also taking a great risk because you are a brand-new business. The last major consideration is that as a startup, you have very few if any hard assets that can serve as collateral. These are the three factors (but not the only ones) that mean that investors will charge you a significant premium for money over what already established firms would need to pay. For the sake of simplicity, you can start by assuming a constant rate of 50%, which is probably too low in your early years and hopefully will be too high in your later years. If you understand the concepts influencing this number, you can change it if it makes sense for your business or industry, but don't be overly optimistic.

You will make your best guess on the above input and proceed but also understand that you will go back and adjust as new information becomes available to you.

How to Calculate Lifetime Value

The LTV is the net present value (NPV) of your profits from year 0 through year 5. As a brand-new business with a very high cost of capital, you will calculate the LTV over a five-year period because

---

[2] William A. Sahlman, "A Method for Valuing High-Risk, Long-Term Investments," Harvard Business School, Case 9-288-006, August 12, 2003.

the years beyond five will be discounted so heavily, it is probably not worth the effort. More explicitly, when projecting more than five years out, the compounded cost of capital for a startup is so high that it negates what value your customer provides you beyond five years. The customer still has value to you beyond five years, but you also have to factor your cost of capital rate into the calculation.

The LTV is expressed in dollars per customer, so to calculate it you will start with the effective price an average new customer will pay you. An average new customer might buy one product or multiple products.

The upfront revenue you get for your product(s) (assuming in this case there is a business model that has a one-time initial charge for the product) will likely be your first source of revenue. Then there could very well be derivative revenue streams, like service or maintenance. For each revenue stream, you will use the gross margin percentage (as it is technically called) to determine the profits. In addition, you will have to assume on retention rates for the ongoing revenue streams.

With all of these revenue streams converted into a time series of numbers, you will then calculate your cumulative profit for the first year ("Year 0"). You will then repeat this for the subsequent five years. (Use the next product purchase rate instead of the retention rate for the years the customer would be expected to replace the product.)

You will then have the total estimated profit for each year across all revenue streams for that given year. Make sure all of this is done in a spreadsheet where your assumptions are clear throughout the whole process so that if you want to change it, it is easy and you can understand it.

You will need to do one more thing before you can add up the profit numbers and get the LTV. The last calculation is called the present value (PV) at Above Cost of Capital, which discounts the profit to take into account that your investors will need to recoup with interest their investment in your business. The PV for year 0 is equal to that year's profits. To calculate the PV for each year's profits beyond year 0, use the following formula:

$$\text{Present Value} = \frac{\text{Profit}}{(1 + \text{Cost of Capital Rate})^t}$$

where t = number of years after year 0.

What does this mean? It means that if you have $1 today, it is worth $1 today because by the formula, anything to the power 0 equals 1. If your cost of capital is 50%, $1 a year from now is only worth $.67 in today's dollars. Likewise, using the formula above, you can see how much $1 every year for five years is worth in today's dollars in Figure 17.1.

Year	0	1	2	3	4	5
Amount in that year	$1.00	$1.00	$1.00	$1.00	$1.00	$1.00
NPV bringing it back to value in today's dollars	$1.00	$0.67	$0.44	$0.30	$0.20	$0.13
Cost of Capital Rate =	50%					

Figure 17.1: Example of effect on NPV calculation with 50% discount rate.

The LTV by itself will not tell you how attractive your business is; for this, you will also need to calculate the CoCA, which you will do in the coming steps. An LTV of $10,000 per customer, for instance, is great if your CoCA is $1,000 per customer, but is poor or at best "challenging" if your CoCA is $50,000 per customer.

LTV Sample Calculation: "Widget" Plus Yearly Maintenance Fee

The following is an example of how to calculate the LTV based on a conceptual case of a company that makes a "widget," that is to say, a generic physical product. In the business model, there is a one-time charge for the widget, with an annual recurring charge for maintenance.

- One-time revenue: The widget is priced at $10,000.
- Recurring revenue: Yearly maintenance fee of 15% of the widget's list price after a six-month warranty period. The fee would therefore be $750 in year 0 and $1,500 in subsequent years.
- Additional revenue opportunities: None.
- Gross margin for each revenue stream: Widget: 65%; Maintenance: 85%.
- Retention rate: Maintenance: 100% per year in the first year; 90% per year in subsequent years.
- Life of product: 5 years.
- Next product purchase rate: 75% of those customers who are still paying the maintenance fee at the time of next product purchase.
- Cost of capital rate: 50%.

As you can see from Figure 17.2, all the above factors matter in determining an estimate for LTV. Some key drivers, however, are the very high cost of capital that new companies have because their limited ability to attract investments gets very expensive. This means that profits tomorrow are much less valuable than today's profits. This makes the subscription and consumables business models not as clear a winner as one would think. The other big drivers are the gross profit margin for your various streams of revenue and your customer retention rate. It is typically cheaper to keep an existing customer than to find a new one, making this a big leverage point.

	Year 0	Year 1	Year 2	Year 3	Year 4	Year 5
Revenue time series: Widget						
Price of widget	$10,000					$10,000
Next product purchase rate (beyond year 0)						75%
Gross margin for widget	65%					65%
Profit from widget	$6,500					$4,875
Revenue time series: Maintenance						
Price of yearly maintenance contract	$750	$1,500	$1,500	$1,500	$1,500	$750
Retention rate (not a direct product of the calculation; instead contributes to cumulative retention rate)	*100%*	*90%*	*90%*	*90%*	*90%*	*n/a (see next product purchase rate) 65.6%*
Cumulative retention rate (cumulative retention rate = r^t where r = retention rate and t = no. of years after year 0)	*100%*	*90%*	*81%*	*72.9%*	*65.6%*	*65.6%*
Next product purchase rate						75%
Gross margin for maintenance	85%	85%	85%	85%	85%	85%
Profit from maintenance	$637	$1,147	$1,032	$929	$836	$313
Sum of profits	$7,137	$1,147	$1,032	$929	$836	$5,188
Cost of capital discount rate	*50%*	*50%*	*50%*	*50%*	*50%*	*50%*
NPV factor based on formula earlier in chapter	*1.00*	*0.67*	*0.44*	*0.30*	*0.20*	*0.13*
PV above cost of capital	$7,137	$768	$454	$279	$167	$674
Net present value of profits (LTV)	$9,479					

Figure 17.2: Detailed widget LTV calculation.

After having done the calculations in Figure 17.2, you must understand that there is an implied level of precision that is not actually possible at this point. So the responsible answer to this example would be the LTV is between $9,000 and $10,000 based on the listed assumptions.

Likewise, there are many factors that entrepreneurs initially overlook in determining LTV, but the biggest one is the cost of capital. When entrepreneurs do this calculation, they are usually surprised at how low their LTV is. If you have access to low-cost capital, it can make a huge difference.

It must also be noted that while you use the cost of capital to determine LTV, there is also value in knowing the absolute number of the revenue stream and users in the out years. This will be a key determinant in the value of the asset you have created, which will make it much easier for you to get lower-cost money and potentially make you an attractive and valuable acquisition target. So while LTV is critically important to make you sustainable and ensure your lack of dependence on others, a deeper understanding than just the single number is important as well.

Overall, it is important for you as a disciplined entrepreneur to operate not with blind optimism but rather with real numbers and to understand what drives those numbers.

Important Considerations

There are many secondary factors to consider when determining the Lifetime Value of your customer. Even if your LTV is too low for your product to be viable, you should first consider whether these elements are correct, then consider whether you can positively impact your LTV with some adjustments.

1. **The Business Model Decision Is Very Important.** Your choice of business model can greatly affect your LTV and the amount of revenue you earn. Recurring revenue models such as subscription models often increase revenue but require additional capital from investors up front, and thus have a very high cost of capital. A one-time charge up front can reduce the amount of capital you need to get started, but is not as lucrative on an ongoing basis.

2. **LTV Is about Profit, not Revenue.** Your gross margin and cost of capital rates are integral to determining an accurate LTV. The most common mistake entrepreneurs make on LTV calculations is they simply tally up the revenue streams, but it is the profit that matters.

3. **Overhead Costs Aren't Negligible.** To simplify the LTV calculation, overhead is excluded, but to account for this the LTV must be substantially higher than the CoCA. These overhead costs, which as mentioned previously include R&D and administrative expenses, are not included when determining the gross margin of a product. These costs can be spread out over the total units of a product sold, so as volume sold goes up, the overhead cost per item goes down.

4. **Gross Margins Make a Big Difference.** Wrapping your lower-margin core product with high-margin add-on products will substantially help your LTV. LARK Technologies started out selling a silent alarm clock, which is a hardware solution, but their business model was not sustainable until they developed an additional revenue stream from a subscription business that produced an expert sleep analysis report for the user. Not only did this increase overall revenue, it produced a much higher-margin recurring revenue stream and allowed LARK to stay in touch with their customers to potentially sell more products to them in the future.

5. **Retention Rates Are Very Important as Well.** The longer you can keep a customer, the better your LTV becomes. This is one of a few levers you can easily control to improve the profitability of your business. A small increase in customer retention rates will mean significant improvements in your cumulative profits.

6. **Finding Additional Real Upselling Opportunities Can Be Very Attractive.** Upselling additional products to your customer can significantly improve your profit, as you see in the LARK Technologies example above. Make sure to drive upselling based on the needs of your Persona, not just to improve your numbers. Companies that over-upsell can lose track of what value they are creating for their customer and also lose the trust and confidence of the customer.

EXAMPLES

Bloom Continued

As discussed in previous narrative and steps, Bloom plans to provide a mobile application to help build and sustain female friendships for a very well-defined target customer group. From Steps 15 and 16, they had determined their business model and pricing should at least start out with a monthly subscription fee of $20. They estimate a retention rate of 85%, which seems reasonable based on the pilots they have run. This revenue stream will effectively have a 100% gross margin percentage—it is very profitable once you have invested in building it.

The team is also very confident that additional revenue will be reaped from each user through their exclusive events and outings, which will be priced in the range of $15–$150 per event. After some modeling based on their primary market research and pilot, they estimate this will be an additional revenue stream of approximately $200 per year. This is not as profitable as the subscription revenue and they estimate a gross margin of 20% on this stream.

Advertising and other upselling opportunities are also in their plans but these are less secure at this point so the LTV calculation will be based on only the above two revenue sources so as to be conservative. All of this leads to the initial LTV calculation for Bloom shown in Figure 17.3.

Calculations to Estimate LTV

Input	t=0	t=1	t=2	t=3	t=4	t=5
One-time revenue (free to download)	0	0	0	0	0	0
Retention rate	–	85%	75%	50%	35%	10%*
Recurring Revenue Amount (2% paying users on $20 monthly subscription)	–	$5	$5	$5	$5	$5**
Recurring Revenue Profit Margin (%)	–	100%	100%	100%	100%	100%
Other Revenue (Event ticketing. Assuming 4 events a year)	–	$200	$200	$200	$200	$200***
Other Revenue Profit Margin (%)	–	20%	20%	20%	20%	20%
Sum of Profit	–	38.25	33.75	22.5	15.75	4.5
Discount Rate	100%	67%	44%	30%	20%	13%
NPV	0	$25.6	$14.9	$6.75	$3.1	$0.6

Assumptions:
Marginal Production Cost of Software = $0
One Time Revenue profit Margin = 100%

*For our Beachhead market, our app targets those between 20-25, and until we target additional populations our retention rate will decrease significantly after 3 years.

**We plan to have a monthly subscription of $20 a month. We estimate that 2% of our users will be paid users. $20 x .02 x 12 = 4.8

*** We plan to introduce exclusive events and tickets for outings. While there will be 10-15 options ranging from $15-150 each month, we held an average estimate of $200 of additional revenue per user annually.

Calculated LTV: ~$50

Figure 17.3: Bloom initial LTV calculation.

What Bloom does next is very important. As you can see in Figure 17.4, they then interpret the calculation so that others can understand it without having to jump into the spreadsheets. They appropriately convert the LTV into a range and make the associated assumptions clear while explaining how they see LTV evolving over time. This is best practice.

Our LTV

$45-65

We are moderately confident about this range. We believe there are key variables on user consumption at events and churn on paid users

Key Variables:

- Monthly Subscription Price. (Currently set to $20)
- Opportunity for additional revenue streams such as advertising
- Event Pricing option/availability
- Addition of targeting new markets such as women 25-30 years.

Short-term	Medium-term	Long-term
Short-term to build out the product effectively, the product will be free, enabling network effects but we will not be revenue or profit generating. In this time, we hope to gain critical mass and prepare for new revenue streams.	Given over the medium-term additional pricing options will be introduced, the retention will now decrease moderately as users convert to paying customers.	Long-term, we anticipate there to be tiered pricing and exclusive access to events so at this point the retention will lower and stabilize to a sustainable rate. We hope to introduce other markets therefore increasing retention and LTV

Figure 17.4: Bloom summary of LTV.

Helios

As discussed in Step 16, Set Your Pricing Framework, Helios had created a coating that deices windshields. They had determined the price should be $100 per unit. This price (the expected net price after discounts) included the window cover and the software to remotely control the deicer on a smartphone for one year.

Based on their business model, pricing decisions, and research on how much the average customer would buy in a typical transaction, the team determined that the yearly revenue per customer in the first year would be $100,000. The typical customer fleet they targeted had 1,000 vehicles (some had more and some had less, but 1,000 was the average fleet size of their target market) and hence the $100K net revenue per new customer estimate for the first year. In subsequent years, an average of 20% of the fleet would be replaced, so the new vehicles would need coating to be applied as well, providing a recurring revenue stream.

As you see in the model in Figure 17.5, it is expected there would be a 5% price increase each year, a 90% customer renewal rate (an aggressive assumption), 97% gross margin because there will be additional marginal service and maintenance costs for each fleet, and a 40% cost of capital, as the business happens to have access to some lower-cost funds to get started. As you can see from the calculations, when the customer unit considered here is a car fleet customer (which is appropriate), the LTV from these assumptions is estimated to be between $125K and $150K.

	Year 0	Year 1	Year 2	Year 3	Year 4	Year 5
Revenue per Year (assumes 5% yearly price increase) =	$ 100,000	$18,900	$17,861	$16,878	$15,950	$15,073
Gross Margin Profits from Revenues =	$ 97,000	$18,333	$17,325	$16,372	$15,471	$14,620
NPV Discount Factor for 40% discount rate	1.00	0.71	0.51	0.36	0.26	0.19
NPV at above Cost of Capital =	$ 97,000	$13,016	$ 8,836	$ 5,894	$ 4,022	$ 2,779
NPV of Profit Stream or LTV per Fleet =	**$131,547**					
Pricing (unit price)	$100	Business Model is a one-time charge with no recurring revenue				
Average Yearly Revenue per Fleet in Year 1	$100K					
Gross Margin	97%					
Price Increase per Year	5%					
Life of Product	5 years					
Retention Rate	90%					
Cost of Capital for Company (est.)	40%					

Figure 17.5: LTV calculation for Helios.

The Helios example raises many interesting points, as is usually the case when doing LTV calculations; they vary greatly and understanding the underlying drivers and leverage points is extremely important.

This new venture was driven to make a big initial sale to a fleet and move on, rather than building a "sticky" product that leveraged happy existing customers to gain additional sales. The business would collect its largest payment in the first year (the $100K to outfit all of the vehicles in an average fleet, a figure that they did not have to discount for cost of capital), so it had weak incentives to continue to work with customers and gain follow-on orders for the 20% annual turnover of vehicles. Further, the 90% retention rate figure, assuming that 90% of the customers who initially installed the product would continue to purchase it for new vehicles added to their fleet, seems aggressive based on other companies' experiences.

So the answer is that Helios estimates an LTV of about $130K of incremental profit per average new customer. The team was surprised that the LTV was not higher, but their choices of the business model and pricing left the company with these economics for LTV. To sell a new fleet would take a lot of time, effort, and, ultimately, cost. The CoCA would be in excess of $30K and probably in excess of $50K because of the high number of sales calls required.

After Helios did their LTV calculation, they saw they would need to revisit their business model and pricing to find if there was a better way to monetize, as well as potentially expand their value proposition by adding more functionality and thinking about new ways to leverage the smartphone app that would activate the deicing system on vehicles.

ADDITIONAL RESOURCES

There are additional resources for this step at www.d-eship.com/step17. For this step you will find:

- Video: LTV Explainers by Bill Aulet and Erdin Beshimov
- Video: Example described and explained in an interview with Humon founders Dan Wiese and Alessandro Babini
- Process Guide
- Worksheet 17.1: Inputs to LTV Calculation
- Worksheet 17.2: LTV Calculation
- Worksheet 17.3: Interpretation of LTV Calculation
- LTV Calculator: Joe Gibson, a lecturer at Clemson University, developed the very useful LTV calculator, which is available for free to download at https://www.d-eship.com/articles/ltv-calculation-spreadsheet/. Thousands of people have found this to be very helpful, but remember, you still need to interpret the results of the calculation!

Additional resources will be added as new and updated examples and information become available.

Summary

The Lifetime Value of an Acquired Customer calculation is the profit that an average new customer will provide, discounted back into today's dollars because you are going to have to spend today's dollars to acquire this new customer. The high discount rate reflects the high cost of acquiring capital that new ventures face. It is important to be realistic, not optimistic, when calculating LTV. You should give a range that reflects the level of precision you are comfortable with. Even more important is to be clear about the assumptions you're making, as changes to those assumptions can drive that LTV higher or lower.

> *NOTE: There is important information in the Glossary about this definition of LTV and how it is similar and dissimilar to other terms often used to convey analogous concepts (e.g., CLVT, ACV, TCV, ARPU). I encourage you to read this as well so you are not confused when you hear or see the terms and can in fact be well prepared to ask questions to understand the information and then use it effectively.*

Design a Scalable Revenue Engine

In This Step, You Will:

- Develop short-term, medium-term, and long-term strategies and plans to generate revenue for your product.

Designing at least a first-draft plan for an effective, efficient, scalable, and adjustable revenue engine is your next key decision.

Why This Step, and Why Now?

- In the last step, you came up with an educated estimate of what the Lifetime Value (LTV) could be for your new venture. That gives you important guidance on the type of go-to-market strategies available to you. Once you have developed your first-draft go-to-market plan, you will then have the critical input you need to estimate the Cost of Customer Acquisition (CoCA) in Step 19 and complete the all-important unit economics test.

Let's Get Started

Since I originally published this book, there have been significant changes in entrepreneurial sales. As such, the title of this step is updated from previous editions to be more specific based on rapidly advancing technology, and techniques in this area. You will also notice a subtle but important tone change in now calling this "revenue," which is more expansive than "sales." This is an important mindset change.

To acquire customers for your product, you will need a sales and marketing strategy. This will involve what have historically been called "channels to market" but today are called "sales and marketing motions." These will be your techniques to generate revenue that are compatible with your customer's acquisition process (Steps 12 and 13) and also economically sustainable, in that they are compatible with the LTV (Step 17) that you estimate for your business. This is the foundation of your go-to-market (GTM) plan, but it will be a first draft and will be refined over time.

All the work done in the earlier steps is going to start to pay off now. Building your Scalable Revenue Engine can be done with great specificity that you would not have had if you had not gotten to this level of detail about your target customer. This step is about getting "channel-market fit" (CMF) where earlier you had been focused on getting "product-market fit" (PMF). As time has gone on, PMF has become table stakes (i.e., something that is necessary but not sufficient). Increasingly, with all the tools to build products now, it is getting easier to build products, and the battle for success in the marketplace is now more focused on who can come up first with the most efficient, effective, scalable, and antifragile GTM implementation.

What Are the Different Sales Motions

There are major levers or "motions" that you should consider:

1. **Field Sales:** Direct salespeople who are employees of the company. They call on prospects in person at some point in the process. They provide high-touch connection and line of communication to the potential customer. Also known as "outside sales."

2. **Inside Sales:** Known as "telesales" in the past, today it is no longer just telephone sales reps. E-mail and other electronic communication are used to create and continue a dialogue with the customer, but they do not visit the customer in person.

3. **Automated Sales:** This is a general catch-all category for sales done by computers through automatically generated e-mails, advertising, big data analysis, social media, preference engines, and so on. The key differentiator is that there is no human in the loop.

4. **Channel Resellers:** These people sell your product but are not employees of your company. They include value-added resellers (VARs), distributors, stores, catalogues, independent sales agents, and the like.

5. **Product-Led Growth (PLG):** There is no human in the loop, but in contrast to automated sales, the product is simply designed to sell itself (e.g., Dropbox, LinkedIn, Calendly, Slack, Zoom).

6. **Customer Success:** Chief revenue officers have found they can drive sales by investing in customer success teams who work with existing customers to make sure they get the desired value out of their usage of the product.

A comparison of the pros and cons of each sales motion is in Figure 18.1.

Option	Pros	Cons
1. **Field Sales**	• Excellent for demand generation when creating new markets; may well be the only option for demand generation. • High-touch approach creates excellent feedback loop. • High-touch approach also generally creates deep customer loyalty.	• Very expensive (salary, bonus, expenses). • Requires an LTV of $50K or likely higher. • Hard to scale up as hiring them is hard and expensive and the success rate is unpredictable. • Takes a long time to become productive. • A challenge to manage.
2. **Inside Sales**	• Much cheaper than field sales. • Maintain direct connection with prospects, potential customers, and customers. • Able to get nuanced feedback from prospects because a human is in the loop.	• Lower touch, resulting in less customer engagement and less demonstration of the company's commitment to the customer. • Still expensive because the salesperson is interacting one-on-one with customers.

Figure 18.1: Sales motions pros and cons.

Option	Pros	Cons
	• High productivity because of lack of travel. • Good systems exist to further increase productivity and track progress of sales funnel and sales reps.	• Some products just can't be sold without an in-person demo or meeting with the customer.
3. **Automated Sales**	• Direct interaction with the customer. • Ability above all others to systematically capture even more data on the customer and track their progress—as well as spot patterns and make intelligent recommendations. • Lowest cost by far. • Actually preferred by some prospects.	• Low touch. • Can't read some nuances that only humans can. • Some prospects do not react well to it. • Privacy considerations. • Can be hard to build customer loyalty. • Risk for high LTV prospects/customers that others who use the higher touch channels above will steal these valuable customers.
4. **Channel Resellers**	• Instant geographic coverage. • Easy to manage. • Understand cultural context and have preexisting contacts in their databases. • Lower cost than field sales. • Don't have to hire, fire, and manage salespeople. • Good for quick demand fulfillment. • Potential temporary solution. • Potential good solution for a mature product.	• They own the customer, not you (very bad!). • They take big commissions on sales, eating into your profit margins. • Because they own the customer relationship, you will likely not have direct interaction with prospects, hence miss important learning about customer needs. • Historically have been poor at demand generation but that is not necessarily true anymore if you design your program carefully. • Similarly, historically most likely have low loyalty to you and your product (just another product in their portfolio) but again that is not necessarily true if you carefully design a program for them.

Figure 18.1: (Continued)

Option	Pros	Cons
5. **Product-Led Growth (PLG)**	• All the same benefits of Automated Sales. • This is just a specialized version of Automated Sales that has become very popular where more of the work is done in the engineering organization.	• Similar to Automated Sales. • Must have bandwidth and expertise to execute in the engineering organization.
6. **Customer Success**	• Decreased abandonment rates. • Creates "negative churn" meaning you keep customers longer and they generate more and better leads for you. • Turns a sales funnel into a flywheel for revenue. • Usually can pay customer success people less than salespeople.	• Limit to how much you can do. • Should be part of a portfolio strategy alongside other motions. • Need to have sufficient customers signed up to start the process.

Figure 18.1: (Continued)

Within each of these six motions, there can be many different variants, as well as hybrids, across the categories—and there should be! For instance, someone in field sales often spends a reasonable fraction of time on the phone, but their training and expertise is in face-to-face closing the sale, and their pay reflects that.

I also must say that with things moving so quickly in this space, I must leave a wild card space called "Other" for creative ways to generate revenue. Feel free to *not* be constrained by these six motions!

Your LTV Will Dictate What Sales Motion Options Are Available

You estimate the LTV first because it gives you a good sense of what motions are available to you. For instance, if your LTV is $100, the field sales option and, in the long term, the inside sales option are not viable for you. Figure 18.2 will guide you on what sales strategies you should be considering based on your LTV.

Estimated LTV	What you can afford for sales channels in the long term
~$30	Only automated sales and/or PLG; no human can be in the loop.
~$300	Predominantly if not all automated sales and PLG, with maybe a very small amount of inside sales for the most important prospects.
~$3,000	Mix of automated sales and inside sales and maybe some channel resellers, especially if the product is mature or requires low support.
~$30K	Mix of all channels, with heavy reliance on inside sales and judicious use of field sales on big accounts. Channel resellers can play a role in this scenario for geographic coverage and quick scale-up.
~$300K	Likely led by field sales and customer success, with support from inside sales and some channel resellers in selected areas for geographic coverage.
~$3M	Dominated by field sales but big element of customer success as well, with other channels in a supporting role.
~$30M	The field sales representatives are the all-powerful dictators with customer success in the second slot taking guidance from field sales; other sales channels don't even look at highly qualified prospects or customers without their approval. Customer intimacy and professionalism are crucial in this scenario.

Figure 18.2: Sales motions you can consider based on your LTV.

Your Sales Process Will Change Over Time

For most ventures, the CoCA will start very high and decrease over time. The sales process necessary to reach and close customers at the founding of a new business requires much more time and investment than the same process does once a business has matured and begins to scale. This is because at the beginning you have to educate the market and create demand for your product. As your company, your product, and the market mature, you shift into more and more fulfilling demand as opposed to creating demand.

That is why I don't call it just a revenue engine, but instead a Scalable Revenue Engine, to emphasize that this plan will drive your business over time. To show this progression over time, you should break down your planning horizon into the short term, medium term, and long term. You will use a different mix of sales methods or motions in each period.

1. **Short Term:** In the short term, the primary focus of your Scalable Revenue Engine is to create demand for your product and then not only fulfill orders for those initial orders for the product but also work to make them successful—and learn yourself what is needed to make your customer successful. This is very high-touch sales. This initial period is often appropriately referred to as the "founder-led sales stage." While your customer-centric focus means you have worked diligently to create a product the customer wants, there will still be some surprises. Your product is still new to the world, so you will need direct interaction with the customer to explain your value proposition and why your product is unique. Even with all your work to date, you will still be making adjustments at the early stages. In addition, the market will not be aware of and properly educated on your product. Doing all this is difficult, and exponentially more so if you funnel sales through intermediaries such as distributors. This is the missionary sales stage and it ends when you start to see demand for your product that you did not directly generate.

   - Direct salespeople—often called "business development" people—are traditionally a wise and effective investment here. However, they are very expensive and they take time to get up to speed. Good ones can be very hard to find and also hard to retain. Despite these challenges, they still might be your only option, and therefore your best one. Oh yes, and "founder-led sales stage" means you are deeply involved, too.

   - Digital marketing tools and techniques such as inbound marketing, e-mail, social media marketing, and telemarketing can help lessen the need for direct salespeople, even at this stage. One of the great benefits of these tools is that you can get extensive analytics on your customer that are not possible through the human channel.

2. **Medium Term:** At this stage, focus shifts more from demand creation toward order fulfillment as word of mouth and distribution channels take on some of the demand creation burden. At this stage, you will also begin client management, which means ensuring you retain existing customers as pilots move to production rollouts. I recommend that entrepreneurs entering this stage try to use lower-cost motions where they maintain direct interaction with customers, if possible. This could include inside sales, automated sales, product-led growth (PLG), or customer success. Another option to be considered in this stage is channel resellers who are often called distributors or value-added resellers (VARs), especially to serve more remote markets, or smaller customers who have a lower LTV.

Your expensive direct salespeople should focus only on larger customer opportunities with a higher LTV. Using distributors or VARs substantially lowers your cost of customer acquisition but requires you to give up some of your profit margin to the distributor—between 15 and 45% or higher depending on the industry. The decreased profit margin per unit is presumably more than offset by the reduction in CoCA that results and the speed at which you can enter new markets through these already-existing distribution channels. In your urgency to move forward and reduce dependency on direct sales, I caution you that you should not sacrifice direct customer ownership and interaction lightly. Remember the maxim I mentioned in Step 16, which I repeat often: "Whoever owns the customer relationship owns the gold."

3. **Long Term:** Your sales strategy should now focus even more on fulfilling customer orders. Your business will do very little demand creation, and will continue client management where appropriate. The inside sales, automated sales, PLG, and customer success motions are most commonly employed in a long-term strategy. There will have to be adjustments made as competitors come into the market along the way, but this is the general path.

Design a GTM Plan Based on a Mix of Revenue-Generating Motions That Evolve

To develop this short-term, medium-term, and long-term sales strategy, you must make a first-pass plan for which sales channels or motions you will use to generate revenue, and how that mix might change over time. You can draw on the work you have already done in the Full Life Cycle Use Case (Step 6).

Key questions that your Scalable Revenue Engine should address include:

- How does your target customer become aware that they have a problem or an opportunity?
- How will the target customer learn that there is a solution to this problem they have, or learn there is the opportunity they did not previously know about?
- Once the target customer knows about your business, what is the education process that allows them to make a well-informed analysis about whether to purchase your product?
- How do you make the sale?
- How do you collect the money?

Once you have developed your Scalable Revenue Engine, vet it with experienced professionals in the industry. Figure 18.3 shows a pretty typical traditional sales and distribution strategy for B2B companies.

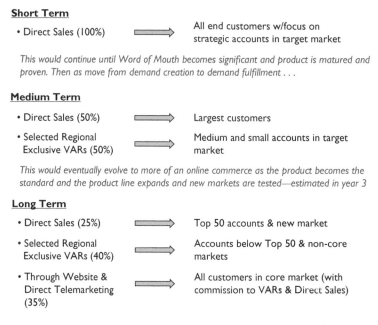

Figure 18.3: Example map of Scalable Revenue Engine.

Updating Your Sales Funnel

In Step 13, you made your first draft of your Sales Funnel and you may have updated it since then. Even if you haven't, now is the time to update it again with more details based on the knowledge you have gained. You should do it for the short, medium, and long term with special focus on increased specificity because you know that is essential for entrepreneurial success.

This is not the last time you will be updating this but at this point you should start to have increased confidence in how your customer acquisition process will evolve over time. You also have to maintain the always required humility to know that whatever you think it will be, it is just your best hypotheses and they will certainly change in some dimension, which is not just fine but very good.

Bloom Continued

Back to our friends at Bloom: you can see a summary of their short-, medium-, and long-term plans in Figure 18.4.

Sales: Short, Medium, Long Term Channel

Revenue Channels for Short, Medium & Long Term

	Short Term Year 1	Medium Term Years 2-4	Long Term Years 5+
% Sales by Revenue	20% field, 10% inside, 70% internet	10% field, 0% inside, 90% internet	10% field, 0% inside, 90% internet
Key Milestones	• Adoption by women in target cities through Facebook Group acquisition	• Organic customer acquisition via word of mouth and referrals begins • Partnerships with companies to enhance employee social wellness	• Returning customers occur as enter new stages of life • Increased focus on upselling and maintaining customers on platform
Key Assumptions	• New grad women aged 20-25 need new friends • New grad women are eager to try new digital tools to make friends • Critical mass obtained on platform	• Women will not feel embarrassed to be on a "friend-finding" platform • Women will refer the platform to their friends and colleagues who are moving	• Beachhead market is conquered • Moving on to conquer secondary markets; existing customers recommend product for new generations of women
Highest Risk Factors	• New grad women feel that current options are sufficient • New grad women have no WTP • Male-identifying customers on platform	• BumbleBFF creating a group-focused product • Inability to onboard enough events to platform to meet growing demand	• Expansion into new markets may result in changes to brand positioning
Summary for Time Period	• Customer acquisition to happen primarily through existing Facebook Groups and by targeting soon-to-graduate women	• Customer acquisition to become more "hands-off" as women join through referrals and ads • Brand names starts to become recognizable	• Customer acquisition continues to occur mainly through low-cost social media advertisement and platform is

Figure 18.4: Bloom initial go-to-market plan over time.

They then converted this into a revised sales funnel with more detail than the first draft created in Step 13, as you can see in Figure 18.5. It is important to continually update your Sales Funnel and this step is one of those critical points to do so.

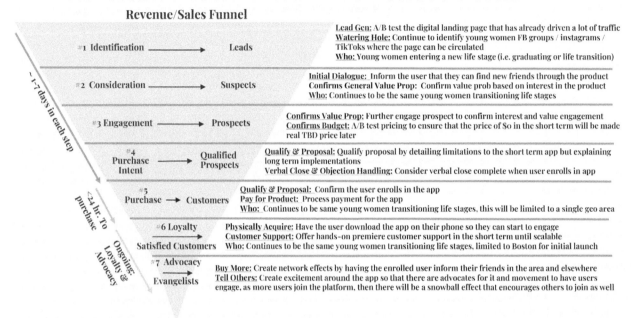

Figure 18.5: Bloom second-draft sales funnel with a lot of more actionable details.

Finally, they summarize their learnings of how the sales funnel will evolve in Figure 18.6, which demonstrates that they understand the logic behind their plan so they can further refine the plan over time.

Will things work out exactly as planned? Absolutely not. They know this, but at least they have a well-thought-out initial plan to get started and then they can learn from the variations to make intelligent adjustments along the way. They have to at a minimum show a path to viability and that they are clear on the assumptions. Again, the final plan recommendation is less important than understanding the logic behind it so you can have a battle plan to interpret results as they come in and then make adjustments and decisions with the best framework possible.

Evolution of the Sales Funnel: Major Changes

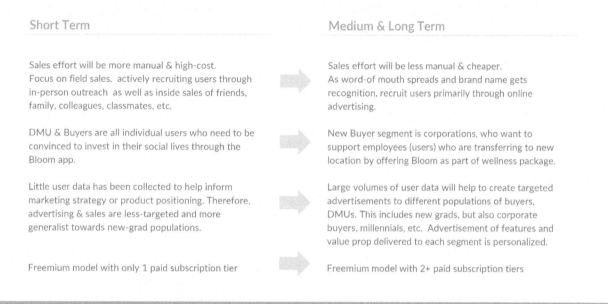

Short Term	Medium & Long Term
Sales effort will be more manual & high-cost. Focus on field sales, actively recruiting users through in-person outreach as well as inside sales of friends, family, colleagues, classmates, etc.	Sales effort will be less manual & cheaper. As word-of mouth spreads and brand name gets recognition, recruit users primarily through online advertising.
DMU & Buyers are all individual users who need to be convinced to invest in their social lives through the Bloom app.	New Buyer segment is corporations, who want to support employees (users) who are transferring to new location by offering Bloom as part of wellness package.
Little user data has been collected to help inform marketing strategy or product positioning. Therefore, advertising & sales are less-targeted and more generalist towards new-grad populations.	Large volumes of user data will help to create targeted advertisements to different populations of buyers, DMUs. This includes new grads, but also corporate buyers, millennials, etc. Advertisement of features and value prop delivered to each segment is personalized.
Freemium model with only 1 paid subscription tier	Freemium model with 2+ paid subscription tiers

Figure 18.6: Capturing lessons learned in Bloom GTM plan development.

LARK Technologies

Silent alarm-clock manufacturer LARK Technologies realized in mapping out its sales process that it would need to educate users about what a silent alarm clock and sleep-coaching product was all about (Figure 18.7). It would take some hard work to get the market moving. CEO Julia Hu developed the following short-term, medium-term, and long-term plans.

Short Term: With no alternative, Julia started by engaging in one-on-one selling to potential customers, even setting up a table on the MIT campus on commencement day to explain her product and its value. Julia also sought and won lots of public speaking opportunities to create awareness of her product. This strategy had a significant cost associated with it because it pulled her away from the core operations aspects of her business.

Many of the first units were sold to family and friends who could spread the word about the product. Julia also engaged her Persona's primary influencers, such as the website *Urban Daddy*, a daily e-mail newsletter specifically targeted at wealthy young urban professionals.

The company created a website where customers could purchase the product. It experimented with search engine optimization (SEO) to help drive traffic to the site. It also started to experiment with social media like Twitter, though with marginal results.

Medium Term: The company signed a deal with Apple to distribute its product in the Apple Store without requiring exclusivity. The strategy gave the LARK product instant credibility, in that it had been approved for sale in the Apple stores by Apple itself, as well as much broader exposure, but the company had to give up a lot of margin. Since the product sold in the store was the hardware component and the store had to carry inventory, LARK's gross margin was significantly affected. However, Julia no longer had to do one-on-one sales, instead focusing on recruiting distributors and improving LARK's website.

Long Term: The website is the key place to get info about the product and purchase it. Julia expects 40% of her orders to come through the website (and other direct online channels), 50% from the retail distribution channel, and 10% from other channels.[1]

Figure 18.7: LARK's display.

---

[1] These numbers were changed to illustrate the point and are not Julia's actual long-term projections.

ADDITIONAL RESOURCES

There are additional resources for this step at www.d-eship.com/step18. These materials include:

- There are no individual videos for this step alone, but rather the materials are integrated into the videos referenced in Step 19, Calculate the Cost of Customer Acquisition (CoCA).
- Process Guide to design a Scalable Revenue Engine
- Worksheet 18.1: Sales Motions for short, medium, and long term
- Worksheet 18.2: Second-draft sales funnel refinement
- Worksheet 18.3: Visual second-draft sales funnel refinement to be redone for each stage
- Worksheet 18.4: Describing the difference between the sales funnels as they move from stage to stage
- Worksheet 18.5: Proposed actions to improve yield rates in sale funnel
- Worksheet 18.6: Areas to watch with most risks and proactive mitigation plans to address them

Additional resources will be added as new and updated examples and information become available.

Summary

Mapping your Scalable Revenue Engine is a thoughtful first pass at how you will enter the market, refine your sales strategy over time, and ultimately establish a sustainable long-term strategy for customer acquisition. The Scalable Revenue Engine includes creating awareness, educating the customer, and handling and processing the sale. The Scalable Revenue Engine drives the CoCA, one of the variables—along with the LTV—that shows your business's profitability.

Remember, a business is about getting paying customers and you have to respect the sales, or more appropriately now, revenue generation process. Don't give this step less attention. It is critically important to build up your knowledge of this part of your business. This is where many of the most important adjustments in your plan will be made, so understanding the levers to pull is mission critical.

STEP 19

Calculate the Cost of Customer Acquisition (CoCA)

In This Step, You Will:

- Estimate how much it costs to acquire a customer over the short term, medium term, and long term, based on the go-to-market (GTM) plan you developed in Step 18.
- Understand the key drivers of these costs and how to influence them over time.

Entrepreneurs consistently underestimate the real costs of customer acquisition.
It is essential that you do realistic calculations.

Why This Step, and Why Now?

The unit economics are a simple but effective indicator for how sustainable and attractive your business will be at any point in time, especially as it scales. You just completed a thoughtful first-draft go-to-market (GTM) plan in Step 18, and now with this critical information it is time to estimate your CoCA. The balance between LTV and CoCA is one of the most generally accepted metrics to decide if you have a viable business, so these calculations should be done before you start to make the heavy investment in product development.

Let's Get Started

Now that you have done a first-pass estimate on LTV, the question becomes: "How much will it cost to successfully acquire that average new additional customer?"

The concept of CoCA is relatively simple, but when they first start, entrepreneurs (myself included for many years until I got retrained) tend to dramatically underestimate how much it costs to gain a new customer.

To truly understand how much you will have to spend on your sales process to gain customers, you will conduct a rigorous, honest assessment based on facts, not hope or optimism.

This started in the last step by mapping out your expected Scalable Revenue Engine, without attaching dollar signs to any of it but instead keeping it at a high level. In this step, you will use that information to develop a more specific estimate of what your sales and marketing initiatives are going to cost on a per customer basis. Once you estimate your CoCA in this step, you will likely go back and change your sales process to lower the CoCA, or maybe even look more energetically for ways to increase your LTV.

The CoCA, in combination with the LTV, helps you understand the dynamics of your business and gives you enough data to make a meaningful first-pass analysis on the sustainability and profitability of your business.

Four Factors Entrepreneurs Often Overlook About Customer Acquisition Costs

Entrepreneurs are inherently optimistic, and tend to remember only customers who responded positively to information about their products or who offered to buy their products relatively quickly. They often fail to account for many factors and scenarios common to the customer acquisition process. The most commonly overlooked factors include:

- **All Marketing and Sales Costs:** The cost behind all of the sales and marketing efforts required to reach their prospects. These may include the salaries of salespeople, creation of sales collateral, development and maintenance of websites, costs of trade show exhibits, advertising in industry publications, development of white papers, among others.

- **Underestimating Sales Cycle:** Long sales cycles that cost a lot of money. Entrepreneurs tend to remember only the shortest sales cycles.

- **Forgetting the Ones Who Didn't Buy:** All the customers who did not buy their product, and the sales and marketing costs associated with reaching those customers. How many frogs did you kiss before you found your prince? (See Figure 19.1.)

- **The Seeming Unusual Occurrences That Are Actually Usual and Need to be Planned and Accounted For:** Reorganization or personnel changes in your customer's DMU often force you to start your sales process over again. New managers bring in preferences for new products as well as often bring in new people to accomplish their goals, which can hamper the effectiveness of an entrepreneur's efforts to sell to the customer. While you might think these are unusual; they are in fact not just usual but you should anticipate they will happen. You are just not sure in exactly when and in what form.

Figure 19.1: To accurately calculate the cost of customer acquisition, you have to take into consideration all the effort, time, and resources you put into trying to sell to those people with whom you were unsuccessful and not just the successful ones.

How Not to Calculate CoCA: A Bottom-Up Perspective

Let's say you are selling a widget with a sales cycle of half a year, and it takes 1/20 of our salesperson's work time to identify, engage, track, support, close, and collect payment for selling to one customer. You pay the salesperson $150,000 per year if they make 100% of their quota (often called on-target earnings).

For this example, assume the salesperson meets their quota. Therefore, how much does it cost to pay one salesperson to acquire one customer? To determine the cost of one salesperson per sales cycle, you multiply their yearly salary by the length of the sales cycle: $150K * 1/2 year = $75K per sales cycle. Then, if the salesperson devotes 1/20 of their time to closing one sale, the cost of the salesperson's salary on each sale is $75K * 1/20 = $3,750. While all of this seems logical, it does not nearly represent the actual Cost of Customer Acquisition. It's merely the cost of one component of the sale—the salesperson.

First, the calculation above does not take into consideration all the other costs associated with closing this deal. The salesperson's benefits package (healthcare, vacation time, 401(k), etc.) typically costs you the equivalent of 25–30% of their salary. Then there are costs for travel and entertainment, demo units, tech support, mobile phone bills, trade show expenses, marketing campaigns to generate leads, Internet data charges, and more. You could do a bottom-up analysis, painstakingly scrutinizing the receipts and invoices and assigning expenses to each customer. You also have to take into account the other expenses associated with having a salesperson: the office furniture, computer, Internet and phone charges, the cost to rent or purchase the building the salesperson works from, and more. Let's say that all these costs, added up and divided by the number of new customers, equals another $2,500 per customer. So is our CoCA actually $3,750 + $2,500 = $6,250? No!

Also, when I said it takes the salesperson 1/20 of their time to close one sale, and divided the salesperson's salary for that sales cycle by 20 to get the cost per customer, I was assuming that the salesperson closes 100% of the sales they work on, totaling 20 sales per six-month sales cycle. This assumption is extremely unlikely because no salesperson closes every deal. If a salesperson is closing even 50% of the customers they engage with, they are probably getting paid much more than $150,000 per year and your startup likely would not be able to afford them!

Even assuming a salesperson closes 25% of sales, which is very aggressive, that means the salesperson is actually selling 5 units during each sales cycle, rather than 20. So, for every 1/20 of a salesperson's time spent on a customer who makes a purchase, another 3/20 of the salesperson's time is spent with potential customers who do not buy. These costs have to be factored into the CoCA as well.

A bottom-up analysis that factors in all these other expenses tends to get messy quickly and can create a false sense of accuracy. In my experience, this method does not work. A completely accurate estimate of the cost to acquire one new customer is hard to project. What you can be sure of is that estimating a CoCA of $6,250 would be dramatically understated, and merely the tip of the iceberg of the CoCA cost. Realistically, the CoCA in this example is probably closer to 10–20 times that number (see Figure 19.2).

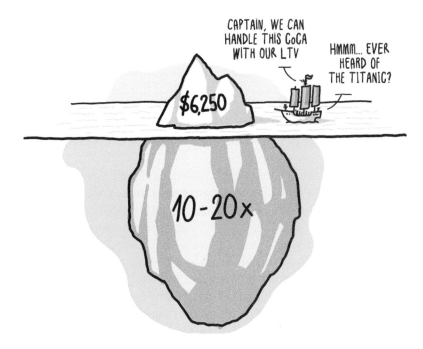

Figure 19.2: Be careful with bottom-up CoCA calculations as they tend to be significant underestimations.

The Right Way to Calculate CoCA: A Top-Down Perspective

A more effective way to calculate an accurate CoCA is much easier and will be more accurate: add up all of your sales and marketing expenses over a period of time, then divide that by the total number of new customers you acquire within that time period. That is really it.

Your CoCA will vary over time, which is why you will refer to it as CoCA(*t*). Ideally it will go down over time because:

- You should be refining and continually enhancing your sales process.
- The market will become educated and you will have to spend less time on demand creation and more on demand fulfillment.
- You should develop strong positive word of mouth within your target customer group.

While often your CoCA will start significantly higher than your LTV, if your business is to be successful it will have to become a fraction of the LTV, as illustrated in Figure 19.3. To capture the variability of CoCA over time without making things too complicated, you should estimate your CoCA over three time periods in order and show how the CoCA is trending. This mirrors the short-term, medium-term, and long-term approach to your Scalable Revenue Engine from Step 18, so you have the information you need already in the right format.

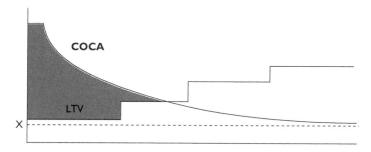

Figure 19.3: In a sustainable business, the Cost of Customer Acquisition (CoCA) will eventually drop below the Lifetime Value of an Acquired Customer (LTV).

Appropriate time periods depend on the life cycle of your product, which is directly related to the amount of time it takes for your customer to realize the value proposition from your product. A typical way to define the first three time periods for a CoCA calculation is by taking your first year of sales, your second and third year of sales, and your fourth and fifth year of sales. Depending on your new venture, these time periods could be different. If in doubt, use year 1, years 2 and 3, and years 4 and 5 as your three time periods.

When aggregating your sales and marketing expenditures, be sure to include all costs for all the key items in your sales and marketing plan, including those often-overlooked factors mentioned earlier in this chapter.

This calculation requires that you understand your sales process well. Do not worry if your calculation is not exactly right but make sure to make all the assumptions/inputs clear so you can adjust them later as needed. It is valuable here if you can enlist an experienced financial modeling person to help develop budget projections.

Dividing the cost of your sales and marketing expenses by the defined time period will yield the Total Marketing and Sales Expenses over Time or TMSE(t) where t is the first, second, or third time period. If a sizeable portion of your TMSE(t) is the cost of retention of existing customers, rather than acquiring new customers, subtract this from the TMSE(t). The cost of retention is referred to as the Install Base Support Expense over Time or IBSE(t). This would include your Customer Success expense.

Once you have these two numbers, the last item you need is the number of new customers you will close during that time period, referred to as New Customers over Time or NC(t). To forecast this number, you need to do a sales forecast that you and your team believe is not only possible but also likely.

Your sales forecast for your first 90 days, and possibly even for your first year, should have specific names of the customers whose sales you are going to record. If the potential customers don't already know you and you know them, it is highly unlikely that they will be buying during this initial time period. Take the number of people you think will be buying and only record a percentage of that on your forecast so that it is more realistic (maybe 80%, but that will vary by situation).

In the longer term, your sales forecast can make more abstract estimates based on growth rate, sales productivity, and market share, but understand that the more abstract the assumptions are in the calculation of the forecast, the less credible and the riskier they are. Have your forecast reviewed and tested by a sales professional. Often, entrepreneurs make forecasts that are wildly overoptimistic.

Given these definitions, you can explicitly define the CoCA calculation for any given time period to be as follows:

$$COCA(t) = \frac{TMSE(t) - IBSE(t)}{NC(t)}$$

$$Cost\ of\ Customer\ Acquisition = \frac{Total\ Marketing\ and\ Sales\ Expenses(t) - Install\ Base\ Support\ Expense(t)}{Number\ of\ New\ Customers(t)}$$

Once you have numbers for each of your first three time periods, plot them on a graph where the x-axis is time and the y-axis is CoCA for that period. You can also draw a best-fit curve.

The graph in Figure 19.4 illustrates a good CoCA, where it decreases over time. The horizontal line at X represents the CoCA's steady state, once sales volume ramps up and the product, company, and market mature, typically achieved during the longer-term stage of your sales process.

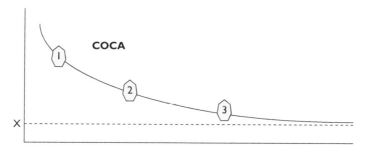

Figure 19.4: Graph of Typical CoCA over time.

How to Reduce CoCA

As you can see in Figure 19.3, the CoCA will most commonly start high—well above the final CoCA and likely higher than the LTV—because you need to first create the market. There is a good chance that you will be surprised at how high the initial CoCA is (and if you are not, you are probably missing a lot of costs). That is a normal and healthy response. Since your unit economics won't work at this initial CoCA, you will look for ways to decrease CoCA.

The easiest way to decrease your CoCA is simply to increase the number of units sold in a given time period. This will bring it down the fastest and most dramatically.

That being said, the market has a capacity and market adoption rate that you will have to acknowledge and not defy. Work with your head sales and marketing person to understand this. Do not make sales forecasts you can't achieve just to meet the CoCA goal. That is one of the first and most common ways entrepreneurs get into trouble. Remember, always look to underpromise and overdeliver.

Assuming you have the forecasts in the right neighborhood, then you have to look to less dramatic but important considerations to drive down CoCA. Here are some of the common ways this can be done:

1. **While Very Powerful, Use Direct Sales Judiciously as It Is Very Expensive:** Hiring a team to do direct sales may be necessary to start, but you'll pay a lot for it. As an alternative,

consider investing instead in technological enablers, from telemarketing to having an effective web presence to engaging through social media to decrease costs as much as possible.

2. **Automate as Much as Possible:** Whenever possible, try to automate the customer acquisition process even if it requires significant investments. If you can promote your product through sites where there are big networks and opportunities to make your message go viral, from Facebook's and LinkedIn's network effects to Amazon's preference engine, these are great channels through which details about your product can be shared. You might also automate your marketing by creating incentive schemes for your users similar to the ones made famous by Avon or Groupon. This leads into the very fertile area of PLG, one of the motions described in Step 18, where the product is designed to drive adoption or sell itself.

3. **Improve Conversion Rates in the Sales Funnel:** Always focus on improving the conversion rates from your leads. As you see in the bottom-up calculations, there is a huge cost associated with chasing deals that you don't close. Getting higher conversion rates on leads opens up the funnel so more deals get through, increasing your revenue and decreasing your CoCA.

4. **Decrease the Cost of Leads and Improve the Quality of Leads:** Getting a bunch of business cards at a trade show may get you a lot of leads (less cost per lead), but they are probably poor-quality leads. You can reduce the cost of leads without sacrificing the quality of the lead with techniques like HubSpot's inbound marketing strategy. Incorporating tools and techniques into your sales process that increase the quality of your leads, and paying attention to where your leads are coming from, will improve your conversion rate.

5. **Speed Through the Sales Funnel:** By focusing on the speed at which prospects are moving through the sales cycle, you can decrease the sales cycle, which will have a dramatic positive effect on reducing the CoCA.

6. **Choose Your Business Model with CoCA in Mind:** The design of your Business Model can dramatically affect your CoCA, as Jim Dougherty learned at IntraLinks, the company providing a secure online space for investment bankers and lawyers to share documents with their clients. His business model was based on usage, but it was hard to sell to customers because they could not easily plan how much they would spend on the product. When he switched to a "cell phone" type of model, where customers paid a fixed amount each month for an agreed-upon type of service, with the flexibility to buy additional service on a usage basis, it became much easier to sell the product to customers, and the sales cycle length decreased dramatically.

7. **Word of Mouth:** The biggest driver of reducing CoCA is positive word of mouth about a company and its product. This tends to dramatically decrease the sales cycle, decrease the customer's desire to push you for discounts, and bring in well-qualified customers who already are good fits for the product, so salespeople can be much more productive in dealing with them. Many companies today, large and small, attempt to drive this by measuring it using the Net Promoter Score (NPS) index and system. They carefully track this and report it in their operations, executive, and even board meetings. Bonuses are tied to it with the belief, validated in real life, that NPS is a good proxy for the strength of word of mouth from your customers.

8. **Stay Focused on the Target Market:** Staying focused on your Beachhead Market from the earliest steps of this process, and not getting distracted by customers outside of your chosen market, will help improve word of mouth and also make your sales reps much more productive. They will become experts in their industry and the sales cycle length will decrease (repetitive selling to the same DMU and Process to Acquire a Paying Customer makes the sales rep much more productive), thereby decreasing the CoCA.

EXAMPLES

Bloom Continued

What Bloom had accomplished in Step 18 was a plan for what type of mix of revenue-generating motions they planned to use in the short, medium, and long term. That is very important information, but the team needed more.

They first needed to build out a forecast of how many customers they planned to acquire at least on a yearly basis for three to five years. That would help them understand how their total marketing and sales costs translate into an estimated average cost to acquire each customer. In the first year, you should have greater specificity on what those revenue and number of customers milestones would be.

Once they had a forecast of customers, the team then built out a marketing and sales plan they were comfortable would allow them to achieve this plan—using the general GTM plan developed in Step 18, Design a Scalable Revenue Engine. They included all digital marketing campaigns, salaries of anyone working on this, consultants used, websites, logo work, video costs, tradeshows, travel expense, and so on. For Bloom, as you can see in Figure 19.5, they plan to keep it very simple. I think these numbers are unreasonably low because they are not valuing their time spent on sales and marketing appropriately.

Total Sales and Marketing Expense List

	Short Term (<1 yr)	Medium Term(1-3 yrs)	Long Term (3+ Yrs)
Goal	*S&M Pre Launch: Build hype*	*Burst Campaigns: Focus on customer growth & partnering with events/businesses*	*Loyalty & Retention: Organic Growth, PR & Partnerships*
Sales Expenses	No Direct Sales Costs for users as app is Free	Sales Team Salary $500k-$1 m/yr Regional sales teams across US to partner with businesses to provide services for app in return for referral %	Sales Team Salary $800k-$2 m/yr Focus on national partnerships with HR departments/Insurance partnerships as a part of women's mental health/wellness initiatives
Marketing Expenses	Social Media Ads $ 50k/yr Influencer Marketing $25k/yr	Social Media Ads $ 100-200k/yr Influencer Marketing $300k/yr Bloom Ambassador Programs at Universities Salary + Swag $250k/yr	Influencer Marketing/Health Professional Social Media marketing $500k-$1m/yr. Marketing to new adjacent markets and through integration with other platforms such as Resy, Opentable, Classpass, Tock, Nextdoor $1-$2m/yr

Even though we expect total sales and marketing costs to increase, our strategy shifts from targeting individual users to corporations and businesses to acquire and retain greater volume of users.

Figure 19.5: Bloom's general description of marketing and sales expenses needed to make the sales targets in their forecast.

In Figure 19.6, you can see that integrating the customer acquisition forecasts with the projected numbers for the marketing and sales resources required to achieve those forecasts allows Bloom to now estimate the CoCA for each of the first five years. Using specific numbers, of course, provides a false sense of precision, so I would summarize their CoCA as starting in the mid-$20s range and going down to the $11–$13 range in steady state.

Estimating the CoCA

Year

	(Pre Launch)	2	3	4	5	Assumptions
New Users Forecasted (High Growth)	5,000	75,000	250,000	750,000	1,000,000	After gaining 20k users on our waitlist pre-launch (tested using a landing page), we believe 25% will convert to new users
All Sales expenses	$ -	$500,000	$1,000,000	$2,000,000	$1,000,000	
All Marketing expenses	$100,000	$650,000	$1,500,000	$2,500,000	$4,000,000	We will have high network effects & virality in years 2-3
Total Marketing & Sales expenses	$100,000	$1,150,000	$2,500,000	$4,500,000	$5,000,000	In Years 1-3, Founders will tap into their professional & social networks to promote the app. (Not accounted for in Sales & Marketing expense, but is an important contributor with very low cost)
High User Growth COCA	$20.00	$15.33	$10.00	$6.00	$5.00	
Conservative User Growth COCA	$26.67	$25.56	$25.00	$24.00	$20.00	
Average CoCA Estimate	$23.33	$20.44	$17.50	$15.00	$12.50	

Product Unit Economics: CoCA

Figure 19.6: Bloom's assumptions and calculations to estimate CoCA.

With the CoCA estimate in hand, Bloom then explained what drives these numbers (Figure 19.7), so they can make intelligent adjustments over time.

Interpreting CoCA & Anticipating Next Steps

What are Key Drivers that will bring CoCA down?	- Expanding to B2C cross-selling, e.g. targeting corporate HR or insurance companies as a mental health benefit - Network effects on social media, virality factor - Improving the effectiveness of campaigns via A/B testing - Improve customer retention by enhancing the product
How risky are the drivers?	**Moderate to high risk**. Strong dependence on virality factor / network effects makes it risky since there is a strong reliance on recommendations / word of mouth. Ultimately will people recommend this to their friends/coworkers/family members?
How to mitigate risk?	Promotional / referral incentives and improved product features for retention

Figure 19.7: Reflecting on the CoCA estimate.

Finally, the team showed the link between CoCA and LTV over time (see Figure 19.8).

Product Unit Economics: CoCA & LTV/CoCA Ratio

Comparison of LTV and CoCA Over Time

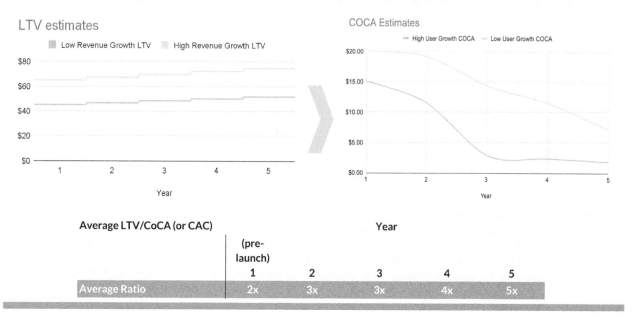

Figure 19.8: Comparing LTV and CoCA for Bloom.

ADDITIONAL RESOURCES

There are additional resources for this step at www.d-eship.com/step19. These materials include:

- Video: CoCA Explainers by Bill Aulet and Erdin Beshimov
- Video: Example described and explained in an interview with Humon founders Dan Wiese and Alessandro Babini
- Process Guidance to calculate the CoCA
- Worksheet 19.1: Time Interval Assumptions for CoCA
- Worksheet 19.2: Total Marketing and Sales Expenses
- Worksheet 19.3: Estimate the CoCA
- Worksheet 19.4: Convert CoCA calculations into an appropriate estimate
- Worksheet 19.5: Ways to Decrease CoCA
- Worksheet 19.6: Visual comparison of LTV versus CoCA over time
- Worksheet 19.7: Overall Summary of Unit Economics

Additional resources will be added as new and updated examples and information become available.

Summary

At this point, you have completed the important steps of determining whether your business has a reasonable path to financial sustainability. The LTV and CoCA analysis checks the economic viability of your new venture. It highlights the importance of keeping an eye on these key factors. It also provides a quantitative way to manage the business to be successful. It is important to understand that unit economics analysis does not fully account for the expenses of research and development as well as general and administration, not to mention some room for profit back to the shareholder, but it is a proven and generally accepted strong indicator. Don't let your optimism blind you in doing the calculations. Make the numbers real and not what you want them to be.

NOTE: There is important information in the Glossary about this definition of CoCA and how it is similar and dissimilar to other terms often used to convey analogous concepts, most specifically but not exclusively CAC. I encourage you to read this as well so you are not confused when you hear or see the terms and can be well prepared to as the right questions and clarify, and then respond appropriately.

Identify Key Assumptions

In This Step, You Will:

- Determine which are the most important assumptions about your business for it to be successful.
- Rank your top 5 to 10 assumptions in order of importance.

Everything is looking and feeling good but before you go and build, step back and revisit again with the benefit of greater wisdom—what are the Key Assumptions that need to go right for your new venture to work?

Why This Step, and Why Now?

Throughout the whole 24-step process, you have been developing well-reasoned and evidence-based hypotheses that you have been then testing and adjusting and gaining confidence. So why do you need a special step now to do test assumptions? Good question.

This is a moment to step back and catch your breath and make sure you don't miss something big. You want to look at the broader landscape you have developed and with the wisdom you have accumulated, and now look for the most critical assumptions that need to be true for your business to be successful. You are doing it at this time because the "price of poker" (i.e., the costs of continuing forward) is about to go up dramatically. Once you start to build the product, your costs will go up significantly.

Also, as you start to transition from being predominantly in inquiry mode (looking to understand your customer's need) to advocacy mode (building and promoting the product you believe meets your customer's need), it will be both economically and emotionally harder to turn back and make changes, as discussed with the IKEA effect in Step 7, High-Level Product Specification.

This is why I dedicate two steps to explicitly identifying and testing your "final" key hypotheses at this point, understanding that testing assumptions never ends, but this is the last opportunity before starting product development to make big changes.

Let's Get Started

Identifying and breaking down your Key Assumptions is not difficult and can be a fun exercise, but entrepreneurs tend to skip over this step, trusting intuition or research to substitute for actual testing of business and customer behavior assumptions. Don't do that. Be disciplined.

Those of you familiar with Lean Startup methodology will see similarities to the concept of a "minimum viable product" or MVP. This can create some confusion. A product is different from a hypothesis. A "product" should be something that is complete enough such that a customer can gain value from it and then someone will pay something for that value created. The Lean Startup MVP framework, by comparison, includes in its definition of "products" actions that merely test individual assumptions about the new venture idea. Therefore, I detail the process of identifying and testing assumptions in Steps 20 and 21, which will be followed in Step 22 by establishing what I call the "Minimum Viable Business Product" (MVBP)—a different concept than the MVP as used in Lean Startup language. The process of establishing an MVBP provides a "systems test" of whether your customer will pay money for what you are offering, not just a channel through which to test an assumption. Much as you do not have a meaningful business until you have a paying customer, your business does not have a product until someone purchases it, gets value from it, and can provide meaningful feedback to you about it.

Over the next two steps, you will unpack your assumptions, breaking them down into a prioritized list to test empirically before you launch your MVBP.

How to Identify Your Key Assumptions

First, review each step of the framework and make a list of the areas in which you have made logical conclusions based on your primary market research. Have you correctly identified your Persona's priorities? Will your customer find the value proposition attractive when it comes time for them to make a purchase? Will the customer make the time and effort to integrate your product into their workflow?

One key area in which you should question assumptions is your gross margin. Are your cost targets accurate? If your product is hardware, review the bill of material and carefully analyze the cost of the most important items in the bill of material. If yours is a software development effort, you will do a similar thing, listing the key development challenges, assumptions, and cost items. Identifying and taking a closer look at these easily testable hypotheses provides an additional level of analysis to the most significant areas.

Two other key areas to test are the Next 10 Customers list and the Decision-Making Unit. Out of the customers you have already identified, are any of them "lighthouse" customers, where other customers will buy if they do? Are any "linchpin" customers, where if they don't buy, others will not? Are there other linchpin customers who you have not yet identified? And, most importantly, are the lighthouse and linchpin customers interested in purchasing your product?

At this point, you should review each step and determine what is the most critical assumption that must be true for you to be successful.

It is important to note that it is not just the production of assumptions, but rather the team discussion that leads to the production of assumptions, which is the most valuable thing. It is critical that you have a fully bought-in team going forward and this step is a chance to reinforce this.

Five Conditions That Make for a Good Key Assumption

There is a skill in carefully crafting good Key Assumptions. This is because our Key Assumptions are hypotheses that you want to test in as scientific a manner as possible. As such, they should meet the follow five criteria:

1. **Specific:** A good hypothesis must be very specific and descriptive in nature, otherwise it is not particularly useful. Much like a Persona needs to be rich in detail, so should your hypothesis.

2. **Singular:** There should only be one factor in the assumption statement. The word "and" is usually a flashing light indicating there is more than one factor at play and the assumption needs to be broken up.

3. **Important:** It must be an assumption that has enormous impact on whether or not your business becomes successful.

4. **Measurable:** It must be an assumption you can quantify, an unbiased way to compare different situations.

5. **Testable:** If it is not testable, it is not a useful Key Assumption. But you do not have to worry about this yet; this is the essence of Step 21.

EXAMPLES

Bloom Continued

At this point, you have been on the journey with Madeleine, Anisha, and Sarah as they built Bloom, so these assumptions should resonate with you.

You can see the identified Key Assumptions in Figure 20.1, along with which of the 24 Steps it is associated with, the risk level, and the impact if the assumption turns out to be false. This is a reasonable start, but there is more work to be done to make them more specific and measurable, which the team refined as they took the exercise out of the classroom.

Sasa

Started by three dynamic young female entrepreneurs—Ella Peinovich, Gwen Floyd, and Catherine Mahugu—Sasa is a for-profit social venture empowering women in Africa by allowing them to sell their art worldwide using mobile phones. As the team looked to launch and grow their business in a capital-constrained situation, they were very careful to identify their assumptions and test them so as not to waste any precious money or time developing the product. As opposed to Bloom, Sasa was a differentiated two-sided market, which required a more complex set of Key Assumptions to be considered, with the producers being the African artisans and the consumers being customers worldwide (with a Beachhead Market in the United States). The team identified several Key Assumptions for each side of the market (see Figures 20.2 and 20.3).

Note that some of the assumptions for the consumer side are not specific enough and will need to be decoupled into multiple assumptions.

Design & Build: Key Assumptions

We Identified the Following Key Assumptions

#	Assumption	Step	Risk Level	Impact if Assumption is Wrong
1	Women view the issue of not having a sufficient social circle as something important enough that they will commit time to it	3, 4, 5, 14	High	Not being able to monetize the product, lack of interest in the product, no positive network effects
2	Women will commit time to forming friendships on app despite other ways to spend time, e.g. TikTok	3, 4, 5, 14	High	Gaining attention on someone's phone is very difficult, if we can't capture interest, product won't be able to grow
3	Willingness to pay - women will pay, long term, to create friends	9, 13, 14, 15	High	Eventually, monetization is a necessity for the product to grow and succeed
4	Meeting others digitally via apps is here to stay	9, 14, 15	Medium	Other mediums of meeting could take over, e.g. return to in-person, which would negate network effects
5	Women prefer to socialize in groups	8, 10	Medium	If women do not prefer to socialize in groups then the differentiating factor of the app is much less
6	There are enough women in a certain geography to form a group	4, 14	Low	Inhibits the network effects if there aren't enough women to interact in-person
7	Women are willing to invest time in creating their canvas	7, 10	Low	If women do not prefer to create a Canvas, then there will need to be a different basis for matching algorithm

Testing Key Assumptions

Figure 20.1: Bloom's identification of Key Assumptions.

Producers Assumptions
1. Craftswomen (i.e., Producers) want to be economically empowered.
2. Craftswomen will adopt the Sasa platform into their market practices.
3. The vendors will earn a sustainable income.
4. Vendors will trust the Sasa technology and services.
5. Existing infrastructures will be consistent and expand with demand.
6. Vendors will earn more using Sasa than by selling in the open-air markets.
7. A vendor can afford to buy a simple feature phone, which is camera-enabled.
8. A vendor is familiar with using SMS.
9. A vendor is able to leverage their knowlege of SMS to quickly adopt the use of MMS.

sasa Customer—Assumptions about the producers

Figure 20.2: Sasa customer assumptions about the producers.

Web Consumer Assumptions
1. Consumers not only value, but prefer handmade goods.
2. Consumers want to know who made their products and how.
3. International consumers will trust the Sasa technology and services.
4. International consumers will be compelled to buy products on the Sasa platform.
5. Sasa customers will return to Sasa to buy more products.
6. International consumers will happily wait for up to three weeks to receive products from Africa.
7. Sasa can profit greatly just from selling jewelry to start.
8. The necessary infrastructure and policy will be consistent and expand with demand.

sasa   Customer—Assumptions about the web consumer

Figure 20.3: Sasa customer assumptions about the web consumers.

ADDITIONAL RESOURCES

There are additional resources for this step at www.d-eship.com/step20. These materials include:

- Process Guide to identify Key Assumptions
- Worksheet 20.1: List of Key Assumptions

Additional resources will be added as new and updated examples and information become available.

Summary

Identifying Key Assumptions is the first part of the process to validate your primary market research by looking for customers to take specific actions, which will happen in the next step. Before the assumptions can be tested, they need to be broken down into their component parts, so that each assumption represents a specific, narrow idea that can be empirically tested in the next step using a single experiment design. Do not worry yet about how you will design the experiment. Focus on breaking out all the Key Assumptions, because if you skip over an assumption fearing that testing it is difficult, you will neglect a potentially important factor in your business's health.

This step does not involve a lot of new work, but it is important. It is nice to have a step that is a bit easier, isn't it? You are getting close to the end now—hang in there!

Test Key Assumptions

In This Step, You Will:

- From your list of top identified assumptions from the previous step, design simple, low-cost, and rapid methods of testing them to see if you can refute them or gain more confidence that they are true.

- Once designed and agreed upon by the team, perform the empirical tests, moving quickly and efficiently to decrease the risk of your startup.

Using the scientific method to test your individual assumptions may not always give you the answer you wanted, but it can be fun and rewarding—and much better to find your problems before your customer does!

Why This Step, and Why Now?

As mentioned in the previous step, the price of poker is about to go up significantly. You need to de-risk as much of your plan as possible now. With all that you have done, you have a strong holistic picture of the potential of the Beachhead Market. With this plan on the verge of being converted into action, the final questions are:

1. Can you build this?
2. Can you execute this in the real world (because there are sure to be surprises)?

The first question is easier to address and you will get to that in Step 22, Define the Minimum Viable Business Product (MVBP). But what trips up a new venture is the second question, so in this step you are looking to build your confidence by running localized tests of those critical factors identified in Step 20, Identify Key Assumptions, that could tank your business, and by doing so, mitigate your risks as much as possible. Better to know sooner rather than later, especially when the cost of being wrong is about to skyrocket.

Let's Get Started

In the last step, one of the criteria for a Key Assumption was that it was "testable." You will now design experiments to test those assumptions in the cheapest, quickest, and easiest ways possible. The goal is to gather empirical, unbiased data that either supports or disproves your assumptions. These experiments will not require much, if any, in the way of building physical goods or writing code, but rather logical thinking to design simple yet effective tests. They should actually be fun to test. Be humble and don't be discouraged by news that negates your hypotheses. You need to know the truth and not just hear what you want to hear.

With the value of hindsight, some of these experiments may seem simple enough that they could have been conducted earlier in this process. But don't worry about this because what you have learned to this point will more clearly point you to the most Key Assumptions. With all of the knowledge you have and the focus of product-market fit, you should be able to design and run efficient experiments.

Furthermore, if you run a bunch of experiments with different hypotheses off the top of your head, and some of the experiments seem to succeed, that by itself does not guarantee success. Remember, in social science research, your do not prove hypotheses so much as disprove hypotheses, so a successful experiment only gives you more confidence that you will have a successful new venture. It does not guarantee you success. The combination of your primary market research and the empirical experiments you will perform in this step will lead you to understand your customer more fully and increase your likelihood of success.

Now That You Have Identified the Assumptions, Test Them

Designing good experiments requires that you be systematic and think creatively. There is an entire field of research—behavioral economics—that explains why people make the decisions they make and how to design proper and efficient experiments that will illuminate this behavior, so I won't go into detail within the confines of this book. Instead, I suggest that you read some of the literature in this field. One book I find immensely useful in describing the value of well-designed experiments as well as the emerging field of behavioral economics and some of its basic principles is *Think Like a Freak* by Steven Levitt and Stephen Dubner, who are well known for their bestselling book *Freakonomics*.

Paul Cheek's book *Disciplined Entrepreneurship Startup Tactics: 15 Tactics to Turn Your Business Plan into a Business* (a valuable companion to this book) is very useful for all steps and it is particularly so for this step. His hacking mentality (he first arrived at our center as the "Hacker-in-Residence") and skills make his guidance especially valuable in this area.

It should be fun to design the experiments that test your assumptions, and you don't need a team of PhD economists, especially if you're only testing one assumption in each experiment. If an experiment is more complex, such as one that tests multiple assumptions at the same time, it gets much more difficult and less fun. Hence, try to decouple assumptions and design your experiments carefully.

When detailing the experiments you plan to run, make sure to define what outcomes will validate your assumption(s). If you don't define your outcomes before the experiment, you will inevitably skew the experiment in favor of your assumptions, making the outcomes worthless as indicators of the strength of your new product's plans.

Don't be surprised if the result of testing your assumption is that you need to do follow-up work. Sometimes the result of a successful experiment is more experiments. You have to be patient.

Notice how simple the tests can be. More complicated is *not* better; it is actually worse. Some may be as simple as calling your vendors to validate your list of how much it costs for each part that goes into your product (the cost of goods sold or COGS), as that cost is often a Key Assumption. Or, if getting a certain highly influential customer in your chosen market segment is a crucial validation point, you'll want to measure their commitment level more energetically, such as getting them to prepay at least partially for a solution or put down a deposit, or at least provide a letter of intent or agree to a pilot. The expectations and commitment thresholds are still low because you should not be communicating to customers that you have a product being sold—you're still in inquiry mode for a bit longer, which is a much better environment for experiments. Enjoy it while it lasts because it will be ending soon!

Finally, remember that a valid assumption is still only an assumption, because only with paying customers do you truly know that your startup has a sustainable market. I will guide you through how to start determining whether customers will actually buy your product in Step 23, Show That "The Dogs Will Eat the Dog Food." An experiment that invalidates an assumption will often tell you more than an experiment that seems to give you confirming evidence regarding an assumption. Nevertheless, the more you test in advance, the more problems you can identify while fixing problems is still relatively inexpensive.

IN THEORY VERSUS IN PRACTICE

Here is one of my favorite stories about why you should be very careful about believing something is true or false until you have tested it in the real world.

The professorship chair I currently hold at MIT, known as the Ethernet Inventors Professor of the Practice of Entrepreneurship, was generously endowed by the legendary entrepreneur Bob Metcalfe. During his acceptance speech upon receiving the Turing Award in 2023, Bob shared a captivating story about his co-inventor, the late David Boggs. Together, they invented and, even more importantly, pioneered Ethernet, a revolutionary computer networking protocol that facilitated communication between computers.

After the successful invention of Ethernet, Bob established a company called 3Com to bring this groundbreaking technology to the commercial market. However, the dominance of IBM, which held significant control over the computer industry at the time, posed a formidable challenge. IBM perceived networking protocols as a threat to its existence and sought to maintain control over them.

IBM launched a relentless attack against 3Com, leveraging its vast resources, extensive industry connections, and reputation. At the time, as 3Com was gaining traction in the marketplace and becoming a major player, David received an invitation to join a panel discussion on the technical merits of Ethernet at a major industry tradeshow. Little did he know, whether intentionally or coincidentally, he was about to find himself in an unenviable position.

The panel consisted of two additional technical experts who spoke prior to David. They discussed the supposed technical limitations of Ethernet compared to IBM's Token Ring architecture, expressing severe doubts about its ability to function as advertised. In fact, it was accurate to say that he was attacked by Token Ring advocates with elaborate computer models demonstrating that Ethernet would not work. As the final speaker, David, who had already built over a hundred Ethernet networks and who was known for his concise communication skills, carefully chose his response. He stated, "Ethernet apparently does not work in theory, only in practice."

Despite the skepticism raised by the previous panelists, Ethernet ultimately triumphed over the Token Ring protocol. It became the foundational technology that powers the internet today, enabling communication for two-thirds of the world's population. No question the dogs ate that dog food. As an entrepreneur myself, I value the facts on the ground more than untested theories, and you should too.

EXAMPLES

Assumption: Smartphone Users Aged 25–34 Access Weather Forecasts on Their Phone to Decide What to Wear

A team proposed this as a single assumption, but within it are two assumptions that must be decoupled. Assumption 1 is that people with smartphones use them to obtain weather forecasts. Assumption 2 is that people consult smartphone-based weather forecasts to decide what to wear.

To test the first assumption, the team approached their target customers (in a health club or restaurant, or on the sidewalk near where the target customer worked) and asked if they had a weather app on their phone and whether they used the app. Over 90% said yes, validating this first assumption. The team also looked at the general market research and found that weather apps were one of the most popular applications for smartphones, further validating this assumption.

The results were mixed when testing the second assumption. In one distinctive group, less than 30% consulted weather forecasts on their phones for the purpose of deciding what to wear, while in another different sampled group, more than 70% did so. The team realized that the first group had the distinguishing characteristic of being male. The second group was female, showing that the team had identified an important segmentation factor and that they had not previously segmented their market enough, given that they found such significantly different priorities existed along gender lines. The experiment provided the team with valuable information they didn't have before that was inexpensive and quick to obtain. Once they had done this, they then validated their assumption to be true but for a much more well-defined target customer group.

Assumption: "Neohippies" Aged 25–35 Use Their Smartphones to Help Them Shop in the Grocery Store

This team wanted to offer a smartphone-based personal shopping assistant to young people who shop at health food stores like Whole Foods Market. The students on the team used their smartphones when they shopped, so they assumed that others did so as well. This was a Key Assumption that needed to be tested.

To test the assumption, the team went to a Whole Foods and observed shoppers who fit the description of their demographic. The experiment was conducted around the time the iPhone was first released in 2007. The team observed that virtually none of the shoppers used a smartphone while in the store. The team was incredulous, but confirmed the result at a different Whole Foods location. The team interviewed shoppers and found that while many of them owned iPhones, they were not interested in using them while shopping because they already had a way of shopping that worked well for them and did not want to change. As a result, the team changed its focus completely and worked on a different mobile app for a different target customer. Maybe someday there would be a market for such an app, but the timing was not right yet.

Assumption: Conducting Opinion Polls Is Much Better on Facebook Than with Traditional Telephone-Based Methods

One student, a political science major, was concerned about political opinion polls and the possibility that the accuracy of polls would be affected by the growing number of people who were canceling landlines in favor of cell phones. American laws prohibit contacting cell phone users with autodialing machines, so pollsters who want to call cell phones have to individually dial each number, making it much more expensive to contact cell phone users versus landline users.

Polls risked being skewed because certain demographics were more likely than others to be cell phone–only users. The student assumed that since Facebook allows you to target ads at certain demographics and access the demographic data for clicked ads, he could use Facebook ads to quickly and cheaply conduct polls that are more accurate and less labor-intensive than telephone-based polls.

The student was able to test his hypothesis overnight with less than $100 in Facebook ads. His initial experiment compared his ad click-through rates against the 2012 New Hampshire presidential primary and the aggregate of the professional polls done of the primary. His click-through rates did not accurately predict the outcome of the primary, so he hypothesized that if he changed the design of the ads, he would achieve more accurate results. Less than a week later, with another $50 in ads, he tried a different format for the headlines of the ads (see Figure 21.1).

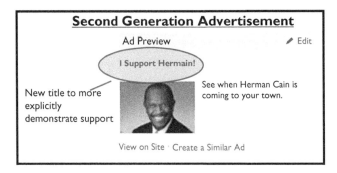

Figure 21.1: Second-generation advertisement for Herman Cain.

This second attempt was compared to a different state's presidential primary, and achieved results similar to the professional polls that cost $100,000 and several days to produce. Interestingly, while validating his hypothesis, he found an even more interesting use for his idea—pollsters were interested in using Facebook's demographic targeting of ads to organize hyper-targeted focus groups, a market opportunity with much broader application than simply predicting the results of an election.

Assumption: People Will Be Inspired to Contribute to Chalkboards That Have Writing Prompts on Them

One student team came up with an idea that seemed illogical and lacked real innovation. The idea was to capitalize on the trends of food trucks and coffee drinking to start a coffee truck that would be in close proximity to college campuses where there are no "good" coffee shops near academic buildings.

The students called their trucks "Inspired" and believed that to attract a loyal following, they could cover the sides of the truck with chalkboards for people to write on (see Figure 21.2). There would be prompts to encourage people to write, and the resulting messages would inspire all the customers. That, in combination with the high-quality coffee the truck would serve, would attract customers. So a key assumption that was fundamental to their business model (but not the only one) was that they could attract people and engage with potential customers by having them write on common blackboards regarding inspirational topics.

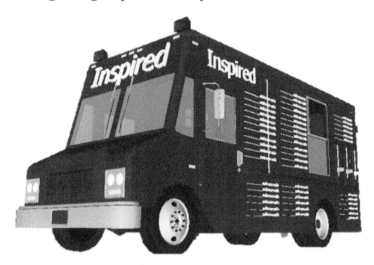

Figure 21.2: The Inspired coffee truck.

The team then set out to test this simple assumption, that people would write inspiring things on chalkboards voluntarily. They found a large blackboard wall in MIT's Stata Center in a heavily traveled corridor for students (similar to the environment where they would want to park a coffee truck) and at 8 a.m. wrote a prompt on it: "_____ makes me Smile" (see Figure 21.3). The team then waited to see if students would fill in the other blanks without any further prompting.

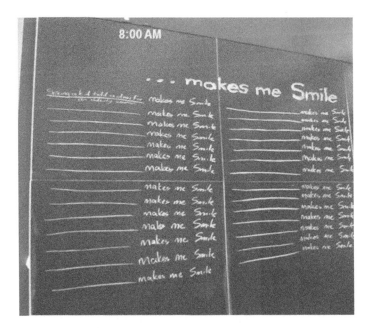

Figure 21.3: The blackboard with "_____ makes me Smile" prompt at 8:00 a.m.

By noon, the entire wall had been filled (Figure 21.4); clearly students had gotten engaged with the process and enjoyed expressing themselves based on the entries, which are not only very clever but also showed many contributors felt compelled to be creative, as well. Interestingly, one of the entries was "Coffee makes me smile," which further helped the student team's case.

The team ran the experiment again on a different day, using a different phrase (see Figure 21.5).

The quote was "Before I die, I want to _____" and lo and behold, by noon the board was not only full, it was overflowing, with additional comments in adjacent space (see Figure 21.6).

Needless to say, the team had validated a key assumption in a much more compelling way than making a logic-based argument because they had real-world data to back it up. I gave them an A for the assignment. Testing this assumption was also a lot more fun for the team than coming up with some abstract rationale—and it was more powerful.

Figure 21.4: The blackboard with "_____ makes me Smile" prompt at noon.

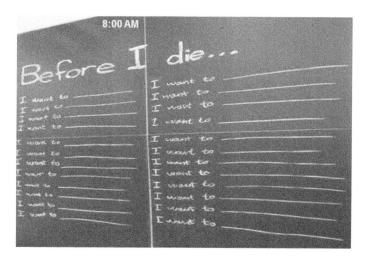

Figure 21.5: The blackboard with "Before I Die" prompt at 8 a.m.

Figure 21.6: The blackboard with "Before I Die" prompt at noon.

EXAMPLES

Bloom Continued

You saw in the last chapter that Bloom identified seven Key Assumptions. They identified three in particular that were of the highest risk. As I mentioned in the previous step, the Key Assumptions were still a bit too general and should have been more specific. Because of this, it is hard to make them measurable, and designing the test becomes more of a struggle for this team. While other steps done by this team are brilliant, this step is one they refined in a follow-on class later in the year. You can see in Figure 21.7 that they were able to make a good first pass in this class on defining some tests and concrete metrics to measure.

Test Key Assumptions

#	Empirical Test	Required Resources	Validating Outcomes
1	Find example women from Beach Head Market & observe how much time they spend trying to make friends online & offline. Proxy could be engagement within existing friendship watering holes, e.g. FB Groups	The ability to shadow a few individuals within the beachhead market or the ability to run data analytics on the conversations taking place in the Facebook groups to see if there are key phrases that indicate friendships are being established offline	If there is good engagement in how women interface online, then this can be a sign that one of the big risk factors - lack of willingness to invest - is mitigated **Metric**: % of women actively engaging in friendship forming activities with new individuals
2	Gauge willingness to participate / engage with the app by assessing willingness to provide personal information / time	Create a lightweight landing page that intakes personal information about women and match women manually into groups to see if there is traction / follow through	If there is good engagement with the landing page and in person, that is a strong indicator that there will be good network effects **Metric**: # of women entering information and % of women who entered their information that attended an event
3	Gauge interest in group hangouts and identify if there are interpersonal dynamics that complicate group engagements	Match women in their geographic area to small groups & have them meet in person @ a Bloom event. See if they attend & satisfaction with experience	Repeat attendees is a sign that the group dynamic is working, lack of returns indicates the contrary **Metric**: % of women who attended a group hang managed by Bloom that return to another
4	Geographic density is sufficient to support in-person meeting	Launch a landing page that intakes geographic information to see if there are hot spots of need / interest	Lots of interest in a geographic area supports in-person meeting **Metric**: # of sign-ups per geographic area

Figure 21.7: Bloom's plans to test Key Assumptions.

ADDITIONAL RESOURCES

There are additional resources for this step at www.d-eship.com/step21. These materials include:

- Process Guidance on how to test Key Assumptions
- Worksheet 21.1: Tests for Key Overall Assumptions

Additional resources will be added as new and updated examples and information become available.

Summary

Testing Key Assumptions, particularly the most significant assumptions, such as cost targets and interest of lighthouse customers, is not hard and is even fun. It complements your PMR-based approach. The convergence of your market research with empirical results from your experiments prepares you to move forward with confidence.

After having completed this step and the previous step, you have de-risked your product at the level of individual assumptions as much as you reasonably can. This accomplishment does not mean that, when all the assumptions are put into one product, the fully assembled solution is assured of market success, but you have done the best you can. Some assumptions will never be able to be fully tested until there is a product and it is put into production. That testing comes in the next two steps.

Define the Minimum Viable Business Product (MVBP)

In This Step, You Will:

- Determine what is the minimum product you need to build to test whether your end user gets value from your product.
- Determine whether the economic buyer is willing to pay for your product.
- Start the feedback loop with your customers to improve your product over time.

It's time! You have done all your homework, so now you have to give your customer a product. But keep it simple to start.

Why This Step, and Why Now?

The previous two steps focused on testing individual assumptions. In this step and the next, you will develop and test them integrated together. To do this you will create a Minimum Viable Business Product (MVBP). The MVBP combines your most important key individual assumptions into one simple but complete product that can be sold. This will be your all-important starting point that you will build off of in Step 24 to grow a bigger business.

Let's Get Started

Once you ship a product, the stakes become much higher, but the quality of feedback becomes much, much better, too. As such, now you have done all you can to test before building, so now you will pivot to building a product and getting feedback from it. Words and surveys only get you so far. Now you will get concrete feedback about whether customers are willing to pay you for your product. If you don't ship a product, you can't be a business.

To reduce the investment, complexity, and time (remember, clock speed is extremely important), the concept of an MVBP is very important. You need to get to the market quickly without overspending, and so you don't want to build out the entire product now, just the smallest amount possible. Getting into an iterative feedback loop with your customers will lead you to the truth. All of the work from the previous steps positions you to do this efficiently and effectively.

The MVBP sets you up to test the two most important overarching assumptions—do you create meaningful value for your customer and are they willing to pay for your product?

Three Conditions of an MVBP

As mentioned in Step 20, the Lean Startup definition of a minimum viable product is too limited and does not accurately describe a "product." A product needs to be complete enough that you can gain meaningful feedback about whether someone will pay for it. As such, there are three conditions that must be satisfied for your MVBP to be sufficient:

1. The customer gets value out of use of the product.
2. The customer pays for the product.
3. The product is sufficient to start the customer feedback loop, where the customer can help you iterate toward an increasingly better product.

The First Part of an MVBP Is That It Must Be Minimal

The first hard part of defining a MVBP is in the first word. It must be absolutely minimal. The more minimal the better, which can be hard for entrepreneurs because they always want to add something else. While what you build must be substantial enough to satisfy the three conditions of an MVBP, you do not have the luxury of time or funding as a startup, so you must focus on what you can test with customers quickly and in a cost-effective manner. Simplicity is the key here.

By now, between the work you did in Step 7 on your High-Level Product Specification, your conversations with potential customers, and other brainstorming your team has done over time, you have probably come up with a lot of ideas for features. Removing features is challenging because people naturally don't want to give up ideas they have already thought of and think are good. The Nobel Prize–winning behavioral economist Richard H. Thaler describes this as the endowment effect, that you attach more value to things you own than similar things you don't. But you must give up on features. Less is more here. So be prepared for some tough conversations on your team.

The level of detail needed for an MVBP will vary depending on your industry. I have heard software entrepreneurs say that if you are not embarrassed when you ship your first product, you shipped too late. That ethos might work well for some software, but it doesn't translate well to every situation. If you are making a product for brain surgery, for instance, your MVBP's core minimal reliability better be rock solid! It can and should have a narrow scope in terms of features and functions, but it can't fail. Much is written about software entrepreneurship and then extrapolated to other industries, so use common sense when applying startup advice to the particular demands of your industry.

"Concierge" Anything You Can

You have probably heard the term "fake it 'til you make it," which sounds a little questionable in character. In this case it is not! You want to make as little of the product as you can until you have evidence that it has high odds of being successful. To do this, I strongly recommend the concept of concierging.

The term "concierge" refers to a specific approach or strategy that involves providing highly personalized and hands-on support to customers or users during the early stages of product development. The concept draws inspiration from the role of a concierge in a hotel, who assists guests with their individual needs and ensures their comfort and satisfaction. It is resource-intensive and not scalable in a cost-effective manner. Rather than creating a fully polished product upfront, the entrepreneurial team works closely with these customers to understand their unique requirements, pain points, and desired outcomes. As a result, you keep your initial costs low, and you have great flexibility so you can move quickly to incorporate feedback from your customers.

One example is Wealthfront, which sought to use software to help people invest their money. Instead of building out the software at first, they employed wealth management advisors who met one-on-one with their first customers. Through these meetings, the team proved out what sorts of advice customers wanted and were willing to pay money for, and they were able to automate that advice over time.

Another startup, Cardmunch, wanted to make it easy for users to scan business cards into their computer and have their data stored electronically. While the team could have spent time developing a sophisticated optical character recognition system, they instead started by using Amazon's Mechanical Turk, a service that connects you with real people who will do small tasks for small payments. They were able to prove out their business value—that customers would pay for digitized business card data—by having humans transcribe the business cards at first. And in this case, users didn't know that their business cards weren't being processed by software.

You should look to do the same with your MVBP wherever possible. Don't make big investments to build out things before you have tested them. Fake it behind the scenes before you make it, and then you will know whether it is worth making and more precisely what to make.

Examples

Home Team Therapy

The student behind this idea, Tim Fu, had gone through physical therapy after ACL reconstructive surgery, and believed there was lots of room for improvement in how physical therapy during recovery was delivered. When the Microsoft Kinect system was released, he saw an opportunity to use it to provide patients with real-time automated feedback when they do their therapy exercises at home. Doctors could also see the home sessions and provide feedback of their own. The Kinect hardware and software system was built to allow users to interact with an Xbox videogame console using gestures, rather than a keyboard, voice, or touchscreen, and the Kinect could work on regular computers as well. While the original product was made for the gaming market, Tim envisioned it as a fundamental enabler for his application.

He found implementing his idea complicated, in part because, as a startup, he had few resources. So he started to define his MVBP based on whether doctors and patients would use and pay for his online system that assists them in physical therapy.

When Tim first started, he emotionally wanted to include the Kinect system in his product. The device was a real attention-grabber; so his first thoughts on a product (note that this is pre-MVBP) looked like what's shown in Figure 22.1.

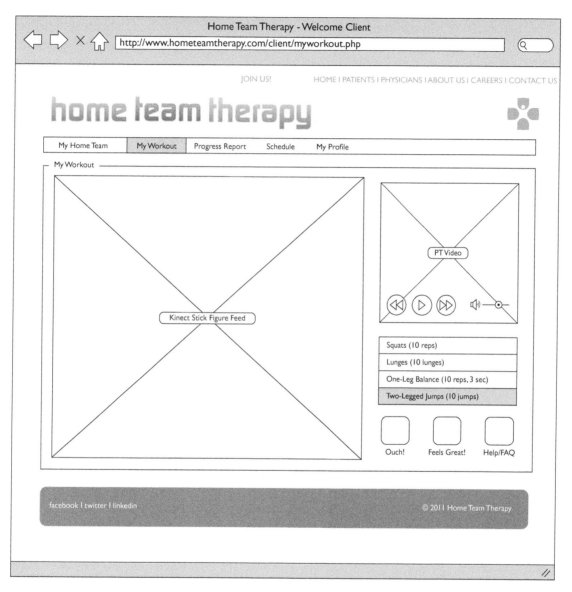

Figure 22.1: Home Team Therapy's stick figure wireframe.

Upon reflection, after asking himself serious questions about what was required to minimally launch to test his core assumptions and get into a feedback cycle with his customer, he simplified it to look more like what's shown in Figure 22.2.

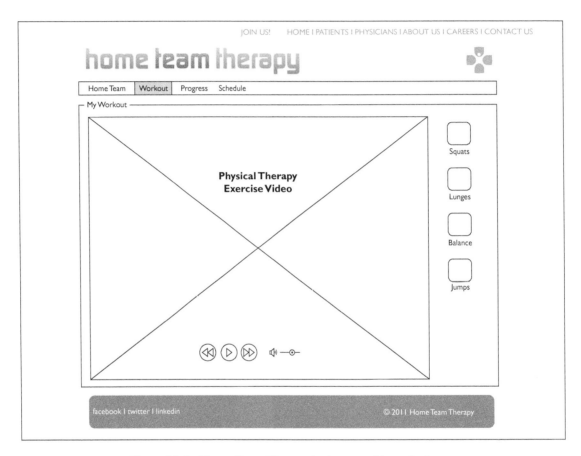

Figure 22.2: Home Team Therapy's therapy video wireframe.

Notice that the elements of the old design that included the Kinect system are gone, which I found disconcerting at first because initially it was the essence of Tim's vision. However, he was right that he could just use an online video for physical therapy and a very simple connection to the physical therapist in his MVBP. This eliminated the technological risk and many other risks, such as how the patient would get the hardware, whether it would be compatible with a computer the patient already had, whether the user would be comfortable using the Kinect, and many other questions.

In this example, determining the MVBP tested the most important assumptions possible to get the iterative learning feedback loop started:

1. Can we get patients to sign up?
2. Will they use the system?
3. Can we get doctors to sign up?
4. Can we get paid for this in general?
5. We've done customer research, but how can we determine if these are the features that customers really want?
6. Are these the features that customers will pay for?
7. Are these the features that customers will always want, or does it appear that their preferences will change over time?

All the other sexy stuff such as the Kinect system could be added later; but for now, Tim had chosen his MVBP wisely and was not distracted by the exciting vision and technology. He had simplified the definition of his MVBP and could now test his key assumptions in a product, beginning the iterative customer feedback loop that would make him successful.

Tim tested these assumptions with friends, family, and ultimately other physical therapy patients. It turned out that instructional videos were most useful to patients when they were still in the information-gathering phase, but they were really looking for other more valuable features in the long term. In developing your own MVBP, it's up to you to determine what those features are and how to design your product offering so you maximize value for your customers and your company.

StyleUp

One of my students, Kendall Herbst, had been a fashion editor at *Lucky* and *New York* magazines, and she had noticed the gap between traditional fashion advice channels and what actually helped a woman decide what to wear or to buy. She came to business school to refine her idea and in her first year got the idea to send women fashion advice that was tailored to each person's taste and to the local weather that day. She suspected women would love a dose of fashion inspiration when they need it most—when they are getting dressed—and that a condensed, personalized dose would be more effective than a cumbersome 600-page magazine. She tested this assumption by sending individual daily e-mails to a handful of female friends with an outfit each woman could re-create, as well as the weather forecast for that day (see Figure 22.3).

Figure 22.3: StyleUp e-mail.
Credit: Aditya Birla Fashion and Retail Limited.

Women loved this idea. The initial group soon grew to almost 40 people. Many of these were Kendall's friends, and she could talk to them about what they liked and what she could improve. In this stage, she learned some of the key products insights. For instance, some women preferred the inspiration the night before and others wanted to receive the e-mails first thing in the morning.

She also learned that women wanted to shop these looks, if they did not own similar items already. Perhaps most importantly, Kendall also looped in women she did not know, and these women consistently opened the e-mails. This hinted the idea could scale, but clearly she needed some technical help.

Classmate Ryan Choi, who before graduate school was an early Salesforce.com engineer, built a system for Kendall to categorize images and deliver them to many women at a time versus one-to-one. Ryan also incorporated many of the early findings like customized time delivery and click-to-purchase links. In this business idea, the primary customer was the woman who received the free daily e-mail; the secondary customer would be a company related to fashion, such as a retailer, who would want access to the primary customer so they could convince the primary customer to buy their products (see Figure 22.4).

Together, Kendall and Ryan created the MVBP:

- A backend system that could categorize images based on weather and style, which they could have concierged but it was just as easy for Ryan to write up some code quickly to do this.

- An easy delivery mechanism to dispense these images every day.

- A database of beautiful images the targeted customer (busy, professional women) would be inspired to see, which included a source link (for copyright issues).

- Analytics to measure how deeply women were engaging with and sharing the service.

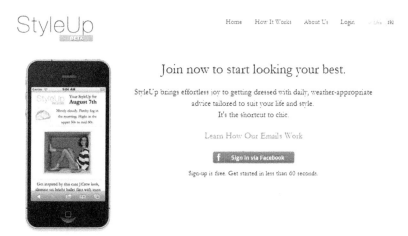

Figure 22.4: StyleUp sign-up page.

Without investing much money or going too far down a single path, Kendall and Ryan's goal was to show that women would like the value proposition enough to sign up, open the e-mails, and tell their friends.

They were very confident they could add more features later; but they wanted to get more guidance after these original foundational features were implemented and used to know which ones to add and in what priority. They wanted to start the feedback loop with their target customers as soon as possible.

This MVBP also set them up well to test whether the secondary customer got value from the product and was willing to pay for access to the primary customer, since the MVBP has links that allow women to click to websites on which clothing items are sold.

ThriveHive

Two students, Max Faingezicht and Adam Blake, with different backgrounds (Max had worked at Intel and Amazon while Adam had worked in small companies) came together in my class and left determined to launch a new company that would provide new-age marketing tools and support to small companies that previously was not possible. Their vision was a platform that would bring together critical information for the brave new world of marketing in a cost-effective manner, including bringing together website analytics, e-mail, social media, and direct mail all under one roof. At the core of their system would be a leads report, which would show the business owner what was working and what wasn't. Every channel would be built through backend integrations to third-party providers, thus reducing the development costs. Customers would pay a monthly subscription for the use of the platform, starting from $99/month.

The first challenge they faced was figuring out how to make an MVBP when their value proposition hinged around bringing all the channels together in a simplified way. Early on they decided to build only the necessary integrations, those that required real-time response: Facebook and Twitter for social media. These were basic features without the bells and whistles. You could link your accounts and schedule a post, but you couldn't comment or even monitor your feeds. They decided also to develop an e-mail builder for customers to send e-mail campaigns. It used a basic e-mail editor, which provided limited editing functionality. Whenever the channels allowed for delays, they would just "fake it before you make it." A good example of this is the Postcard Builder. When a user hit the button to send a postcard, they would be able to upload a file and a list. They would see the additional cost right there and then they would hit "Send." Instead of building a system integration with a partner, in reality this sent an e-mail to the team with the details around the postcard. Someone would then login to the third-party provider website and set the postcard to get printed, posted, and delivered on the date it was scheduled for. This is a wonderful example of concierging. By faking it, they were able to see if people would use and be willing to pay for certain features before having to make the major investments to build them.

EXAMPLES

Bloom Continued

As you have been able to follow the Bloom example throughout this book, you can see the team had identified their key assumptions, so now it was time to see if their target audience will show up and really engage.

There was actually a lot going on in parallel in this step but I will serialize it here. Their first decision was whether they would run their product on an existing platform, in this case Facebook, or they would develop their own app. As you can see from Figure 22.5, after a detailed analysis and discussion, the team opted for a no-code standalone app.

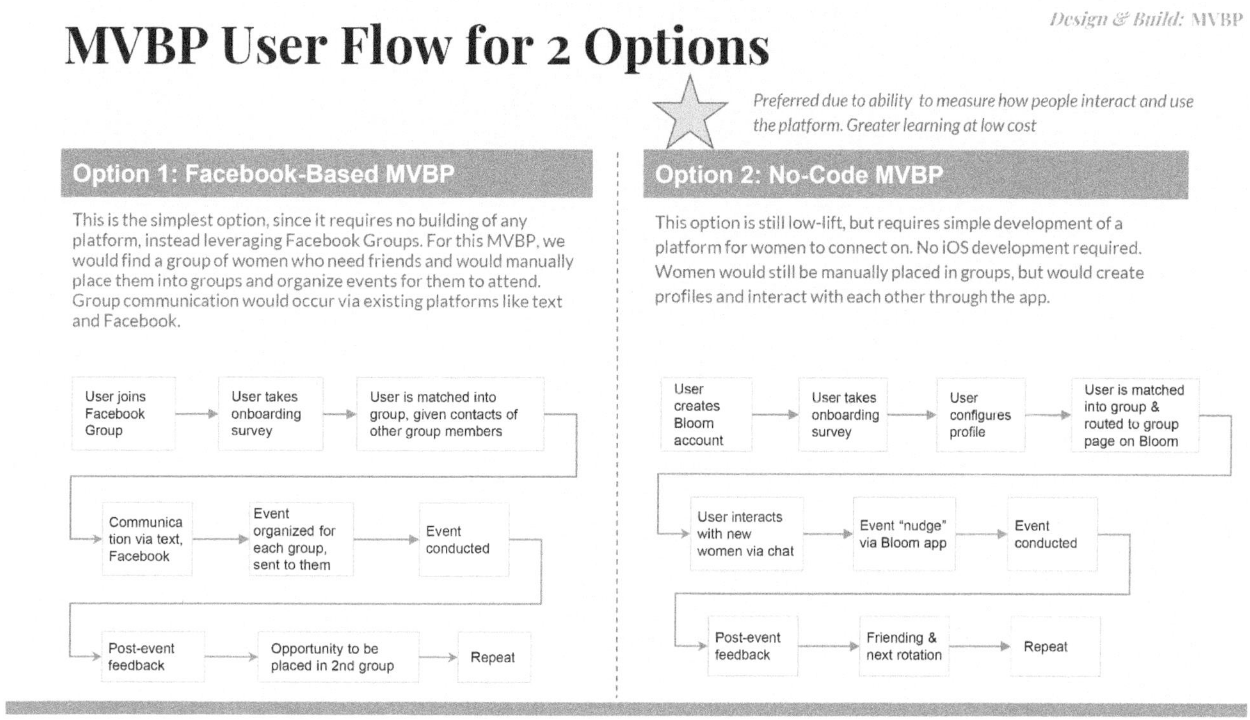

MVBP User Flow for 2 Options

Preferred due to ability to measure how people interact and use the platform. Greater learning at low cost

Option 1: Facebook-Based MVBP

This is the simplest option, since it requires no building of any platform, instead leveraging Facebook Groups. For this MVBP, we would find a group of women who need friends and would manually place them into groups and organize events for them to attend. Group communication would occur via existing platforms like text and Facebook.

Option 2: No-Code MVBP

This option is still low-lift, but requires simple development of a platform for women to connect on. No iOS development required. Women would still be manually placed in groups, but would create profiles and interact with each other through the app.

User joins Facebook Group → User takes onboarding survey → User is matched into group, given contacts of other group members →

→ Communication via text, Facebook → Event organized for each group, sent to them → Event conducted →

→ Post-event feedback → Opportunity to be placed in 2nd group → Repeat

User creates Bloom account → User takes onboarding survey → User configures profile → User is matched into group & routed to group page on Bloom →

→ User interacts with new women via chat → Event "nudge" via Bloom app → Event conducted →

→ Post-event feedback → Friending & next rotation → Repeat

Figure 22.5: Analysis of what platform to use for Bloom MVBP.

In parallel with this decision, the team had done an analysis about what they could do in concierge mode and the impact it would have. This made them comfortable that they would gain benefit from having their own app, despite the limitations of a no-code approach, because they could concierge some parts of their MVBP to overcome those limitations (see Figure 22.6).

Concierge Opportunities in MVBP

√√√ High Impact
√√ Medium Impact
√ Low Impact

Opportunity	Decrease Time to Market?	Decrease Investment?
1. Build No-Code MVBP prior to investing in iOS full stack development	√√√ Yes- quicker out-of-box development with no-code app, but less functionality	√√ Yes - don't need iOS developer, but still need to invest a lot of time from existing resources
2. Manual Group Matching	√√ Formal algorithm does not need to be done prior to launch, can instead be built concurrent with MVBP as we are learning from feedback	√√ Integration of data capture, algorithm and cloud computing is not required
3. Manual Event Organization & Event Creation in System	√√√ Book events as you would today and manually add to the no-code platform. No agreements with businesses or app integration required	√ High cost of initial events for testing, no partnerships or discounts yet developed

Figure 22.6: Analyzing the concierge opportunities for Bloom and the impact.

Finally, the team engaged in an intense process of defining what minimal features would be required. You can see in Figure 22.7 what they came up with for the MVBP mockups. I would really question whether all of these features are necessary, but considering this was their first and fast pass through the 24 Steps, the work they did here is a great starting point for discussion.

MVBP Chosen: No-Code Mock-Ups

No-code MVBP allows information about how women will navigate & interact with a mobile app to be collected, guiding future development

Design & Build: MVBP

User profile picture, information & bio

User "Canvas", designed to showcase interests & personality for more informed matching. This format is closer to current forms of media enjoyed by Gen-Z

User profile pictures placed below the canvas

Group name & member overview. Includes the names of members & profile pictures

Chat function within group → place where primary communication will happen between women.

Event pop-up. In MVBP, events manually scheduled & programmed into app.

Figure 22.7: Bloom detailed description of MVBP.

Finally, they recalibrated at the end to make sure the MVBP satisfactorily meets the three essential criteria of an MVBP (see Figure 22.8).

Our MVBP Meets the 3 Key Objectives:

Provides Value

Users are guaranteed to be matched with a group of other women who they have similarities with, increasing the success in finding new friends and social groups.

The manual effort of sifting through Facebook groups and the awkwardness of 1:1 meetings is cut out, making the experience effective and pain-free.

User Will Pay

To test for adoption and willingness to pay, we plan to offer a premium level of service that unlocks additional functionality and access. This includes event reservations, interest group access and personality overlap analytics.

Users have already demonstrated willingness to pay for optimized matching and group activities.

Creates Feedback Loop

Our MVBP rollout will occur in Boston with a small controlled group of women.

We will elicit detailed feedback from them in a variety of ways, including through live discussion, Bloom events, focus groups and CSAT surveys. Tracking feature-based usage will also provide us with feedback as to what is most valuable.

Figure 22.8: Bloom validating that it meets the three essential criteria for an MVBP.

ADDITIONAL RESOURCES

There are additional resources for this step at www.d-eship.com/step22. These materials include:

- Process Guidance for creating your MVBP
- Worksheet 22.1: Update Your High-Level Product Specification
- Worksheet 22.2: How Your Proposed MVBP Meets the Three Objectives of an MVBP
- Worksheet 22.3: Concierge Opportunities

Additional resources will be added as new and updated examples and information become available.

Summary

You have previously tested individual elements of your business; however, the MVBP represents the first full systems test of your product. It must now actually provide value to the customer. You must actually get someone to pay something for it. And importantly, it starts the real-world feedback loop to test your value proposition and GTM strategy that is critical to allow you to iterate to make your product, value proposition, GTM execution, and business better.

Show That "The Dogs Will Eat the Dog Food"

In This Step, You Will:

- Develop a dashboard of key metrics to track once your MVBP is available and with customers.
- Determine in a quantitative manner the level of engagement and adoption rate of your customer.
- Develop metrics that indicate the level of word of mouth your MVBP is creating among customers.

Now that you have launched your product, you have something you have not had before: real marketplace feedback on how the customer is receiving your product. The customer is the final arbiter of your success.

Why This Step, and Why Now?

Numbers don't lie. Entrepreneurs have an ability to create great passion for a vision, but now is the time for reality, to show concrete evidence that your product, and specific features of it, are succeeding. Qualitative information and conceptual logic are not sufficient. You do this step now because you finally have the MVBP and you need to validate it before moving forward.

Let's Get Started

In this step, you make sure you are grounded in not your conceptual understanding but in the verifiable facts on the ground. You will now take your Minimum Viable Business Product (MVBP), put it in front of your target customer, and test whether this integrated system of assumptions will be accepted and paid for . . . and then adjust!.

"THE DOGS WILL EAT THE DOG FOOD"

This step is named after the following fictional story, but it is based off parallels to many very real companies I have dealt with:

> Once upon a time in a land called Ivory Tower, not so far away from here, there was a chemist who wanted to make better dog food. He studied to see what kind of food would improve the health, happiness, and financial and spiritual well-being of dogs.
>
> In his lab, he came up with a breakthrough formula that was better for everyone and cost one-tenth the price of the cheapest dog food on the market. Dogs would sleep better at night, have a better demeanor, shed less hair, have whiter teeth, be friendlier to strangers, obey their owners more, and so on. They had tested all this in the lab from a chemical standpoint. They were also told that there were tests in the lab that showed it would even taste better than any of the alternatives. Everything made logical sense. It was a business opportunity that was almost too good to be true.
>
> He sprang into action, raising a large sum of money and spending $3 million to build a plant to produce the dog food. He signed up distributors and kicked off a huge marketing campaign. To paraphrase Jackie Gleason from *The Honeymooners*, "This thing is going to the moon, Alice!"
>
> The product shipped. Owners put the food in front of their dogs. And the dogs refused to eat the dog food. The company crashed and burned in a spectacular fashion.

"That's crazy! That wouldn't happen in real life," you may say. But it happens all the time. Just ask Coca-Cola with their infamous "New Coke" debacle, which took place in 1985 and is considered one of the biggest marketing blunders in history. And they are not alone at all.

When I worked at IBM during the 1980s and early 1990s, we saw that "electronic medical records" made all the logical sense in the world, so lots of smart people spent lots of time and money working on making it a reality. But guess what? For decades, even though the technology was capable and the logic compelling, the doctors simply wouldn't use electronic medical records—they wouldn't eat the dog food when it was put in front of them. This was in spite of the fact that we had tested it with willing doctors and believed they represented the greater population. Turned out they had selection bias in their process. Their PMR was just with the very few doctors at the time who were interested in computers and of course they loved it. It has finally changed, but only after two decades and billions of dollars had been spent by IBM and others on the conceptually brilliant and seemingly feasible idea.

This will happen to you as well in some ways but you just don't know which ones yet. Based on every detail you've uncovered about your product and your customer, it might make sense that your product would be viable, but ultimately a person is going to have to accept your new product and humans are not always rational. Some behavioral economists have made a name for themselves in focusing their research on irrational human behavior. So, after you have made your logical plans with individual experiments along the way, as in our fable above, and before you invest large amounts of time and money, make sure the dogs will eat the dog food! And, oh yes, make sure the dog's owners (or friends) will *pay* for the dog food, too.

How to Measure Adoption

Your qualitative observations can help guide you on how your product and go-to-market plan are working, but they can also lead you astray. It is imperative that you combine them with quantitative data (where the data gets the last word) or you will very likely be in a blindly optimistic world. As quoted in in Step 8, Lord Kelvin expressed this concept well: "When you can measure what you are speaking about, and express it in numbers, you know something about it; but when you cannot measure it . . . your knowledge is of a meager and unsatisfactory kind."

There are many different ways to quantitatively measure your adoption rate. A few include:

1. **Initial Interest:** Once your target customers are exposed to your value proposition, what percentage of them actively seek to learn more?

2. **Conversion Rates:** Monitor the conversion rate for each step as a potential customer engages with your sales process, purchases the product, becomes a repeat customer, and starts

evangelizing your product to others (i.e., once the target customer is in the sales funnel, the yield rates going from section to section of the funnel are extremely important numbers to understand, both the absolute numbers but also the trends).

3. **Purchase and Pay:** The ultimate conversion. Whether the customer pays for your product is one very important indication of whether the customer is getting value. The initial price of the product is not as important as showing that target customers will pay for the adoption of your product. It is good to "beta-test their wallet," as HubSpot co-founder Dharmesh Shah calls it. As you establish your value proposition and hopefully grow it, you will be able to command a higher price. How long it takes the customer to pay, and what percentage of customers end up not paying after making an initial commitment (the "default rate"), are also interesting numbers to watch.

4. **Retention Rates:** It is always telling to monitor retention rates, often referred to in the negative modality of "churn rate," especially in subscription businesses. One way to measure retention rates is through support or maintenance contracts for post-purchase support. If the customer buys the product but doesn't sign up for a maintenance contract at the end of the warranty period, in some industries that is a bad sign and you should take note immediately.

5. **Customer Advocacy:** There is a huge difference between a satisfied customer and a very happy, evangelizing one. The simplest and most commonly used way to measure customer advocacy is the Net Promoter Score (NPS). You gather the necessary data by asking customers a single question: On a scale of 1 to 10, with 10 being the highest, how likely is it that they would recommend your product to a friend or colleague? By tallying the percentage of responses that are 9s and 10s ("promoters") and subtracting the percentage of responses that are 6s and below ("detractors"), you get your score, which can be as low as 100 (all detractors) and as high as 100 (all promoters).

6. **Cost of Customer Acquisition (CoCA) and Lifetime Value (LTV):** Estimate these numbers again now that you have some sales. They are much easier to estimate the second time around! They are valuable, albeit imperfect, indicators of your success. If there are surprises in these numbers, then quickly dive into them and understand why.

7. **Gross Margin:** Your gross margin—the difference between what it costs to make one unit of product and what you sell that unit of product at—should go up over time, indicating that you are getting strong word of mouth for your product. If it goes down, then you are possibly providing too many discounts on your product, so the number of customers may be going up because the price is artificially low. The gross margin trend is an imperfect indicator on its own (much like the other indicators here), but make sure you monitor it.

Don't feel constrained by this list. There are plenty of other metrics that will be equally or more valuable for your situation. While it is hard to capture all of these metrics, especially at the beginning, they will be highly useful to you, especially within the framework of the sales process from Step 18.

Before you release your product, make sure you clearly define what metrics you will be observing, how you will observe them, what time period you will measure for, and what constitutes success against those metrics. If you release your product without carefully defining what constitutes success, it is all too easy to pretend that whatever results you get are indicators that you have a good product. Don't fall into that trap!

Even if the dogs do not eat nearly as much dog food as you thought, you can now learn a tremendous amount because you have real data on your MVBP. You are now in an iterative learning feedback loop with your customer, which is where you will start to mine the gold that will make you rich: customer preferences. With today's tools, there are so many ways to measure if the dogs are eating the dog food, so entrepreneurs should take full advantage of these tools.

EXAMPLES

Bloom Continued

Since the examples I am showing you from the Bloom team are from their semester-long class project, this step is simply a first draft that shows a few key metrics they could monitor over time. As you can see in Figure 23.1, the key metrics that the Bloom team will be tracking are from the sales funnel. As they refine their plans, I would strongly encourage them to add other ones, but this is a good first draft and indicates how this process starts.

StyleUp

Once Kendall and Ryan released their MVBP, it was time to first measure the engagement and adoption of their target customer. They needed to see if women would respond to the service and encourage their friends to sign up. Consistent engagement and growth were the key metrics to value the progress and validate a business opportunity. Engagement included both whether women opened the e-mails and whether they clicked through to webpages where they could purchase the merchandise they saw in the e-mails, which was a potential way to monetize the product.

StyleUp's analytics showed that women were opening the e-mails every day, and some women were opening each e-mail an average of five times—which either means the recipient reopened the

Key Success Metrics

Funnel Stage	Description	Est. Industry Conversion	Conversion Goal	Actual Conversion
Identification & Consideration	Our target market is very large with room for growth potential as we expand into tangential markets. Still, we expect large conversion rates based on our initial landing page conversion rate of 36% over 3 weeks*	30%	30%	36%*
Purchase Intent & Purchase	Social discovery apps similar to Bloom have low conversion rates for payment of premium services. Therefore, we expect the same and aim for 1.5% of paying premium users	2%	1.5%	To be tested
Loyalty (Retention)	Apps like Bloom are meant to support women in certain stages of life, and therefore we expect churn to be relatively high, but new profile creation to keep up at a similar rate.	20%	30%	To be tested
Advocacy (Referrals)	Women make up the majority of consumers and love to share referrals with friends when a service is good, therefore we expect this to be high	15%	20%	To be tested

Figure 23.1: Bloom's first-draft success metrics.

message, or the recipient forwarded the message to her friends. The company's e-mail open rate is 70%, compared to an industry average of 14% (see Figure 23.2). The metrics showed that women were engaged and were looking forward to receiving the e-mails.

They also received key anecdotal support. Google's shopping editor Adelle McElveen wrote, "StyleUp inspires me to think about what I'm going to wear the next day, and how to not just dress for the weather, but to dress stylishly for the weather."

Beyond daily engagement, Kendall and Ryan could see that women were also telling their friends to sign up for StyleUp. It was easy to track this quantitatively via the referral link through which members signed up. Despite not spending money on marketing in the first few months, word spread to 1,500 people based on pure word-of-mouth traction and minimal press coverage. Even when they reached nearly 8,000 members, StyleUp had committed minimal capital and time to marketing and yet continued to see 20% month-over-month growth. The goal to create a product women love so much that they naturally share it was working and they had data to back it up.

Figure 23.2: StyleUp e-mail open rates.

Of course, additional customer satisfaction metrics, like Net Promoter Score, would be a valuable additional piece of data to gauge the long-term viability. This indicates the strength of the word of mouth for your product as well as their likelihood to be a repeat customer.

They also needed to prove that the dogs, or someone associated or wanting to be associated with the dogs, would pay for the dog food. That is, clearly the women were taking to the product, but now the questions were "Can StyleUp get paid for this customer engagement? Can StyleUp monetize the situation it has created?"

TechCrunch reported that StyleUp was using an affiliate model for monetization.[1] So to show that secondary customers—affiliates—would find value from StyleUp and be willing to pay to reach StyleUp's primary customers, three important metrics to measure would be click-through rates on the e-mails that were opened, the amount of money in sales that affiliates realized from the click-throughs, and the payments made to StyleUp for these sales. One might think that only the last of these three factors matters; but it is very valuable to know all three in order to provide a robust data set if the business model needs tweaking. In such a manner, they will be able to better understand the sustainable nature of the economics of the new venture.

With this combination of metrics, StyleUp will have developed a case that should be extremely compelling to themselves first, and then to any potential strategic partners (like investors). While it would not guarantee success, it would indicate that the odds of success are quite high.

---

[1] Leena Rao, "YC-Backed StyleUp Recommends Daily Personalized Outfits Tailored To Your Style And Location," TechCrunch, March 18, 2013, http://techcrunch.com/2013/03/18/yc-backed-styleup-recommends-daily-personalized-outfits-tailored-to-your-style-and-location

ThriveHive

As introduced in Step 22, Define the Minimum Viable Business Product (MVBP), ThriveHive is a marketing platform for small but ambitious businesses. To test their MVBP, they signed up a small group of beta testers and offered the platform for free for a limited time in exchange for providing feedback sessions.

After a few months of private beta, they had gathered enough feedback to figure out which features people were using and which new features people were asking for. While great, the private beta had not yet proven if the dogs would eat and pay for the dog food; this was yet to come. All they had done was eat for free so far but the moment of truth was coming. As they ended the private beta, and gave each beta tester one full month to decide whether to start a paid subscription, they simultaneously began offering the product to the public with a 30-day free trial. The proof of whether the dogs would really eat the dog food and pay for it (because it created real value that exceeded the price) would be evident in their conversion rate to start with. This was the moment of truth.

Fortunately for Max and Adam, of the beta testers, 74% converted to a paid subscription, showing the team they had a successful MVBP—customers got value from the product and would be willing to pay to continue using it. Another metric that would help the case would be signups from the public.

With the momentum of this success, Max and Adam continued to develop their product, and while the above testing is sufficient for the basic requirements of this step, their more-robust testing of whether the dogs would keep eating the dog food is valuable as well as you think beyond the 24 Steps into execution and scaling.

Specifically to make the business economically sustainable and scalable, Max and Adam focused on three key areas for further testing:

- Market Access: Can they generate leads in our target market using repeatable techniques?
- Sales Process: Can they sell to customers with unit economics that make sense?
- Deliver Value: Can they deliver more value than they capture?

Market Access: ThriveHive decided to target very small businesses (<20 employees), so the question became: What are the most scalable and effective ways to reach that target? While some businesses like SCVNGR were using a direct sales approach to reach this market, ThriveHive decided instead to use only online methods in the beginning, due to the ability to start small and scale.

ThriveHive launched an organic content play to start building a presence in online search and social media, but that would take time to get off the ground. To start getting data fast, the team ramped up a Google AdWords campaign that could drive targeted traffic quickly.

All the work was done with the idea to generate enough leads to feed a single salesperson so the unit economics could be proven.

After about six months of work, the team had built a lead pipeline generating hundreds of qualified leads per month at a cost per lead that was in line with the unit economics model that was coming together on the sales side. More importantly, ThriveHive had shown the ability to scale the lead generation quickly as the company growth would demand.

Sales Process: The sales process was a challenging model to prove out. Focusing again on the unit economics, ThriveHive brought on board a single inside sales rep to begin selling to the leads being generated. There were literally hundreds of variables at play, from the salesperson himself, to the process used to bring a customer on board, to pricing. The challenge was to figure out what was working and what wasn't, with almost no data. The sales process was slow and the numbers were so small that it was hard to know when the process needed to be tweaked when things were off track, or whether only more time was needed.

Similar to the market access, after about six months the unit economics started to work. Three major tweaks helped everything come together:

1. Achieve better balance on the give-and-take during the sales and onboarding process (there was a 30-day free trial).[2]

2. Create an account manager role to help ensure customer success during the free trial.

3. Generate enough leads to feed a single salesperson.

Delivering Value: ThriveHive decided to focus on delivering more value than it captured. While it might seem obvious, there are many successful companies built on exactly the opposite philosophy. Think about infomercials that sell you products you buy and never use; they can be great businesses, but ThriveHive felt that the only path to long-term success in this very small business market was to generate more value than it captured. The cost of acquiring the customers was going to be too high to survive if they left too quickly.

---

[2] Better balancing the give-and-take during the free trial is referring to a very carefully sequenced customer acquisition process that was developed. Instead of asking for everything from the customer upfront, ThriveHive created a process that brought them through a series of steps, giving the prospect something before asking them for the next step. Specifically, it was:

1. GIVE: the customer a free e-book download.
2. TAKE/ASK: customer to accept a phone call from their sales rep.
3. GIVE: Sales rep would give free advice from the e-book tailored to the prospect's business.
4. TAKE/ASK: Customer would get asked to schedule a call for sales rep to do a demo of the software.
5. GIVE: The sales rep would show how the software could solve problems specific to the business owner.
6. TAKE/ASK: Close the deal.

To measure progress on the value delivery front, ThriveHive tracked three critical metrics: monthly churn, customer referrals, and qualitative success metrics (what the customers were saying). On the churn front, ThriveHive decided to start without any contracts (even though the product is fundamentally one that delivers value over time). This left the company as exposed as possible to feedback.

By the time the market access and sales process had been vetted, ThriveHive was able to show results on all three value delivery fronts, which led the team to believe that they were successfully delivering more value than was being captured:

- Churn was already at the low end of industry comparables, even with a very immature product.
- More than 15% of the customer base was consistently being driven by existing customer referrals (without incentives).
- More than 50% of the businesses that had been with ThriveHive since the launch of the paid product were expanding their businesses due to marketing success that they attributed in large part to ThriveHive.

It was only when all three of the areas came together that ThriveHive felt that the dogs were genuinely and repeatedly eating the dog food in an economically and scalable manner.

ADDITIONAL RESOURCES

There are additional resources for this step at www.d-eship.com/step23. These materials include:

- Process Guidance
- Worksheet 23.1: Define Units of Time for Metrics
- Worksheet 23.2: Examples of Key Metrics to Determine if the Dogs Are Eating the Dog Food
- Worksheet 23.3: Interpreting the Results and Taking Action on Customer Adoption Metrics

Additional resources will be added as new and updated examples and information become available.

Summary

Take your MVBP to the customers to see if they will actually use and pay for the product. Collect data to see if they are really using it and how engaged they are as users. Determine if they, or someone associated with them, will pay for it and also if they are advocating for your product with word of mouth. After you collect data over time, analyze it and especially look for trends and understand underlying drivers. Make sure you are intellectually honest and rely on real-world data and not abstract logic.

Develop a Product Plan

In This Step, You Will:

- Describe how you will improve your product so that you can fully capture your Beachhead Market and then start to address follow-on markets.

- Revisit the adjacent markets you prioritized to attack in Step 14, Calculate the Total Addressable Market Size for Follow-on Markets, and now reprioritize as appropriate.

- Develop a technological and product development road map that will enhance your competitive position and give you unfair advantage as you enter new markets.

It is time to revisit your Follow-on Market TAM and develop a Product Plan so that your product is not just an island but the start of a great business.

Why This Step, and Why Now?

Putting together a growth strategy allows your team to have a plan for greatness. You have built a solid foundation for winning your Beachhead Market with the first 23 steps but now you want to expand your business and increase your impact, as was always the goal. You have not achieved your goals if you simply win the Beachhead Market, because it will be the first of many victories for you. You laid out the general plan for greatness in Step 14 and now you are adding more details on how to execute your plan. It should be noted that even though this is the last step in the 24 Steps, it never ends. You repeat this process for each market and even for the markets you have already won. Markets and technologies are always changing and every success has an expiration date on it. You must stay close to your market and keep revisiting the 24 Steps framework if you want to have continued success.

Let's Get Started

Once you have shown that you have won your Beachhead Market, it is time to move forward to expand. Central to this expansion will be a thoughtful Product Plan that allows you to methodically take advantage of your building up of assets to gain an unfair (good for you in this case) edge as you enter your next markets. This will most likely start out with enhancements to your first product but it could also start to include new products as well. It is a plan for development to capitalize on your success and start to significantly increase your impact. You started to think about this in Step 14 and now you will add a specific development plan to this thinking so you can move quickly once you win your Beachhead Market.

When you established your MVBP in Step 22, you most likely took a number of features and put them on hold to concentrate on the bare minimum feature set required. In the Product Plan, you will select which of these features, based on your Persona's needs, to incorporate back into the product in follow-on releases.

It is important to also institute a protocol within the development of your product where you continuously ensure a high level of quality through process and mindset. When new features or functionality are released, even with the best of intentions, it usually takes a while in the marketplace to work the bugs out and refine the product. While functional enhancement releases are more exciting than improved quality of existing features releases, you need both in balance. It is good to implement a process to validate the quality of the releases so that a focus on quality is built into the fabric and mentality of the company. If a company plans to drive growth by continually releasing new features quickly without ensuring and improving quality, a company is destined to have quality problems. This is why well-run companies alternate between feature-focused product releases and quality-focused product releases. It is an important balance to build into your culture.

It is also important to think about **when** you should expand your market. Your Persona is for one specific market, your Beachhead Market, but once you achieve a strong position in that market—you become the de facto standard and achieve dominant market share for your solution (generally 20% and usually higher)—you should then shift your strategy. You should take those "hunters" in your company who love the challenge of creating new markets and move them on to the next new market. You would then replace them in the now successfully conquered Beachhead Market with "farmers" or people who are more interested in growing an existing market. I have found that these are generally different types of people.

That next market, or "pin" in the bowling alley metaphor, could have a different Persona but should still leverage your Core and be a logical next step for your business. The product for this next market will be very similar but will be customized in various dimensions, not just product but also in your GTM strategy to meet the new Persona's needs. This will leverage the expertise you have developed in the product area.

If you will be selling to the same Persona in your Beachhead Market, upselling them a new product, then your plans will be focused on what are the easiest things you can do in your Product Plan to give them increased value that will be beneficial to your business objective as well.

The Product Plan is subject to change as you move forward, so don't sweat the details and don't spend too much time on it. However, you should have a general vision of where you see things going next so that you capture some of the broader TAM.

EXAMPLES

Bloom Continued

As you think about Step 24, there is not just a question of what you will produce for this step but also the timing. This is very important, as you don't want to start expanding until you have secured the Beachhead Market and have a strong base on which to build. The Bloom team was very intentional about what indicators will make them comfortable that they have successfully won the Beachhead Market (see Figure 24.1).

Scaling: Product Plan for Beachhead Market

Nailing the Beachhead Market

We will consider our beachhead market successfully captured when we have completed the following:

Capturing the Market	Positive User Metrics	User Referrals
✓ The app is live in all 1st and 2nd tier cities, with critical mass reached	✓ Majority of users are logging on 3-5 times per week	✓ Word of Mouth marketing via TikTok and Instagram witnessing steady organic growth
✓ Critical mass measured by the number of unique groups of 8 women we can rotate each user through - goal to have 10 options at all times	✓ Majority of users are attending an average of 2 Bloom affiliated events per month	✓ New downloads of Bloom exceed downloads of HeyVina
	✓ NPS at or above 15 (benchmarking against BumbleBFF)	✓ Referral offer conversion rate at 20%

Figure 24.1: Bloom setting milestones they believe will indicate success in Beachhead Market.

The Bloom team then looked back at what they had done in Step 14 for the initial follow-on plan (see Figure 24.2), and building off this initial thought process refined it further (see Figure 24.3).

This thought process gives them a five-year Product Plan (see Figure 24.4). This Product Plan is very much a first draft. They know it will not be right but it is a plan that will be useful and they can iterate on going forward.

Follow-on Market Considerations

 ⭐ Our Next Focus

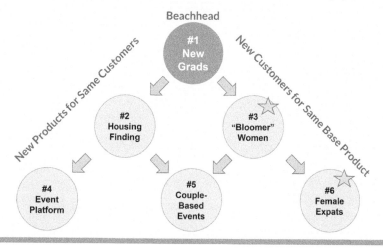

Figure 24.2: Bloom's initial work on Step 14, which they used as an input to Step 24.

Follow-on Markets for Acquisition

Beachhead Market

Core Product
- Match users into groups of 5-8 to enable connection
- Rotate user groups to support further connections
- Simple algorithm to support users to match to women they are most compatible with

Core Product Expansion - Event Support
- Plan activities for users, facilitating their in-person connection via event planning / logistics
- Support feedback from matches / events to better improve the experience
- Improved machine learning algorithm for better matching women and learning from group rotations

Follow-On Market

Expand to "Bloomer" Women (Estimated TAM ~$36M)
- Expand to adjacent market of women who are slightly older than college age, who could be moving, etc.
- Expand event functionality to ensure that there are events appropriate for this age demographic
- Support age filtering / other relevant filters to provide users more control on who they're matched with

Expand to Female Expats (Estimated TAM ~$7M)
- Expand event planning capabilities to be functional abroad
- Automate and steam-line event venue on-boarding to support faster international growth
- Support "Bloom" creation across geographies to support women in more remote locations

Figure 24.3: Bloom integrates new knowledge and product development perspective for refined follow-on markets plan.

5-Year Product Plan

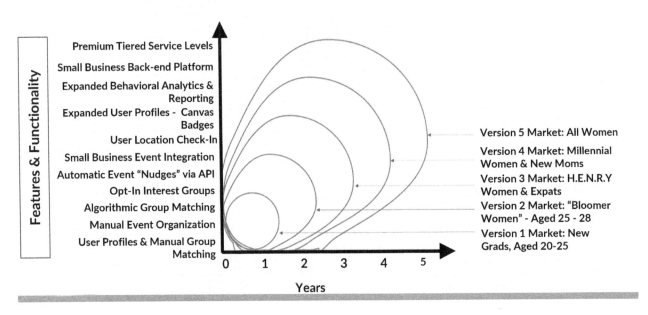

Figure 24.4: Bloom first-draft five-year Product Plan to expand business and impact.

SensAble Technologies Continued

Once we had become the standard in the toy and footwear industry, we planned to move to additional markets off the center of this bell curve (Figure 24.5), like jewelry, animation, consumer products, electronics, and automotive.

As we researched more closely these other industries we wanted to expand into, we realized that we were going to have to expand our functionality in two major areas. First, we would need to do more than just sculpted forms. We would have to expand into other, less organic or irregular forms that could be more easily represented mathematically, specifically geometric or regular forms, and highly stylized forms. Second, to fit into the workflow of these new markets, we would need to support more file formats for our final digital output to their downstream systems. We would have to continue to support the standard rapid prototyping file formats (specifically the .stl file format), but we would have to add NURBS (Non-Uniform Rational B-Splines) support, which is the standard file format for CAD/CAM packages in all manufacturing industries, which more

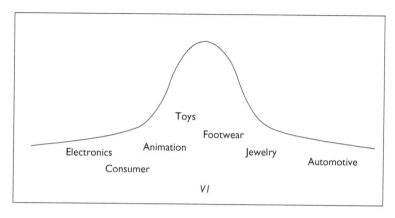

Figure 24.5: SensAble's version 1 Product Plan.

precisely represents the geometric shapes generated in the design process. In addition, as we continued to grow, we would have to add polygon support because this was the accepted file format for a number of the markets we were expanding into, most specifically the Digital Content Creation (DCC) market for 3D animation movies at places like Pixar.

Version 1 of our product focused on the Beachhead Market (toy and footwear), then we planned to branch out into the jewelry market in version 2 (Figure 24.6).

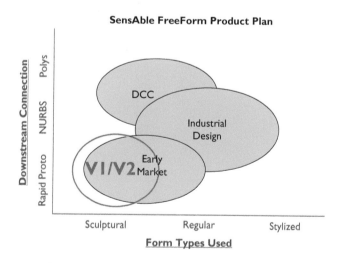

Figure 24.6: SensAble's version 2 Product Plan.

Upon achieving success in these early markets, we planned to expand our markets to include jewelry and furniture by adding support for the creation of geometric or regular forms in the product and also support the export of our files in the NURBS for a broader group of industrial designers. To make it attractive to these new markets, we planned for version 3 of our product to be capable of creating both sculpted and regular forms, such as those used in jewelry and furniture. It would also be able to export to traditional CAD/CAM packages such as Pro/E, CATIA, SolidWorks, or UniGraphics, which were crucial to our expanding business operations, especially as we expanded into industries with more sophisticated manufacturing operations. This version 3 of our FreeForm product is represented in Figure 24.7.

You can see the product increasing in its functionality. Because we were closely tying this to a target market, it would also be increasing the market opportunity in a very systematic way.

In the plan for FreeForm version 4, this trend continued and the market further increased with specific functional enhancements (Figure 24.8).

Finally, with FreeForm version 5, we were shooting for the stars but had a vision of how to get there. We were aiming to achieve a ubiquity in the industrial design marketplace and become a tool that all industrial designers had to have in their toolbox (Figure 24.9).

While this plan gave us a good starting point, allowing us to capture certain market requirements and group them into buckets within the plan, we knew from the start that our actual product progression would differ from the plan and that this would be okay.

As the famous general, president, and war hero Dwight D. Eisenhower once said, "Plans are nothing; planning is everything." By preparing a plan, you allow yourself to consider new

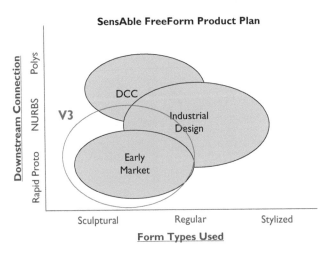

Figure 24.7: SensAble's version 3 Product Plan.

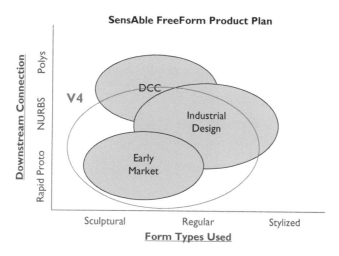

Figure 24.8: SensAble's version 4 Product Plan.

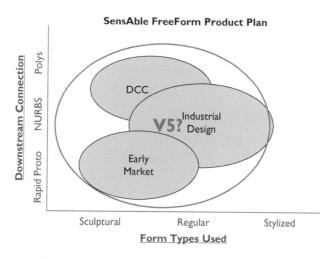

Figure 24.9: SensAble's version 5 Product Plan.

possibilities, envision potential obstacles, and generally get your mind around what you are trying to accomplish. So the plan, while not unimportant, is simply a means to an end. It's a place to start, even if you know you will finish elsewhere.

ADDITIONAL RESOURCES

There are additional resources for this step at www.d-eship.com/step24. These materials include:

- Process Guidance to develop a Product Plan
- Worksheet 24.1: First-Draft Product Plan for Version 2
- Worksheet 24.2: First-Draft Product Plan for Version 3
- Worksheet 24.3: Other Activities to Expand Value Created for Beachhead Market
- Worksheet 24.4: Framework to Discuss Prioritization of Initiatives to Move Beyond Beachhead Market
- Worksheet 24.5: Visual Representation of Long-Term Product Plan

Additional resources will be added as new and updated examples and information become available.

Summary

Establishing a Product Plan is similar in mindset to Step 14, Calculate the Total Addressable Market Size for Follow-on Markets, where you did a first-pass calculation of the broader TAM. The idea is to get you thinking ahead so you raise your sightlines and don't get too bogged down in your Beachhead Market as the end game. The beachhead is only your first step as a business; you want to expand from it. This last step gives you a long-term vision that keeps you reaching and thinking ahead, especially in the design of your product and organization. Do not spend too much time here, though, because you still need to get the dogs to eat the dog food today, or else you will run out of money long before entering adjacent markets. Plans will change as you learn more from the beachhead, but not to have a plan is to put yourself in the hands of luck as opposed to your own methodical process.

 WHAT ELSE?

Beyond the 24 Steps

It Never Ends

Congratulations on making it through the full 24 steps of this book—for the first time. You are now trained to do it again and again. And the good news is that it gets easier and more fun each time.

The great singer and songwriter Bob Dylan wrote, "He not busy being born is busy dying." Success in business always has an expiration date on it. The question is how do you build into your business and products the process of being born over and over again. That comes from repeating the 24 Steps because, as Figure 25.1 summarizes, success is increasingly temporary.

Figure 25.1: Success always has an expiration date, so you must keep innovating and entrepreneuring.

It is clear when you look at the arc of history that change is coming at a faster and faster pace. Adaptation to change is becoming a survival skill. This is what entrepreneurship offers and the skill set to do this is embodied in these 24 steps. You won't just survive change; you will thrive in change. This is what we call being "antifragile," using the term coined by Nassim Nicholas Taleb.[1]

But all of this being said, the 24-step framework by itself does not make a successful business. You should be aware there are other dimensions that we did not have enough time and space to get into in this book in sufficient depth that are critical to your success. They include:

- Selecting and developing a strong founding team[2]
- Entrepreneurial financial literacy[3]
- Growing and building a company culture[4]
- Product development
- Selling and sales execution
- Servicing your customer and building customer success processes
- Considerations in scaling your business
- Raising money to scale your business
- Entrepreneurial leadership
- Building and utilizing good corporate governance

And much more. But all of that is for another time.

I hope this book has given you clear guidance on how to get started and I can assure you it will improve your odds of success. But this book will do no good unless you put it into action. Entrepreneurship is not a spectator sport. It is action that makes things happen and how we make progress and learn, but not any action—specifically intelligent and adaptive action. We entrepreneurs want to constantly be moving forward and making progress, testing our imperfect ideas and products on real customers and spiraling toward success.

Ten years ago, when this book was originally released, I had no idea the profound effect it would have. It has sold hundreds of thousands of copies worldwide and has been translated into over two

---

[1] For much more on this topic, see our free online speaker series at https://entrepreneurship.mit.edu/antifragile-speaker-series/

[2] The gold standard for this topic is *The Founder's Dilemmas: Anticipating and Avoiding the Pitfalls That Can Sink a Startup* by Noam Wasserman.

[3] For more on this topic, there is a free online course at https://www.edx.org/course/fundamentals-of-entrepreneurial-finance-what-every-entrepreneur-should-know

[4] For more information on this, see the article I wrote for TechCrunch, "Culture Eats Strategy for Breakfast," https://techcrunch.com/2014/04/12/culture-eats-strategy-for-breakfast/

Figure 25.2: An entrepreneurial venture is more than a product or a way to make money. It is a group of people with a common vision, shared values, and complementary skills doing something meaningful that has never been done before.

dozen languages. It has been the basis of online courses taken by hundreds of thousands and it is used in probably over a thousand of the top educational institutions globally. It is safe to say that it has helped create or made better millions of entrepreneurs. That being said, I always felt there was more to be done and something missing. In this regard, I could not be more excited that alongside this new expanded and updated version of *Disciplined Entrepreneurship*, there will also be released at the same time *Disciplined Entrepreneurship Startup Tactics: 15 Tactics to Turn Your Business Plan into a Business*[5] which will give even more guidance on how to implement all of these steps and more. The book you are reading now provides some theory and a lot of practice with its framework, but the DE Tactics book, written by my good friend and esteemed MIT colleague Paul Cheek, will take you even further into how to implement these principles (Figure 25.3).

---

[5] Link to Disciplined Entrepreneurship Tactics website: startuptactics.net

Figure 25.3: To get even more value out of this book, I highly recommend combining it with the Disciplined Entrepreneurship Tactics book.

Yet the solution to any of your business questions does not lie solely in any book, but rather by applying the frameworks of these books to the marketplace for a customer who has an unmet need or unrealized opportunity. All that books or videos can do is help you think about how you can systematically produce a solution that will be economically sustainable and positively impact the world in a scalable manner.

Now more than ever, with the enormous challenges our world faces that will only get more dire going forward, the world needs more and better entrepreneurs. Historically, the intrepid spirit, skills, and way of operating of entrepreneurs are what have solved the world's challenges. I have faith that this will happen again and again until the end of time. So hopefully this framework will make you a more confident and successful entrepreneur. Go forth now and make the world a better place through action.

GLOSSARY

adjacent market   A new market that you can easily enter from the market you are currently in; requires its own Persona.

Beachhead Market   The first market your business sells in.

Business   A viable organization created to achieve a goal that does not depend on outside charitable contributions.

cash-flow positive   When the cash received by the company exceeds the cash that is paid out in a particular month.

Competitive Position   How well you meet your customer's top two priorities compared to any existing or likely competition, including the status quo for the customer.

Core   The central element to your business that gives you a sustained advantage over your competitors.

Cost of Customer Acquisition (CoCA)   The marginal amount of costs your business will incur to acquire one more average new customer. This involves only the marketing and sales costs and not the product and development or general and administrative costs. Unfortunately, there is not a standard or Generally Accepted Accounting Principle with regard to this, so whenever you hear the term (often expressed as CAC, or Customer Acquisition Cost), it is important to understand what the assumptions are in that business's calculation. This book gives you an explicit definition in Step 19 but others have other interpretations. If you understand the concepts and calculations in this book, you will be able to adjust to other definitions, but make sure you are explicit about assumptions and calculations.

follow-on market   A market you enter after gaining significant market share in the market you are currently in, which for this book will be the Beachhead Market. Either an adjacent market buying the same application as the Beachhead Market, or an additional application for your current Persona.

go-to-market (GTM)   The plans and execution to create and fulfill demand, and today increasingly the customer success elements of your business, for your product that will ultimately generate sustained revenue for your business.

gross margin   The difference between revenue and marginal costs for your product. Most often expressed as a percentage, so a 20% gross margin means your revenue from each unit of product is 20% higher than your cost of making a unit of a product.

Innovation   A new-to-the-world idea or invention that gets commercialized, either by an existing business or through starting a new business. It may be technology, process, business model, market positioning, or other. It can also be for each of these disruptive, incremental, or lateral. It must create value for the end user.

innovation-based entrepreneurship   Starting a new business based on a new-to-the-world idea or invention.

Lifetime Value (LTV) of an Acquired Customer   The average profits you will get when you acquire one new average customer in today's dollars (or equivalent currency). This is the net present value of the gross margin that new average customer will generate for the company. Like with CoCA, there is no official GAAP (Generally Accepted Accounting Principle) for LTV so you have to be diligent to understand and be clear about what is included in your calculation and to remain consistent in your approach. This important metric is also often referred to as CLTV (Customer Life Time Value), which is the same concept. Terms such as ACV (Annual Contract Value), TCV (Total Contract Value) or ARPU (Annual Revenue Per User) are similar but not the same and should not be used interchangeably with LTV but could be important inputs to calculate LTV.

Market   A system in which the trade of goods and services takes place, characterized by three conditions: customers buy similar products, customers have similar sales cycles and value propositions, and there is word of mouth between customers.

marketing communications   Getting word out to potential customers about your product with the primary purpose to increase exposure and to generate leads. Not to be confused with "product marketing."

Net Promoter Score (NPS)   A simple and easy-to-implement metric used to measure customer satisfaction and loyalty. It gauges the likelihood of customers to recommend a company's products or services to others.

primary market research   Information gained by talking directly with, interacting directly with, and/or directly observing, customers and potential customers.

Product   Physical goods, a service, or the delivery of information.

product–market fit   When your product matches what customers in a specific market are interested in buying.

product marketing   The process of finding product–market fit by finding out what the customer wants and mapping a product to it. Actual messaging to potential customers is called "marketing communications."

sales funnel   A systematic, simple, and visual way to represent the process a venture goes through to acquire a new customer, and then make them successful such that they will promote the product acquired to others.

secondary market research   Information obtained from market research reports and from indirect sources like the Internet or analyst reports.

target customer   A group of customers in a market that you intend to sell the same product to. They share many characteristics and would all reasonably buy a particular product.

Total Addressable Market (TAM) Size   The amount of annual revenue your business would earn if you achieved 100% market share in a market. Expressed in terms of dollars per year. This can be for any market segment or for all the segments combined and it is important to specify which market segments you are referring to when using this term.

ACKNOWLEDGMENTS

ALL ACKNOWLEDGMENTS FOR THIS book must start with my dear friend, Romanian entrepreneur, and Renaissance man Marius Ursache, who not only did the illustrations for this book but has provided a sounding board over multiple decades on the raison d'être for this book and then its implementation. Much as his illustrations will bring you joy as you fight through this book, they did to me when I was writing it. I was always like a kid on Christmas morning when I saw his e-mails come in with new drawings because I was so excited to see them and he never let me down. Secondly, I must give a huge thank you to the third member of our band, my editor-in-chief Chris Snyder. This is the third time we have gotten the band back together and it has not only been a productive relationship, but it has been fun too, loaded with laughs.

On the first version of this book, I was very fortunate to have editorial advisor Nancy Nichols on our team. On this new version, we were blessed to have Wiley developmental editor Julie Kerr assigned to our team. She jumped right in and became a fourth band member to finalize the book and get it out the door at a level we were all proud of.

A special thanks goes out to the rest of the team at John Wiley & Sons, led by the creative, efficient, and fun Shannon Vargo, along with her team, including Leah Zarra and Gabriela Mancuso, and who brought this book to production in record time and with utmost professionalism. To finish the job on the Wiley team, they brought in the closers, Deborah Schindlar (the pride of NYC and a joy to work with) and Suganya Selvaraj, who were essential to get the book to the finish line on time and with the quality we all demanded. A special thanks to former students, entrepreneurs, and just great people Madeleine Cooney and Anisha Quadir for providing such a great longitudinal example for this new version.

Ryan Strobel, Sam Broner, Ben Spector, Sarah Moseson, Ian Hinkley, Alex Wright-Gladstein, Gaëtan Bonhomme, Jason Norris, Sarah Malek, Lauren Abda, Yevgeniy Alexeyev, Greg Backstrom, Christina Birch, Michael Bishop, Adam Blake, Young Joon Cha, Vishal Chaturvedi, Ryan Choi, Kevin Clough, Yazan Damiri, Charles Deguire, Deepak Dugar, Max Faingezicht, Daniel Fisberg, Patrick Flynn, Tim Fu, Pierre Fuller, Megan Glendon, David Gordon, Melinda Hale, Katy Hartman, Kendall Herbst, Nick Holda, Julia Hu, Max Hurd, Ricardo Jasinski, Max Kanter, Freddy Kerrest,

Mustafa Khalifeh, Zach LaBry, Jake Levine, Michael Lo, Dulcie Madden, Vasco Mendes de Campos, Aditya Nag, Madeline Ng, Inigo De Pascual Basterra, Ella Peinovich, Giorgi Razmadze, Adam Rein, Izak van Rensburg, Miriam Reyes, Sophia Scipio, Colin Sidoti, Sam Telleen, Jocelyn Trigg, Pedro Valencia, Eduard Viladesau, and Leo Weitzenhoff all need to be acknowledged for their contributions to and/or reviews of sections of this book. Thank you also to 3D Systems and Dollar Shave Club for their permission to include certain images.

Erdin Beshimov has been a colleague and friend on this path from almost the beginning. His leadership in online learning and then with the MIT Bootcamps with Vimala Palaniswamy and team has benefitted hundreds of thousands of aspiring entrepreneurs around the world, as well as me in refining the concepts in this book and creating new materials and avenues to distribute it. It has been a great ride that is not over.

This book came about because I have been able to work at MIT for the past 15 years and interact with the best entrepreneurship faculty in the world. I have been honored to work with them. Of the many who have made enormous intellectual contributions, special acknowledgment must go to my original mentor Ed Roberts and my colleague in teaching this material for many years, the great Howard Anderson. Others in the MIT sphere who richly merit recognition as well include Bengt Holmström, Scott Stern, Michael Cusumano, Nelson Repenning, Charlie Fine, Antoinette Schoar, Matthew Rhodes-Kropf, Simon Johnson, Ezra Zuckerman, Fiona Murray, Pierre Azoulay, Charlie Cooney, Desh Deshpande, Matt Marx, Catherine Tucker, Eric von Hippel, Paul English, Katie Rae, Reed Sturtevant, Elaine Chen, Peter Levine, Lou Shipley, Brian Halligan, Peter Hirst, Trish Cotter, Kit Hickey, Donna Levin, Carly Chase, Sue Siegel, Georgina Campbell Flatter, Kosta Ligris, Kirk Arnold, Kevin Johnson, Tod Hynes, Francis O'Sullivan, Libby Wayman, Eugene Fitzgerald, Martha Gray, Don Sadoway, Dina Katabi, Jonathan Fleming, Andrey Zarur, Shari Loessberg, Nagarjuna Venna, Dip Patel, Andrea Ippolito and Emmanuelle Skala. Also, thanks to Mark Gorenberg, Scott Maxwell, Jean Hammond, David Skok, Thomas Massie, Tom Ellery, Jim Dougherty, Andrew Hally, Bernard Bailey, Marc Dulude, Jim Baum, Bill Warner, Dan Schwinn, Bob Coleman, Ken Morse, Jon Hirschtick, Chuck Kane, Brad Feld, Marty Trust, Sal Lupoli, Joi Ito, Sanjay Sarma, Bruce Hansen, Max Carnecchia, Jim Hale, Jane Thompson, Jim DeBello, Scott Carter, Donna Wells, Jason Gray, Pete Hart (especially you, Coach Pete) and team Mitek, David Baldwin, and the many mentors and collaborators I have been so fortunate to have had over the years. They all contributed heavily to the intellectual content of the book, but I take responsibility for the interpretations on how to apply and integrate it for practical implementation, which is the goal herein. Any errors made in this document are mine and no one else's.

The support I have gotten at MIT to sustain this imperfect journey has been beyond anything I deserve and I want to give a special acknowledgment in this regard to MIT Sloan Dean David Schmittlein and MIT School of Engineering Dean Anantha Chandrakasan. Historically and even continuing to the present day, MIT President Emerita Susan Hockfield has provided more support than she will ever know.

The content of this book has come from far beyond MIT. Domestic and international collaborators who deserve acknowledgment are Ted Zoller, Jon Fjeld, David Robinson, Kyle Jensen, Marc Randolph, Jocko Willink, Tom Byers, Danny Warshay, Daniela Ruiz Massieu, Ana Bakshi, Pranjul Shah, Fiona Bennington, Adele Ward, Jon Breslin, Jeff Larsen, John Knapton, Megumi Takata, Alex Bergo, Eleanor Shaw, Donna Chisholm, Nicola Douglas, Tim Barnes, Alberto Rodriguez de Lama, Andrés Haddad Di Marco, Thomas Andrae, Christian Potthoff-Sewing, Frank Rimalovski, Vassilis Papakonstantinou and team Greece, Rowena Barrett, Glen Murphy, Graham Fellows, and the whole QUT team past and present.

A key enabler of this book as well has been the fabulous team of disciplined pirates we have at the Martin Trust Center for MIT Entrepreneurship, including Christine Hsieh, Macauley Kenney, Amrutha Killada, Jenny Larios Berlin, Ylana Lopez, Susan Neal, Ben Soltoff, George Whitfield, and Greg Wymer, carrying on the lineage of fabulous entrepreneurship, educators only out for the best interests of the students. They provide encouragement, perspective, and a sanity check every day I am in the center.

This center would not be possible without the philanthropic support of such fabulous friends and supporters who have also become my kitchen cabinet in additional dimensions, including Frederic Kerrest, Bob Pozen, Robert Huang, Diana Mackie, Elliot Cohen, Gary Bergstrom, Jean-Jacques Degroof, Ivy Head, George Petrovas, as well as others already mentioned in these acknowledgments elsewhere.

A lifetime acknowledgment goes to the late Edwin Barlow, high school teacher, who believed in me before I did and got me on the right track. He gave me my first book for what he said would be my library going forward and I treasure it to this day.

As I close out these completely insufficient acknowledgments, it would be a felony not to give extra special recognition to three people.

Bob Metcalfe endowed the professorship chair I am honored to hold today. We have had many animated and productive discussions over the years even before he won the Turing Award, and while we may disagree on some things, we are in complete agreement that the world needs more entrepreneurs, and the path for this is better entrepreneurship education. Generations to come will benefit from his commitment to this perspective, as I have.

Today, I could not be more blessed to work directly, day in, day out, with Alicia Carelli and Paul Cheek, who keep me going—and in the right direction. Alicia and I have worked together for well over a decade and she just knows what I should do and makes sure it gets done, with a smile. Paul has been in our center for less than a decade but two years ago became the executive director. To say he is amazing is an understatement. He excels in so many dimensions that our center has risen to yet another level. He pushed me to do this new version and helped provide the space to get it done. Extremely importantly, he is authoring a new complementary book to this one called *Disciplined Entrepreneurship Startup Tactics: 15 Tactics to Turn Your Business Plan into a Business* (Link to Disciplined Entrepreneurship Tactics website: startuptactics.net) that I believe will take entrepreneurship education globally to a new level, just as he has done with our center. I can't wait to see how the two books are implemented together beyond MIT. Without these two people, there would be no "Updated and Revised" edition.

Finally, I want to acknowledge the thousands of students and entrepreneurs all over the world with whom I have had the privilege to work; you all give us such energy and hope every day, and increased wisdom through your willingness to go onto the battlefield fearlessly. We all want to help you so much, as you are our hope for the future.

ABOUT THE AUTHOR

BILL AULET is the Ethernet Inventors Professor of the Practice of Entrepreneurship at the MIT (Massachusetts Institute of Technology) Sloan School of Management. In addition, for the past 15 years he has been the managing director at the Martin Trust Center for MIT Entrepreneurship, serving all of MIT.

As an educator, in 2021, he was named by the United States Association for Small Business and Entrepreneurship (USASBE) as the Entrepreneurship Educator of the Year. In 2019, the Deshpande Foundation recognized him for Outstanding Contributions to Advancing Innovation and Entrepreneurship in Higher Education. In the past few years he has also been recognized by multiple organizations such as the *Boston Globe, Poets & Quants* (Favorite Professor), and MIT itself for his leadership in the field.

While broadly responsible for overseeing practical entrepreneurship education at MIT, he has also directly designed, created, and taught over 10 courses at MIT, ranging from introductory to advanced courses. In addition, he likewise created a suite of co-curricular programs such as the MIT Climate and Energy Prize, delta v summer accelerator, fuse micro-accelerator, and the t=0 festival of entrepreneurship.

Beyond MIT, his five free online courses on MITx/edX have been taken by hundreds of thousands of students in over 199 countries. His materials are today used by well over a thousand schools and other organizations globally and have positively influenced millions of entrepreneurs.

Prior to joining MIT, Bill had a 25-year track record of success in business. He has directly raised more than $100 million in funding for his companies and, more importantly, led the creation of hundreds of millions of dollars in market value in those companies. He worked at IBM for 11 years, from 1981 to 1993, and was featured in the movie *Silicon Cowboys*, for his work on the IBM Personal Computer. From 1993 to 2005, he founded and led two companies (Cambridge Decision Dynamics and SensAble Technologies) and then led a third (Viisage Technology) that were all MIT spinouts. They were increasingly successful and accumulated over 24 awards and recognition including a two-time *Inc.* magazine 500 Fastest-Growing Private Company.

As an author, he has written two books (*Disciplined Entrepreneurship: 24 Steps to a Successful Startup* and *Disciplined Entrepreneurship Workbook*). The former has been translated into over two dozen languages and become an award-winning international bestseller.

To stay current in a rapidly changing world, Bill also continues to sit on public and private boards as well as to look for other opportunities to broaden his perspective. These have included keynote talks and workshops globally, as well as visiting professorships at places like Strathclyde University, Duke University, and the University of North Carolina.

Bill lives in Cambridge, Massachusetts, with his wife of over 40 years, and they have four grown sons and two grandchildren. He is a former professional basketball player in England and recently won a gold medal in the sport at the 2023 U.S. National Senior Games.

Bill holds a bachelor's in engineering from Harvard University and a master's degree from the MIT Sloan School of Management.

More information is available at www.disciplinedentrepreneurship.com.

INDEX